Retiring in FRANCE

David Hampshire

SURVIVAL BOOKS • LONDON • ENGLAND

First published 2007
Second Edition 2008

Survival Books Limited
26 York Street, London W1U 6PZ, United Kingdom
☎ +44 (0)20-7788 7644, 📄 +44 (0)870-762 3212
✉ info@survivalbooks.net
🖥 www.survivalbooks.net

British Library Cataloguing in Publication Data.
A CIP record for this book is available
from the British Library.
ISBN: 978-1-905303-61-8

Printed and bound in India by Ajanta Offset

ACKNOWLEDGEMENTS

I would like to thank everyone who contributed to the successful publication of this book, including numerous retirees for their invaluable thoughts on retiring to France and countless staff at government offices and local councils for their help with queries. Some people who deserve a particular mention for their excellent research include Joe Laredo (revision and updating for second edition), Graeme Chesters, Selwyn Glick, Martin Hills and Trevor Zutshi. Kerry Laredo for proof-reading, Di Tolland for the page design and indexing, Jim Watson for the illustrations, cartoons and maps – and last, but not least, the many photographers (listed on page 326), whose superb images help bring France to life.

THE AUTHOR

David Hampshire was born in England and after serving in the Royal Air Force, was employed for many years in the computer industry. His work has taken him around the world and he has lived and worked in many countries, including Australia, France, Germany, Malaysia, the Netherlands, Panama, Singapore, Spain, and Switzerland. David is the author, co-author or editor of around 20 titles, including *Buying a Home in France* and *Living and Working in France*. David lives with his partner in England and Panama.

WHAT READERS & REVIEWERS

'If you need to find out how France works then this book is indispensable. Native French people probably have a less thorough understanding of how their country functions.'

Living France

'It's everything you always wanted to ask but didn't for fear of the contemptuous put down. The best English-language guide. Its pages are stuffed with practical information on everyday subjects and are designed to compliment the traditional guidebook.'

Swiss News

'Rarely has a 'survival guide' contained such useful advice – This book dispels doubts for first-time travellers, yet is also useful for seasoned globetrotters – In a word, if you're planning to move to the US or go there for a long-term stay, then buy this book both for general reading and as a ready-reference.'

American Citizens Abroad

'Let's say it at once. David Hampshire's Living and Working in France is the best handbook ever produced for visitors and foreign residents in this country; indeed, my discussion with locals showed that it has much to teach even those born and bred in l'Hexagone – It is Hampshire's meticulous detail which lifts his work way beyond the range of other books with similar titles. Often you think of a supplementary question and search for the answer in vain. With Hampshire this is rarely the case. – He writes with great clarity (and gives French equivalents of all key terms), a touch of humour and a ready eye for the odd (and often illuminating) fact. – This book is absolutely indispensable.'

The Riviera Reporter

'A must for all future expats. I invested in several books but this is the only one you need. Every issue and concern is covered, every daft question you have but are frightened to ask is answered honestly without pulling any punches. Highly recommended.'

Reader

'In answer to the desert island question about the one how-to book on France, this book would be it.'

The Recorder

'The ultimate reference book. Every subject imaginable is exhaustively explained in simple terms. An excellent introduction to fully enjoy all that this fine country has to offer and save time and money in the process.'

American Club of Zurich

HAVE SAID ABOUT SURVIVAL BOOKS

'The amount of information covered is not short of incredible. I thought I knew enough about my birth country. This book has proved me wrong. Don't go to France without it. Big mistake if you do. Absolutely priceless!'

Reader

'When you buy a model plane for your child, a video recorder, or some new computer gizmo, you get with it a leaflet or booklet pleading 'Read Me First', or bearing large friendly letters or bold type saying 'IMPORTANT - follow the instructions carefully'. This book should be similarly supplied to all those entering France with anything more durable than a 5-day return ticket. – It is worth reading even if you are just visiting briefly, or if you have lived here for years and feel totally knowledgeable and secure. But if you need to find out how France works then it is indispensable. Native French people probably have a less thorough understanding of how their country functions. – Where it is most essential, the book is most up to the minute.

Living France

A comprehensive guide to all things French, written in a highly readable and amusing style, for anyone planning to live, work or retire in France.

The Times

Covers every conceivable question that might be asked concerning everyday life – I know of no other book that could take the place of this one.

France in Print

A concise, thorough account of the Do's and DONT's for a foreigner in Switzerland – Crammed with useful information and lightened with humorous quips which make the facts more readable.

American Citizens Abroad

'I found this a wonderful book crammed with facts and figures, with a straightforward approach to the problems and pitfalls you are likely to encounter. The whole laced with humour and a thorough understanding of what's involved. Gets my vote!'

Reader

'A vital tool in the war against real estate sharks; don't even think of buying without reading this book first!'

Everything Spain

'We would like to congratulate you on this work: it is really super! We hand it out to our expatriates and they read it with great interest and pleasure.'

ICI (Switzerland) AG

CONTENTS

IMPORTANT NOTE

Readers should note that the laws and regulations regarding retirement and buying property in France aren't the same as in other countries and are liable to change periodically. Those who aren't nationals of an EU country will need to obtain a residence permit to retire permanently in France. I cannot recommend too strongly that you always check with an official and reliable source (not necessarily the same) and obtain expert legal advice before making plans to retire in France or buying or renting a home there. Don't, however, believe everything you're told or read – even, dare I say it, herein!

To help you obtain further information and verify data with official sources, useful addresses and references to other sources of information have been included in all chapters and in Appendices A to C. Important points have been emphasised throughout the book in **bold** print, some of which it would be expensive or foolish to disregard. **Ignore them at your peril or cost!** Unless specifically stated, the reference to any company, organisation, product or publication in this book doesn't constitute an endorsement or recommendation.

Author's Notes

- Times are shown using the 24-hour clock, e.g. 10am is shown as 10.00 and 10pm as 22.00, the usual way of expressing the time in France.

- Prices quoted should be taken only as estimates, although they were mostly correct when going to print and fortunately don't usually change greatly overnight. Although prices are sometimes quoted exclusive of value added tax (*hors taxes/HT*) in France, most prices are quoted inclusive of tax (*toutes taxes comprises/TTC*), which is the method used when quoting prices in this book.

- His/he/him also means her/she/her – please forgive me, ladies. This is done to make life easier for both the reader and the author, and isn't intended to be sexist.

- Most spelling is (or should be) British, not American English.

- Frequent references are made in this book to the European Union (EU), which comprises Austria, Belgium, Bulgaria, Cyprus, the Czech Republic, Denmark, Estonia, Finland, France, Germany, Greece, Hungary, Ireland, Italy, Latvia, Lithuania, Luxembourg, Malta, the Netherlands, Poland, Portugal, Romania, Slovakia, Slovenia, Spain, Sweden and the United Kingdom, and the European Economic Area (EEA), which includes the EU countries plus Iceland, Liechtenstein and Norway.

- Warnings and important points are shown in **bold** type.

- The following symbols are used in this book: ☎ (telephone), 🗐 (fax), 🖳 (internet) and ✉ (email).

- Lists of further information sources, further reading and useful websites are contained in **Appendices A**, **B** and **C** respectively.

- For those unfamiliar with the metric system of weights and measures, imperial conversion tables are shown in **Appendix D**.

- Useful maps of France are contained in **Appendix E** and on page 6.

- Airline and airport information is provided in **Appendix F**.

Amboise, Loire Valley, Indre-et-Loire

INTRODUCTION

Millions of people dream of retiring to a home abroad where they can enjoy a slower, more relaxed lifestyle and a milder climate. A numbers of surveys in recent years have concluded that as many as one in five Britons aged over 50 are planning to retire abroad by 2015-2020, and there are signs of similar trends in Germany and other northern Europeans countries. One of Europe's most popular retirement destinations is France, which is already home to thousands of foreign retirees whose favourite retirement spots include Brittany, Dordogne, Normandy, Provence and the Côte d'Azur.

Among France's many attractions are its generally mild climate (particularly in the south); beautiful beaches and villages, and vibrant cities; high standard of living; outstanding healthcare (among the best in the world); superb food and wine; spectacular countryside; and good (low-cost) air connections, particularly with northern European countries.

Many retirees find that a move to France results in a much-improved quality of life and most claim they feel fitter and younger, boasting that retirement to France has not only taken years off their life, but also helped them to live longer! However, retiring to France isn't always a bed of roses and obstacles such as bureaucracy, language difficulties, poor social services for the elderly, a lack of nursing homes and boredom are all potential barriers to a happy and fulfilling retirement.

As with all life-changing decisions, the key to a successful retirement in France is planning ahead and doing as much research as possible before you go, which is where this book will prove invaluable. Written specifically for retirees (and prospective retirees) in France, **Retiring in France** is worth its weight in *joie de vivre*.

Within these pages you will find information and advice on a wide range of essential topics, including buying a home, the cost of living, retirement hot spots, getting to and from France, public transport, motoring, healthcare and financial matters. Suggestions are also provided to help smooth your 'settling-in' period and help you make the best use of your new-found leisure time. In short, everything you need to make your retirement as fulfilling and successful as possible.

Most retirees in France would agree that, all things considered, they love living there – and wild horses couldn't drag them away. Retiring in France, even for part of the year, is a wonderful way to enrich and revitalise your life. I trust this book will help you to avoid the pitfalls and smooth your way to a happy and rewarding future in your golden years.

Bonne Chance!

David Hampshire

March 2008

Château de Villandry, Loire Valley

1.
WHY RETIRE TO FRANCE?

R etiring in France, whether permanently or for just part of the year (so-called 'seasonal retirement'), is an increasingly popular choice, particularly among retirees from countries with inclement climates and/or high property prices. It's estimated that there are almost 34,000 pensioners living in France – out of a total British expatriate population of around 200,000.

For many people, the dream of spending their golden years in the French countryside has become an affordable option, although retiring in France (even for part of the year) isn't without its pitfalls and shouldn't be attempted without careful consideration and planning. Before deciding where, when or indeed, whether to retire to France, it's important to do your homework thoroughly and investigate the myriad implications and possibilities. Recognising and preparing for potential difficulties in advance is much easier than dealing with disappointment – or even a crisis – later. However, if you do decide to take the plunge, you'll be in good company. Tens of thousands of people have successfully retired in France.

It isn't unusual for people to uproot themselves and after some time wish they had chosen a different part of France – or even that they had stayed at home! It's worth bearing in mind that a significant number of people who retire abroad return home within a few years.

The first question to ask yourself is **exactly** why you want to retire to France. Do you wish to live there permanently or spend only part of the year there? For example, some retirees spend the winter in southern France and return to their home country for the summer. Do you primarily wish to live somewhere with a lower cost of living? If you're planning to retire abroad for health reasons, the climate will be an important consideration. Do you want to make frequent return trips to your home country, to visit your family and friends? What do your family and friends think about your plans to live in France? Can you afford to retire there? What about the future? Is your income secure and protected against inflation?

☑ SURVIVAL TIP

As when making all major life decisions, it isn't wise to be in too much of a hurry. Many people make expensive (even catastrophic) errors when retiring in France, often because they don't do sufficient research or take into account the circumstances of their partners and family members.

You'll need to take into account the availability and cost of accommodation,

Port of Antibes, Alpes-Maritimes

communications, travelling time (and cost) to and from your 'home' country, security, health facilities, leisure and sports opportunities, culture shock, the language, the cost of living and local taxes, among other things. Many retirees wishing to retire to France are North Americans or northern Europeans, who can often buy a home abroad for much less than the value of their family home. The difference between the money raised on the sale of your family home and the cost of a home in France can be invested to supplement your pension, allowing you to live comfortably in retirement, particularly if France also has a lower cost of living. However, if you plan to buy a second home in France, you'll

need to maintain two homes, although the running costs can usually be offset by letting your home(s) when you're absent.

ADVANTAGES & DISADVANTAGES

Before planning to live abroad permanently, you must take into account many factors. There are both advantages and disadvantages to retiring in France, although for most people the benefits far outweigh the drawbacks.

Advantages

The benefits of retirement in France may include the following:

Agreeable Climate

In parts of France (primarily the south and Corsica), one of the primary attractions to its millions of annual visitors and many retirees is the weather. Much of the south has mild winters and hot summers and one of the principal benefits is improved health as a result of living in a warmer climate and a more relaxing environment. Your general sense of well-being is greatly enhanced when you live in a warm and sunny climate.

However, if you're planning to retire abroad for health reasons, you should ask your doctor for his advice regarding suitable locations, and if you want warm rather than mild winters, you'll need to head further afield than France (even the south and Corsica can experience cold winters).

Living in a warmer climate often results in an increased life expectancy for retirees (France has one of the world's highest life expectancies – around 83 for women and 75 for men). A warmer climate also provides ample opportunities to enjoy outdoor activities during your increased leisure time. On the financial side, you'll save a considerable sum on heating bills, although you shouldn't automatically assume that because your retirement destination is hot in the summer it will also be warm in winter. For example, in most of France (including the south and Corsica) it can be surprisingly cool in winter (particularly at night), when you'll need some form of heating, and the hot, humid summers in some areas may make costly air-conditioning necessary. It's wise to visit the region of your choice at different times of the year before making a decision, to find out exactly how cold and hot it **really** is in the winter and summer.

Good International Communications

Almost all regions have international airports and some are served by inexpensive flights from various European destinations. There are cheap flights from several British airports (especially London Stansted, from where Ryanair, for example, flies to around 20 French cities – see **Appendix F**), while Eurostar and the *TGV* (France's high-speed train service) also provide easy access for the British.

Higher Standard of Living

Depending on the country you're moving from, you may find that France offers you a higher standard of living, particularly regarding healthcare and public transport (see below). If you include 'quality of life' in your evaluation (see also below), your standard of living is likely to increase significantly.

Increased Leisure & Sports Options

In many parts of France, the availability of a wide range of leisure and sports activities at an affordable cost is an added attraction. Many areas have excellent leisure and sports facilities, such as cycling, boating, hiking, fishing and a wealth of golf clubs (France has the second-largest number of golf courses in Europe, after the UK) with reasonably-priced membership.

☑ SURVIVAL TIP

If you retire to an area with a mild climate, you'll also have more time and opportunities to enjoy your chosen sport or activity, which will rarely be interrupted by rain!

Lower Cost of Living

Although the cost of living in France isn't low, the price of everyday goods is around the same as in most northern European countries, and many items are relatively inexpensive, while services tend to be cheaper. Among the things that are particularly good value are eating in restaurants, alcohol (a reasonable bottle of wine needn't cost more than €3), cigarettes and transport; public transport, where available (see page 60), is among the cheapest and best in western Europe.

Paris is France's most expensive place to live by far; its cost of living, including property rent, ranks it 11th of the 71 world cities featured in the UBS Prices and Earnings survey (🖥 www.ubs.com/1/e/ubs_ch/wealth_mgmt_ch/research.html) last published in 2006 (Lyon, the only French city rated, came 31st). London is the world's most expensive city, followed by New York, Oslo, Tokyo, Zurich, Copenhagen, Geneva, Dublin, Chicago, Los Angeles (LA). When rents are excluded, Paris still ranks 11th, behind Chicago and LA but ahead of Stockholm and Helsinki.

For further information regarding prices, see **Cost of Living** on page 53.

Lower Property Prices

Property prices in North America and northern Europe (and in most of the world's capital cities) have risen considerably in recent years, and many people find themselves trapped in a spiralling property-price web, unable to buy a home that represents good value. Prices have also risen considerably in France in recent years, but many areas still offer affordable homes and in some lesser-known regions bargains can be found (e.g. prices can be as little as a third of those in the UK). See **Cost of Property** on page 114.

Quality Healthcare

The World Health Organization regularly reports that France has the best healthcare system in the world. This is a big attraction for anybody considering living in France, but is particularly important for retirees – provided, of course, you qualify for state healthcare (see **Chapter 7**).

Relaxed Lifestyle

The French generally have a slower pace of life than people in the UK and the US, and sensibly devote more time and effort to the appreciation of good food and wine, friends and, above all, family.

Space

France is Western Europe's largest country and, particularly compared to the UK and the Netherlands, is sparsely populated with vast areas of unspoilt countryside. The average density of the population of mainland France is around 100 people per km² (260 per mi²), one of the lowest in Europe. However, the density varies enormously from region to region.

Paris is one of the most densely populated cities in the world, with over 20,000 inhabitants per km² (over 52,000 per mi²); when Paris is excluded, the population density for the rest of the country drops to around 50 people per km² (130 per mi²)

Well Established Expatriate Communities

France is already home to tens of thousands of foreigners, concentrated mainly in the south-west and south, where there are well established expatriate communities, particularly Portuguese, British, German, Dutch and Scandinavian. There are small, localised expatriate communities in other areas, including Brittany and Normandy. In these areas, it's easier to find your feet and avoid language problems due to the numerous expatriate clubs, associations and activities.

Disadvantages

There are also potential disadvantages to retiring in France and you should consider these and their implications carefully before making a decision. However, it's worth noting that the majority are avoidable or surmountable, provided you do your homework before retiring there.

Boredom & Isolation

Although most people look forward to retirement, many find the reality of not working difficult and the prospect of full-time leisure daunting. The question 'What are you going to do all day?' can be difficult to answer – even more so in France, where there may not be the same facilities and familiar leisure activities that you have in your home country and a language barrier preventing you from enjoying those that do exist. You may miss your social life back home and find it difficult to be accepted into (or to accept) your new expatriate or French community. It's wise to visit your prospective retirement destination a number of times at different times of the year and to rent a property (see page 68) before buying a home and making a long-term commitment.

Bureaucracy

France is notorious for its bureaucracy and red tape, which, if you aren't prepared for it, can be frustrating and daunting. The situation is improving, but until the French finally shake off their obsession with paperwork, you would be wise to engage a

Roman amphitheatre, Nîmes, Gard

translator or professional to help you deal with the red tape.

Communication Problems

For many, the main disadvantage of retiring abroad is the separation from family and loved ones, particularly from grandchildren who have a habit of growing up fast. This barrier can be reduced by keeping in touch regularly by phone (many companies offer inexpensive international calls) and email (broadband internet access is available in most of France) – see **Keeping in Touch** on page 39 – and by choosing to live in an area that has easy access to your home country (see **Getting There** on page 28).

Culture Shock

Many people find that coping with retirement and the lack of structure to life without a daily work regime is made doubly stressful by the sense of isolation (and possible frustration) created by a new culture and language (see below). Are you prepared to be in a minority and to be treated as a foreigner? Are you open to different ways of doing things? Do you make friends easily? Can you cope with a slower pace of life and a high level of bureaucracy?

Many retirees underestimate the cultural isolation you can feel living in France, particularly if you plan to move to a part of the country where there are few of your compatriots. It's commonly assumed that French attitudes and manners differ little from those in other developed countries; nothing could be further from the truth, as the French have (and jealously guard) many unique character and behavioural traits, which can be frustrating and baffling to foreigners – even those from neighbouring countries. For details of French culture and how to cope with it, refer to *Culture Wise France* (Survival Books – see page 317).

A new culture doesn't, however, have to make your life more frustrating and can do much to enrich it, although it's important to be aware of the potential difficulties. Culture shock can be significantly reduced if you retire to an area of France with an established expatriate community (see above). See also **Culture Shock** on page 253.

Language Problems

Another common and erroneous assumption is that most French people speak English. Most don't, thanks to their outdated education system, or won't, for fear of making mistakes and embarrassing themselves.

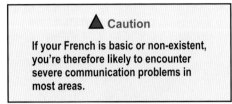

> ### ⚠ Caution
>
> **If your French is basic or non-existent, you're therefore likely to encounter severe communication problems in most areas.**

Moreover, it's generally accepted that the older you are, the more difficult it is to learn a new language (see **Learning the Language** on page 47). Linguistic difficulties can be mitigated by dedicated study before as well as after you retire to France, but you may never feel completely accepted by the French, for whom being able to communicate is less important than eloquence.

On the plus side, you can buy British and many other foreign newspapers in some French cities and tourist areas, and thanks to satellite television you can also enjoy your favourite TV programmes (for example, all British terrestrial channels are available via Sky).

Financial Problems

Retirement to France can involve unforeseeable financial problems, such as those caused by exchange rate fluctuations and poor investment returns if you're relying on foreign savings and investment income. Tax and cost of living benefits may also turn out to be lower than originally thought; French taxes and social security costs are high, as are the costs of some goods and services. Consult financial experts to help you do your sums before making a final decision. See **Chapter 3** for further information about the financial implications of retiring in France.

Old Age & Infirmity

Before making plans to live in France, you should consider how you would cope if your mobility was restricted. France's facilities and support for those with disabilities are improving – especially since the passing of a law called the Loi pour l'Egalité des Droits et des Chances des Personnes Handicapées in early 2005, which was designed to give disabled people equal rights with the able-bodied regarding employment, education, leisure activities and physical access – but are still inadequate in some areas.

Dying isn't something you'll want to think about but you must carefully consider whether you wish to spend your last years – possibly in illness or infirmity – and be buried or cremated in a foreign country. Many people prefer to be surrounded by their loved ones as death approaches, which may mean moving back home sooner or later.

OTHER CONSIDERATIONS

The following points should also be taken into account when considering whether or where to retire to in France:

● Decide whether you would like to retire permanently to France or just for part of the year. This decision is important because it will influence where you decide to live in France and your finances, particularly taxation.

● If you're planning to retire to France with your partner, ask yourselves if you **both** want to go. It's vitally important that the decision should be one you're both happy with. While it isn't a happy subject, you should both think ahead and consider what you'll do if one of you becomes seriously ill or dies.

● Consider whether you'll need to return regularly to your home country, e.g. for visits to relatives and grandchildren or medical appointments or to keep your affairs in order. If so, you should choose a location near a port or airport with easy access to your home country.

● Think carefully about how you'll feel being separated from your loved ones. Most of France is within a few hours of the UK and other neighbouring countries, but even this means you won't be able to meet friends for coffee or have the family round for Sunday lunch. **One of the main reasons retirees move back to their home country after relocating to France is that they cannot cope with the separation from family and friends.**

● Ask yourself 'why' you're considering retiring in France and write a list of the reasons. Make sure most or (preferably) all of the reasons are positive; an abundance of negative reasons may mean you're running away from problems in your home country. Bear in mind that a change of country doesn't necessarily mean that existing problems will go away. It may be better to stay in your home country and sort out your

problems before making a decision about retirement in France.

● Think about the 'pleasantness' of your chosen retirement location. You should be aware that an area can change considerably over a period; for example a village may be quiet and undeveloped when you buy a property and retire there, but it could rapidly become a major tourist spot or property investment target. This is particularly true of parts of the coastline where previously unspoilt and 'undiscovered' resorts are now bustling concrete jungles. Conversely, a thriving village could soon be deserted as people move nearer to surrounding towns. Before committing yourself to a location, make sure that you're aware of the regional and local authorities' plans for it.

● Be cautious about choosing your favourite holiday destination as your place of retirement. Holiday memories tend to be recalled through rose-tinted spectacles; the reality of daily life can be very different, and your perspective and requirements as a resident are quite different from those of a tourist.

● Investigate local public transport thoroughly. This is particularly important if you're elderly, as you may not always be able (or wish) to drive. There's little point in choosing an isolated spot or somewhere with a limited public transport system, when in a few years' time you may have to rely on just such services. You should also consider the terrain of your chosen home, as a location with lots of hills or steps can become an insurmountable problem if you have mobility restrictions or become disabled. It's advisable to avoid property in hilly areas; although hillside homes offer wonderful panoramic views, you'll need a car for everything and the climb will become much more difficult as you get older!

☑ SURVIVAL TIP

Before buying a home you should visit an area at different times of the year and rent a property for an extended period (up to six months) before taking the plunge (see page 68).

● Do as much research as possible on your prospective retirement destination, preferably by visiting the area several times, before making a decision. If you're planning to retire to France with a partner, you should do the research together, so that both of you are aware of the benefits and drawbacks. Survival Books publish many other best-selling publications for foreigners in France, including *Buying a Home in France*, *Living and Working in France*, *Rural Living in France* and *The Best Places to Buy a Home in France* (see page 327).

● **Most importantly – and it bears repeating – if you're planning to live in an unfamiliar area, rent for a period (up to six months) so that you can become familiar with a region or town and are certain you will enjoy living there. Don't burn your bridges before you're absolutely certain you want to retire to France!**

Annecy, Haute-Savoie

2.
BE PREPARED

O nce you've decided you'd like to retire to France, you need to consider the practical aspects of the move. This chapter contains information about permits and visas; getting to France by air, bus, train and ferry; getting around by public transport and car; keeping in touch (by telephone, post and internet and via published and broadcast media); and learning French.

VISAS & PERMITS

Before making any plans to visit France or live there, you must ensure that you have the necessary identity card or passport (with a visa if necessary) and, if you're planning to stay long-term, the appropriate documentation to obtain a residence and/or work permit. There are different requirements for different nationalities and circumstances, as detailed below.

French bureaucracy (euphemistically called *administration*) is legendary, and you should be prepared for the frustration caused by time-wasting and blatant obstruction on the part of officials. (This isn't necessarily xenophobia – they treat their fellow countrymen in the same way!) Note also that immigration is an inflammatory issue in France, where non-EU citizens are regarded with particular suspicion.

Permit infringements are taken very seriously by the French authorities, and there are penalties for breaches of regulations, including fines and even deportation for flagrant abuses.

While in France, you should carry your passport or residence permit (if you have one) at all times, as this serves as an identity card. You can be asked to produce your identification papers at any time by the police or other officials and, if you don't have them, you can be taken to a police station and interrogated.

☑ SURVIVAL TIP

Immigration is a complex and ever-changing subject, and the information in this chapter is intended only as a general guide. You shouldn't base any decisions or actions on the information contained herein without confirming it with an official and reliable source, such as a French consulate.

Visitors

Citizens of other EU countries can visit France for up to 90 days with a national identity card or passport only. Visitors from EU countries plus Andorra, Canada, Iceland, Japan, Monaco, New Zealand, Norway, Singapore, South Korea, Switzerland and the US don't require a visa, although French immigration authorities may require non-EU visitors

d'entrée sur le territoire français). **Note also that as a visitor you may not remain in France for more than 180 days a year.**

Non-EU citizens (except citizens of Andorra, Monaco and Switzerland and spouses of French citizens) who are staying with friends or family must obtain a 'certificate of accommodation' (*attestation d'accueil* – formerly *certificat d'hébergement* and sometimes referred to as *attestation d'hébergement*), valid for 90 days, before departure and present it on their arrival in France. Your hosts must apply for the *attestation* at their local town hall, police station or gendarmerie, which they can do up to six months in advance of your arrival, and send it to you.

Visas

Visitors from EU countries plus Andorra, Canada, Iceland, Japan, Monaco, New Zealand, Norway, Singapore, South Korea, Switzerland and the US don't require a visa to enter France. Other nationals need a visa to enter the country, for whatever purpose. Note, however, that some countries (e.g. Ireland and Italy) allow foreigners with close ancestors (e.g. a grandfather) who were born there to apply for a passport for that country, which can allow non-EU citizens to become 'members' of the EU. Visas may be valid for a single entry only or for multiple entries within a limited period. A visa is stamped in your passport, which must be valid for at least 90 days **after** the date you plan to leave France.

to show a return ticket and proof of accommodation, health insurance and financial resources. All other nationalities need a visa to visit France (see **Visas** below).

Retired and non-active EU nationals don't require a visa before moving to France, but they must apply for a residence permit within a week of their arrival (see page 27). If you're a non-EU national, it isn't normally possible to enter France as a tourist and change your status to that of a resident. You must return to your country of residence and apply for a long-stay visa (see below).

Note that you must spend at least 90 days outside France before you're eligible for another 90-day period in the country. If you're likely to want to return and require proof that you've spent the required period abroad, you should have your passport stamped at a police station, customs office or an office of the national police (*gendarmerie*) near your point of entry into France. You should ask to make a declaration of your entry (*déclaration*

The following websites provide further information about visas for France:

🖳 www.consulfrance-washington.org/spip.php?rubrique98 – for US nationals

🖳 www.globalvisas.com/worldwide_visas/france_visa.html

🖳 www.learn4good.com/travel/fr_visa.htm

For details of the application procedure, see *Living and Working in France* (page 325).

There are two main types of visa in France, as described below.

Short-stay Visa

A short-stay visa (*visa de court séjour*), also referred to as a short-term visa, tourist visa, travel visa, visit visa, business visa and 'Schengen Visa', is valid for 90 days and is usually valid for multiple entries as well as for free circulation within the group of EU nations that are signatories to the Schengen agreement (Austria, Belgium, Denmark, Finland, France, Germany, Greece, Italy, Luxembourg, the Netherlands, Portugal, Spain and Sweden). A short-stay visa may be valid for single or multiple entries, although the latter must be within the 90-day period, and costs between around €25 and €50.

 Caution

If you require a visa to enter France and attempt to enter without one, you'll be refused entry. If you're in doubt about whether you require a visa to enter France, enquire at a French consulate before making travel plans.

Long-stay Visa

A long-stay visa, valid for up to six months, isn't necessary for EU nationals planning to stay longer than 90 days in France, although they may need to apply for a residence permit (see opposite). A non-EU national intending to remain in France for more than 90 days must obtain a long-stay visa (*visa de long séjour*) **before** arriving in France and must apply for a residence permit within a week of arrival. If you arrive in France without a long-stay visa, it's almost impossible

to change your status after arrival and, if you wish to remain for longer than 90 days, you must return to your country of residence and apply for a long-stay visa. Long-stay visas cost between around €50 and €140.

Non-EU parents with children aged under 18 must also obtain long-stay visas for their children. Non-EU retirees should make a visa application to their local French consulate at least four months before their planned departure date.

Residence Permits

All foreigners remaining in France for longer than 90 days in succession (for any reason) require a residence permit (*titre de séjour*). Where applicable, a residence permit holder's dependants are also granted a permit. Different types of residence permit are issued according to your status, including permits for long-stay visitors (*visiteur*) and family members (*membre de famille*). For details of the application and renewal procedures, refer to *Living and Working in France* (Survival Books – see page 325).

There are two main categories of residence permit in France: a *carte de séjour* (short-stay residence permit) and a *carte de résident* (long-stay residence permit), as detailed below.

Carte de Séjour

Until November 2003, a resident permit (*carte de séjour*) was required by all foreigners aged 18 and above, both EU and non-EU nationals, who were to remain in France for more than 90 days (around 120,000 are issued each year). A new law (called the *loi Sarkozy*) introduced in November 2003 is generally believed to have waived the requirement for EU citizens to obtain a *carte de séjour*, although the actual wording of the law is ambiguous. EU citizens are therefore advised to contact their departmental *préfecture* in order to check whether a *carte de séjour* is required – particularly as you can be fined up to €1,500 for failing to apply for one! The information below is provided on the assumption that a *carte de séjour* is required.

Retired and non-active EU nationals must provide proof that they have an adequate income or financial resources to live in France without working or becoming a burden on the state. The minimum amount necessary is roughly equivalent to the French minimum wage (*SMIC*), which is currently €8.27 per hour (around €1,255 per month, depending on the number of hours worked, or around €15,000 per year), although it should be less if you aren't paying a mortgage or rent. It's normally necessary for non-EU retirees also to show proof of private health insurance.

The period of validity of a *carte de séjour* varies according to your circumstances, e.g. five years for pensioners and 'non-active' EU nationals.

A *carte de séjour* automatically becomes invalid if you spend over six months outside France and it can be revoked at any time if you no longer meet the conditions for which it was issued (or if you obtained a permit fraudulently). After three years of continuous residence in France, the holder of a *carte de séjour* can obtain a *carte de résident* (see below).

> **☑ SURVIVAL TIP**
>
> Whether or not you require a *carte de séjour*, you must meet the criteria for residence in France, i.e. adequate financial means of support and, unless you qualify for state health benefits, private health insurance.

Carte de Résident

Once you've lived (legally) in France for five consecutive years, you can apply for a *carte de résident* (the exception is the foreign spouse of a French resident, who's automatically granted a permanent residence permit after one year of marriage), provided you're practising a profession in France or have sufficient financial resources to maintain yourself and your dependants. A *carte de résident* authorises the holder to undertake any professional activity (subject to qualifications and registration) in any French department, even if employment was previously forbidden.

In order to be granted a *carte de résident*, you must provide evidence of your intention to remain in France for a considerable time and of your integration into French society, which requires a 'sufficient' knowledge of French and of the principles governing the Republic. The local mayor may be asked to confirm that such integration has taken place. You may also be asked to confirm your means of support and the status of any professional activity. A *carte de résident* is renewable automatically, unless you've committed a serious offence.

GETTING THERE

Even if you're planning to retire permanently in France, you're likely to want

to be able to visit your family and friends in your home country (and them to visit you) a number of times a year. One of your major considerations will therefore be the cost of getting to and from France and how long it will take. You should answer the following questions:

- How long will it take to get to a home in France, taking into account journeys to and from airports, ports and railway stations?

- How frequent are flights, ferries or trains at the time(s) of year when you plan to travel?

- Are direct flights or trains available?

- Is it feasible to travel by car?

- What is the cost of travel from my home country to the region where I'm planning to buy a home in France?

- Are off-season discounts or inexpensive charter flights available?

If a long journey is involved, you should bear in mind that it may take you a day or two to recover, especially if you suffer from jet lag. Obviously, the time and cost of travelling to a home in France will be more significant if you're planning to spend frequent weekends there rather than a few long stays a year. When comparing the cost of using public transport (e.g. air, train or bus) with driving via the Channel Tunnel or ferry, you need to take into account the cost of motorway tolls (see page 36), fuel, meals and, possibly, overnight stops.

Airline Services

All major international airlines provide scheduled services to Paris, and many also fly to other main French cities, such as Bordeaux, Lyon, Marseille, Nice and Toulouse. The French state-owned national airline, Air France, is France's major international carrier, flying to over 30 French, 65 European and 120 non-European destinations in over 70 countries. Air France and its various subsidiaries (known collectively as Groupe Air France) has a fleet of over 200 aircraft and carries some 16m passengers annually. It provides a high standard of service and, as you would expect, excellent in-flight cuisine.

☑ **SURVIVAL TIP**

Allow plenty of time to get to and from airports, ports and railway stations, particularly when travelling at peak times, when traffic congestion can be horrendous, and also allow for airport security checks.

Air France shares its monopoly on many international routes with just one foreign carrier and is thus able to charge high fares. The lack of competition means that international flights to and from most French airports, and French domestic flights, are among the world's most expensive. However, some opposition is starting to appear and high fares on some transatlantic flights have been reduced in recent years by travel agents such as Nouvelles Frontières. There are regular scheduled flights to Paris CDG from many North American cities, including Atlanta, Boston, Chicago, Dallas, Detroit, Houston, Los Angeles, Miami, Montréal, Newark, New York, Philadelphia, San Diego, San Francisco, Seattle, Toronto and Washington, to Lyon from Montréal, and to Nice from Montréal, New York and Toronto. There are also transatlantic charter flights to other French airports, e.g. to Toulouse from Montreal and Toronto.

In recent years, British and Irish visitors have been particularly well served by cheap flights (as well as less inexpensive services) from a number of airports – especially London Stansted – to many regional French destinations. The major budget carrier is Ryanair, but low-cost flights are also offered by a number of other British operators. For a summary of services current in late 2007, see **Appendix F**. Note, however, that the low-cost airlines are notoriously fickle and frequently change services according to 'demand' (i.e. profitability), so you should check current services with the airline **and** the airport (who may well provide you with different information!). Take into account also any seasonal charter flights, e.g. to Nice in the summer and Chambéry and Lyon in the winter, and, if you plan to live near one of France's borders, flights to airports in neighbouring countries, such as Italy and Switzerland.

Airports

The main French airports handling flights from the UK, Ireland and North America are Paris Roissy-Charles de Gaulle, Lyon-Saint-Exupéry (formerly Satolas), Nice-Côte-d'Azur and, surprisingly, Bergerac in Dordogne. Charles de Gaulle (CDG) is the country's busiest airport and handles 95 per cent of the direct flights from North America (see **Appendix F**), followed by Nice, which offers direct scheduled flights to around 80 cities worldwide.

Depending on your destination, it's sometimes cheaper or quicker to fly to an international airport outside France, such as Luxembourg for north-eastern France and Geneva for eastern France.

Long and short-term parking is available at major airports, including reserved parking for the disabled, and car hire is also available at Paris and principal provincial airports.

The Aéroports de Paris website (🖳 www. aeroportsdeparis.fr) has information on both CDG and Orly with maps and even pre-ordering from the airport duty-free shops! Details of all French airports and their current services can be found on 🖳

www.aeroport.fr. Selected airline websites and phone numbers are listed in **Appendix F**.

Brive-Souillac airport was supposed to be open for international flights by the end of 2007 but may not be operational until late 2008 at the earliest and no operators or routes had been announced at the time of publication.

International Rail Services

There are direct trains to France from most major European cities, including Amsterdam, Barcelona, Basle, Berlin, Brussels, Cologne, Florence, Frankfurt, Geneva, Hamburg, London (see **Eurostar** below), Madrid, Milan, Munich, Rome, Rotterdam, Venice, Vienna and Zurich. Some international services run at night only and daytime journeys may involve a change of train. The high-speed *Thalys* service links Paris with Brussels and Amsterdam.

Some non-*TGV* international trains such as *Trans-Europ-Express* (*TEE*) and *Trans-Europ-Nuit* (*TEN*) are first class only.

The operators of a number of European high-speed trains, including Eurostar (see below), *Thalys* and *TGV*, have teamed up to offer 'seamless' international rail travel through an agency called Railteam (🖳 www.railteam.eu).

Eurostar

The Channel Tunnel (the world's most expensive hole in the ground) joins France with England by rail and runs from Sangatte (near Calais) in France to Folkestone. Trains are operated exclusively by Eurostar and, since the opening of a separate, high-speed line from Folkestone to London in October 2003 and the transfer of the London terminal from Waterloo to St Pancras four years later, link London and Paris in just two hours. Speed and convenience come at a cost, however: a standard return fare costs over €400, although a return trip including a weekend booked at least three weeks in advance can save you €250 and return tickets for under €100 can be had from London to other French cities.

The 'hub' of the Eurostar network is Lille, Paris being the 'end of the line' for most trains, although a direct London to Avignon route, taking six hours, was inaugurated in summer 2003.

You can obtain train information in English or make a booking by calling UK ☎ 08705-186186 or ☎ 01233-617575 or France ☎ 01 70 70 99 49 or via the Eurostar website (🖥 www.eurostar. com). Note that a £5 booking fee is made for telephone bookings. For car-train services through the Channel Tunnel, see **Eurotunnel** on page 33.

tram, Bordeaux, Gironde

Motorail

Motorail

Motorail is a European network of special trains (known as *auto-trains*), generally running overnight, carrying passengers and their cars or motorbikes over distances of up to 1,500km (900mi); caravans cannot be taken on Motorail trains. The SNCF provides an extensive Motorail network of some 130 routes linking most regions of France. The principal Motorail services from the UK operate from Calais and Dieppe to Avignon, Biarritz, Bordeaux, Brive-la-Gaillarde, Narbonne, Nice and Toulouse. Trains don't run every day and on most routes operate during peak months only.

Motorail journeys are expensive (e.g. a minimum or £230 for a family to travel from London to Brive-la-Gaillarde one way) and it's cheaper for most people to drive, although it's usually slower and not as relaxing (trains are now equipped with a 'bar car'!). The main advantage of Motorail is that you travel overnight and (with luck)

arrive feeling refreshed after a good night's sleep. Note that there's a big difference between fares during off-peak and peak periods.

A comprehensive timetable (*Guide Trains Autos et Motos Accompagnées*) is published for bookings made through a railway station or travel agent in France, containing routes, tariffs, general information and access maps for Motorail stations. UK Passengers can obtain a brochure, *Motorail for Motorists – the Expressway into Europe*. Further information can be found on the French Motorail website (🖥 www.raileurope.co.uk/ frenchmotorail) or by calling ☎ 08448-484064 in the UK.

International Bus Services

Eurolines (☎ **08717-818181,** 🖥 www. eurolines.com or 🖥 www.eurolines.fr – in French) operates regular services from the UK to over 50 French cities, including Bordeaux, Cannes, Lyon,

Marseille, Montpellier, Nice, Orléans, Paris, Perpignan, Reims, Saint-Malo, Strasbourg and Toulouse.

International Ferry Services

Ferry services operate year round between France and the UK/Ireland. There's a wide choice of routes from the UK, depending on where you live and your intended route, but only one for Irish travellers. These are (from east to west):

● **Dover/Dunkerque** – Norfolk Line (UK ☎ 0870-870 1020, 🖳 www.norfolkline. com), providing conventional ferry services;

● **Dover/Calais** – P&O Ferries (UK ☎ 08716-645645, France ☎ 08 25 12 01 56, 🖳 www.poferries.com) and Sea France (UK ☎ 08705-711711, France ☎ 03 21 17 70 33, 🖳 www.seafrance. co.uk), providing conventional ferry services, with over a dozen crossings in each direction per day;

● **Dover/Boulogne** – Speed Ferries (UK ☎ 0870-220 0570, 🖳 www.speedferries. com), which provides a three- to five-times daily fast ferry service with a crossing time of 50 minutes;

● **Newhaven/Dieppe, Newhaven/Le Havre & Portsmouth /Le Havre** – Transmanche Ferries (UK ☎ 0800-917 1201, France ☎ 08 00 65 01 00, 🖳 www.transmancheferries.com) and LD Lines (UK ☎ 0844-576 8836, France ☎ 02 35 19 78 78/08 25 30 43 04, 🖳 www.ldlines.co.uk), conventional ferry services;

● **Portsmouth/Caen, Portsmouth/ Cherbourg & Portsmouth/Saint-Malo** – Brittany Ferries (UK ☎ 0870-907 6103, France ☎ 08 25 82 88 28, 🖳 www.brittany-ferries.co.uk), a conventional ferry service;

● **Portsmouth/Cherbourg & Portsmouth/Saint-Malo** – Condor

Ferries (UK ☎ 0845-609 1024, 🖳 www. condorferries.co.uk), conventional and fast ferry services, the latter operating via Guernsey and Jersey;

● **Poole/Cherbourg** – Brittany Ferries (see above);

● **Poole/Saint-Malo & Weymouth/Saint-Malo** via Guernsey and Jersey – Condor Ferries (see above);

● **Plymouth/Roscoff & Cork/Roscoff** – Brittany Ferries (see above).

Some services operate during the summer months only, and the frequency of services varies from dozens a day on the busiest Calais-Dover route during the summer peak period to one a week on longer routes.

> **Services are less frequent during the winter months, when bad weather can also cause cancellations.**

On the longer routes (i.e. Portsmouth/Le Havre and further west), there are overnight services.

Fares

Since Speed Ferries began operating between Dover and Boulogne in 2003, undercutting the Dover/Calais operators, there has been an intense price war (and not a few unsavoury practices, such as preventing boats from docking) and fares have generally been reduced, although they remain notoriously variable and unpredictable and can vary by hundreds of pounds (depending on the operator, time of year, time of day, duration of return ticket and, it would appear, sheer luck), peak rates still being outrageously high. For example, a standard Calais/Dover return with P&O for a vehicle up to 5m (16ft) in length costs around £385 (£190 single) including only the driver and one passenger, which works out at over £7 per mile! It isn't necessarily an advantage to book early, although P&O recently announced the introduction of an 'airline-style' system, whereby the earlier you book, the cheaper the fare.

It's worth ringing the ferry operators to ask about offers, but otherwise finding the cheapest fare is best done online, as staff won't be able to tell you the cheapest times to travel but will merely give you a price for each of the criteria you give, exactly as will their websites. An alternative to checking the sites of each operator separately is to use a comparative site, such as Channelcrossings.net (🖳 www.channelcrossings.net), Cross-Channel Ferry Tickets (🖳 www.cross-channel-ferry-tickets.co.uk), Direct Ferries (🖳 www.directferries.com), International Life Leisure 2000 (🖳 www.ferrysavers.com) and Intoferries (🖳 www.intoferries.co.uk), although finding the best fare is still a laborious matter of entering endless permutations of dates and times. Brochures rarely include the range of fares and never indicate all the variations. Children under four years old usually travel free and those aged 4 to 14 travel for half fare. Students may be entitled to a small discount during off-peak periods. Bicycles are transported free on most services. A new ferry booking agency, Ferrygreen (☎ 0870-264 2644, 🖳 www.ferrygreen.com), offers an environmentally-friendly ticket-less service and gives cross-Channel travellers the chance to offset their carbon emissions.

Some operators offer discounts to regular travellers. For example, Brittany Ferries runs a Property Owners' Travel Club, offering savings of up to 30 per cent on single and standard return fares, although you must pay a registration fee of £70 and an annual membership fee of £55, and P&O offers a 'season ticket' for three or more return crossings per year;

Provence

there's no membership fee and if you book nine returns they cost just £54 each (£84 at peak times) for a standard car with passengers. Most operators offer travel and accommodation packages, and in some cases these work out cheaper than the crossing alone!

Eurotunnel

Eurotunnel (formerly Le Shuttle) operates a shuttle car train service between Coquelles (near Calais) and Folkestone via the Channel Tunnel. There are three trains per hour during peak periods and the crossing takes just 35 minutes. Each train can carry around 180 cars. Fares are generally higher than those charged by ferry operators, e.g. a peak (summer) club class return costs around £430 and an off-peak (January to March) return around £200 for a vehicle and all passengers. It's wise to book in advance, and you shouldn't expect to get a place in summer on a 'turn up and go' basis, particularly on Fridays, Saturdays and Sundays.

Trains carry all types of vehicle, including cycles, motorcycles, cars, trucks, buses, caravans and motor-homes, although

rail service, particularly between cities served by the *TGV*, one of the world's fastest trains. France is also served by a good domestic airline service. On the negative side, bus and rail services are poor or non-existent in rural areas and it's generally essential to have a car if you live in the country.

Paris in particular has one of the most efficient, best integrated and cheapest public transport systems of any major city in the world. In addition to its world-famous *métro*, public transport services include the *RER* express rail system, an extensive suburban rail network, comprehensive bus services and, since 2006, a tram system. Other cities have similar systems, and several have reintroduced trams in recent years.

> Thanks to government subsidies, public transport is generally inexpensive in France, although this doesn't stop the French from complaining about the cost.

Various commuter and visitor discount tickets are also available.

For further details of domestic transport services in France, refer to *Living and Working in France* and *The Best Places to Live in France* (Survival Books – see page 325 & 323).

Domestic Flights

Sadly, most of France's regional airlines have been swallowed by Air France, which now dominates the domestic flight market, although there are still a few other operators, including Airlinair (🖥 www.airlinair.com), which operates to a number of destinations from Paris Orly and between certain regional airports, e.g. Bordeaux/Brest, Bordeaux/Rennes, Lyon/La Rochelle, Lyon/Poitiers and Mulhouse/Rennes, and CCM Airlines (🖥 www.aircorsica.com), operating from Bordeaux, Clermont-Ferrand, Lille, Lyon, Marseille, Montpellier, Nantes, Nice, Paris Orly, Quimper, Strasbourg and Toulouse to

you pay more for vehicles over 1.85m (6ft 1in) high. Note also that caravans and motor-homes must have their gas supplies disconnected and gas bottles must be shut off (gas bottles are routinely inspected, so make sure they're accessible).

Eurotunnel (UK ☎ 0870-535 3535 or France ☎ 08 10 63 03 04, 🖥 www. eurotunnel.com) is constantly changing its incentives for regular users. It currently offers a scheme called 'Frequent Traveller Fares' which allows you to book ten single crossings (at certain times) for £39 each over the course of a year.

GETTING AROUND

Public transport (*transport public*) services in France vary considerably according to where you live. They're generally excellent in cities, most of which have efficient local bus and rail services, many supplemented by underground railway and/or tram networks. French railways provide an excellent and fast four Corsican airports. Most recently, British airline easyJet established bases as Paris Charles de Gaulle and Lyon airports, offering flights to Biarritz, Bordeaux and Toulouse as well as international services.

Air France (☎ 08 20 32 08 20 for bookings, 🖳 www.airfrance.fr) offers domestic services between major cities such as Paris, Bordeaux, Lyon, Marseille, Mulhouse/ Basel, Nice, Strasbourg and Toulouse. Its domestic services to and from smaller airports operate mainly to the capital, and many domestic flights are timed to connect (*correspondance*) with international departures and arrivals.

Competition on major domestic routes from *TGV*s (see below), e.g. Paris-Lyon and the new three-hour Paris-Marseille route, has helped reduce air fares, and flying is sometimes cheaper than travelling by train and quicker on most routes. Any destination in mainland France or Corsica can be reached in less than 100 minutes by air, although security procedures now mean that check-in times can be up at least an hour before departure.

Domestic Rail Services

French railways are operated by the state-owned Société Nationale des Chemins de Fer Français (SNCF), which operates one of the most efficient rail systems in Europe, and employees and the French public take great pride in their trains. French railways are operated as a public service and charge reasonable fares and offer a wide range of discounted fares, all of which help increase passenger numbers, thus reducing road congestion and environmental damage. French high-speed trains compete successfully with road and air travel over long distances, both in cost and speed. The French railway network extends to every corner of France, although most routes radiate from Paris, there are few cross-country routes and services in most rural areas are limited.

The SNCF operates high-speed trains (*train à grande vitesse*, abbreviated to *TGV*) on its main lines, which are among the world's fastest, capable of over 550kph (around 350mph). *TGV* services operate to over 50 French cities. It takes just three hours to travel from Paris to Marseille by *TGV*. Standard trains have either electric (*Corail*) or gas turbine (*Turbotrain*) locomotives, which, although not in the *TGV* league, are fast and comfortable. Some branch lines operate *express* and *rapide* diesel trains. The slowest trains are the suburban *omnibus* services (some with double-deck carriages), which stop at every station. A *direct* train is a through train, usually classified as an *express* or *train express régional* (*TER*), stopping only at main stations and second in speed to the *TGV* (see above). A *rapide* is faster than an *omnibus* but slower than a *direct* or *express*. Smoking isn't permitted on trains in France.

All SNCF telephone enquiries are now centralised on a premium-rate telephone number (☎ 36 35); information can also be obtained and bookings made via the SNCF websites (🖳 www.sncf.com and 🖳 www.voyages-sncf.com), where offers are available ... on Tuesdays! The SNCF has offices in many countries, including the UK (Rail Europe, ☎ 08448-484064, 🖳 www. raileurope.co.uk).

> The SNCF publishes a free quarterly magazine in some countries, e.g. Top Rail in the UK, plus a wealth of free brochures and booklets detailing its services, including Le Guide du Voyageur, available from French stations.

Senior Discounts

Those who are over 60 (known in 'French' as *les seniors* – pronounced 'sen-your') can buy a *Carte Senior*, which costs €50 and provides a 50 per cent reduction in off-peak periods and a 25 per cent reduction in peak periods. There's also a 25 per cent reduction on international journeys to 27 European countries, and the card can be used on the national railway networks of several European countries. The *Carte Senior* is valid on all trains except regional trains in Paris and can be purchased from SNCF offices abroad as well as in France.

Carte Senior holders are also entitled to discounts of up to 50 per cent on entertainment and museum fees and other travel discounts. Discounts are often listed in entertainment publications such as *Pariscope*. Even without a card, those over 60 are entitled to a 25 per cent reduction on all journeys starting in an off-peak period (known as the *tarif découverte senior*).

Domestic Bus Services

There's a nationwide campaign for 'car-free' cities, and there are excellent bus services in Paris and other major cities, some of which (including Bordeaux, Caen, Le Mans, Lyon, Montpellier, Nancy, Nantes, Nice, Orléans, Rouen, Strasbourg, Toulon, Valenciennes and now Paris itself) also have trams or trolley buses. The town of Châteauroux (in Indre) recently became the first in France to offer free bus travel in order to persuade citizens to abandon their cars, and in Lille commuters are offered half-price bus travel.

In rural areas, however, buses are few and far between, and the scant services that exist are usually designed to meet the needs of workers, schoolchildren, and shoppers on market days. This means that buses usually run early and late in the day with little or nothing in between, and may cease altogether during the long summer school holiday period (July and August). A city bus is generally called an *autobus* and a country bus a *car* or *autocar*. Smoking isn't permitted on buses in France.

The best place to enquire about bus services is at a tourist office or railway station. In large towns and cities, buses run to and from bus stations (*gare d'autobus/routière*)

usually located next to railway stations. In rural areas, bus services are often operated by the SNCF and run between local towns and the railway station. An SNCF bus, on which rail tickets and passes are valid, is shown as an *autocar* in rail timetables. The SNCF also provides bus tours throughout France. Private bus services are often confusing and uncoordinated and usually leave from different locations rather than a central bus station. Some towns provide free or discount bus passes to senior citizens (over 60) on production of an identity card, passport, or *carte de séjour* and proof of local residence. There are no national bus companies in France operating scheduled services.

Driving

France has a good road system that includes everything from motorways to forest tracks. The quality of roads varies enormously, however: while motorways are generally excellent and most other main roads good, urban roads and minor roads in rural areas

can be poorly maintained. Trunk roads vary from almost motorway standard dual-carriageways to narrow, two-lane roads passing through a succession of villages where the speed limit is 50kph (30mph).

You can drive in France for at least a year with most foreign licences, unless you incur a driving penalty, in which case you must obtain a French licence. This may be to your advantage in any case, as French driving licences are valid until the age of 75, after which you must pass a medical examination every two years.

Motorways

France boasts one of the best motorway (*autoroute*) networks in Europe, totalling over 9,500km (6,000mi). Unfortunately they're among the world's most expensive roads, most of them being toll roads (see below). Because of this, driving on motorways is considered a luxury by many French people and they therefore have the lowest traffic density of any European motorways. Partly for this reason, motorways are also France's safest roads (but note that this is a relative term!) – with the notable exception of the Paris *Périphérique*, an eight-lane race track around the city centre on which there's an average of one fatal accident a day!

☑ SURVIVAL TIP

Because of the continuous expansion of the network, you shouldn't use a motoring atlas that's more than a year old.

Tolls: Most French motorways are toll roads (*à péage*) and are among the most expensive in Europe, although there are plans to privatise half the motorways in the south, which could reduce charges by up to 30 per cent. Rates aren't standardised throughout France and vary with the age of the motorway and the services provided. There are no tolls on the

sections of motorways around cities. A new system of tolls has been introduced in some areas with higher rates during peak periods. On average, however, motorway travel costs around €0.07 per kilometre for a car. There are five vehicle categories on most motorways, and tolls for motor-homes and cars towing trailers or caravans are higher than for cars.

The approximate costs of driving a standard car from Calais or Le Havre to various French towns are shown in the table below.

Town	Cost
Biarritz	€70
Bordeaux	€65
Cahors	€40
Clermont-Ferrand	€50
Dijon	€40
Grenoble	€55
Lyon	€70
Marseille	€70
Nancy	€30
Nantes	€60
Nice	€85
Paris	€20
Perpignan	€60
Poitiers	€50
Strasbourg	€40

There's no longer an *Autoroute Tarifs* leaflet, but you can calculate the cost of a particular journey by entering the details under '*Itinéraires*' on the website of the Association des Sociétés Françaises d'Autoroutes, 3 rue Edmond Valentin, 75007 Paris (💻 www.autoroutes.fr – in French only, though an English version is promised for early 2008; click on the map on the home page for details of proposed improvements to the motorway network in a particular area). The above website gives details of laybys and service stations with disabled facilities; click on 'Services aux personnes à mobilité réduite' under 'INFOS SERVICES'.

Tolls are also levied to use the Mont Blanc tunnel (Chamonix-Entrèves, Italy, 11.6km/7.2mi), the Fréjus tunnel (Modane-Bardonecchia, Italy, 12.8km/8mi), the Bielsa tunnel (Aragnouet-Bielsa, Spain, 3km/1.86mi), and a number of bridges, including the Ponts de Normandie, Tancarville and Saint-Nazaire and the spectacular new Millau Viaduct. If you're travelling long distances, it may be cheaper to fly or take a TGV and will almost certainly be quicker and less stressful.

Other Roads

Unlike French motorways, main trunk roads (*route nationale*) are jammed by drivers (including those of heavy goods vehicles) who are reluctant to pay or cannot afford the high motorway tolls. If you must get from A to B in the shortest possible time, there's no alternative to the motorway (apart from taking a plane or train). However, if you aren't in too much of a hurry, want to save money **and** wish to see something of France, you should avoid motorways. The money saved on tolls can pay for a good meal or an inexpensive hotel room. *Routes nationales* and other secondary roads are often straight and many are dual carriageways, on which you can usually make good time at (legal) speeds of between 80 and 110kph (50 to 70mph). On the other hand, many trunk roads pass through towns and villages, where the speed limit is reduced to 50kph (30mph), which can make for slow progress.

Information

In June each year, the French Ministry of Transport issues a 'wily bison' map (*Carte de Bison futé*) showing areas of congestion and providing information about alternative routes (*itinéraire bis*), indicated by yellow or

green signs. The map is available free from petrol stations and tourist offices in France and from French Government Tourist Offices abroad, which also provide information about motorways, tolls and driving rules in France. Similar information can be found on the 'wily bison' website (🖳 www.bisonfute. equipement.gouv.fr). There are around 90 information rest areas throughout France, indicated by a black 'i' and an *Information Bison futé* sign. Green-arrowed holiday routes (*flèches vertes*) avoiding large towns and cities are also recommended.

A colour system is used to indicate the state of the roads – orange for bad, rouge for very bad and noir for appalling – and this is announced on the radio and television.

Route planning is simple thanks to the internet, where several sites can help you find the quickest and most economical route to your French home, including 🖳 www.mappy.com, 🖳 www.rac.co.uk, 🖳 www. theaa.com and 🖳 www.viamichelin.co.uk (all in English).

Up-to-date information about French roads can be obtained from the Ministère de l'Ecologie, du Développement et de l'Aménagement Durables (🖳 www. equipement.gouv – in French only; click on 'Infrastructures et transports'). Details of current roadworks can be found by phoning Bison futé (within France ☎ 08 26 02 20 22 or from abroad ☎ +33 892 687 888 – in French only) or visiting the website (🖳 www. bisonfute.equipement.gouv.fr) or by tuning in to Autoroute Info on 107.7FM. Details of planned new roads are provided in The Best Places to Buy a Home in France (Survival Books – see page 323).

KEEPING IN TOUCH

An important consideration when thinking about retiring in France is how easy it is to keep in touch with your friends and loved ones, and with current affairs back in your home country.

Telephone Services

France enjoys a high standard of telephone services (including fax, internet and mobile phones). The telephone system is operated by France Télécom (FT), which is 55 per cent state-owned (and one of the world's most indebted companies!), but several companies, including FT, provide services for local as well as inter-departmental and international calls. Information and help is available in English on ☎ 08 00 36 47 75 (or ☎ +33 1 55 78 60 56 from abroad) during normal office hours Mondays to Saturdays. The essentials of French telephone services are outlined below; for further details refer to Living and Working in France (Survival Book – see page 319).

Installation & Registration

If you're planning to move into a property without an existing telephone line, you'll need to have one installed. In this case, you must visit your local France Télécom agent, which you'll find in the yellow pages

under Télécommunications: service. You'll need to prove that you're the owner or tenant of the property in question, e.g. with an electricity bill, confirmation of purchase (attestation d'acquisition) or a lease. You'll also require your passport or residence permit (carte de séjour). France Télécom publishes a Set Up Guide in English.

⚠ Caution

If you buy a property in a remote area without a telephone line, it may be expensive to have a telephone installed, as you must pay for the line to your property. Contact France Télécom for an estimate.

If you're restoring a derelict building or building a new home, you should have trenches dug for the telephone cable if you want a below ground connection (you may be able to have an above ground connection via a wire from the nearest pylon). This work can be carried out by France Télécom, but their charges are high and it's possible to do it yourself, although you must observe certain standards. Details of the required depth of trenches and the type of conduit (gaine) to use, etc. can be obtained from France Télécom.

When you go to the France Télécom agency, you'll need to know what kind of telephone sockets are already installed in the property, how many telephones you want, where you want them installed, what kind of telephone you want (if you're buying from France Télécom) and whether you want to upgrade a line (e.g. to ADSL – see Broadband below). If you want a number of telephone points installed, you should arrange this in advance.

You may be given a telephone number on the spot, although you should wait until you receive written confirmation before giving it to anyone. **Note that it isn't possible simply to take over the telephone number of the previous occupants, as France Télécom always changes the telephone number when the ownership or tenancy of a property changes.** If you own a property and are letting it for holidays, you can arrange to have outgoing calls limited to the local area, or to regional or national calls only, but you cannot limit the service just to incoming calls.

To have a line installed takes from a few days in a city to weeks or possibly over a month in remote rural areas, although 90 per cent of new customers have a line installed within two weeks.

When moving into a new home in France with a telephone line, you must have the account transferred to your name and a telephone number issued to you. To do this, you can simply dial ☎ 1014 or go to the France Télécom website (🖳 www.francetelecom.com) and follow the links to *l'agence sur le net*. Some information is available on the English-language section of the website, but it's limited to business services and investment details.

☑ SURVIVAL TIP

If you move into a property where the telephone hasn't been disconnected or transferred to your name, you should ask France Télécom for a 'special reading' (*relevé spécial*).

If you're taking over an existing line, you can usually have it connected within 48 hours. The cost of installing a new line (known elaborately as *frais forfaitaire d'accès au réseau*) is normally around €110; if you're taking over a line from a previous user, there's a charge of €55.

Broadband

Broadband (*le haut-débit*) via ADSL (*l'ADSL*) is available in most urban areas but extension of the network to rural areas is proving slow, as France Télécom struggles to absorb the cost of upgrading its outdated infrastructure. For reasons best known to FT, broadband is sometimes available in one part of a village but not another! To find out if broadband is available in your area, go to 🖳 www.agence.francetelecom.com, click on '*internet*' and '*abonnement express*' on the right, then enter your current telephone number (or a neighbour's). You can simply enter the number of the department in which you live or intend to live but this won't tell you whether broadband is available in a particular village or part of a village. If broadband is available, installation of ADSL costs the same as a standard line (see above). France Télécom offers various combined phone and internet access packages for compulsive internet surfers (see **Internet** on page 43).

If it's available, you can upgrade an existing line to an ADSL at no extra charge; if it isn't available and you aren't in a 'cabled' area, an integrated services digital network ISDN (*RNIS* but referred to by France Télécom *as Numéris*) line is an option, although an expensive one.

For those whose French (let alone their 'techno-speak') isn't up to the complexities of all this, French telecom company Téléconnect offers an 'AngloPak' consisting of an English-language helpline (☎ 08 05 02 40 00) and English translations of all documentation and contracts. The service costs €29.95 per month, including two hours of 'free' calls; for details go to 🖳 www.teleconnectfrance.com.

Alternative Providers

There are currently around 20 alternative telephone service providers in France, some of which advertise in the English-language press (see **Appendix B**). If you

International Calls: It's possible to make International Direct Dialling (IDD) calls to most countries from both private and public telephones. A full list of country codes, plus area codes for main cities and time differences, is shown in the information pages (*les info téléphoniques*) of your local yellow pages. To make an international call you first dial 00, then the country code, the area code without the first zero and the subscriber's number.

For international (and domestic) directory enquiries, you must instead choose between umpteen services and endure a barrage of advertising (without being told how much you're being charged for the privilege!) before being given the number you want. All directory enquiries numbers begin 118. Details of all directory enquiries services can be found on a dedicated website, 🖳 www.appel118.fr. Only some of these services provide numbers outside France.

France subscribes to a Home Direct service (called *France direct*) that allows you to call a number giving you direct and free access to an operator in the country that you're calling, e.g. for British Telecom in the UK dial ☎ 08 00 99 00 44. The operator will connect you to the number required. Note, however, that this service can be used only for reverse charge (collect) calls. To obtain an operator from one of the major US telephone companies dial ☎ 08 00 99 00 11 (AT&T), ☎ 08 00 99 00 87 (Sprint) or ☎ 08 00 99 00 19 (Worldphone).

wish to use another provider (or several providers, for different types of call), you'll need to open a separate account with each one. Note, however, that you must still have an account with France Télécom for line rental.

Using the Telephone

Using the telephone in France is simplicity itself. All French telephone numbers have ten digits, beginning with a two-digit regional code (01 for the Ile-de-France, 02 for the north-west, 03 north-east, 04 south-east and 05 south-west), and followed by another two-digit area code. Note that, if you're calling within France, you must **always** dial all ten digits, even if you're phoning your next-door neighbour.

Numbers beginning 06 are mobile (*portable*) numbers (see **Mobile Phones** on page 42), and those beginning 08 and 09 are charged at various rates, from free to several euros per minute; refer to *Living and Working in France* (Survival Books) for details.

see **Mobile Phones** on page 42

☑ SURVIVAL TIP

For both domestic and international numbers, it's easier and cheaper to use an online telephone directory, e.g. 🖳 www. pagesjaunes.fr for France.

These companies also offer long-distance calling cards, which provide access to English-speaking operators, and AT&T offers a 'USA Direct' service, whereby you can call an operator in any state (except Alaska). To reach an operator in any other country from France, you must call directory enquiries (see above) and ask for the relevant *France Direct* number; there's no longer a list of Home Direct codes in French telephone directories. You can also use the *France Direct* service from some 50 countries to make calls to France via a France Télécom operator.

France Télécom publishes a useful free booklet, *Guide du Téléphone International*, containing information in both French and English.

Emergency & Service Numbers

The national emergency numbers (*services d'urgence et d'assistance*) in France are:

Number	Service
15	Ambulance (*Service d'Aide Médical d'Urgence/SAMU*)
17	Police (*police-secours*)
18	Fire (*sapeurs-pompiers/feu centrale d'alarme*)

Public Telephones

Despite the increasing use of mobile telephones (see below), public telephone boxes (*cabine téléphonique*) can be found in all towns and villages: in post offices, bus and railway stations, airports, bars, cafés, restaurants and other businesses, and of course, in the streets. Most telephone boxes are aluminium and Perspex kiosks, and most public telephones (*téléphone publique*) accept telephone cards, *Cartes France Télécom* and bank (i.e. debit) cards, although many won't accept credit cards, particularly those without a microchip.

Mobile Phones

Lower prices due to increased market competition have ensured rapid growth in the use of mobile phones, and there are currently three mobile phone service providers: Bouygues – pronounced 'bweeg' – (🖥 www.bouyguestelecom.fr), Orange – actually France Télécom in disguise – (🖥 www.orange.fr), and SFR (🖥 www.sfr.fr). None of them have bothered to have their site translated into English.

As in most countries, buying a mobile phone is an absolute minefield, as not only are there different networks to choose from and the option of a contract or 'pay-as-you-talk', but there's also a wide range of tariffs covering connection fees, monthly subscriptions, insurance and call charges. To further complicate matters, the providers have business ties to one or more of the fixed telephone services (SFR, for example, is part of Vivendi, which owns and operates Cégétel) and offer various deals for those who combine mobile and fixed phone services.

> ☑ SURVIVAL TIP
>
> If you don't use a mobile phone much but just want one for emergencies and to receive calls, buy an inexpensive pay-as-you-talk phone.

If you use a foreign mobile in France, you can be liable for high 'roaming' charges, but it's usually possible to buy a French SIM card, which will give you a French mobile number and allow you to make and receive calls at normal rates.

Charges

Deregulation of the telecommunications market has resulted in an intense price war, and considerable savings can be made on national as well as international calls by shopping around for the lowest rates. However, as there are around 20 alternative providers in France, it's impossible to list all their tariffs here; in any case, each company offers different packages, which disguise the charge per call in different ways. Comparisons between the rates offered by a number of service providers can be found via the internet (e.g. 🖥 www.comparatel.fr and 🖥 www.budgetelecom.com). Line rental and call charges are explained below; for information about installation and registration charges, see page 39.

Line Rental: A monthly line rental or service charge (*abonnement*) of €30 is payable to France Télécom irrespective of the service provider you choose. If you use an alternative provider, there may be a separate monthly fee in addition to your call charges, although most providers have dropped these.

International Calls: France Télécom has eight tariff levels for international calls, listed on its website. All international calls are subject to an initial charge of €0.11 for a period varying from 5 to 27 seconds, depending on the tariff. Calls to western Europe and North America (except Hawaii and Alaska) are charged at the lowest tariff and cost €0.069 per minute. Calls to Australia and New Zealand cost €0.23 per minute.

Other telephone providers have different tariff structures for international calls. Most alternative providers also offer a variety of discount plans, such as half price on all calls to a designated 'favourite country' or to specific overseas phone numbers frequently called.

Internet

The internet in France got off to rather a slow start due to competition from its (French) precursor, Minitel, but it's

now widely used and the availability of broadband connection is among the highest in the EU. There has recently been a proliferation of internet service providers (*fournisseur d'accès/FAI* or *serveur*), over 200 currently offering a variety of products and prices. France Télécom offers Orange (formerly Wanadoo), a package that includes email (see below) and on-line shopping. AOL Compuserve France is the other major internet contender; between them, Orange and AOL have some two-thirds of the market, although AOL has recently been taken over by Neuf (see below). Contact details of some of the major French internet service providers (ISPs) are as follows:

- **Alice France** (formerly Tiscali) – 🖥 www.aliceadsl.fr;

- **AOL** – 🖥 www.aol.fr. Recently bought by Neuf (see below) and soon to be phased out;

- **Club Internet** – 🖥 www.club-internet.fr;

- **Free** – 🖥 www.free.fr;

- **FreeSurf** – 🖥 www.freesurf.fr;

- **Neuf Télécom** – 🖥 www.neufportail.fr;

- **Orange** – 🖥 www.orange.fr;
- **Tele2** – 🖥 www.tele2.fr.

For a comparison of ISP services and charges, consult one of the dedicated internet magazines, such as *Internet Pratique* and *Net@scope*, or visit the Budgetelecom website (🖥 www.budgetelecom.com), which provides information on current offers, customer evaluations and direct links to provider websites.

Charges

France has a number of 'free' internet access services, where you pay only for your telephone connection time, not for access to the internet provider. Alternatively, most service providers (including the free ones) offer various monthly plans which include all telephone charges for your online connections, usually at a rate that's lower than the telephone charges alone. For as little as €6 to €10 per month, you can usually spend five or ten hours online.

⚠ Caution

Note that, if you already have an AOL account with a fixed monthly fee for unlimited access, you may (or may not!) have to pay for connection time in France but, if you're registered in another country, you won't be able to change your registration and must cancel your email address(es) and re-register new ones in France (or the same ones if you're lucky!).

Broadband

For faster internet connections, you can have an ADSL or ISDN line installed (see **Installation & Registration** on page 39). Most providers, including France Télécom, offer combined telephone and internet

access packages (*forfaits*). In Paris, and other urban centres with cable television, it's often possible to have cable internet access, which offers speeds comparable to a broadband telephone line.

Modems

Foreign modems will usually work in France, although they may not receive faxes (Big Dish Satellite, 🖥 www.bigdishsat.com, sells converters for this purpose).

Postal Services

French postal services are poor by western European standards. The French Post Office (La Poste) is a state-owned company, although privatisation of the postal service is in progress and La Poste's monopoly on the handling of letters between 50 and 100g was due to end in 2006 (although in December 2007 no alternative services were available and it's likely that these will be confined to 'express' services, as has happened in other EU countries). There are around 17,000 post offices, 60 per cent of them in communes of fewer than 2,000 inhabitants but, as in other countries, those in the least populated areas are gradually being closed. Signs for post offices in towns vary widely and include *PTT* (the old name for the post office), *PT, P et T, Bureau de Poste* or simply *Poste*. Post offices are listed in the yellow pages under *Poste: Services*.

In addition to the usual post office services, a range of other services are provided. These include telephone calls, telegram and fax transmissions, domestic and international cash transfers, payment of telephone and utility bills, and the distribution of mail-order catalogues. Recently, La Poste has also started offering email services, including free and permanent email addresses as well as e-commerce services for small businesses. The post office also provides financial and banking services, including cheque and savings accounts, mortgages, retirement plans, and share prices. Post offices usually have photocopy machines and telephone booths.

The Post Office produces numerous leaflets and brochures, including the handy *Tarifs Courrier – Colis*, or you can obtain information via La Poste's website (🖥 www. laposte.fr), although only limited information is available in English. The site offers a search tool to help you find the address and telephone number of your nearest post office (enter the town name or postal code). Unfortunately, the listings don't include the opening hours or the times for the last collection each day. For further details of French postal services, refer to *Living and Working in France* (Survival Books – see page 325).

English-language Publications

Major foreign European newspapers are available on the day of issue in Paris and a day or two later in the provinces. Some English-language daily newspapers are widely available on the day of publication, including *USA Today*, *International Herald Tribune* (edited in Paris), *Wall Street Journal Europe*, the *Guardian* and the *European Financial Times*, printed in Frankfurt. The price of foreign newspapers sold in France is usually listed on the front or back page.

Many British and foreign newspapers produce weekly editions, including the *Guardian Weekly*, *International Express* and the *Weekly Telegraph*, which are available on subscription. Most English-language newspapers can also be accessed via the internet, either free or for a small subscription fee.

Le Monde publishes a supplement in English on Saturdays. Two monthly English-language newspapers covering French news are published in France: *The Connexion* and *French News* (see **Appendix B**). A number of other English-

language publications are available in newsagents' and major supermarkets and on subscription (see **Appendix B**).

Most French book shops don't stock English-language books. There are, however, English-language book shops in most large towns and cities. English-language book shops in Paris include the Abbey Bookshop (5th *arrondissement*), Librairie Albion (4th), Brentano's (2nd), Galignani (1st), San Francisco Book Co. (6th), Shakespeare & Company (5th), WH Smith & Son (1st), Tea and Tattered Pages (6th), and the Village Voice (6th). English-language books are also sold at the Virgin Megastore on the Champs-Elysées. However, imported English-language books are expensive (except for those published by Survival Books, which are an absolute bargain!), usually costing around double their 'recommended' home country price. Americans in particular will be appalled at the cost.

Many expatriate organisations and clubs run their own libraries or book exchange schemes, and some French public libraries

keep a small selection of English-language books.

English-language Television & Radio

French television (TV) uses a different standard from TV in other countries – SECAM-L, which is incompatible not only with the North American NTSC system and the PAL systems used in the UK and other European countries but also with other SECAM standards. This means that imported TV sets won't work in France; and imported video cassette tapes may play only in black and white on French TV sets.

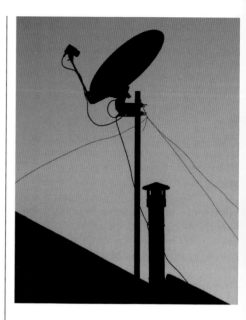

Television Licence

In 2008, those over 65 with low incomes are entitled to a 50 per cent reduction on the French TV licence fee, currently €116 per year and included in your *taxe d'habitation*, but unless the law is changed they will have to pay 100 per cent from 2009.

There's very little English-language programming on French terrestrial TV; most foreign-language films, soaps, documentaries, etc. are dubbed into French rather than subtitled. If you live close to a French border and have the appropriate aerial, you may be able to receive foreign stations. In the Nord-Pas-de-Calais region, for example, it's possible to receive British and Belgian stations, those in northern Lorraine can receive Luxembourg TV, and in Alsace you can watch German and Swiss TV. Otherwise, those wanting to watch TV in English (or another language) are limited to broadcasts (see below) or recorded programmes (e.g. DVDs); cable TV is available only in French.

Satellite TV

France is well served by satellite TV (*télévision par satellite*); there are a number of satellites positioned over Europe carrying over 200 stations broadcasting in a variety of languages. BBC channels can now be received unencrypted (as can CNN, Euro News, Sky News and a few other channels); information is available on the BBC's main website (🖳 www.bbc.co.uk). The BBC's commercial subsidiary, BBC World Television (formerly BBC Worldwide Television), broadcasts two 24-hour channels: BBC World (24-hour news and information) and BBC Prime (general entertainment). BBC World is free-to-air, while BBC Prime is encrypted. For more information and a programme guide contact BBC World Television, PO Box 5054, London W12 0ZY, UK (☎ 020-8433 2221). A programme guide can be found on the internet (🖳 www.bbc.co.uk/worldservice) and both BBC World and BBC Prime have their own websites (🖳 www.bbcworld.com and 🖳 www.bbcprime.com). When accessing them, you need to enter the name of the country (e.g. France) so that schedules appear in local time.

Any digital satellite receiver can receive the BBC and other 'free-to-air' channels.

To receive some ITV channels, however, you need a Sky digibox and a Sky card, obtainable only if you have a UK address. A new digital satellite receiver costs around €350 and a card around €30. If you live in the Nord-Pas-de-Calais region and have the appropriate aerial, you may also be able to receive British stations without a satellite system.

Radio

Around 60 per cent of popular music broadcast on French radio is in English. On the other hand, there's little English-language radio programming, although in a few areas there are English stations run by expatriates (e.g. Riviera Radio on 106.5FM in the south of France, Sud Radio on 96.1FM in the south-west and Lot radio on 88–89FM). Radio France Internationale (RFI) broadcasts in English for three-and-a-half hours every day in the Paris region on 738MW. The BBC World Service is broadcast on short wave on several frequencies (e.g. 12095, 9410, 7325, 6195, 3955, 648 and 198kHz) simultaneously and you can usually receive a good signal on one of them. The signal strength varies according to where you live in France, the time of day and year, the power and positioning of your receiver, and atmospheric conditions.

The World Service is also available on medium wave (648MW) in northern France. You can also receive BBC national radio stations (on long wave) in some northern and western areas of France, and all BBC radio stations, including the World Service, are available via satellite (see below). BBC radio stations can also be received via a computer (PC) using a Radio Player (which can be downloaded free from 🖥 www.bbc.co.uk/radio). If you're desperate, you can also hear recordings of BBC radio programmes on your computer via 🖥 www.bbc.co.uk/worldservice/schedules/frequencies/eurwfreq.shtml. For frequency

information, refer to the main BBC website (🖥 www.bbc.co.uk). If you have satellite TV, you can also receive many radio stations via satellite. For example, BBC Radio 1, 2, 3, 4 and 5, BBC World Service, Sky Radio, Virgin 1215 and many foreign-language stations are broadcast via satellite. Digital satellite TV subscribers also have a choice of many French and international radio stations. Details are usually available in the monthly satellite subscriber newsletter. Satellite radio stations are listed in British satellite TV magazines such as the *What Satellite and Digital TV*. Those with internet access can 'tune in' to Expats Radio, a new radio station aimed at expatriates (🖥 www.expatsradio.com); you can even contribute to its broadcasts!

LEARNING THE LANGUAGE

Although English is the international *lingua franca* and all French people are taught the language for at least five years at school, it isn't widely spoken in France; in fact, in most areas it's rare to encounter anyone who speaks English fluently and still rarer to find anyone willing to speak to you in English, as the French are taught not to make mistakes rather than to communicate in foreign languages (and their own) and have an ingrained fear of making mistakes and 'losing face'. (In a recent survey, 66 per cent of French people claimed to speak only French and a mere 22 per cent admitted to speaking English 'well'.) The French are also extremely proud of their language (to the point of hubris) and – quite rightly – expect everyone living in France to speak it.

If you come to France without being able to speak French, you'll therefore have difficulty making yourself understood and even more difficulty understanding what is being said to you. You'll be excluded from society and will feel uncomfortable, embarrassed and helpless. For people retiring permanently to France permanently, learning French isn't an option, but a necessity. You **must** learn French if you wish to have French friends.

However bad your grammar, poor your vocabulary and terrible your accent, an attempt to speak French will be much better appreciated than your fluent English. Don't, however, be surprised when the French wince at your torture of their beloved tongue, pretend not to understand you even though you've said something 'correctly', or correct minor grammatical or pronunciation errors! The French honestly believe they're doing you a favour by pointing out your mistakes to you while they're fresh in your mind. (This also explains much of their hesitance to use English in public, for fear of being corrected themselves.)

> ### ⚠ Caution
>
> **The most common reason for negative experiences among foreigners in France, both visitors and residents alike, is that they cannot (or won't) speak French.**

If possible you should have French lessons before arriving in France, and you should take evening classes or a language course **before you leave home**, as you'll probably be too busy for the first few months after your move, when you most need the language; and you should continue to take lessons after arriving. It's a mistake to assume that you'll 'pick up' the language once in France, especially as you won't be working (although you might consider taking a menial or even a voluntary job, as this is one of the quickest ways of improving your French).

If you don't already speak good French, don't expect to learn it quickly, even if you already have a basic knowledge and take intensive lessons. It's common for

foreigners not to be fluent after a year or more of intensive lessons in France. If your expectations are unrealistic, you'll become frustrated, which can affect your confidence. **It takes a long time to reach the level of fluency needed to be able to communicate satisfactorily in French.**

Note that France has a number of regional languages, including Alsatian (spoken in Alsace), Basque (south-west), Breton (Brittany), Catalan and Occitan (Languedoc-Roussillon) and Corsican (Corsica), although you won't need to learn anything other than French in any region of France. On the other hand, however fluent your French, you may still have problems understanding some accents – particularly those of southern France – and local dialects (*patois*).

Although it isn't easy, even the most non-linguistic person can acquire a working knowledge of French. All that's required is a little hard work, perseverance and some help, particularly if you have only English-speaking friends.

Self-help

There are numerous self-study French courses available, including those offered by the BBC (⌨ www.bbc.co.uk/education/languages/french), Eurotalk (⌨ www.eurotalk.co.uk) and Linguaphone (⌨ www.linguaphone.co.uk). Websites offering free tutorials include ⌨ www.france-pub.com/french, ⌨ www.frenchassistant.com and ⌨ www.frenchtutorial.com. A quarterly publication, *bien-dire* (*sic*), is aimed at adult learners (⌨ www.learningfrench.com), and the About French language website (⌨ www.french.about.com) provides copious information about the language and tips to help you learn.

There are several things you can do to speed up your language learning, including watching television (particularly quiz shows where the words appear on the screen as they're spoken) and DVDs (where you can select French or English subtitles), reading (especially children's books and product catalogues, where the words are accompanied by pictures), joining a club or association, and (most enjoyable) making French friends.

Finding a French 'penfriend' (*correspondant/e*) while abroad is a good way to improve your language skills, and there are a number of websites aimed at putting people in touch for this purpose, including ⌨ www.friendsabroad.com and ⌨ www.mylanguageexchange.com.

There are many language schools (*école de langues*) in cities and large towns. One of the most famous French language teaching organisations is the Alliance Française (AF, ⌨ www.alliancefr.org), a state-approved, non-profit organisation with over 1,000 centres in 138 countries, including 32 centres in France, mainly in large towns and cities. The AF runs general, special and intensive courses, and can also arrange a homestay in France with a host family. Note, however, that the AF's teaching is somewhat 'old-fashioned' in being grammar-centred – and exclusively in French!

Another non-profit organisation is Centre de Liaisons et d'Echanges Internationaux (⌨ www.clei.asso.fr), offering intensive French language courses for juniors (13 to 18 years) and adults throughout France. Courses include accommodation in their own international centres, with a French family, or in a hotel, bed-and-breakfast or self-catering studio. Junior courses can be combined with tuition in a variety of sports and other activities, including horse riding, tennis, windsurfing, canoeing, diving and dancing.

The British organisation CESA Languages Abroad (UK ☎ 01209-211800, ⌨ www.cesalanguages.com) offers advice and arranges language courses.

Most language schools run various classes, and which one you choose will depend on your language ability, how many hours you wish to study a week, how much money you want to spend and how quickly you wish to learn. Language classes generally fall into the following categories: extensive (4 to 10 hours per week); intensive (15 to 20 hours); total immersion (20 to 40 or more). Some offer telephone lessons, which are particularly practical if you're busy or don't live near a language school.

Don't expect to become fluent in a short time unless you have a particular flair for languages or already have a good command of French. Unless you desperately need to learn French quickly, it's better to arrange your lessons over a long period. However, don't commit yourself to a long course of study, particularly an expensive one, before ensuring that it's the right course. The cost of a one-week total immersion course is usually between €2,500 and €3,000! Most schools offer free tests to help you find the appropriate level and a free introductory lesson.

Individual Lessons

You may prefer to have individual lessons, which are a quicker, although more expensive way of learning a language. The main advantage of individual lessons is that you learn at your own speed and aren't held back by slow learners or left floundering in the wake of the class genius. You can advertise for a teacher in your local newspapers, on shopping centre/supermarket bulletin boards and university notice boards, and through your or your spouse's employer. Otherwise, look for advertisements in the English-language press (see **Appendix B**). Don't forget to ask your friends, neighbours and colleagues if they can recommend a teacher.

A recent innovation is teaching via webcam, which offers one-to-one tuition without either you or your teacher needing to leave the comfort of your homes.

Individual lessons by the hour cost from around €50 at a school or €15 to €35 with a private tutor, although you may find someone willing to trade French lessons for lessons in your native language, especially if it's English. In some areas (particularly in Paris), there are discussion groups that meet regularly to converse in French and other languages; these are usually advertised in the English-language press (see **Appendix B**).

Information

The Best Places to Buy a Home in France (Survival Books – see page 321) includes lists of language schools in the most popular regions of France. A comprehensive list of schools, institutions and organisations providing French language courses throughout France is contained in a booklet, *Cours de Français Langue Étrangère et Stages Pédagogie de Français Langue Étrangère en France*. It includes information about the type of course, organisation, dates and costs, and other practical information, and is available from French consulates and from the Association pour la Diffusion de la Pensée Française (ADPF, 🖥 www.adpf.asso.fr).

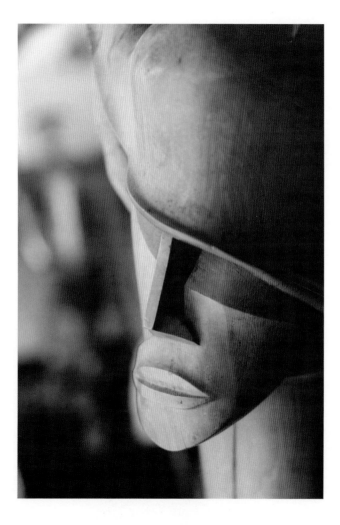

Villefranche-sur-mer, French Riviera, Alpes Maritime

3.
CAN YOU AFFORD IT?

A prime consideration when contemplating retiring in France is whether you can afford it! It's important to do your sums carefully and consider all the financial implications of spending your retirement in France. It isn't uncommon to hear tales of retirees forced to return to their home country because they didn't do their homework and found out later that they couldn't afford to live in France. You need to consider not only day-to-day living expenses but also your long-term financial prospects. If your income is generated in a currency other than euros (e.g. a UK or the US pension), you must take into account currency fluctuations and allow for periodic gains and losses. Sound financial advice from an expert familiar with the French tax system and your home country's tax system is essential.

This chapter contains essential information about the cost of living in France, along with money-saving tips, and your entitlement to pensions and social security benefits when resident in France. Information about French currency, banking and taxation is provided in **Chapter 8**.

> ☑ SURVIVAL TIP
>
> It's important to plan ahead, invest wisely and make the most of any legal opportunities to save or avoid tax.

COST OF LIVING

Contrary to popular belief, France isn't a cheap place to live. Inflation in France in 2006 was around 2 per cent, having risen from an all-time low of 0.5 per cent in 1999, largely as a result of the introduction of the euro, which provided manufacturers and retailers with a convenient smoke-screen for price increases! Moreover, the combined burden of social security contributions, income tax and indirect taxes make French taxes among the highest in the EU.

Anyone planning to live in France, particularly retirees, should take care not to underestimate the cost of living, which has increased considerably in the last decade. France is an expensive country by American standards, particularly if your income is earned in US$, and in recent years many US visitors have found it difficult or impossible to remain within their budgets. (Americans are particularly shocked by the price of gasoline, electricity, clothing, paper products and English-language books.) Some products are particularly expensive in France and are worth importing. These include electronic and audio equipment, cosmetics, furniture, books, paint and similar products, and almost anything that's manufactured outside the EU. However, many things remain cheaper than in northern European countries, including property (with the exception of the Paris, the Côte d'Azur and a few other places), property taxes, good food, alcohol, hotels, restaurants, public transport and general entertainment.

Your cost of living obviously depends on your lifestyle – what you eat (and drink), where you shop, the size and type of property you buy, whether you use public transport or run a car, and the type and amount of entertainment you indulge in. If you want to minimise your costs, you'll almost certainly have to change your lifestyle, as an attempt to continue living as you did in your home country – e.g. importing a car and food – is likely to prove costly.

Bargain Shopping

French retailers are among the world's most competitive and have smaller profit margins than those in many other countries. Price fixing isn't permitted, except on books, although the Loi Lang (named after Culture Minister Jack Lang) allows only up to a 5 per cent discount off manufacturers' 'recommended retail prices'. Prices of bread and pharmaceuticals are government controlled.

There are relatively few bargain shops in France (certainly compared with the UK or US), although there's usually at least one cheap 'bazaar' in each town, selling cheap new goods, and maybe a dépôt-vente, selling second-hand items. Brocantes can be a source of good value second-hand furniture and other items, but many are full of overpriced junk. Markets are generally not the place to go for cheap products, other than CDs and DVDs and some clothing – certainly not for food. Another source of second-hand items is the chain of Emmaüs outlets (🖳 www.emmaus.asso.fr).

'Boot sales' (known as foires à tout in the north and vide grenier in the south) are becoming increasingly common, and are usually held in the spring and autumn; products on offer range from collectors' items to worthless junk. There are second-hand book shops in most large towns and cities. If you're into buying (or selling) second-hand items online, you might like to investigate France's answer to eBay, Troc Anglaise (🖳 www.trocanglaise.com – in English).

It's possible to buy goods direct from factories, with discounts of between 30 and 70 per cent, although factory shops aren't nearly as common as in the US. Most of them are to be found in the north and east of France, although the factory-shopper's Mecca is Troyes in Aube, where there are around 250 'factory' outlets. Keen bargain hunters may want to track down The Factory Shop Guide for Northern France by Gillian Cutress & Rolf Stricker, which is now out of print, Le Guide France-Europe des Magasins d'Usine (Editions du Seuil) and Paris Pas Cher (Flammarion).

You should be on the lookout for fake goods, as some 70 per cent of all fake products are copies of French brands, reckoned to cost the country 30,000 jobs and €6bn in lost sales annually.

Perfumes are a favourite target, but counterfeit goods include leather products, CDs and DVDs, household goods and food. Even French truffles, which can cost as much as €650 per kilo, have been 'counterfeited' by the Chinese in recent years!

Regional Variations

Not surprisingly, Paris, Lyon, Nice and other large cities are France's most expensive places to live, although up-market areas such as the Côte d'Azur and popular winter and summer resort towns in other regions such as Chamonix, Deauville and Le Touquet provide close competition. In general, prices are higher in resort areas, where savvy locals inflate prices for tourists and resident foreigners, and cheaper inland

and in coastal areas that aren't popular with foreigners. Similarly, prices vary within a town or city according to location, e.g. you can expect to pay €3 to €5 for a coffee or beer at a seafront café or a tourist venue, whereas you may pay only €2 at a local bar.

☑ **SURVIVAL TIP**

Even in the major cities and popular resorts, the cost of dining out is generally reasonable by international standards and you can get a meal with wine in most places for around €15 to €20.

Food

Eating out is also considerably cheaper than most northern European countries, though less so than in North America, and in many establishments the *menu du jour* (three our four courses, plus a drink and bread) costs between €8 and €12. On the other hand, food in shops isn't particularly cheap – especially if you buy from small, specialist retailers (see sample prices below). However, you can save money on food by:

- buying French products rather than imported ones – imported items can cost up to five times more than a similar French product, e.g. a 500ml bottle of French-made tomato ketchup costs around €0.50, the imported equivalent €2; imported marmalade can cost €3 or more, while French-made marmalade (*confiture à l'orange*) costs around €1; Quality Street chocolates and toffees, widely available in France, cost over €7 for a 480g pack, while similar French brands cost around €4.50 for the same amount.

- buying food that's in season, which is also usually of better quality;

- comparing the prices of packaged and loose fruit and vegetables, as the former is surprisingly often cheaper;

- shopping around the hypermarkets and supermarkets. The national hypermarket chains, such as Auchan, Carrefour and Géant, are fiercely competitive on price and many offer to refund the difference should you find an equivalent product cheaper within a radius of say, 20 to 30km. Even so, it's worth shopping around, as similar 'own brand' products can be half the price in one chain compared with another and short-term promotions often provide exceptional bargains and the lines each chain (and even each outlet within a chain) discounts vary.

- looking out for produce that is nearing its 'sell-by' date (*date limite de vente*), which is often reduced in price.

Good-value food and drink includes biscuits, bottled water, chocolate, coffee, cola, dry dog and cat food, fish, fruit juices (especially orange), honey, jam, milk (long-life), mustard, olive oil and other oils, packet soups (tinned soups aren't available), pasta sauces, tinned sweetcorn (fresh sweetcorn isn't sold but fed to

Item	Quantity	Cost
Drinks		
Beer	6 x 250ml	€3.50
Coffee (ground)	250g	€1.50
Coffee (instant)	100g	€1.50
Fizzy drink	2 litres	€1.00
Milk	litre	€0.75
Tea	50 bags	€3.00
Water	1.5 litres	€0.30
Wine (drinkable)	75ml	€2.00
Fresh Fish		
Salmon	1kg	€11.50
Sardines	1kg	€8.00
White fish	1kg	€8.00
Meat		
Beef	1kg	€8.00
Chicken	1kg	€2.50
Lamb	1kg	€6.00
Pork	1kg	€4.00
Cooked meats	1kg	€8.00
Bread		
Bread	baguette	€0.50
Bread	loaf	€1.20
Dairy Produce		
Butter	250g	€3.00
Cheese	1kg	€10.00
Eggs	6	€1.00
Margarine	500g	€1.30
Yoghurt	4x100g	€4.00
Fruit & Vegetables		
Apples	1kg	€1.10
Bananas	1kg	€1.30
Carrots	1kg	€0.75
Green beans	1kg	€3.00
Oranges	1kg	€2.20
Potatoes	1kg	€0.25
Tomatoes	1kg	€1.50
Tins, Packets & Jars		
Baked beans	tin	€1.50
Biscuits	packet	€1.00
Cereal	375g	€0.60
Cooking oil (olive)	1 litre	€4.50

animals!), salad dressings, salt, soft drinks, steak, sweeteners, stock cubes, wine and spirits and most vegetables and dairy products (cheese, *crème fraîche*, *fromage frais*, mayonnaise, yoghurt, etc.). Note, however, that it isn't common practice in France for shops to sell cheap at the end of each day fruit and vegetables that won't keep until the following day, as in the UK.

Other good-value products include aluminium foil, audio-visual and photographic equipment, bicycles and bicycle and car accessories, cat litter, coffee makers, disposable contact lenses, DIY and gardening equipment, glasses (to drink out of), kettles, luggage, pots and pans, shampoo, shavers and shaving products, swimming pool chemicals (e.g. chlorine tablets), tissues and toilet and kitchen paper, tobacco products, toothpaste, water softeners and washing powder.

Shopping Basket

The following table is a rough guide to the lowest price of certain food items (own brand included) in an average supermarket in France. The prices don't take into account offers or bulk buying. A guide to current prices of many foodstuffs and other items can be found at 🖳 www.day-tripper. net.

Cooking oil (sunflower)	1 litre	€1.25
Crisps	250g	€2.00
Flour	1kg	€0.30
Jam	350g	€1.20
Pasta	500g	€2.30
Rice	1kg	€1.60
Sardines	tin	€0.50
Sugar	1kg	€0.95
Tuna	3 tins	€2.00
Toiletries & Cleaning Products		
Shampoo	250ml	€1.80
Shower gel	750ml	€6.60
Toilet paper	6 rolls	€1.65
Toothpaste	tube	€2.50
Washing powder	27 washes	€4.00
Washing-up liquid	500ml	€1.00

Leisure & Sport

Prices for leisure and sporting activities are generally reasonable in France. The following list is a general guide to the cost of some activities:

Leisure

The following prices apply to major venues.

Cinema	from €5
Concert	from €20
Museum	from €5
Musical	from €20
Theatre	from €15
Theme park or zoo	from €12

There are no senior discounts for most leisure activities, except for *Carte Senior* holders (see **Senior Discounts** on page 27), but sometimes museums allow free entry one day a month (e.g. the first Sunday in each month), and on the third weekend in September (*les journées du patrimoine*) various places of interest not normally open to the public can be visited free of charge.

Websites (all in French only) offering tickets to all kinds of events, though not necessarily at discounted prices, include 🖥 www.carrefourspectacles.com, 🖥 www. ticketnet.fr and 🖥 www.viafrance.com.

Miscellaneous Items

Newspaper (French)	€0.85
(foreign)	from €3.00
CD	from €10
DVD	from €10
DVD Rental	from €2

English-language books, including (in some cases) second-hand books, are available from specialised shops in cities, resort areas and towns with a large expatriate population. New English-language books can be purchased at discount prices from 🖥 www. amazon.co.uk and 🖥 www.amazon.fr.

Sports

Month's gym membership	from €25
One-day ski pass	from €30
Round of golf (18-hole)	from €20
(from €60 on the Côte d'Azur)	
Tennis court per hour	from €5

Property

Spiralling prices in the last five years have made property in France an excellent investment – many buyers have seen huge returns – but it remains good value, particularly in comparison with property in the UK. In some areas bargains can still be found, although these are usually in remote areas or 'undiscovered' regions – or consist of dilapidated properties in need of major restoration.

> Although prices are still rising at above the rate of inflation, the rate of increase slowed between 2005 and 2008.

The average price of resale properties countrywide fell slightly between November 2006 and January 2007, stabilised in

February and March, picked up in April to June, fell again in July and August before rising again slowly at the end of the year, for an overall annual increase of around 3.7 per cent – compared with increases of 7.2 per cent in 2006, 10.9 per cent in 2005, 15.5 per cent in 2004 and 14 per cent in 2003. The average price of houses rose slightly more than that of apartments (4.5 per cent compared with 3.2 per cent). In Ile-de-France, including Paris, prices rose by just under 8 per cent between mid-2006 and mid-2007 compared with over 14 per cent from mid-2005 to mid-2006; the fastest rises (over 8.5 per cent) were in Paris and Yvelines, the slowest (under 7 per cent) in Essonne, Seine-et-Marne and Val-de-Marne.

The slow-down in the property market is expected to continue for the rest of the decade, some forecasters predicting a fall of up to 18 per cent between 2008 and 2010 – which is good news for buyers.

Property taxes (see page 195) are low in France compared with those in some other countries, e.g. the UK, although this is changing. In recent years, central government has devolved many responsibilities to the regions and departments, which has allowed them to lower or stabilise income tax levels, but local taxation has risen to make up the difference. On the other hand, fees and taxes payable when buying a property are high at around 10-15 per cent of the purchase price. Note also that maintenance costs can be high if you buy a property with a pool or large garden, or if you need someone to look after your property when you're away or you let it.

For further information on property prices and what you can buy for your money, see **Cost of Property** on page 114.

Cars

New car prices are higher in France than in most other European countries (although lower than those in the UK) and many French people buy their cars in Belgium, Luxembourg or Portugal, where most new cars are up to 20 per cent cheaper than in France. However, French dealers compete in offering discounts, guarantees, financing terms and deals, so it pays to shop around. Second-hand cars are expensive (i.e. cars hold their value well) and often come with an assortment of dents and scratches as standard!

The table below gives a guide to basic motoring costs in France:

Motoring Costs	
Item	**Cost**
New basic car (e.g. Renault Twingo)	€11,350
Second-hand basic car (five years old)	€5,500
Registration (one-off)	€200
Road tax	€0
Vehicle test (every other year after first four years)	€55
Annual insurance for 70-year-old with good record (third-party) to (comp)	€380 €880
Fuel (diesel) (unleaded petrol) per litre	€1.15 €1.35
Service (interim) (main)	€140 €250

Insurance

Most car insurance policies are reasonably priced in France, although the actual price depends on the cover and policy. Third-party car insurance (the minimum legal requirement) is inexpensive for those with a no-claims bonus (the maximum in France is 50 per cent) or if you choose to pay an excess.

For further information see **Car Insurance** on page 209.

Road Tax

French-registered private vehicles no longer require a road tax certificate (*vignette automobile*), with the exception of certain camper vans, but since January 2006 a tax has been added to the cost of a registration document for cars that emit more than a certain amount of carbon dioxide.

The use of most motorways (*autoroute*) and certain bridges and tunnels is 'taxed' in the form of tolls.

Fuel

As in other European countries, the cost of fuel in France has increased considerably in recent years and the days of cheap petrol are long gone. Even so, fuel prices in France are lower than in some other EU countries, including the UK. Diesel is slightly cheaper than petrol, but only by a few cents. Prices are usually set by individual petrol stations, so it's worthwhile shopping around for the lowest price (usually to be found at hypermarkets). The average prices of petrol and diesel in France and other European countries can be found on ⌨ www.day-tripper.net/pricespetrol.html.

The environmentally-conscious can do even better than buying a dark-green-label car (see above) by investing in a vehicle that runs on a mixture of propane and butane, known as liquid-petroleum gas (LPG – *gaz de pétrole liquéfié*, *GPL* or *Gépel* in French). You can also convert a conventional car to run on LPG, which produces less harmful emissions than petrol, including around 15 per cent less carbon dioxide as well as less carbon monoxide. There are around 200,000 LPG-powered cars on French roads, and they're manufactured by Daihatsu, Ford, Opel and others.

> All new cars sold in France must be labelled with their 'energy efficiency' (i.e. the amount of carbon dioxide their engines emit for every kilometre travelled), with colour codes ranging from dark green for the most environmentally-friendly models (emissions of less than 100g/km) to red for the most polluting (over 250g/km) and there's a surcharge on the cost of a registration document for high-emission cars.

Although new LPG cars cost around €1,500 more than ordinary cars (and conversion of an ordinary car costs between €2,000 and €3,500), tax credits of between €1,525 and €2,300 are available and fuel costs around half as much as petrol, so major savings can be made. Engine wear and noise are also reduced. Note, however, that LPG-powered cars aren't permitted to use certain road tunnels and there have been a number of spectacular explosions involving LPG-powered vehicles. The *Guide GPL* is available from petrol stations supplying LPG and from the Comité Français du Butane et du Propane (💻 www.cfbp.fr).

If you retire to Paris, you can even buy an electric car – they're tax-free and entitle you to free parking (if you can find a space) – and hope that the promised 100 charging points (*bornes de recharge*) are installed before your batteries go flat! Further information and maps showing the location of charging points can be found on 💻 www.paris.fr/portail/deplacements/Portal.lut?page_id=5775.

Public Transport

Public transport is generally inexpensive in France and if you purchase a season ticket savings are considerable. You can also save money by travelling at off-peak times and by booking. Those over 60 are entitled to discounts of 25 (peak) or 50 per cent (off-peak) on all rail journeys with a *Carte Senior* (see page 27). See **Getting Around** on page 34 for general information about public transport.

Utilities

Electricity

France has the EU's cheapest electricity, although prices have risen considerably in the last few years. The cost depends on your power supply and tariff. You can save on electricity bills by using the peak/off-peak tariff (*option heures pleines/heures creuses*), with a reduced rate period (or periods) of a total of up to eight hours a day, when you can run high-power appliances such as water heaters and night storage heaters.

You can also install solar power (for heat and electricity production) and buy low-consumption appliances (look for those with an 'A' classification) to save on electricity bills. Generous grants are available for solar power installations from both central and local government, although even taking these into account it

still takes eight to ten years to recoup the initial outlay.

You're normally billed for your electricity every three months but may receive bi-monthly or monthly bills if your consumption is above a certain level, or you can choose to make regular monthly payments by direct debit. See chapter 5 for further information.

Gas

Mains gas (*gaz de ville*) is available in around 80 towns and cities in France and is inexpensive. If you live in a rural area you'll have to use bottled gas, which is more expensive than mains gas. Bottles come in 35kg, 13kg and 5/6kg sizes. A small one used just for cooking will last an average family around six weeks. Bottles can be bought at most petrol stations and super/hypermarkets, but you should trade in an empty bottle for a new one; otherwise it's much more expensive. An exchange 13kg bottle costs around €25. If you need to buy a gas bottle, you'll be asked to register and pay a deposit (e.g. €40). If you want to run central heating by gas and don't have access to mains gas, you'll need a gas tank (*citerne*) installed on your property; see 127 for more information.

Water

French mains water is among the most expensive in the world, although the cost varies by up to 100 per cent from region to region, according to its abundance or scarcity. It can cost as much as €3.60 per cubic metre or as little as €1.75; the national average is around €2.75 (or 0.275 centimes per litre). However, if you have a septic tank (*fosse septique*) as opposed to mains drainage (*tout à l'égout*), your water bill will be much lower, e.g. €0.75 per cubic metre, as water rates also pay for mains sewerage. Most properties are metered, so that you pay only for the water you use.

Many rural properties have access to 'free' water from wells or springs (*eau de forage*). This is mostly used for watering gardens, etc. but it may also be used domestically if the quality is good enough (you need to have it analysed).

> ⚠ **Caution**
>
> **Some people drill for water but this is expensive, particularly if water is at great depth or no water is found, and the cost of pumping water to the surface can also be high. Moreover, extensive development in some areas has seriously lowered the water table and it's likely that restrictions will be placed on both drilling and the use of *eau de forage* before long.**

Water shortages are rare in towns but fairly common in some rural areas during hot summers, when the water may periodically be switched off. It's possible to have a storage tank installed for emergencies and you should also have a rainwater or household waste tank for watering the garden and washing cars. You can reduce your water consumption by installing a 'water saver' that mixes air with water (available from hypermarkets and DIY stores).

You're billed by your local water company annually or every six months and can pay by direct debit. In community properties, the water bill for the whole building is usually divided among the apartments according to their size, although they may be individually metered.

Telephone

Landlines: Deregulation of the telecommunications market has resulted in an intense price war between some 20 providers, and considerable savings can be made on both national and international calls by shopping around for the lowest rates (many people use different companies for different types of call). Tariffs are continually changing, so keep an eye on the latest deals. Comparisons between the rates offered by different service providers can be found on the internet (e.g. 🖳 www.comparatel.fr and 🖳 www.budgetelecom.com).

Mobile phones: After a slow start in introducing mobile telephones (*portable* or, increasingly, *mobile*), France has one of Europe's fastest-growing cellular populations. Mobile phone rates vary hugely according to the company and the type and duration of calls you make. The best deals are available on contract arrangements, although you must usually pay a minimum monthly amount, but 'pay-as-you-talk' options are better value if you don't use a mobile much. It may be

cheaper to make a mobile to mobile call than a mobile to landline call or vice versa.

Internet: There has been a proliferation of internet service providers (ISPs), called *fournisseur d'accès/FAI* or *serveur* in France, in recent years and there are now over 200 offering a variety of products and prices. As in other countries, a price war is raging and it's worth comparing prices to find the cheapest provider for your needs. Dial-up internet connections generally cost the same as local calls, but most companies offer services that allow you to buy a fixed number of access hours per month at a discount. For as little as €6 to €10 per month, you can usually have five or ten hours online, although most ISPs offer packages including broadband and telephone for around €30 per month. For details of French ISPs see page 43.

Internet telephony: If you have a broadband internet connection, you can make long-distance and international 'phone calls' free (or almost free) to anyone with a broadband connection. 'Voice over internet protocol' (VOIP) is a new technology that's revolutionising the telecommunications market and will eventually (some say within five years) make today's telephone technology (both land lines and mobile networks) obsolete. A leading company in this field is Skype (🖳 www.skype.com), recently purchased by eBay, which has over 50m users worldwide. Microsoft also has a popular system, MSN Messenger (🖳 http://messenger.msn.co.uk), and there are numerous other companies in the market – a web search on 'internet phone' will throw up many other internet phone providers. All you need is access to a local broadband provider and a headset (costing as little as $10) or a special phone. Calls to other computers anywhere in the world are free, while calls to landlines are charged at a few cents per minute.

For further information about telecommunications, see **Keeping in Touch** on page 39.

PENSIONS & SOCIAL SECURITY BENEFITS

Pensions

Retirees receiving a state pension from another EU country can continue to receive it in France and are entitled to the same health benefits as French retirees. Americans who retire in France can receive their pensions (and other benefits) via the social security department of the French Embassy in Paris (see **Appendix A** for the address). However, your pension and benefits will be paid in the currency of the country of origin (e.g. £GB or $US) and will therefore be vulnerable to currency exchange swings when converted into euros. Note also that tax-free lump sums from a foreign (e.g. UK) pension fund aren't tax-free in France, where they're regarded as taxable income.

Non-EU citizens entitled to a state retirement pension in their home country will probably be able to receive it in France.

Under EU law, social security contributions made towards a state pension scheme in any EU country count towards a state pension in another EU country. If you qualify for a state pension, you can claim it from any EU country where you've made contributions or from the EU country you're living in when you retire. All EU countries have different regulations regarding the qualifying age, the number of contributions and the amount paid. If you apply for your pension in France, the authorities will consult your social security contributions record in other EU countries and you may qualify for a higher pension than is usually paid in France. This process takes some considerable time and you're advised to start the application process at least six months before you retire.

> ☑ SURVIVAL TIP
>
> You should inform the pension authorities in your home country well in advance about your move to France and provide details of your French bank account so that your pension can be paid directly in France (if desirable).

If you plan to retire while living in France, you should check that your pension contributions are up to date, either in France or in your previous country of residence. If you won't be entitled to a full French state pension (e.g. you won't have worked there for a sufficient number of years), you may be able to continue to make contributions to your pension fund in your previous country of residence. Britons should contact HM Revenue & Customs, Centre for Non-Residents (Newcastle), Longbenton, Newcastle-upon-Tyne NE98 1ZZ (☎ 0845-915 7800 or ☎ 0191-203 7010). A French state pension is paid only when you cease full-time employment and isn't paid automatically; you must make an application to your regional sickness insurance fund office (Caisse Régionale d'Assurance Maladie/CRAM).

UK Pensioners

If you're entitled to a UK state pension, payments can be made to you in France and your pension payments are index-linked, i.e. subject to annual increases in line with inflation rates in the UK (not those in France). You can choose to have payments made by cheque and sent by post or transferred directly to a French bank account. The latter method is cheaper and more efficient – you don't lay yourself open to the vagaries of the French postal system. For payment via bank transfer, you must provide the authorities with the name and address of your bank, your account number (20 digits) and IBAN. Payments are made every 4 or 13 weeks (you can choose) unless your pension payment is very small, in which case payment is made once a year.

Unless you have an armed forces or government pension, which are taxed in the UK, your pension will be taxed in your country of residence, i.e. France if you spend more than half the year there (see **Liability** on page 191). If your pension provides a lump sum rather than an annual income, you may be able to avoid French tax by taking it before leaving the UK; seek expert advice.

UK nationals planning to move to France before retirement age can obtain a pension forecast from their local Social Security office (by completing form BR19) or from the Retirement Pension Forecasting and Advice Unit of the Department of Work & Pensions (☎ 0191-218 7585, 💻 www. thepensionservice.gov.uk). Those already living in France should ask for form CA3638.

Social Security Benefits

EU retirees coming to live permanently in France are entitled to the same social security benefits as French retirees. Those over 60 aren't required to make contributions, although they must still register (and present form E106 or E121 – see page 156). France also has reciprocal social security arrangements with the following countries: Algeria, Andorra, Bosnia-Herzegovina, Cameroon, Canada, Cape Verde, Chile, Congo, Croatia, Gabon, Israel, Ivory Coast, Macedonia, Madagascar, Mali, Mauritania, Monaco, Morocco, Niger, Philippines, Senegal, Serbia and Montenegro, Togo, Tunisia, Turkey and the US. These agreements differ in extent, however, and you should check your social security entitlements in France before making any arrangements to retire there.

If you don't qualify for benefits but your household has an annual income of less than €8,644 (until 30th September 2008; the 'ceiling' (*plafond*) is increased annually on 1st October), you may be entitled to basic social security cover under the *Couverture Maladie Universelle* (*CMU*) scheme, introduced in 2000. Information is available from your local CPAM office and a dedicated government website (💻 www. cmu.fr – in French only). If you earn more than this amount, you may earn entitlement to *CMU* by paying a contribution of 8 per cent of your income above the ceiling. *CMU* entitles you to standard reimbursements, so you must usually pay part of the cost of medical treatment (see page 174). If you earn even less than this, you may be entitled to *Couverture Maladie Universelle Complémentaire* (*CMUC*), which provides you with 100 per cent reimbursement.

UK Pensioners

Depending on your status, you may be entitled to additional benefits from the UK government when you move to France.

Long-term incapacity benefit

If you qualify for this in the UK, you'll continue to receive it in France, but the amount is calculated at the same rate as the French authorities pay to French nationals, so you may find the benefit significantly reduced.

Winter fuel allowance: If you're over 60 and qualify for this benefit in the UK (and were claiming it before you left), you may continue to receive the allowance, which is worth £200 or £300 depending on your age and circumstances, after moving to France. Contact the Winter Fuel Payment Centre, Southgate House, Cardiff Central, Cardiff CF91 1ZH, UK (☎ 0845-915 1515 or ☎ 029-2042 8635, 💻 www. thepensionservice.gov.uk/winterfuel).

See also **Health Insurance** on page 219.

Provence

4.
LOCATION, LOCATION, LOCATION

O nce you've decided to retire to France – and that you can afford to – you'll need to choose the area where you wish to settle (the subject of this chapter) and what sort of home to buy (see Chapter 5).

The secret of finding the right place to retire is research, research and more research – the right choice of location may make the difference between a dream and nightmare retirement. You may be fortunate and buy the first place you see without doing any homework and live happily ever after. However, successful retirement is much more likely if you thoroughly investigate the towns and communities in your chosen area, compare the range of amenities and facilities available, and research property prices to ensure that you can afford to buy or rent there.

Where you choose to retire will depend on a number of factors, including your preferences, whether you plan to buy or rent a property, whether you intend to retire to France permanently or for just part of the year, and, not least, your financial resources. When seeking a permanent home, don't be too influenced by where you've spent an enjoyable holiday or two. A town or area that was enjoyable for a few weeks' holiday may be far from suitable for a retirement home, particularly regarding the proximity to shops, medical facilities and other amenities.

It's worth bearing in mind that France is a large country (the largest in western Europe) and is home to a wealth of varying landscapes, climates and cultures; these differ so much that France could almost be several countries (and there's a lot of variation within some regions). You also need to be aware that standards vary from region to region, e.g. some regions spend more on healthcare than others, and it's worth taking this into account when choosing your retirement location.

The 'best' area to retire to depends on a range of considerations, including the proximity to a town, shops (e.g. a supermarket), public transport, sports facilities, beach, etc. When looking for a home, bear in mind the travelling time and costs to shops and local amenities such as the health centre, restaurants, and sports and social facilities. If you buy a remote country property, the distance to local amenities and services could become a problem, particularly as you get older and less mobile. If you live in a remote rural area you need to be much more self-sufficient than if you live in a town and will need to use a car for everything, which can add significantly to the cost of living.

RENTING BEFORE BUYING

If you haven't decided on your retirement destination or cannot decide between several locations, it's advisable to rent a furnished property for a period. If you plan to retire to France permanently or for long periods, it's advisable to rent for at least six months and preferably a year. An area that's quiet and relaxing between November and March can become noisy, congested and stressful between April and October, particularly if it's a popular holiday area. Conversely, somewhere that's attractive in the summer can virtually 'close' in winter or the weather can be depressing. If you cannot rent long term, try to visit an area for a week or two in each of the four seasons.

If possible, you should rent a similar property to the one you're planning to buy, during the time(s) of year when you plan to occupy it.

☑ **SURVIVAL TIP**

If you plan to let your property in your home country, make sure that you choose a reputable management company to look after both the property and the rentals, and take expert advice on the tax implications.

If you're looking for a long-term rental property, it's best not to rent unseen, but to rent a holiday apartment for a week or two to allow yourself time to look around for a longer-term rental. You may even wish to consider renting a home in France long term (or 'permanently'). Some people let their family homes abroad and rent one in France for a period (you may even make a 'profit'!).

Properties for rent are advertised in local newspapers and magazines, particularly expatriate publications, and can also be found through property publications in many countries (see **Appendix B)** and numerous websites (see **Appendix C**).

The advantages of renting include the following:

- It allows you to become familiar with the weather, the amenities and the local people, to meet other foreigners who have made their homes in France and share their experiences, and to discover the cost of living at first hand.

- It 'buys' you time to find your dream home at your leisure.

- It saves tying up your capital and can be surprisingly inexpensive in many regions.

On the other hand, the disadvantages of renting should be taken into consideration, including the following:

- Annual property price increases in most areas are higher than interest rates, which means that you may be better off putting your money into property than investing it elsewhere while you rent.

- Taking a long-term rental before buying means in effect moving house twice within a year or two – and moving is said to be one of life's most stressful experiences.

- You may not find the type of rental property you want, which will colour your experience of living in a particular area and possibly in France generally.

village, Beaujolais

For short-term rentals, France has an abundance of furnished, self-catering accommodation and the widest imaginable choice. You can choose from literally thousands of cottages, apartments, villas, bungalows, mobile homes, chalets, and even *châteaux* and manor houses. Many short-term lets are *gîtes*, which literally means a home or shelter but is nowadays used to refer to most furnished, self-catering holiday accommodation. A typical *gîte* is a small cottage or self-contained apartment with one or two bedrooms (sleeping four to eight and usually including a sofa bed in the living room), a large living room/kitchen with an open fire or stove, and a toilet and shower room.

Standards vary considerably, from dilapidated, ill-equipped cottages to luxury villas with every modern convenience. In certain parts of France, notably the overcrowded Côte d'Azur, *gîtes* may be concrete 'rabbit hutches', built to a basic standard with minimal facilities. Check whether a property has the facilities you require, in particular central heating if you're planning to rent in winter.

Most property let on a short-term basis is intended for holidays and you're normally limited to one or two weeks only, particularly during the peak summer season, when the rent can be prohibitive. Longer lets are sometimes available, but generally only in low season. Furnished properties that aren't holiday accommodation are sometimes available for as little as three months, but the usual minimum period is a year. Note that to rent a furnished property, you must provide evidence that it isn't your principal residence. The minimum rental period for unfurnished property is three years, so this is unlikely to be an option.

Information (in French) on renting can be found on the website of the Union des Chambres Syndicales de Proprétaires et Copropriétaires (UNPI, 💻 www.unpi. org – click on *Questions/Réponses* for a list of topics).

Finding a Rental Property

Your success or failure in finding a suitable rental property depends on many factors, not least the type of rental you're seeking (a one-bedroom apartment is easier to find than a four-bedroom detached house), how much you want to pay and the area. France has a strong rental market in most areas, although long-term rentals are more difficult to find in rural areas.

☑ **SURVIVAL TIP**

When looking for rented accommodation, try to avoid the months of September and October, when French people return from their summer holidays and (in university towns and cities) students are looking for accommodation.

Ways of finding a property to rent include the following:

- Visit accommodation and letting agents. Most cities and large towns have estate agents (*agents immobiliers*) who also act as letting agents. Look under *Agences de Location et de Propriétés* in the yellow pages. It's often better to deal with an agent than directly with owners, particularly with regard to contracts and legal matters. Builders and developers may also let properties to potential buyers.

- Contact travel agents, French Government Tourist Offices (who are agents for Gîtes de France) and local tourist offices, who may deal with short-term rentals.

- Look in local newspapers and magazines, particularly expatriate publications, and foreign property publications (see **Appendix B** for a list of the most popular publications).

- Check newsletters published by churches, clubs and expatriate organisations, and their notice boards.

- Look for advertisements in shop windows and on notice boards in shopping centres, supermarkets, universities and colleges, and company offices.

- Search the internet: useful sites are listed in **Appendix C** (under **Property & Accommodation**).

- Ask at the local town hall or *mairie*, which may have details of properties to rent long term.

- Contact owners directly via the publications listed in **Appendix B**.

Companies that offer long-term 'holiday' rentals include Cottages4you (☎ 0870-782100, 🖳 www.cottages4you.co.uk

– up to six weeks), French Locations (☎ 01275-856691, 🖳 www.french-locations. co.uk – from three months).

Rental Costs

Rental costs vary considerably according to the size and quality of a property, its age and the facilities provided. Prices are calculated according to the number of rooms (*pièces*) – **excluding** the kitchen, bathroom(s), toilet(s) and other 'utility' rooms – and the floor area (in square metres). A one-room apartment has a combined living and sleeping room (it may have a separate kitchen and bathroom) and is called a *studio*. A two-room (*deux-pièces*) apartment usually has one bedroom, a living room, kitchen and bathroom. A three-room (*trois-pièces*) apartment has two bedrooms, a four-room (*quatre-pièces*) apartment may have three bedrooms or two bedrooms and separate dining and living rooms, and so on. The average size of a two-room apartment is around 50m² (500ft²).

Rental prices are also based on the prevailing market value of a property (*indice*), and the most significant factor affecting rental prices is location: the region of France, the city and the neighbourhood. Like everywhere, rental prices in France are dictated by supply and demand and are higher, for example, in Cannes, Grenoble, Lyon and Nice than in Bordeaux, Marseille, Strasbourg and Toulouse. Rental accommodation in Paris is in high demand and short supply, and the prices are among the highest in Europe and often double those in other French cities. In Paris, you should expect to pay at least €25 per m²; a tiny studio apartment of around 20m² (215ft²) in a reasonable area costs around €500 per month, while a two or three-bedroom apartment (125m²/1,345ft²) in a fashionable *arrondissement* can cost up to ten times as much.

The lowest prices are found in small towns and rural areas, although there isn't so much choice. As a general rule, the further a property is from a city or large town (or town centre), public transport or other facilities, the cheaper it is. In the provinces you can rent a two-bedroom apartment or cottage for €300 or less per month. Houses can be rented in most rural areas and on the outskirts of some towns; for a three-bedroom house, you can expect to pay at least €500 per month – double that in parts of Ile-de-France and the south-east, including the Alps. In late 2007, the average monthly property rental price nationwide was €12.40 per m²; the average apartment (52m²) renting for around €640 and the average house for €880.

Rental prices are often open to negotiation and you may be able to secure a 5 to 10 per cent reduction if there isn't a queue of customers behind you. For details of prices and availability of long-term lets in different regions, refer to *The Best Places to Buy a Home in France* (Survival Books – see page 323).

For short-term lets the cost is calculated on a weekly basis (Saturday to Saturday) and depends on the standard, location, number of beds and facilities provided. The rent for a *gîte* sleeping six is typically from €250 to €350 per week in June and September, and €350 to €500 in July and August. The rent is higher for a *gîte* with a pool. However, when renting long-term outside the high season, you can rent a two-bedroom property for around €500 per month in most regions.

> A tax known as 'right to a lease' (*droit au bail*) of 2.5 per cent is added to rental charges.

In addition to rent, you may incur some or all of the following costs:

● agency fee (*frais d'agence*) – equivalent to two months' rent, but may be shared between you and your landlord. Some agencies charge an additional 'inspection fee' and/or registration fee.

- deposit (*caution*) – to cover any damage you might cause to the property or its furnishing or fittings, which is usually equivalent to two months' rent, although it's refundable if you don't damage anything;

- heating, electricity and water charges (see **Utilities** on page127) – which aren't normally included in the rent;

- maintenance/service charges;

- residential tax (*taxe d'habitation*) – which you must pay if your rental period includes 1st January, unless otherwise agreed with the lessor.

Rental Contracts

A rental contract, whether for an unfurnished or a furnished property, must be signed by all parties involved, including the agent handling the contract, if applicable. Next to their signature each party must also write the words *lu et approuvé* (read and approved). A contract for a furnished property is called a *contrat de location de locaux meublés*, while a seasonal contract is an *engagement de location meublée saisonnière*.

French rental laws (and protection for tenants) don't extend to holiday lettings. For holiday letting, the parties are free to agree such terms as they see fit concerning the period, rent, deposit and the number of occupants permitted, and there's no legal obligation on the landlord to provide a written agreement. However, you should never rent a property without a written contract, which should be drawn up or checked by a notary for long-term rentals. This is important if you wish to get a deposit returned. You should also ensure that there's a detailed inventory (*état des lieux*),

or you could be charged at the end of your tenancy for 'damage' you haven't caused.

If you rent for more than a year, you (and the lessor) become subject to minimum notice periods (a month for the lessee, three months for the lessor), which are increased if you rent for more than three years.

In certain circumstances it's possible to enter into a *contrat de location accession*, whereby you spend a period (agreed between you and the owner – known as the *période de jouissance*) in a property during which you decide whether or not you wish to buy it. During the 'trial' period, you must pay an indemnity (*redevance*) and all running costs, as if you were renting.

Home Exchange

An alternative to renting is to exchange your home abroad with one in France. This way you can experience home living

in France at low cost. Although there's an element of risk involved in exchanging your home with another family, most agencies thoroughly vet clients and many have a track record of successful swaps (a recent UK Consumers' Association survey found that 99 per cent of house swappers were happy with their experience).

Apart from the obvious advantage of providing you with free accommodation, home exchange has the major benefit of putting you in direct touch with people who live in the area that you're interested in moving to (i.e. the owners of the home you're occupying).

There are home exchange agencies in most countries. Global Home Exchange (☎ 250-740 1740, 🖳 www.4homex.com) is based in Canada and Swaphouse.org (🖳 www.swaphouse.org) in Italy. Those in the US include Home Exchange.Com or HomeExchange.com Inc. (☎ 310-798-3864, 🖳 www.homeexchange.com), Home Exchange (or House Swap) International (🖳 www.singleshomeexchange.com) and HomeLink International (☎ 305-294 7766 or 800-638 3841, 🖳 www.homelink.org or 🖳 www.swapnow.com), which has some 16,500 members in around 50 countries. HomeLink also has an office in the UK (7 St Nicholas Rise, Headbourne Worthy, Winchester SO23 7SY, ☎ 01962-886882, 🖳 www.homelink.org.uk), which publishes a *Directory* of homes and holiday homes for exchange. Other UK-based exchange agencies are Home Base Holidays, 7 Park Avenue, London N13 5PG, UK (☎ 020-8886 8752, 🖳 www.homebase-hols. com) and Intervac Home Exchange, 24 The Causeway, Chippenham, Wiltshire SN15 3DB (☎ UK 01249-461101, 🖳 www. intervac.com), which has representatives in some 30 countries. Green Theme International is a British agency based in France, at 9 rue des Insurgés, La Maillerie

Ouest, 87130 Linards (☎ 05 55 08 47 04, 🖳 www.gti-home-exchange.com).

Most agencies charge (usually between £40 and £100 per year) to advertise your property and allow you to view other properties, which means that only bona fide house swappers have access to your details.

CHOOSING THE LOCATION

The most important consideration when buying a home anywhere is usually its location – or, as the old adage goes, the three most important considerations are location, location and location! If you're looking for a good investment, a property in reasonable condition in a popular area is likely to be much better than an exceptional property in an out-of-the-way location. Even if you aren't concerned with making money from your property, there's little point in buying a 'dream home' if it's right next to a motorway or a rubbish dump or is so inaccessible that a trip to the baker's is a major expedition. France offers almost everything that anyone could want, but you must choose the right property in the right spot.

Many people's choice of location for a home is based on holiday experiences, friends' recommendations or simply an area's reputation. However, if you're likely to be spending a (hopefully) long retirement in your new home, it's worth taking the time and trouble to consider every aspect of its location first hand. When choosing a permanent home, don't be too influenced by where you've spent an enjoyable holiday or two. A place that was acceptable for a few weeks' holiday may be far from suitable for year-round living.

The 'best' place to live in France obviously depends on your preferences and lifestyle and there isn't one ideal location that would suit everyone. The climate, lifestyle and cost of living can vary considerably from region to region (and even within a particular region). The important thing is to identify the positive and possible negative aspects of each of your selected locations in order to help you choose the one that best suits you and your family.

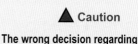

Caution

The wrong decision regarding location is one of the main causes of disenchantment among retirees who purchase property in France.

If you have little idea about where you wish to live, read as much as you can about the different regions of France (see **Regions** on page 80 and *The Best Places to Live in France* by Survival Books – see page 323) and spend some time looking around your areas of interest. A publication that claims to provide up-to-the-minute reports on French property hotspots and other matters related to buying a home in France is *France Property Alerts*, a weekly subscription newsletter circulated by email (🖳 www.francepropertyalerts.co.uk). The results of a survey of the suitability for retirees of each of France's departments, published by *l'Express* magazine in December 2007, are included in **Appendix G**.

If possible, you should visit an area a number of times over a period of a few weeks, both on weekdays and at weekends, in order to get a feel for the neighbourhood (don't just drive around, but walk!). A property seen on a balmy summer's day after a delicious lunch and a few glasses of *vin blanc* may not be nearly so attractive on a subsequent visit *sans* sunshine and the warm inner glow.

You should also try to visit an area at different times of the year, e.g. in both summer and winter, as somewhere that's

Fountain, Place de la Concorde, Paris

wonderful in summer can be forbidding and inhospitable in winter (or vice versa). If you're planning to buy a retirement home in a mountain area, you should also view it in the summer, as snow can hide a multitude of sins! In any case, you should view a property a number of times before making up your mind to buy it. If you're unfamiliar with an area, most experts recommend that you rent for a period before deciding to buy (see **Renting Before Buying** on page 68). This is particularly important if you're planning to buy a retirement home in an unfamiliar area. Many people change their minds after a period and it isn't unusual for people to move once or twice before settling down permanently.

You should also check the medium-term infrastructure plans for the area, with the local town hall and, if possible (it often isn't!), relevant regional and national authorities, particularly with regard to planned road and railway construction. Although a rural plot may seem miles from anywhere today, there could be plans for a motorway passing along the boundaries within the next five or ten years.

Bear in mind that foreign buyers aren't welcome everywhere, particularly when they 'colonise' a town or area (see **Community** on page 76). There has been some resistance to foreigners buying property in certain areas and a few towns have even blocked sales to foreigners to deter speculators. Understandably, the French don't want property prices driven up by foreigners with more money than sense to levels they can no longer afford. However, foreigners are generally welcomed by the local populace (and in most areas are infinitely preferable to Parisians!), not least because they boost the local economy and in rural areas often buy derelict properties that the French won't touch. Permanent residents in rural areas who take the time and trouble to integrate with the local community are invariably warmly welcomed.

The 'best' place to live in France depends on a range of considerations, including the following.

Accessibility

Is the proximity to public transport, e.g. an international airport, port or railway station, or access to a motorway important? Note that the motorway network is continually being expanded and will eventually cover the whole country, and the expansion of the *TGV* rail network (see map in **Appendix E**) means that many remote areas are now linked to Paris and other major cities in just a few hours. Don't, however, believe all you're told about the distance or travelling times to the nearest motorway, airport, railway station, port, beach or town, but check it for yourself.

If you buy a remote country property, the distance to local amenities and services could become a problem, particularly as you get older. Check the local public transport, as you may not always be able (or wish) to drive. See also **Getting Around** on page 34.

☑ SURVIVAL TIP

Although it isn't so important if you're buying a retirement home in France and planning to stay put, one of the major considerations when buying a part-time retirement home is how easy and cheap it will be to travel (by road, rail or air) to and from your home country (or anywhere you wish to visit frequently, such as Paris).

Although budget airlines have recently made previously remote parts of France accessible, such services are notoriously fickle and it isn't wise to buy in a particular area purely because it's served by cheap flights; airlines create and cancel routes (and are bought and sold) at the drop of a hat and you could be left stranded. Many buyers discovered this to their cost after the acquisition of Buzz airline by Ryanair, after which Ryanair discontinued services from some French airports.

Amenities

What local health and social services are provided? How far is the nearest hospital with an emergency department? What shopping facilities are provided in the neighbourhood? How far is it to the nearest town with good shopping facilities, e.g. a supermarket/hypermarket? How would you get there if your car was out of commission? If you live in a remote rural area you'll need to be much more self-sufficient than if you live in a town.

Don't forget that France is a **BIG** country, and those living in remote areas need to use the car for everything. It has been calculated that it costs some €7,000 a year (including depreciation costs) to run a new small car doing 15,000km (9,300mi) a year, which is less than average. **The cost of motoring is high in France and is an important consideration when considering retiring there.** Note also that many rural villages are dying and have few shops or facilities, and they aren't usually a good choice for a retirement home.

Climate

For most people the climate is one of the most important factors when buying a home in France, particularly a holiday or retirement home. Bear in mind both the winter and summer climate as well as the position of the sun and the direction of the prevailing wind. The orientation or aspect of a building is vital and you must ensure that balconies, terraces and gardens face the right direction: west-facing properties are the hottest in the summer, while north-facing properties receive practically no sun at all except in the height of summer. A home facing south has the best prospect of morning and afternoon sun but may be excessively hot in the middle of the day.

If you're coming to France from northern Europe, it might be one of your priorities to escape wet weather, but parts of northern and western France are as wet as the UK, and many other areas experience occasional torrential rain. Conversely, drought is common and water shortages frequent in parts of the south.

France experiences many strong, cold and dry winds (*vent violent*) including the *Mistral* and the *Tramontane*. The *Mistral* is a bitterly cold wind that blows down the southern end of the Rhône valley into the Camargue and Marseille. The *Tramontane* affects the coastal region from Perpignan, near the Pyrenees, to Narbonne. Corsica is buffeted by many winds, including the two aforementioned plus the *Mezzogiorno* and *Scirocco*. There are over 800 other named winds in France, listed and described in the *Petite Encyclopédie des Vents de France* (J. C. Lattès) – fascinating reading for wind buffs.

Community

When choosing the area, you need to decide whether you want to live among your own countrymen and other foreigners in a largely expatriate community, such as those in Dordogne and parts of Provence and Brittany, or whether you prefer (and are prepared) to integrate into an exclusively French environment.

However, unless you speak French fluently or intend to learn it, you should think twice before buying a property in a village. Note that the locals in some villages resent 'outsiders' moving in, although those who take the time and trouble to integrate into the local community are usually warmly welcomed (although it's also worthwhile checking the local mayor's views on foreign residents!).

> ☑ **SURVIVAL TIP**
>
> If you're buying a permanent home, it's important to check your prospective neighbours, particularly when buying an apartment. For example, are they noisy, sociable or absent for long periods? Do you think you'll get on with them?

Crime

What is the local crime rate? In some areas the incidence of burglary is high, which not only affects your security but also increases your insurance premiums. Is crime increasing or decreasing? Note that professional crooks like isolated houses, particularly those full of expensive furniture and other belongings, which they can strip bare at their leisure. You're much less likely to be a victim of theft if you live in a village, where strangers stand out like sore thumbs. See also **Crime** on page 251.

Hunting

Hunting is a jealously guarded 'right' in France, and you should check whether hunting is permitted on your land if you don't want it invaded by armed men every Sunday between September and February. In any case, in rural areas you may have to put up with the sound of gunfire, hunting horns and barking dogs, although shooting isn't permitted within 150m of a dwelling.

Local Council

Is the local council well run? Unfortunately, some are profligate and simply use any extra income to hire a few more of their cronies or spend it on grandiose schemes. While some councils have active 'social committees', which organise activities and functions throughout the year, others may not even bother to arrange a party on 14th July. What are the views of other residents? If the municipality is efficiently and enthusiastically run, you can usually rely on good social, sports and other activities.

Natural Phenomena

Check whether an area is particularly susceptible to natural disasters, such as floods, storms, forest fires and lightning strikes (which are common in the south-east and Corsica – for details, refer to *The Best places to Buy a Home in France* (Survival Books – see page 323). If a property is located near a waterway, it may be expensive to insure against floods, which are a constant threat in some areas.

Noise

Noise can be a problem in some cities, resorts and developments. Noisy neighbours account for around half of all police complaints in France, and 50 per cent of Parisians complain that their neighbours make too much noise. Although you cannot choose your neighbours, you can at least ensure that a property isn't located next to a busy road, industrial plant, commercial area, discotheque, night club, bar or restaurant (where revelries may continue into the early hours). Look out for objectionable neighbouring properties which may be too close to the one you're considering and check whether nearby vacant land has been 'zoned' for commercial use. In community developments (e.g. apartment blocks) many properties are second homes and are let short-term, which means you may need

to tolerate boisterous holidaymakers as neighbours throughout the year (or at least during the summer months).

Don't assume, however, that rural life is necessarily tranquil. Other kinds of noise can disturb your peace and quiet, including chiming church bells, barking dogs, crowing cockerels and braying donkeys, and aircraft if you live near a civil or military airfield. On the other hand, those looking to buy a rural property should note that there may be times when noisy activities such as lawn mowing are prohibited, e.g. at lunchtime on Saturdays and all afternoon on Sundays.

Parking

If you're planning to buy in a town or city, is there adequate private or free on-street parking for your family and visitors? Is it safe to park in the street? In some areas it's important to have secure off-street parking if you value your car. Parking is a problem in many towns and most cities, where private garages or parking spaces can be very expensive (e.g. up to €5,000 in Provence!). An apartment or townhouse in a town or community development may be some distance from the nearest road or car park. How do you feel about carrying heavy shopping hundreds of metres to your home and possibly up several flights of stairs? Traffic congestion is also a problem in many towns and tourist resorts, particularly during the high season.

Property Market

Do houses sell well in the area, e.g. in less than six months? Generally you should avoid neighbourhoods where desirable houses routinely remain on the market for six months or longer (unless the property market is in a slump and nothing is selling).

Radon

Radon (radon), a radioactive gas emitted by granite, is found in significant quantities in parts of Brittany, Corsica, and the Massif Central and Vosges mountains, and some 300,000 homes are estimated to have dangerous levels of radon. Although there's evidence that exposure to high levels of radon can cause cancer, particularly among smokers, there's no proven danger in long exposure to low levels.

☑ **SURVIVAL TIP**

If you're worried about radon levels and want a property checked, contact the Agence Nationale pour l'Amélioration de l'Habitat (ANAH), whose regional and departmental offices are listed on its website (🖳 www.anah.fr – click on 'L'adresse de *votre délégation*').

Sports & Leisure Facilities

What is the range and quality of local leisure, sports, community and cultural facilities? What is the proximity to sports facilities such as a beach, golf course, ski resort or waterway? Bear in mind that properties in or close to ski and coastal resorts are considerably more expensive, although they also have the best letting potential. If you're interested in a winter holiday home, which area should you choose? Be sure to check the local snowfall record and whether it's stable or decreasing (thanks to global warming, the winter sports season is shortening, particularly in resorts at lower altitudes).

Termites

Termites (*termites*) or white ants are found in over 50 departments – particularly in the south-west – the worst-affected departments being Landes, Gironde, Charente-Maritime and Lot-et-Garonne in that order. In certain communes, an inspection is required (known as *un état parasitaire*).

Details of areas affected can be obtained from your regional Observatoire de Lutte Xylophages (look in the phone book or ask at your town hall) or via the internet (e.g. 🖥 www.xylophages.com) and a list of recognised treatment companies from your local Direction Départementale de l'Equipement (DDE), the Centre Technique de Bois et de l'Ameublement/CTBA (☎ 01 40 19 49 19, 🖥 www.ctba.fr or 🖥 www.termite.com.fr, where there's also a map showing affected areas) or the Union Nationale des Experts et Techniciens en Parasitologie Immobilière (☎ 05 56 43 63 00, 🖥 www.unectpi.com).

Note that a *certificat de non-infestation* is only valid for three months, so in the average purchase procedure the inspection cannot be carried out until after you've signed the *compromis de vente*, in which case you must keep your fingers crossed that the result is positive. If it isn't, you can withdraw from the sale and have your deposit returned, negotiate a reduction in the selling price to allow for termite treatment (which can cost between €2,500 and €5,000) or ask the seller to have the treatment done before proceeding with the sale.

Tourists

Bear in mind that if you live in a popular tourist area, e.g. almost anywhere in the south of France, you'll be inundated with tourists in summer. They won't only jam the roads and pack the public transport, but may even occupy your favourite table at your local café or restaurant!

Although a 'front-line' property on a beach or in a marina development may sound attractive and be ideal for short holidays, it isn't usually the best choice for permanent retirees. Many beaches are overcrowded in the high season, streets may be smelly from restaurants and fast food outlets, parking impossible, services stretched to breaking point, and the

beach, Nice, Alpes-Maritimes

incessant noise may drive you crazy. You may also have to tolerate water restrictions in some areas.

If you want to live in (or avoid) one of France's most beautiful villages, contact the Association des Plus Beaux Villages de France, 19500 Collonges-la-Rouge (🖥 www.villagesdefrance.free.fr), which has selected around 150 villages of fewer than 2,000 inhabitants for this accolade.

Town or Country?

Do you wish to be in a town or do you prefer the country? Bear in mind that if you buy a property in the country, you'll probably have to put up with poor public transport (or none at all), long travelling distances to a town of any size, solitude and remoteness. You won't be able to pop along to the local *boulangerie* for a *baguette* and *croissants*, drop into the local bar for a glass of your favourite tipple with the locals, or have a choice of restaurants on your doorstep. In a town or large village, the weekly market will be just around the corner, the doctor and chemist close at hand, and if you need help or run into any problems, your neighbours will be close by.

On the other hand, in the country you'll be closer to nature, will have more freedom (e.g. to make as much noise as you wish) and possibly complete privacy, e.g. to sunbathe or swim *au naturel*. Living in a remote area in the country will suit nature lovers looking for solitude who don't want to involve themselves in the 'hustle and bustle' of town life (not that there's much of this in French rural towns). If you're seeking peace and quiet, make sure that there isn't a busy road or railway line nearby or a local church within 'donging' distance (see **Noise** above).

▲ Caution

Many people who buy a remote country home find that the peace of the countryside palls after a time and they yearn for the more exciting night-life of a city or tourist resort.

If you've never lived in the country, it's wise to rent first before buying. Note also that, while it's cheaper to buy in a remote or unpopular location, it's usually much more difficult to find a buyer when you want to sell.

REGIONS

The following section contains information about France's regions. This book's sister publication, *The Best Places to Buy a Home in France* (see page 323) contains more comprehensive surveys of France's regions and a wealth of information about the facilities and amenities in each area.

Alsace

Alsace (population 1.7m) is one of the smallest regions, containing just two

departments: Bas-Rhin (67) and Haut-Rhin (68) – Lower and Upper Rhine. It's located in the extreme east bordering Germany, to which it has belonged at various times in its colourful history. Not surprisingly it has a Germanic feel, which is reflected in its architecture, cuisine, dress, dialects (German is still widely spoken), names and people (called Alsatians). Sandwiched between the Vosges mountains and the Rhine, Alsace is gloriously scenic and largely unspoiled, with delightful hills (cross-country skiing is a popular winter sport), dense forests, rich farmland and pretty vineyards. It's noted for its many picturesque villages, particularly on the Wine Road (*Route du Vin*) stretching from Marlenheim west of Strasbourg down to Thann beyond Mulhouse. Alsace is famous for its beer (such as Kronenbourg) and white wines (particularly gewürztraminer). Surprisingly, Alsace has more Michelin restaurant stars than any other region of France!

The regional capital is Strasbourg (67), home of the European Parliament, the European Court and the European Commission on Human Rights. Other notable towns include Colmar and Mulhouse, a prominent industrial city. Property prices are higher than the average for France and there are few bargains to be found. Rundown or derelict rural properties for sale are rare in Alsace, where (unlike many other regions) there hasn't been a mass exodus from the farms and countryside. The region has excellent road connections with Paris, the south of France, Germany and Switzerland.

Aquitaine

Aquitaine (population 2.9m) is made up of the following departments: Dordogne (24), Gironde (33), Lot-et-Garonne (47), Landes (40) and Pyrénées-Atlantiques

(64). Aquitaine is perhaps most famous for its wines, beaches, surfing and of course, Eleanor of Aquitaine, mother of Richard the Lionheart. In the north of the region is the Bassin d'Arcachon, a natural inland sea with the largest beach in Europe (where incidentally 90 per cent of French oysters are grown), while the south of Aquitaine includes the so-called *Landes de Gascogne*.

Aquitaine owes its name to the Romans, who logically named the area Aquitania, as it had many rivers running through it (to which canals were later added). It has had a somewhat chequered history and, like Normandy, was once ruled by the kings of England, although it has been under French rule since 1650. The region, which covers an area of 41,310km^2 (16,135mi^2) and has a population of 2.7m, is largely agricultural, unspoiled and sparsely populated, and is noted for its temperate climate. Crops include corn and peppers (the hot variety), which are hung from the window ledges and beams of houses to dry. Aquitaine is one of the most varied regions of France; although predominantly flat (the majority of the region lies less than 250m/825ft above sea level), the land rises in the south at the foothills of the Pyrenees. It has over 270km (170mi) of spectacular beaches along the Atlantic coastline, known as the *Côte d'Argent* ('Silver Coast'), 30km (20mi) of which are considered to offer the best surfing in Europe.

'The Landes' is a flat, sandy plain (*lande* means 'moor'), roughly triangular, bounded by the sea and dunes to the west and stretching from Bordeaux (33) in the north to Dax (40) and the Golfe de Gascogne in the south and east as far as Nérac (47) and therefore covering roughly the whole of the department of Landes, as well as a good deal of Gironde and parts of Lot-et-Garonne. It was transformed during the 19th century by the planting of pine trees, which now cover virtually the entire area, creating

La route des Vins, d'Alsace

purportedly the largest forest in Europe (the trees are now used for making paper). Part of the forest, corresponding roughly to the basin of the river Eyre, was designated a regional park (the Parc régional des Landes de Gascogne) in 1970. As a result, Aquitaine comprises 45 per cent woodland, the highest percentage in France. The Landes is known as *'le pays de la bonne bouffe'* ('the land of good grub'), where traditional dishes include *cruchade* (a dessert), *garbure* (soup), *millas* (corn-cake) and *saupiquet* (fried ham). Gironde to the north is also generally flat (its highest point is just 165m/535ft) and much of the land is given over to vineyards.

Pyrénées-Atlantiques is part of the Basque Country (*Pays basque*), which extends from around 160km (100mi) south of Bordeaux, where the Landes give way to the foothills of the Pyrenees, across the mountains into Spain and east along the river Nive as far as Saint-Jean-Pied-de-Port. The Basque Country has its own language, style of architecture, sport (*pelota*) and traditions and is itself divided into ancient 'regions', such as Labourd, Soule and Basse-Navarre. Apart from the conurbation of Bayonne, Anglet and Biarritz (known locally as the 'BAB'), where property is fairly expensive, Pyrénées-Atlantiques is sparsely populated. To the east of the Basque Country is Béarn (famous for its *sauce béarnaise*), another ancient 'region' (its capital is Orthez) surrounding the valleys of the Aspe, Barétous and Ossau in the east of Pyrénées-Atlantiques. The inland department of Lot-et-Garonne is undulating and largely rural and agricultural. It's one of the largest fruit-growing areas in France, producing apples, apricots, melons, nectarines, peaches, plums (including the mouth-watering *prunes d'agenais*) and strawberries, as well as tobacco, among

other crops. (There's a famous fruit fair at Prayssas, between Agen and Villeneuve-sur-Lot.)

> With the exception of Dordogne (see below), Aquitaine hasn't been especially popular with foreign property buyers, but with access becoming easier by air, rail and road, coupled with reasonable property prices, a pleasant climate and (of course) wonderful food and wine, the region has seen an increase in the purchase of second and retirement homes – especially by the British and other Europeans.

Dordogne

One of the most popular French departments among foreign homebuyers and retirees (particularly the British) is Dordogne. The ancient province of Périgord, Dordogne is France's third-largest department, covering an area of 9,060km^2 (3,533mi^2), with a population of just under 400,000. Like many French departments, Dordogne is named after the main river flowing through it. It's split into four territories. In the north is 'Green Périgord', so called because of its green valleys irrigated by a multitude of streams. This territory contains the Périgord-Limousin Regional Natural Park and its main towns include Brantôme, Nontron and Riberac. In the centre is 'White Périgord', which takes its name from the limestone plateaux and contains the departmental capital, Périgueux. In the south-west corner of Dordogne is the newly identified territory of 'Purple Périgord', which includes the Bergerac area, famous for its wine grapes (hence 'purple'), and French and English fortified towns, castles and *châteaux* built during the Hundred Years War (Dordogne boasts some 10 per cent of France's 40,000 *châteaux*). In the south-east is 'Black Périgord', so called on account of the ancient oak trees covering large parts

some of the country's prettiest and most dramatic towns and villages, including Brantôme, Domme, La Roque-Gageac, Sarlat-la-Canéda and Trémolat. Domme and Sarlat are the jewels of Dordogne and are so popular that they're in danger of being ruined by tourism (it's almost impossible to find a grocer amongst the tourist shops and artist's galleries along the main road in Domme).

Most of what makes Dordogne memorable is to be found in a 15km (10mi) stretch of the river between Bergerac and Souillac (in Lot), but every village has historical buildings, whether churches, *châteaux* or ordinary houses inhabited by the same family for generations. Dordogne is also a treasure trove of caves filled with prehistoric paintings up to 30,000 years old. Lascaux and Les Eyzies are the two major sites and perhaps the best known. The river itself provides other distractions for inhabitants and holidaymakers, although the latter can be a nuisance to the former in high season. Local cuisine includes truffles and *pâté de foie gras* (the best French *foie gras* is considered to come from Sarlat) and is noted for its duck and goose dishes.

of the area and home to the valleys of the rivers Dordogne and Vézère. Perhaps the territory best known to foreigners, Black Périgord has been inhabited since prehistory and contains the famous caves at Lascaux and Les Eyzies (among others) and the picturesque towns of Saint-Cyprien and Sarlat-la-Canéda.

Dordogne has for a long time been a holiday and migration destination for Britons (the French call the area around Ribérac 'little England') and more recently Dutch and Germans. During the late '80s, the demand was so great for ruined farms and houses that a mini-boom was created. Prices are more reasonable now and bargains can still be found, but it's still the most expensive department in this area for the simple reason that it's one of the most scenic departments in France and contains

Auvergne

Situated south of the centre of France, Auvergne (population 1.3m) covers an area of 26,000km^2 (16,250mi^2) at the heart of the Massif Central (the volcanic region in the centre of France). Auvergne includes the departments of Allier (03), Cantal (15), Haute-Loire (43) and Puy-de-Dôme (63). In the area around Clermont-Ferrand (63), the mountains reach a peak of 1,885m (6,180ft). From north to south, with a small ascent around the Plateau Millevaches (978m/3,200ft) the terrain becomes flatter and rockier. Economically, Auvergne is a poor region, and the department of Haute-Loire in particular is suffering from the decline of agriculture and an ageing population.

The main towns are Ambert, Aurillac, Clermont-Ferrand, Le Puy-en-Velay, Moulins and Vichy. The region is unique in France, as Europe's largest group of volcanoes (now extinct) have created a landscape of mountains (Mont Dore reaches 1,885m/6,180ft), craters, lakes, rivers (the Dordogne springs from near Mont-Dore), springs (including Arvie, Mont-Dore, Saint-Yorre, Vichy and Volvic), spas and lava flows, all of which combine to create a huge geological park. The region contains two regional parks and two nature parks, and in February 2002 a volcano theme park opened, including volcano-related exhibits and a guided tour around the crater of an extinct volcano.

This natural heritage is complemented by a rich cultural and historical heritage: more than 500 Romanesque churches (some of which are considered France's best), almost 50 *châteaux* and ten spa towns. Auvergne also contains ten of the 'most beautiful villages of France', four of which are in Haute-Loire. The regional capital, Clermont-Ferrand (headquarters of Michelin, the tyre manufacturer and tourist guide producer), is mainly built from dark basalt, making an impressive and unusual townscape. There are nine ski centres, 200km (125mi) of downhill runs and over 800km (500mi) of cross-country trails.

Water plays an important part in the economy of the region. Many lakes have formed in valleys blocked by lava streams, e.g. at Aydat and Guéry, or where volcanoes have erupted in valleys, e.g. at Chambon and Montcineyre. Many anglers and watersports enthusiasts use these lakes, along with rivers such as the Allier and the Cher. The many hot springs in the area also owe their existence to volcanic activity. Water temperature ranges from 10C (50F) to over 80C (Chaudes-Aigues is the hottest spring in Europe at 82.3C/180F) and the springs are sought after by people who wish to 'take a cure'.

> Vichy, in Allier, is probably the best known spa town, having waters that are used for drinking and for balneology, and is also famous for its bottled water.

The region is predominantly agricultural with tourism slowly becoming more important. Cows are much in evidence and are used both for meat and for milk, which is made into a number of well known cheeses: Bleu d'Auvergne, Cantal, Forme d'Ambert and Saint-Nectaire. Green lentils have been cultivated in Puy-en-Velay (43) since Gallo-Roman times and are the first vegetable to be given a quality classification as for wine. Excellent wine (both red and white) is also made from the Saint-Pourçain vineyard (one of the oldest in France) stretching along the banks of the Allier.

Brittany

Brittany (*Bretagne*), which has a population of 2.9m, is the westernmost region of France (and Europe) and comprises the departments of Côtes-d'Armor (22), Finistère (29), Ille-et-Vilaine (35) and Morbihan (56). Brittany has some 3,000km (1,875mi) of Atlantic coast – over 25 per cent of the French coastline. The west coast is characterised by dramatic cliffs and rock formations, the north coast boasts attractive coves and tiny harbours, and the south coast has wide estuaries and long, sandy beaches.

Brittany is popular with sailors, although the sea is not without its dangers – all those who die at sea are supposed to meet in the Baie des Trépassés ('Bay of the Departed') near Douarnenez, from where they're ferried to a mythical island of the blessed! More than a third of French lighthouses are in Brittany, mostly in Finistère. The inland region, known as the *Argoat* ('land of woods'), is almost flat; only two ridges and a solitary peak rise above 250m (800ft), although the Bretons call them mountains – the Montagnes Noires (Black Mountains), the Monts d'Arrée (Arée Mountains) and the Montagne de Locronan. Inland Brittany is also largely agricultural, unspoiled and scenic, with delightful wooded valleys, lakes and moors.

Vegetables and fruit are Brittany's two main agricultural products, and the department of Ille-et-Villaine was France's biggest cider producer until the mid-20th century (when there were over 300 varieties of cider apples; today there are fewer than 100). The average Breton is reputed to drink over 300 litres of cider per year! Brittany is also a major producer of pork, poultry, milk and fish, as well as seaweed, which is used in food additives, fertilisers and cosmetics. Cancale is reputed to be a gastronomic Mecca, and

the entire region is a paradise for seafood lovers. Local culinary specialities include *crêpes* and *galettes* (different types of pancake used for sweet and savoury fillings respectively), *cotriade*, a sort of paella without the rice (the Breton equivalent of *bouillabaisse*) and *cervoise*, a beer reputed to be the favourite drink of the Gauls (or Vikings, according to which history you read).

Brittany's population is just under 3m, and the regional capital, Rennes, is its largest city, with just over 200,000 inhabitants. The next largest town is Brest with around 155,000. Other main towns in Brittany include Dinan, Dinard, Lorient, Quimper, Saint-Brieuc, Saint-Malo, Vannes and Vitré.

The local people (Bretons) are of Celtic origin with a rich maritime tradition and a unique culture (preserved mainly in the more isolated west). Proud and independent (they claim that Brittany is a country apart), they even have their own language which has been revived in recent years. Rennes University is a centre of Breton studies. Like Ireland, Brittany is a land of legend and folklore – the jagged coastline is said to have been carved out by the giant Gargantua, and the Forest of Broceliande is claimed to have been the hide-out of the Arthurian sorcerer Merlin. Traditional Breton costume is still worn on special occasions; one of the most colourful of these is the *Fête des Filets bleus* ('Festival of the Blue Nets'), which is held in the fishing village of Concarneau in August.

Brittany has long been a popular region for foreign buyers, particularly the British on account of its sea connections (via the ports of Roscoff and Saint-Malo, and the nearby Normandy ports of Caen and Cherbourg-Octeville) and a similar climate and countryside, as well as their historical and cultural kinship. Great Britain in French is 'big Brittany' to distinguish it from the French region, which was founded

Bigouden), and very expensive on the islands (many of which are inhabited by rich Parisians and French celebrities). The triangle of land between Dinan, Dinard and Saint-Malo is also popular, which is reflected in relatively high prices. The interior is generally quieter and cheaper (nowhere in Brittany is more than an hour's drive from the coast), although the extreme west coast of Finistère is also good value if, obviously, the least accessible part of the region.

Burgundy

Burgundy (*Bourgogne*) has a population of 1.6m and contains the departments of Côte-d'Or (21), Nièvre (58), Saône-et-Loire (71) and Yonne (89). The region has few industries, which means that it's almost totally unspoiled and one of France's most beautiful and fertile areas (it has been dubbed the 'rural soul' of France). It's a timeless land where little has changed over the centuries – a haven of peace and serenity (particularly the Parc du Morvan at its heart).

The name Burgundy is synonymous with magnificent wines such as Nuits-Saint-Georges, Meursault, Beaune, Puligny-Montrachet, Gevrey-Chambertin and Pouilly-Fuissé, grown on the 60km (37mi) Côte d'Or hillside, as well as fine cuisine, including *boeuf bourguignon* (made with Charollais beef), *coq au vin* (with Bresse chicken), Morvan ham and snails, generally served with rich sauces, as well as *pain d'épices* ('spicy' bread) and *kir* (white wine with a dash of blackcurrant liqueur).

The region is also renowned for its many canals and canal boats, and has some 1,200km (750mi) of navigable waterways, including the Burgundy Canal and the rivers Saône and Yonne. Burgundy has a rich and colourful history (it was an independent kingdom for some 600 years), celebrated in numerous festivals and pageants, and a wealth of Romanesque churches, cathedrals, medieval villages

by Cornish settlers fleeing Anglo-Saxon invaders in the fifth century. They took their language with them (curiously, Breton survives more successfully than Cornish) and remain proudly Celtic. It wasn't until 1532 that Brittany officially became part of France. There are also more recent cultural ties between the region and the UK, with twinnings (e.g. Rennes with Exeter) and frequent cross-Channel exchanges. There's even the unlikely *hot dog Breton*, a sausage in a pancake, and Breton whisky, distilled at Lannion!

In fact, there has been an 'invasion' of British buyers in recent years, which has pushed up property prices but has also helped to regenerate many previously moribund rural areas. Property is expensive on the coast, particularly around Quimper and Bénodet (an area known as the Pays and historic towns. Its most important towns include Autun, Auxerre, Beaune, Chalon-sur-Saône, Dijon (21), famous for its mustard and the regional capital, Fontenay, Mâcon, Nevers, Paray-le-Monial and Vézelay.

> Somewhat surprisingly, Burgundy isn't popular with foreign property buyers, perhaps because of its relative isolation, and there are few holiday and retirement homes there.

It rarely features in international property magazines and, although the region has a wealth of beautiful *châteaux*, manor houses and watermills, these (and vineyards) are rarely on the market. Prices tend to be higher than average for France, but inexpensive, habitable village houses and farmhouses in need of restoration can be found in most areas. Burgundy is located just 100km (around 65mi) south of Paris and 80km (50mi) north of Lyon, and has excellent connections with both the north and south of France via the A6 and A31 motorways and the TGV (see the maps in **Appendix E**).

Centre-Val-de-Loire

The central region of France, known officially as Centre-Val-de-Loire but often called simply Centre (population 2.4m), contains the departments of Cher (18), Eure-et-Loir (28), Indre (36), Indre-et-Loire (37), Loir-et-Cher (41) and Loiret (45), the Loire and its tributary, the Loir, giving their names to several of the departments.

The Loire is France's longest river (1,020km/628mi), with its source in the Vivarais mountains (south of Saint-Etienne) and its outlet at Saint-Nazaire in the Pays de la Loire. It's considered to be the dividing line between the colder regions of northern France and the warmer south, although the change is gradual.

The Loire valley is noted for its natural beauty and fertility, consisting of pleasant undulating woodland, lakes, rivers, orchards, and fields of maize and sunflowers (it's the market garden of France), as well as for its plethora of *châteaux*, widely considered to be among the most beautiful in the world. The principal *châteaux* are in Loir-et-Cher (Chambord, the largest; Chaumont; and Chéverny) and neighbouring Indre-et-Loire (Azay-le-Rideau; Chenonceaux, romantically built over the water; and Villandry, boasting magnificent gardens).

The region's main towns include Blois, Bourges, Chartres, Orléans and Tours (37), the regional capital. In fact, these last two towns were recently rated the second and third-best places to live in France by *Le Point* magazine. One of its most attractive areas is the old province of Berry (comprising the departments of Cher and Indre), whose ancient capital was the majestic city of Bourges.

The Loire valley is unspoiled by industry, mass tourism or a surfeit of holiday homes, although it's quite popular with retirees and second homeowners. Property prices vary considerably depending on the proximity to major towns, although they're generally well above the French average and bargains are rare. The region has excellent road connections via the A10, A11 and A71 motorways, which converge on Paris, as well as via the TGV from Paris to Poitiers and Bordeaux (see the map in **Appendix E**).

Champagne-Ardenne

The Champagne-Ardenne region (population 1.3m), which is often called simply Champagne, contains the departments of Ardennes (08), Aube (10), Marne (51) and Haute-Marne (52). The region is celebrated for the sparkling wine after which it's named, and the production of champagne dominates most aspects of life in the region. Its main towns include

Charleville-Mézières, Épernay, Reims, and Troyes (10), the regional capital. Reims is home to the *Grandes Marques* of champagne, such as Veuve Cliquot and Charles Heidsieck, although Épernay is the centre of champagne production. Reims cathedral is one of the most beautiful in France as well as historically the most important, being where the country's kings were crowned.

The region is highly cultivated and, although not one of France's most attractive areas, is noted for its rolling landscape, immense forests (Verzy forest contains beech trees that are over 1,000 years old), deep gorges and vast rivers. Champagne-Ardenne also contains one of Europe's largest artificial lakes, the Lac du Der-Chantecoq near Saint-Dizier. Ardennes (which shares a border with Belgium) is the region's most picturesque department and its rolling, wooded landscape is dotted with ramparts, fortified castles and farmhouses.

> The Champagne-Ardenne region isn't popular with foreign homebuyers, despite property being relatively inexpensive, particularly in Ardennes. However, it becomes more expensive the nearer you get to Brussels in the north and Paris in the west (the western Aube is the most expensive area).

The area has good road connections and is served by the A4 and A26 motorways.

Corsica (*Corse*)

Containing the departments of Corse-du-Sud (2A) and Haute-Corse (2B), the island of Corsica (*Corse*) has population of 260,000 and covers an area of 8,721km^2 (3,367mi^2) with a coastline of around 1,000km (620mi). It's situated 160km (99mi) from France and 80km (50mi) from Italy, with which it has strong historical ties, having been an Italian possession until 1768, when France purchased it from the Genoese. Corsica is quite different from mainland France, not only in its geography but in its people, culture and customs. (Corsican men are reputed to be among the most chauvinistic in France – which is saying something!) The island even has its own language, Corsican, spoken regularly by around 60 per cent of the people, although it has no official status and French is also universally spoken and understood. There's a strong local identity (and independence movement) and Corsica enjoys a greater degree of autonomy than the mainland regions.

The island is sparsely populated with huge areas devoid of human life and has a stark, primitive beauty with superb beaches and picturesque hillside villages; Corsica is considered by some to be the most beautiful Mediterranean island (it's known as the *Ile de Beauté*) and is a popular holiday destination (particularly the western coast). Mountains cover most of its surface, including some 200 peaks over 2,000m (6,500ft), the highest reaching over 2,700m (9,000ft) so that skiing is possible in winter. Around half the island is covered in vegetation, including beech, chestnut and pine forests and the ubiquitous *maquis*, a dense growth of aromatic shrubs (heather and myrtle) and dark holm oak. Corsica also boasts some of Europe's most beautiful Romanesque art.

Tourism is the island's main industry (many French mainlanders holiday here), although it remains almost completely unspoiled and a haven for outdoor-lovers (hikers and bikers) and those seeking peace and serenity. Not surprisingly, Corsica has a slow pace of life, which is epitomised by its ancient and spectacular mountain railway. The main towns include Ajaccio (the regional capital and birthplace of Napoleon), Bastia, Bonifacio, Calvi and Porto-Vecchio, all situated on the coast. It's popular with holiday homeowners, particularly Italians, and prices have risen in recent years following increased interest. It has, however, avoided the devastation wrought in many other Mediterranean islands by high-rise developments; buildings are restricted to two storeys and construction is forbidden close to beaches. Corsica has good air connections with France and most other European countries and Sardinia is only a short boat ride away.

Franche-Comté

Franche-Comté (population 1.1m), meaning literally 'free country', contains the departments of Doubs (25), Jura (39), Haute-Saône (70) and the Territoire-de-Belfort (90). It's a little-known region in eastern France bordering Switzerland, with which it shares much of its architecture, cuisine and culture. It's known for cheeses such as Comté and Morbier, Jura wines, and Morteau and Montbéliard sausages. Franche-Comté is acclaimed for its beautiful, unspoiled scenery (more Swiss in appearance than French) and recalls a fairy-tale land where time has almost stood still. It's reputed to be the greenest region in France.

Sandwiched between the Vosges range to the north and the Jura mountains to the south, Franche-Comté boasts a landscape of rolling cultivated fields, dense pine forests and rampart-like mountains. Although not as majestic as the Alps, the Jura mountains are more accessible and are a Mecca for nature lovers and winter sports fans. The Doubs and Loue valleys (noted for their timbered houses perched on stilts in the river) and the high valley of Ain are popular areas. The region's main towns include Belfort and Besançon (25), the regional capital on the river Doubs.

Franche-Comté is largely ignored by foreign tourists and homebuyers, although it has many attractions. Property prices are higher than the French average, although bargains can be found, particularly if you're seeking a winter holiday home. Besançon is served by the A36 motorway and has good connections with the centre and south of France, Germany and Switzerland via TGV (see the map in **Appendix E**).

Ile-de-France

The region of Ile-de-France (population 11m), in northern central France, comprises eight departments. The city of Paris, a department unto itself (see below), is the heart and soul of Ile-de-France, which is sometimes referred to as the *région Parisienne*. The three departments immediately adjacent to Paris, which make up the so-called *petit couronne* ('small crown' or 'small wreath') are Hauts-de-Seine (92), Seine-Saint-Denis (93) and Val-de-Marne (94). The outer circle of departments is called the *grand couronne* ('large crown' or 'large wreath') and consists of Seine-et-Marne (77), Yvelines (78), Essonne (91) and Val-d'Oise (95).

Ile-de France means 'island of France' and, although the region isn't literally an island, it's more or less surrounded by rivers and was therefore considered an island throughout much of French history.

Ile-de-France covers 12,070km^2 (around 4,700mi^2), a little over 2 per cent of France's land mass, but houses over 15 per cent of France's population. (Those who live in Ile-de-France are called *Franciliens* or *Franciliennes*.) As these figures indicate, Ile-de-France is the most densely populated region in France, with an average of around 900 inhabitants per km^2 overall. Paris is Europe's most crowded capital, with over 20,000 people per km^2 (over 50,000 per mi^2), almost five times the population density of London, although you don't have to travel far from the city to be in the countryside. Overall, however, the region is a mixture of arable land, grassland, urban areas and woodland.

Ile-de-France is also, not surprisingly, the wealthiest region in the country in terms of the number of people with high incomes. Ile-de-France contains six of the seven wealthiest towns in France – Saint-Germain-en-Laye and Versailles (78), Boulogne-Billancourt, Neuilly-sur-Seine and Rueil-Malmaison (92) and Paris itself (the other is Cannes in Alpes-Maritimes). Together, these are home to almost 37 per cent of the country's richest people (almost 17 per cent of French people liable for wealth tax live in Neuilly!).

> The Ile-de-France region offers a wide variety of living environments and kinds of accommodation, as do the various districts (*arrondissements*) and neighbourhoods of the city of Paris.

Each department and each district has a general character and reputation, although there are exceptions and 'atypical' towns and districts in each area.

Paris

The 'City of Light' is the most popular tourist destination in the world, having some of the world's great museums and galleries, as well as world renowned restaurants, cafés and *bistros*, and enjoys a deserved reputation for fashion, romance and passion.

The city is divided into 20 *arrondissements*, each of which is a distinct political unit with its own town hall (*mairie*), mayor (*maire*) and police headquarters (*préfecture*) handling day-to-day administrative matters for local residents, including marriages, birth records, death certificates and voting. (The Mairie de Paris is an administrative centre for the 20 district governments and isn't usually open to the public.)

The numbering system for the *arrondissements* starts at the Palais du Louvre, formerly the French king's primary residence located roughly at the centre of the city, and proceeds in a clockwise spiral out to the city limits. Almost all addresses and directions in Paris include the relevant *arrondissement* number (as well as the name of the nearest underground station). For example, the post code 75016 indicates an address in the 16th *arrondissement*.

In an effort to lessen dependence on Paris, the government established five satellite towns in the mid-'60s, with the intention of making these 'new towns' (*villes nouvelles*) self-sufficient in terms of employment, local commerce and public services. The *villes nouvelles* are Cergy-Pontoise in Val-d'Oise to the north, Saint-Quentin-en-Yvelines to the west, Evry in Essonne to the south, and Marne-la-Vallée and Sénart in Seine-et-Marne to the east. Although the experiment wasn't entirely successful, the *villes nouvelles* have managed to dilute the concentration of jobs, people and services in the capital to a certain extent and offer a less frenetic alternative to the urban intensity of Paris itself.

Languedoc-Roussillon

The Mediterranean coast of France is one of the most popular areas for retirees. The western part of the coast is in the region of Languedoc-Roussillon (population 2.3m), which comprises the departments of Aude (11), Gard (30), Hérault (34), Lozère (48) and Pyrénées-Orientales (66). The popularity and spiralling property prices of Provence-Alpes-Côte d'Azur has prompted many to look instead towards Languedoc-Roussillon, which currently has only half as many British residents, for example, as PACA.

Languedoc-Roussillon is often referred to as 'the Languedoc' (after one of the two ancient languages of France, the *langue d'Oc*, the Roussillon part corresponding roughly to the Pyrénées-Orientales department) or by the French, confusingly, as *le Midi*, although a new name, Septimanie, has recently been proposed. It covers an area of 27,376km² (17,010mi²), containing the coastal departments (from east to west) of Gard, Hérault, Aude and Pyrénées-Orientales, as well as Lozère, inland, which is France's most sparsely populated and highest department, with an average altitude of 1,000m (3,280ft). The region resembles a hammock stretched between Mount Lozère 1,700m (5,580ft) in the north and Mount Canigou 2,784m (9,135ft) in the south. Bordered by the Pyrenees, Andorra and Spain in the south, Languedoc-Roussillon extends north as far as the Massif Central. It has a long Mediterranean coastline of virtually uninterrupted sandy beaches, stretching some 180km (110mi) from the Petite Camargue nature reserve in Gard, through Hérault, Aude and Pyrénées-Orientales,

with its beautiful beaches and cliff inlets (*calanques*) of pink rock, to the Spanish border.

Few French regions are more steeped in history than Languedoc (home of the heretical Cathars), which also offers an abundance of excellent (but under-rated) wines such as Corbières, Minervois and Côtes du Roussillon. It encompasses the largest wine production area in Europe (Béziers claims to be France's wine capital!). The region has a vast range of scenery and landscape, including the beautiful Cévennes national park and Tarn valley areas (famously written about by Robert Louis Stevenson in his *Travels with a Donkey*), the tranquil Canal du Midi, the gentle rolling hills of the Pyrenees, home to a handful of protected bears, and the dramatic beauty (not always appreciated by the Tour de France cyclists) of the high Pyrenees peaks.

Languedoc is noted for its relaxed pace of life and is a popular hideaway for those seeking peace and tranquillity. It has its own ancient language (*Occitan*) and many towns close to the Spanish border have a Catalan feel (Catalan is also spoken here).

> A number of purpose-built resorts have been created on the *Côte vermeille* (Vermillion Coast) in the last few decades, including Argelès-sur-Mer, Gruissan, Saint-Cyprien, Port Bacarès, Port Leucate and Cap d'Agde, where apartment blocks are mostly unattractive if you're looking for a home with character. Collioure, on the other hand, known as the 'jewel of the Vermillion Coast', is a most attractive (and expensive) port.

Limousin

Situated south-west of the centre of France, Limousin (population 710,000) is the name of the old province surrounding the town of Limoges. It covers an area of 16,942km^2(10,600mi^2) with a population of less than 725,000 and is composed of just three departments: Corrèze (19 – the department of President Jacques Chirac and his wife, who is a town councillor), Creuse (23) and Haute-Vienne (87). The main towns are Brive-la-Gaillarde (19), Guéret (23) and Limoges (87). The region is world-renowned for Limoges porcelain and enamels and the tapestries of Aubusson. Limousin has also given its name to a school of painting known as the Crozant school, after the place where Monet painted his first series, and is home to the Centre for Contemporary Art at Vassivière.

Limousin is predominantly agricultural with very little heavy industry, which makes it largely unpolluted and unspoilt by modern industrial buildings. Being in the foothills of the Massif Central, the region features rolling hills and valleys (the lowest point, around Brive-la-Gaillarde, is almost 200m/655ft above sea level and the highest is 978m/3,200ft) without the bleakness of some mountainous areas, and almost 35 per cent of the area is forested (compared with 27 per cent nationally). Its mountains and forests, coupled with the many lakes, rivers and streams that flow into either the Loire or the Garonne, make Limousin a rural holiday paradise, and it's becoming increasingly popular with foreign homebuyers. Limousin also boasts a vast man-made lake, the Lac de Vassivière (1,100ha/2,700 acres), the largest used for water-sports in the country and featuring beaches and adjoining holiday complexes, and is noted for its chocolate and Golden Delicious apples (reputed to be the best in the world).

Economically, Limousin is a poor area, Creuse in particular suffering from the decline of agriculture and an ageing population.

Lorraine

Lorraine (population 2.3m), or Lorraine-Vosges as it's also called, is situated in the north-eastern corner of France bordering Germany, Belgium and Luxembourg, and contains the departments of Meuse (55), Meurthe-et-Moselle (54), Moselle (57) and Vosges (88).

Like Alsace, Lorraine has been fought over for centuries by France and Germany, between whom it has frequently swapped ownership (the region retains a strong Germanic influence). Although mainly an industrial area, Lorraine is largely unspoiled and is popular with nature lovers and hikers. It's noted for its meandering rivers, rolling hills, wooded valleys and delightful medieval towns and villages.

Lorraine is famous for its Moselle wines and *quiche*, but regional cuisine also includes mouthwatering tarts, *clafoutis*, *soufflés* and gratins, and the local beer is highly regarded. Glass and crystal making are ancient traditions. Lorraine's main towns include Nancy (54), the regional capital, and Metz, and there's a wealth of picturesque villages, including Bussang, Ferrette, Le Hohwald, Saint-Amerin and Schirmeck, plus resort towns such as Masevaux and Plimbières-les-Bains. Lorraine has few foreign residents and is largely ignored by retirees and second homebuyers despite the low cost of living and reasonable property prices. The region has good road access via the A4 and A31 motorways.

Midi-Pyrénées

France's largest region (bigger than Switzerland!), Midi-Pyrénées (population 2.6m) comprises Ariège (09), Aveyron (12), Haute-Garonne (31), Gers (32), Lot (46), Hautes-Pyrénées (65), Tarn (81) and Tarn-et-Garonne (82). The Midi-Pyrénées borders Spain in the south, Languedoc-Roussillon to the east and Aquitaine to the west, and encompasses the French Pyrenees with Toulouse, its capital, at the centre. The region boasts a wide variety of stunning, unspoilt scenery, ranging from the majestic snow-capped peaks of the Pyrenees in the south to the pastoral tranquillity of the Aveyron, Lot and Garonne valleys in the north.

The department of Gers is widely regarded as the heart of the ancient province of Gascony (sometimes called 'Guyenne' by the French), which is often described as France's 'Tuscany' due to its rolling green countryside and numerous pretty villages. Neighbouring Haute-Garonne is dominated by Toulouse but reaches right down to the Pyrenees, while Hautes-Pyrénées is a largely mountainous department boasting many ski resorts.

In the north-east of the region, Aveyron offers a variety of landscapes, including the wild, rocky area known as Les Causses, south of Millau, the town being regarded as the gateway to the Tarn Gorges – spectacular cuts through the lower Massif Central and a Mecca for hikers, canoeists, climbers and campers (the viewpoint at the top is appropriately called the Point

Sublime). The departments of Tarn and Tarn-et-Garonne in the east of the region have recently become extremely popular with foreign homebuyers, particularly the British (in many parts, you're almost certain to have British neighbours), and prices have risen accordingly.

In the south-east corner of Midi-Pyrénées, the department of Ariège has stunning scenery and is popular with a number of British and European notables, including former British Prime Minister Tony Blair, who has spent part of his summer holidays here for the past several years. (Perhaps he has been trying to strike it lucky: around 50kg/110lb of gold is panned every year from the department's rivers!) The decline of agriculture means that there are plenty of inexpensive properties to be found, and the department has the dual advantages of being near the Pyrenees and close to Toulouse.

> On the Spanish border is the principality of Andorra, which offers its own ski resorts, as well as tax-free shopping.

The Pyrenees are popular for year-round outdoor activities, including cycling, hiking and, of course, skiing. There are more than 30 ski resorts in the area, which are generally much less expensive than the Alpine resorts, although less challenging for advanced skiers. There are also numerous spa towns in the Midi-Pyrénées, owing to the region's many thermal springs. Lourdes, in Hautes-Pyrénées, is probably the most visited place in the region, millions of people flocking to the Roman Catholic holy shrine each year, many in search of miracle cures.

Named after its principal river, Lot (the 't' is pronounced) is geographically diverse, which contributes to its climatic variations. The altitude rises from west to east as you approach the Massif Central, and the highest point in the department is 780m (2,550ft) above sea level. Two major rivers cross the department: the Dordogne in the north and the Lot, with its many tributaries, in the south. The Dordogne basin is lush with small valleys, bubbling streams and tall cliffs (on which are perched many dramatic *châteaux*). In the southern half of the department are the *causses*, rocky plateaux and hills full of caves, and *Quercy blanc* ('White Quercy') – so called because of the white limestone used in the area's distinctive buildings. These plateaux are mainly hot and dry with little cultivation. In the extreme south, hemmed in by cliffs, are the plains of the Lot valley, covered with the vines of Cahors.

The department is rich in history and boasts many ancient and picturesque towns, including Souillac, 'where culture and history meet' (according to the tourist guides) and Rocamadour, a town built into the cliffs and France's second-most visited place outside Paris (after the Mont Saint-Michel in Brittany). Like many other departments in central France, Lot is suffering from a declining agricultural sector and has an ageing population and some parts are poor, although in the area around Cahors (with its wine industry and tourism) the economy is thriving. However, according to the last census in 1999, Lot's population has risen back to its level of 1936. This is in part due to the influx of both French and foreigners (mainly British) to the area. Tourism has contributed greatly to the economy of the department, as it has a lot to offer both tourists and the many people with second homes here (one in five houses is a second home). Surprisingly, a recent survey concluded that properties for sale in Lot were on average the second-most expensive in France outside Paris!

The people of the Midi-Pyrénées have long regarded themselves as a breed apart – brave and free-spirited, typified by the statue of D'Artagnan (famous as one of the 'Three Musketeers' in the novel of that name by Alexandre Dumas) in the shadow of the cathedral at Auch (32). In fact, D'Artagnan is reputed to have been modelled on Charles de Batz, Captain of the King's Musketeers and a native of Auch.

Examples of the earliest forms of human art, 30,000-year old cave paintings depicting deer, bison and other animals, can be found in the grottoes of the Ariège department, and the region also retains influences of the Celts, who settled here in pre-Christian times, Romans and Moors (Arabs), who occupied the area for some 800 years. The local culture and especially the cuisine have therefore developed from both Roman and Arab roots and are celebrated in the region's many festivals

Several classic French dishes originate in this region, including *cassoulet*, made from Toulouse sausage, *magret de canard* (duck cutlet) and that most politically incorrect (but most typically French) of foods, *pâté de fois gras* (goose-liver pâté). Roquefort cheese is made here (in the town of Roquefort-sur-Soulzon in Aveyron) and another famous Gascon product is armagnac, a grape brandy similar to (but subtly different from) cognac, which is made in neighbouring Poitou-Charentes. (Many connoisseurs rate armagnac above cognac, claiming that is has a richer flavour thanks to its single distillation and oak casking.) Many armagnac producers also make a fine aperitif called Floc de Gascoigne, which is a blend of armagnac and wine, along with a number of armagnac-based liqueurs.

Nord-Pas-de-Calais

The Nord-Pas-de-Calais region in the far north is one of France's smallest regions, containing just two departments: Nord (59) and Pas-de Calais (62). It shares a border with Belgium, from where it derives its Flemish influence and beer-producing traditions. Nord-Pas-de-Calais (along with Picardy) was the birthplace of 19th century manufacturing in France and contains the country's only major conurbation outside Paris, that of Lille.

Although derided as being industrialised and over-populated (and with high unemployment), with a flat, uninspiring landscape and the country's worst climate, Nord-Pas-de-Calais has many beautiful areas and is noted for its clean beaches, undulating countryside, secluded woods, scenic river valleys (particularly the Canche and Authie), colourful market gardens, fine golf courses and many pretty, peaceful villages. For Belgian, British and Dutch second home-buyers, its principal attraction is its proximity to home, offering the opportunity to enjoy a French lifestyle every weekend.

> The region experiences no extremes of temperature on account of the influence of the warm Gulf Stream flowing up the Channel from the North Atlantic, but the weather is changeable and often cloudy and wet.

In fact Nord-Pas-de-Calais has the least sunshine of any part of France, with only 1,600 hours per year and around 120 days' rain annually. Particularly rainy areas are Artois, Haut-Boulonnais and Avenois. There's seldom snow or ice, although the hills of Ardennes, on the Belgian border, experience some. On average it snows on 18 days per year. Average maximum/minimum temperatures along the coast are around 20/14C (68/57F) in summer and 6/2°C (43/36F) in winter.

The region's main towns include Arras, Boulogne, Calais, Cambrai, Dunkerque, Lille (the regional capital), Montreuil, Roubaix, Saint-Omer, Tourcoing and Valenciennes. The region's coastline, known as the *Côte opale* ('Opal Coast'), has a number of pleasant resorts, including Berck, Boulogne, Etaples, Hardelot, Le Touquet (the most fashionable and known as 'Paris Plage') and Wimereux.

The region's popularity among British buyers in particular means that house prices have risen quite quickly, particularly at the lower end of the market, where there are few small farmhouses left for renovation. Nevertheless, homes in the region remain inexpensive compared with those in most parts of Normandy and Brittany, although coastal areas are naturally more expensive than the interior.

As well as frequent ferry services to the UK via Boulogne, Calais and the Channel Tunnel (*Tunnel sous la Manche*), the area has excellent road connections with Paris and the rest of France via the A26 and A25 motorways, and with Belgium and northern Europe, and is also linked with Brussels, London, Paris and the rest of France by *TGV* and Eurostar trains (see the map in **Appendix E**). Paris CDG airport is accessible from southern parts of the region, offering flights to most worldwide destinations. Lille airport (59) offers flights throughout France, and to and from Frankfurt, Munich and towns in Italy, Portugal, Spain and Switzerland, but no direct flights to and from the UK. There's a *TGV* connection to the city centre.

Normandy

Normandy (*Normandie*) has long been popular with foreign buyers, particularly the British on account of its proximity and similar climate and countryside, as well as its historical and cultural kinship. Like Britain, Normandy was invaded by the Vikings – 200 years before the Normans themselves invaded Britain – and it was part of England in the early Middle Ages (the Queen is still 'Duke of Normandy'!). There are also more recent cultural ties between the two regions and the UK, with 'twinnings' (e.g. Honfleur with Sandwich in Kent, and the department of Calvados with Devon) and frequent cross-Channel exchanges.

Despite a widespread movement to reunite Normandy, it's currently divided into two official regions: Lower Normandy and Upper Normandy (see below). This fairly recent (1972) administrative division, however, has neither a historical nor a geographical basis. Historically, Upper and Lower Normandy were separated by the Seine, which now runs roughly along the dividing line between the departments of Eure and Seine-Maritime in Upper Normandy.

Geographically, Normandy can be said to be divided into three areas: the eastern 'plains' (roughly corresponding to Upper Normandy), interrupted by the Seine valley; the western *bocage*, a landscape of fields and hedges resulting from 19th century methods of dairy farming; and a central area divided vertically between plains to the west of the river Orne and *bocage* to the east. (Confusingly, the word *bocage* is used to describe both the area south-west of Caen and any similar landscape in Normandy or France as a whole.) Within the central area, south of Caen, is 'Swiss Normandy' (*La Suisse Normande*), so called because of its similarity to the Swiss landscape, with deep gorges and rocky peaks, although the highest point, Mont Pinçon, is only 365m (120ft) above sea level.

Normandy was originally divided into 'lands' (*pays*), many of which are still referred to and even marked on maps (although they often straddle departments and even the division between Upper and Lower Normandy), e.g. the Pays d'Argentan, Pays du Houlme and Pays du Perche in Orne, the Pays d'Auge (around Caen), the Pays de Bray (near the border with Picardy), the Pays de Caux (a largely rural and agricultural area between Rouen and Dieppe), the Pays d'Ouche (between Bernay and Verneuil-sur-Avre) and the Pays du Vexin Normand in north-east Eure.

Normandy is noted for its lovely countryside and wide variety of scenery, including lush meadows, orchards, rivers and brooks, quiet country lanes, and over 600km (370mi) of coastline (100km/60mi of which were the scene of D-Day landings in June 1944).

Normandy is a rich agricultural region, producing meat, milk, butter, cheese (most famously Camembert, but also numerous other cheeses, including Livarot, Neufchâtel and Pont l'Evêque), apples, cider and calvados – a spirit distilled from apple juice

(Upper Normandy is sometimes referred to as 'calvaland'). It's also renowned for its cuisine, with local specialities including shellfish dishes (Calvados is a major shellfish producer) and apple tart.

Normandy is an important maritime centre, with no fewer than 50 ports along its coast, including Cherbourg-Octeville, Dieppe, Fécamp, Granville, Le Havre, Honfleur, Port-en-Bessin and Tréport, as well as the major inland ports of Rouen and Caen.

Normandy has four regional *parcs naturels* – Boucles de la Seine Normande (between Rouen and Le Havre), Marais

du Cotentin et du Bessin (north of Saint-Lô on the Cotentin peninsula), Perche (east of Alençon, in Orne, stretching into Eure-et-Loir) and Normandie-Maine (west of Alençon). It also has three areas of marshland: around the mouth of the Vire in Manche (where the Parc régional du Cotentin et du Bessin is Europe's largest 'wetland'), around the mouth of the Orne in Calvados and around the mouth of the Seine in Seine-Maritime.

Normandy has long been popular with the British for holidays and second homes, particularly in and around the Channel ports and resorts. Two-thirds of foreign buyers are British. With the exception of Nord-Pas-de-Calais and Picardy, it's the most accessible region from the UK via the ports of Caen, Cherbourg-Octeville, Dieppe and Le Havre. Coastal property is relatively expensive (homes with a sea view command a steep premium) and prices increase the closer you get to Paris (Parisians weekend on the Normandy coast).

Honfleur has a surfeit of British residents and Deauville is packed with chic Parisians, and both are very expensive. On the other hand, there are still bargains to be found (particularly for British buyers), especially in the department of Orne.

Lower Normandy

Lower Normandy (*Basse-Normandie*) is the western 'half' of Normandy (population 1.4m) and contains the departments of Calvados (14), Manche (50) and Orne (61), covering a total area of 17,600km^2 (7,000mi^2). Demographically, Lower Normandy is more rural and 'traditional' than Upper Normandy. The largest city by far is Caen (117,000), the administrative capital, other major towns including Alençon, Lisieux, Mortagne-sur-Perche and Verneuil-sur-Avre. Some 50 per cent of

Lower Normandy is grassland (the highest percentage in France); the north-west of Calvados is known as the Bessin – land of grass, milk and marshes. A further 30 per cent is arable land.

Upper Normandy

Upper Normandy (*Haute-Normandie*) comprises the departments of Eure (27) and Seine-Maritime (61). It covers an area of around 12,500km^2 (5,000mi^2) and has a population of around 1.8m. Upper Normandy is more urbanised and Paris-influenced than Lower Normandy – the department of Eure in particular is said to be in the shadow of the capital. Its largest cities are Rouen (population around 400,000), the administrative capital of Upper Normandy and Le Havre (193,000), other major towns including Dieppe, Evreux, Les Andelys, Louviers, Pont-Audemer and Yvetot.

Pays-de-la-Loire

The Pays-de-la-Loire (population 3.2m) covers an area of 32,082km^2 (12,512mi^2) on the Atlantic coast and comprises five departments: Loire-Atlantique (44), Maine-et-Loire (49), Mayenne (53), Sarthe (72) and Vendée (85). The Loire is France's longest river (1,020km/628mi), with its source in the Vivarais mountains (south of Saint-Etienne in the department of Loire) and its outlet at Saint-Nazaire in Loire-Atlantique. It flows through the middle of the Pays-de-la-Loire, dividing the departments of Maine-et-Loire and Loire-Atlantique horizontally, and is fed by a number of important tributaries in the area, notably the Vienne (which flows through the department of the same name), the Thouet (which joins the Loire at Saumur), the Mayenne (which joins it at Angers and is a favourite among watersports enthusiasts), and the Sèvre Nantaise (which joins it at the great coastal port of Nantes).

Pointe de Penhir, Brittany

Along the coast to the west is the industrial town of Saint-Nazaire and beyond it several attractive and fashionable seaside resorts. Inland are vineyards that produce the famous Muscadet and Rosé d'Anjou wines, and to the north the department of Mayenne, named after the river that runs into the Loire – an attractive area for boating, walking and cycling.

The most easterly part of the region is Sarthe, which centres on Le Mans, notable not only for its 24-hour motor races but also for its spectacular cathedral. This part of the region is less than an hour from Paris by *TGV* or under two hours' by car and, with its fields, hedges and beech woodlands, is popular with Parisians, many of whom have second homes here.

On the southern part of the coast, much of Vendée is flat and windy (its symbol is a windmill). Inland parts of Vendée feature gently rolling countryside with small fields, hedges, trees and woodlands called *le bocage* and similar to that found in parts of Normandy. The department has a dark history of mass slaughter during the religious and revolutionary wars, but now the land is smiling, with its almost endless beaches, seaside resorts and fishing villages, and a soft and sunny climate which encourages mimosa.

In the last few thousand years, the sea has been receding along the west coast leaving a flat plain. Along the border between the Pays-de-la-Loire and Poitou-Charentes (see below) is land which has been reclaimed from the sea, known as the *Marais Poitevin* (Poitevin Marsh). Part of the Marsh hasn't been drained, however, and consists of a pattern of tree-lined canals between small fields used for market gardening and cattle rearing – an area known as '*la Venise verte*' ('Green Venice') and one of the most unusual landscapes in France.

Coastal areas benefit from tourism but are also attracting an increasing number of retired people, as well as foreigners. The department of Vendée in particular is attracting an increasing number of foreign homebuyers and property prices are rising fast.

The Pays-de-la-Loire is noted for heavy industry, with shipyards at Saint-Nazaire and factories near La Rochelle.

Picardy

The region of Picardy (*Picardie*), one of the least known regions of France, has a population of 1.9m and contains the departments of Aisne (02), Oise (60) and Somme (80). It's mainly famous for its battlegrounds from the first and second world wars, particularly the Somme, although the region is rich in earlier history and architecture. Picardy has a generally flat and uninteresting agricultural

La turbie, French Riviera

landscape, with just a 37km (23mi) coastal strip around the mouth of the river Somme near Abbeville, although this is one of a number of attractive areas, including the valleys of the Aisne, Oise and Somme rivers. The region's main towns include the regional capital Amiens (80), Beauvais, Compiègne, Chantilly, Saint-Omer and Saint-Quentin. Picardy has some of the lowest property prices in France, although it isn't popular with foreign buyers. The Oise department is the most expensive of the three on account of its proximity to Paris. Picardy is crossed by the *TGV* line from Paris to Lille (see the map in **Appendix E**) as well as by the A1, A16, A28 and A29 motorways and is within easy reach of England, via the Channel Tunnel and Calais ferries.

Poitou-Charentes

Poitou-Charentes (population 1.6m) covers an area of 25,809km^2 (10,066mi^2) and is made up of four departments: Charente (16), Charente-Maritime (17), Deux-Sèvres(79) and Vienne (86). The Poitou-Charentes region is almost completely unspoiled with virtually no industry and is one of the most tranquil in France. Its long Atlantic coastline is noted for long, sandy beaches, marinas, golf courses and islands, which make it an ideal summer holiday destination. Two large islands, the Ile de Ré and the Ile d'Oléron, with their pine-shaded beaches and superb shellfish, were connected by road bridges to the mainland a generation ago and have seen their populations grow rapidly as a result; camp sites have also proliferated.

> No cars are allowed on the smaller island of Aix, where Napoleon spent his last night in France before leaving for Saint-Helena.

The marshes along the estuary of the Seudre have been converted into oyster beds with lines of thick wooden posts, on which mussels are also farmed. In fact, the region is France's biggest centre for the production of oysters and other shellfish. Elsewhere, the flat shore is used for drying out sea water in shallow pans to make salt.

Inland, the landscape is flat, particularly in Charente, and the land is used for mixed farming and livestock breeding. The gently rolling chalk hills of Charente and Charente-Maritime are covered with vines (mostly for white wine and cognac), poultry farms and grazing for dairy herds, with wooded hilltops rising to over 160m (500ft).

The region is crossed by the medieval routes used by pilgrims on their way to the shrine of Saint James at Compostella in Spain, a practice which is currently being revived. These routes were also used by the stone masons who built the region's many Romanesque churches, such as Saint Pierre at Aulnay (17). Other notable monuments include the 15th century church tower built by the English at Marennes (79), the fourth century baptistery in Poitiers (86) and the collection of 11th century frescos in the church at Saint-Savin (86). There are numerous other places of historical interest, including the fortified town of Brouage, abandoned as a port when the sea receded, the 17th century naval port of Rochefort which replaced it, and the Vieux Port at La Rochelle (all in 17). In contrast, present-day attractions include Futuroscope near Poitiers and what is reputed to be France's best zoo at La Palmyre.

Poitou-Charentes is a popular region with tourists, holiday homeowners and retirees, particularly British property buyers, many of whom favour the area around Cognac (16) and Saintes (17). There's a huge difference between the cost of property on the coast and inland, where homes are good value.

Provence-Alpes-Côte d'Azur

For many people, both French and foreigners, the jewel in France's crown is the eastern Mediterranean coastal region known officially as Provence-Alpes-Côte d'Azur, abbreviated to PACA but simply referred to as Provence by most people. It comprises the departments of Alpes-de-Haute-Provence (4), Hautes-Alpes (05), Alpes-Maritimes (6), Bouches-du-Rhône (13), Var (83) and Vaucluse (84). The magazine Le Point has more than once

elected Aix-en-Provence (13), the 'capital' of Provence, the best French town to live in, and The Riviera Times recently wrote with reference to the Côte d'Azur: "Sun, blue skies, warm sea, delicious food and tasty wines, idyllic villages and an allure of luxury. Surely that's the life we are all looking for?"

Slightly larger than its Mediterranean neighbour, Languedoc-Roussillon, the PACA region occupies an area of 31,400km^2 (19,510mi^2) and has a population approaching 4.6m. Economically, it's the second most important region in France after Ile-de-France. Overall, 40 per cent of PACA is woodland (the second-highest proportion in France).

The Provence area comprises the Alpes-de-Haute-Provence, Bouches-du-Rhône and Vaucluse departments and part of the Var, although opinions differ as to exactly where Provence ends and the Côte d'Azur (Azure Coast) begins. The Côte d'Azur was 'discovered' by the British, who dubbed it the 'French Riviera' and helped to create the world's first coastal playground for the rich and famous. At the end of the 19th century, Queen Victoria was influential in developing the area's popularity through her visits to Hyères (just east of Toulon), which was then considered the western extremity of the Côte d'Azur. Today, many people regard Saint-Tropez, 45km (28mi) further east along the coast, as the limit of Provence and the start of the Côte d'Azur (known locally as la Côte).

Another school of thought (whose members understandably include many local estate agents) believes that the Côte d'Azur lies between Hyères and the conurbation of Fréjus-Saint-Raphaël (east of Saint-Tropez). There are also those who consider the French Riviera as the stretch of coastline from Menton, close to the Italian border, to just beyond Cannes, the Côte d'Azur encompassing the

French Riviera and extending to Saint-Tropez. (Note that Monaco, although geographically part of the Riviera/Côte d'Azur, is a separate principality and not part of France.)

> Wherever it begins and ends, Provence is a fascinating land of romance, history (it has its own ancient language, Provençal, now spoken only in Italy) and great beauty, and is celebrated for its excellent climate, attractive scenery, fine beaches, superb cuisine and fashionable resorts.

It's one of the most exclusive areas of France, and few places in Europe can compete with its ambience and allure, glamorous resorts and beautiful people. However, it's also a region of stark contrasts, with a huge variety of landscape and scenery, encompassing extensive woodlands, rugged mountains, rolling hills, spectacular gorges (the Grand Canyon du Verdon is the deepest cleft in Europe), dramatic rock formations, lush and fertile valleys carpeted with lavender, extensive vineyards (which stretch to the foot of the Alps in Vaucluse), and a ravishing coastline dotted with quaint fishing villages and fine beaches.

A journey through Provence is an indulgence of the senses, and its diverse vegetation includes cypresses, gnarled olive trees, almond groves, umbrella pines, lavender, wild rosemary and thyme, all of which add to its unique and seductive sights and smells. Provence produces a number of excellent wines and includes the prestigious vineyards of Châteauneuf-du-Pape, Gigondas (mostly red) plus popular and drinkable wines such as Côtes du Lubéron and Côtes de Provence.

The region contains many naturally beautiful areas, notably the Lubéron National Park (Parc naturel régional du Lubéron), the heart of the provençal countryside and still a fashionable area for holiday homes and visitors, in spite of (or perhaps because of) Peter Mayle. The Camargue, between Arles and the sea (from which it was reclaimed), is one of the most spectacular nature reserves in France and famous for its wild white horses.

Provence also contains a wealth of beautiful historic Roman towns and dramatically sited medieval villages, and both Marseille and Nice provide sea links to Corsica and North Africa, where the holiday resorts of Morocco and Tunisia are popular with the French (being former protectorates where French is still widely spoken).

Although the Alpes-Maritimes and Bouches-du-Rhône departments have very little coastline which isn't built-up, Var has perhaps the most attractive, unspoilt coastline in the PACA region, between Hyères and Fréjus-Saint-Raphaël.

Not surprisingly, Provence-Alpes-Côte d'Azur is the most popular region in France for holiday and retirement homes and has a large foreign community, British, Germans and Italians being among the largest buyers of second homes. In 2001 there were around 8,000 official British residents (Peter Mayle's televised book, *A Year in Provence*, caused countless Brits to pack up and head south). Popularity, of course, has its price, notably in respect of property costs, which have risen beyond the reach of many, who now look instead towards Languedoc-Roussillon, which currently has only half as many British residents as Provence.

Rhône-Alpes

The Rhône-Alpes region (population 5.6m) runs from Lac Léman ('Lake

Savoie and Drôme. Mont Blanc, altitude 4,807m (15,767ft) in Haute-Savoie is the highest peak in Europe (excluding the mountains of Georgia). The Mont Blanc road tunnel and the Tunnel du Fréjus road and rail tunnel cut through the Alps, from Haute-Savoie and Savoie respectively, linking France with Italy.

The Alps area is, of course, noted for its majestic mountain scenery, which is unrivalled at most times of the year, and it's probably France's most picturesque region with its dense forests, lush pasture land, fast-flowing rivers, huge lakes and deep gorges. It's a paradise for sports fans and nature lovers with superb summer sports, such as rock-climbing and canyoning (abseiling and water-chute descents), hiking and walking, all-terrain cycling, hang-gliding and paragliding, and white-water sports, while winter sports and ski resorts offer some of the best facilities in Europe for downhill (Alpine) and cross-country (Nordic) skiing and snowboarding. Albertville (73), Chamonix (74) and Grenoble (38) have all been venues for the Winter Olympic Games. Top ski resorts include Chamonix, France's mountaineering capital, Courchevel, Megève, Méribel and Val d'Isère. The Alps therefore have two high seasons: the usual summer period, and the winter skiing season (December to April), the two peaks within the latter being the school holidays at Christmas and Easter.

The Alps is the third most popular tourist area in France, after Paris and the Côte-d'Azur, and Annecy is one of the most popular tourist towns in France after Paris, although property prices are well below those of Paris and prestigious towns on the Riviera. Lower property prices than neighbouring Switzerland attract many Swiss, who live in the area and commute to work in Geneva and other Swiss cities.

Geneva'), the largest lake in western Europe, southwards towards the Mediterranean and is bounded by the Italian border to the east and the Rhône to the west. It includes the departments of Ain (01), Ardèche (07), Drôme (26), Isère (38), Loire (42), Savoie (73), Rhône (69) and Haute-Savoie (74). (The former province of Dauphiné corresponds approximately to the north-eastern part of Drôme and the Isère and Hautes-Alpes departments.)

Rhône-Alpes is the most mountainous area of France, the Alps being Europe's biggest mountain range, 'shared' between France, Italy and Switzerland. The average altitude of the mountains in the Alps is 1,150m (3,772ft); the eastern area of the Alps has the highest peaks and forms a natural barrier with Italy. The most mountainous department is Isère, followed by Hautes-Alpes, Savoie, Haute-

Lyon (69), which is the regional capital and France's second-largest city as well as its gastronomic capital, has a beautiful medieval quarter. The Rhône river (whose source is high in the Swiss Alps) is a vital artery for river, road and rail traffic between the north and south of France. Rhône's other major towns include Bourg-en-Bresse, Privas and Saint-Etienne.

> Although largely unspoiled by development, the Rhône valley is one of France's major industrial regions.

The price of property in the Rhône-Alpes region is well above the average, although the most expensive areas are mostly in the Alps. Ardèche with its spectacular gorge is increasingly popular with foreign buyers and is consequently becoming more expensive. Like Franche-Comté, Rhône-Alpes is popular with the Swiss, many of whom live in the region and commute to their workplaces in Geneva and other Swiss cities. The region is noted for its extremes of temperature and is usually freezing in winter and hot in summer, and most pleasant in spring and autumn. The Rhône-Alpes has excellent road, rail and air connections, and Lyon is just two hours from Paris by TGV (see the map in **Appendix E**).

Beziers, Hérault

5.
YOUR DREAM HOME

O nce you've chosen your retirement spot, you need to find a property. France has a wealth of property options for all pockets, tastes and circumstances; the choice can be bewildering, so you need to be absolutely sure you're buying the right type of property for yours.

☑ SURVIVAL TIP

Experts advise renting for a period before buying a property in order to avoid making a costly and stressful mistake (see page 68).

Property in France is generally cheaper than in most northern European countries, so your property in your home country can usually be sold for a higher price than a home in France and you can use the equity released as a financial safety net or to supplement your pension. However, the reasonable price of French property tempts many people into buying a home that's larger than they need or with more land than they can cope with. Think carefully before buying a large country property with acres of land, bearing in mind the high cost and amount of work involved in its upkeep. If it's to be a seasonal retirement home, who will look after the house and garden when you're away? Do you want to spend your time there mowing the lawn and cutting back the undergrowth? France's climate means that grass, plants and trees grow **fast** (up to three times as fast as in

the UK, for example)! Do you want a home with a lot of outbuildings? What are you going to do with them? Can you afford to convert them into extra rooms, guest accommodation or *gîtes* and, if so, will be you be able to attract holidaymakers to stay in them? Retirees should take the opportunity to downsize, not to expand!

This chapter includes essential information on what to buy, the cost of property and letting your French property when you aren't using it. Information is also provided about home security, utilities (electricity, gas and water – connections and general information), and heating and air-conditioning.

For comprehensive information about buying a property in France and the purchase procedure, refer to this book's best-selling sister publication, *Buying a Home in France* by David Hampshire (see page 322).

TYPES OF PROPERTY

In most areas, properties range from derelict farmhouses and barns to modern townhouses and apartments with all modern conveniences, from crumbling *châteaux* and manor houses requiring

papered. When wallpaper is used, it's often garish and may cover everything, including walls, doors and ceilings! Properties throughout France tend to be built in a distinct local (often unique) style using local materials. There are stringent regulations in most areas concerning the style and design of new homes and the restoration of old buildings.

In older rural properties, the kitchen (*cuisine*) is the most important room in the house. It's usually huge with a large wood-burning stove for cooking, hot water and heating, a huge solid wood dining table and possibly a bread oven (*four à pain*). French country kitchens are worlds apart from modern fitted kitchens and are devoid of shiny Formica, linoleum and plastic laminates. They're often comparatively stark, with stone or tiled floors and a predominance of wood, tiles and marble. Kitchens in older apartments in Paris and other cities may be very basic, although modern fitted kitchens (with dishwashers, cookers and refrigerators) are usually found in new properties, and 'American kitchens' (i.e. open plan kitchens separated from the living or dining room by a bar or counter) are increasingly common.

New homes usually also contain many 'luxury' features, e.g. deluxe bathroom suites, fitted cupboards, smoke and security alarms, and coordinated interior colour schemes. New homes are usually sold *décorée*, which means not only that they're decorated but also that they have a fitted kitchen.

Refrigerators (*frigidaire* or *frigo*) and cookers (*cuisinière*) are generally quite small. Cookers in rural homes are usually run on bottled gas or a combination of bottled gas and electricity. Many homes have a gas water heater (*chaudière* or *chauffe-eau*) that heats the water for the bathroom and kitchen. Most houses don't have a separate utility room and the washing machine and drier are kept in the

complete restoration to new luxury chalets and villas.

French homes are built to high structural standards and, whether you buy a new or an old home, it will usually be extremely sturdy. Older homes often have thick walls and contain numerous rooms. Most have a wealth of interesting period features, including vast fireplaces, wooden staircases, attics, cellars (*caves*), and a profusion of alcoves and annexes. Many houses have a basement (*sous-sol*), used as a garage and cellar (*cave*). In most old houses, open fireplaces remain a principal feature even when central heating is installed. In warmer regions (and even in the north) floors are often tiled and walls painted rather than papered, while elsewhere floors are carpeted or bare wood, and walls are more likely to be kitchen or basement. A separate toilet (*toilette* or *WC/water*) is popular, and the bathroom (*salle de bains*) often has a bidet as well as a bath (*baignoire*) and/or a shower (*douche*). Baths are more common than showers in older homes, although showers are found in most modern homes. Note that many old, unmodernised homes don't have a bath, shower room or inside toilet.

Many rural properties have shutters (*volets*), both for security and as a means of insulation. External shutters are often supplemented by internal shutters that are fixed directly to the window frames. In France, windows open inwards rather than outwards. In the south and south-west, many rural homes have outdoor swimming pools, and homes throughout France have a paved patio or terrace, which is often covered. Old farmhouses invariably have a number of outbuildings such as barns, which can usually be converted into additional accommodation.

A huge variety of new properties is available in France, including city apartments and individually-designed, detached houses. Many new properties are part of purpose-built developments (see **Community Properties** below). Note, however, that many developments are planned as holiday homes and they may not be attractive as permanent homes (they're also generally expensive). If you're buying an apartment or house that's part of a development, check whether your neighbours will be mainly French or other foreigners. Some people don't wish to live in a *commune* of their fellow countrymen and this will also deter French buyers if you want to sell. Prices of new properties vary considerably with their location and quality (see **Cost of Property** on page 114).

The French generally prefer modern homes to older houses with 'charm and character' (which to the locals mean 'expensive to maintain and in danger of falling down'!), although new homes often have pseudo-period features such as beams and open fireplaces. France's bold and innovative architecture, as portrayed in its many striking public buildings, doesn't often extend to modern private dwellings, many of which seem to have been designed by the same architect – or not designed at all! However, although new properties are often lacking in character, they're usually spacious and well endowed with modern conveniences and services, which certainly cannot be taken for granted in older rural properties.

Standard fixtures and fittings in modern houses are more comprehensive and of better quality than those found in old houses. Central heating, double glazing and good insulation are common in new houses, particularly in northern France, where they're essential. Central heating may be electric, gas or oil-fired. However, on the Côte d'Azur, where winter temperatures are higher, expensive insulation and heating may be considered unnecessary (don't you believe it!). Air-conditioning is rare, even in the south of France.

> ⚠ **Caution**
>
> **Many apartments don't have their own source of hot water and heating, which is shared with other apartments in the same building.**

Note that most French families live in apartments or detached homes, and semi-detached and terraced properties are relatively rare. Some 45 per cent of the population lives in apartments (although less than 10 per cent in tower blocks), which are more common in France than in most other European countries. In cities and suburbs, most people have little choice, as houses are in short supply and prohibitively expensive. In the major cities there are many *bourgeois* apartments, built in the 19th or early 20th century, with large rooms, high ceilings and huge

With regard to the distance and travelling time to amenities, shops and public transport (etc.), don't accept what you're told by estate agents (brokers). According to some agents' magical mystery maps, everywhere in the north is handy for Paris or a Channel port and all homes in the south are a stone's throw from Lyon or Nice. Check distances, times and the ease of access for yourself and bear in mind that during peak periods they can be much longer.

When house hunting, obtain large scale maps of the area where you're looking. The best maps are the Institut Géographique National (IGN) series of 74 maps with a scale of 1cm = 1km, *cartes de promenade* (1cm = 1km), both of which series are blue, and town and local maps (various scales). These maps show every building, track and waterway as well as contour lines, so it's easy to mark off the places that you've seen. You could do this using a grading system to denote your impressions. If you use an estate agent, he will usually drive you around and you can return later to those that you like most at your leisure (provided you've marked them on your map!).

windows. Unless modernised, they have old-fashioned bathrooms and kitchens and are expensive to decorate, furnish and maintain.

See also **Community Properties** below.

For details of typical homes in the most popular regions of France, refer to *The Best Places to Buy a Home in France* (Survival Books – see page 323). You can also buy a piece of land and have a house built to your own specifications; for information on building your own home, refer to *Buying a Home in France* (Survival Books – see page 322).

Before looking at properties, it's important to have a good idea of the kind of home that you're looking for and the price you wish to pay, and to draw up a shortlist of the areas or towns of interest. If you don't do this, you're likely to be overwhelmed by the number of properties to be viewed. Estate agents usually expect serious buyers to know where they want to buy within a 30 to 40km (20 to 25mi) radius and some even expect clients to narrow it down to specific towns and villages.

Community Properties

In France, properties with common elements (whether a building, amenities or land) shared with other properties are owned outright through a system called 'co-ownership' (*copropriété*), similar to a condominium in the US, but are referred to here as community properties to avoid confusion with part-ownership schemes such as timeshare. Community properties include apartments, townhouses, and detached homes on a private estate with communal areas and facilities. Almost all French properties that are part of a development are owned *en copropriété*. In general, the only properties that aren't community properties are detached houses on individual plots in public streets or on rural land. Under the system of *copropriété*, you own not only your home (*parties privatives*) but also a share (*quote-part* or *tantième*) of the common elements (*parties communes*) of a building or development, including foyers, hallways, lifts, patios, gardens, roads, and leisure and sports facilities, according to the size or value of your property.

Community properties are also often in locations where owning a single-family home would be prohibitively expensive, e.g. a beach-front or town centre. Many modern community developments are located near coastal or mountain resorts and they may offer a wide range of communal facilities, including a golf course, swimming pool, tennis and squash courts, a gymnasium or fitness club, and a restaurant. Most also have landscaped gardens, high security and a full-time caretaker (*gardien/ gardienne*), and some even have their own 'village' and shops. At the other extreme, some developments consist merely of numerous cramped, tiny studio apartments. Bear in mind that community developments planned as holiday homes may not be suitable as permanent homes. Other advantages and disadvantages of community properties are listed below.

> Further information about community properties can be obtained from the Association des Responsables de Copropriété (ARC), 29 rue Joseph Python, 75020 Paris (☎ 01 40 30 12 82, ⌨ www.unarc.asso.fr – in French only).

Advantages & Disadvantages

The advantages of owning a community property may include the following:

- increased security;
- lower property taxes than detached homes;

- a range of sports and leisure facilities;
- community living with lots of social contacts and the companionship of close neighbours;
- no garden, lawn or pool maintenance;
- fewer of the responsibilities of individual home ownership.

The disadvantages of community properties may include the following:

- restrictive rules and regulations;
- excessive community fees (owners may have no control over increases);
- a confining social environment and lack of privacy;
- noisy neighbours (particularly if neighbouring apartments are rented to holidaymakers);
- limited living and storage space;
- expensive covered or secure parking;
- acrimonious owners' meetings, where management and factions may try to push through unpopular proposals.

Note also that communal facilities in a large development may be inundated during peak periods; for example, a large swimming pool won't look so big when 100 people are using it, and getting a game of tennis or using a fitness room may be difficult.

Checks

Before buying a *copropriété*, it's wise to ask current owners about the community. For example:

- Do they like living there?
- What are the fees and restrictions?
- What are the parking facilities like during peak times?
- Are owners required to pay part of the *taxe foncière* as well as the *taxe d'habitation*?

- How noisy are other residents?
- Are the recreational facilities readily accessible?
- Is the community well managed?
- Would they buy there again (why or why not)?

You may also wish to check on your prospective neighbours. Permanent residents should avoid buying in a development with a high percentage of rental units, i.e. units that aren't owner-occupied. If you're planning to buy an apartment above the ground floor, you may wish to ensure that the building has an efficient lift. Upper floor apartments are both colder in winter and warmer in summer and may incur extra charges for the use of lifts; they do, however, offer more security than ground floor apartments. Note that an apartment that has apartments above and below it will generally be more noisy than a ground or top floor apartment.

Houseboats

France boasts extensive navigable waterways (rivers and canals), which are perfect for those whose ideal home is one that floats. Floating homes are usually restored and converted barges, which can offer extensive and luxurious accommodation. You can choose between a fixed mooring (there are even berths in the centre of Paris) and a peripatetic life, travelling from one part of the country to another.

Expect to pay upwards of €200,000 for a luxury houseboat. As well as the cost of fuel (if you plan to be mobile) and maintenance, you should allow between €25 and €60 per day, €100 to €200 per month or €1,000 to €2,000 per year (depending on the size of your boat) for moorings.

> ⚠ **Caution**
>
> **You need a 'driving licence', which costs around €300, and permits for the use of waterways.**

Further information about French waterways and operating a boat on them can be obtained from the French national waterways board, Voies Navigables de France (🖥 www.vnf.fr).

Retirement Homes

Traditionally, the French expect to care for elderly relatives within the family unit (indeed adults are legally obliged to provide for their parents in old age, depending on their means), so retirement homes

Bibliotheque Nationale de France, Paris

(*résidence pour retraités/seniors*) are less common than in many other developed countries. However, they're becoming more common and there are now over 5,000 retirement homes throughout France. There are several types of retirement home, including the following:

● Conventional retirement homes (*maison de retraite* or *maison de repos*), which may be public or private but are almost all French-speaking. i.e. they aren't designed for expatriates. They may have specialist care facilities (*avec section de cure médicale* or *médicalisée*) but can be rather depressing places.

● Sheltered apartments for those on low incomes (*foyer logement* or *foyer soleil* – the former being in blocks occupied entirely by elderly people, the latter in mixed occupancy blocks) are for those who want and can cope with some autonomy but prefer (or need) supervision and special services. You rent an individual apartment, which you furnish, and share services such as a restaurant and laundry.

● Serviced apartments (*résidence avec services pour personnes âgées* or simply *résidence services*) are similar to sheltered apartments but are usually available for purchase as well as rent, and some are unfurnished.

● Retirement villages (*village retraite*), which are still rare in France. Retirement villages have many advantages, including security, on-site amenities and services, and a ready-made community. Amenities may include a communal swimming pool, lounge, library, exercise and music rooms and a restaurant, and services may include caretaking, cleaning, administrative help, pet-sitting, meal delivery, hairdressing, physiotherapy and excursions, lectures, games, shows and films.

Médica (💻 www.medica-france.fr) operates some 120 *maisons de retraite* throughout the country – in all regions except Corsica and Lower Normandy, those with the largest number of homes being Ile-de-France, PACA and Rhône-Alpes.

Most retirement villages are in the south of France, e.g. 12 operated by the Ramos Group – 💻 www.ramos.fr – with ten more under development), although there are others elsewhere, e.g. the Village Seniors du Grand Logis near Saintes in Charente-Maritime (💻 www.legrandlogis. com). Developments usually consist of 60 to 120 one- and two-bedroom villas (*pavillon*). Homes built by the Ramos Group are single-storey and semi-detached (sometimes in blocks of four, back-to-back) and vary in area from 60 to 85m². All have two-bedrooms and cost between around €180,000 and €300,000. Villas can be rented, for between €300 and €600 per month, or purchased. A villa at the Grand Logis costs from around €100,000 depending on the size. The cost depends on which of three purchase options is chosen: outright freehold purchase, fixed term leasehold or lifetime leasehold.

Most retirement developments levy monthly service charges (usually between €150 and €500), which may include a certain number of weeks' nursing care per illness per year in a residents' nursing home. Service charges usually cover heating and air-conditioning, hot and cold water, satellite TV, and the other amenities and services listed above. The costs for other types of retirement home vary depending on the facilities offered.

A traditional retirement home can cost up to €2,000 per month and a long-stay hospital over €1,000 per month (more in Paris). On the other hand, for those who qualify, *foyer-logements* can cost as little as €300 per month.

Details of facilities for the elderly are contained in *Le Guide des Maisons de*

Retraite (Pétrarque) and *Le Guide du Logement Senior* (Balland). Websites providing information about retirement and lists of retirement homes in France include 💻 www.capretraite.fr, 💻 www.distrimed.com/retraite, 💻 www.happysenior.com, 💻 www.lesmaisonsderetraite.fr, 💻 www.maisonderetraitedefrance.com, 💻 www.maisons-retraite.com and 💻 www.plan-retraite.fr (the site of the Association Française de Protection et d'Assistance aux Personnes Agées) – all in French only.

COST OF PROPERTY

Apart from obvious points such as size, quality and land area, the most important factor influencing the price of a house is its location. A restored or modernised two-bedroom house might cost €100,000 in a remote or unpopular area but sell for two or three times as much in a popular location. The closer you are to the coast (or Paris), the more expensive a property will be, with properties on the Côte d'Azur the most expensive of all. A Charente farmhouse with a barn and land costs around the same as a tiny studio apartment in Paris or on the Côte d'Azur.

⚠ **Caution**

Note that when people talk about inexpensive or 'bargain' homes, they invariably mean a dilapidated property that needs restoring, which usually necessitates spending as much as the purchase price (or much more) to make it habitable (see Renovation & Restoration on page 194).

In some rural areas it's still possible to buy a ruin for as little as €25,000.

Despite the recent increase in property prices, a slice of *la bonne vie* needn't cost the earth, with habitable cottages and terraced village homes available from around €100,000 and detached homes from as little as €125,000. Modern studio and one-bedroom apartments in small towns cost from around €40,000 and two-bedroom apartments from €50,000.

A modern two-bedroom bungalow costs from around €75,000 and a rural two-bedroom renovated cottage from around €100,000. However, if you're seeking a home with several bedrooms, a large plot and a swimming pool, you'll need to spend at least €200,000 (depending on the area), and luxury apartments in Paris and villas in the south of France can cost many hundreds of thousands of euros.

Prices in Paris are similar to other international cities (e.g. London). In central Paris, €200,000 barely buys a one-bedroom apartment in some areas and it isn't unusual to pay €2m for a luxury apartment in a fashionable area. Prices are calculated per m^2 and in mid-2007 averaged €6,128 for an apartment in the capital, €3,707 in the inner suburbs and €2,918 in the outer suburbs; the table below shows average property prices in each *arrondissement* of Paris with the percentage increase in prices since mid-2006 (source: *Les Echos*). Excluding Paris, the average price of apartments in the 100 largest cities and towns in France in 2007 was between €1,266 per m² (Nevers in Nièvre) and €5,546 per m² (Boulogne-Billancourt in Hauts-de-Seine).

The average price of a house in the inner suburbs of Paris in late 2007 was just over €340,000 and in the outer suburbs just under €290,000.

To get an idea of the variation in property prices across the regions of France, see *The Best Places to Buy a Home in France* (Survival Books) and check the prices of properties advertised in French and English-language property magazines and newspapers (see **Appendix B**). Property price indexes for different areas are published by some French property magazines, although these should be taken as a guide only.

The table overleaf indicates the types of property available (in late 2007) in various price categories in the most popular parts of France.

In addition to the purchase price, you must allow for various costs associated with buying a house in France, which are higher than in most other countries (see **Fees** below). Note that prices may be quoted inclusive or exclusive of agency fees (see **Selling Agent's Fee** on page 122).

Paris Property Prices per m²		
Arrondissement	Annual Increase 2006-07	Average Price per m²
1	+ 12.9%	€7,535
2	+ 12.9%	€6,597
3	+ 12.9%	€7,010
4	+ 13%	€8,348
5	+ 5.6%	€7,569
6	+ 9.3%	€8,818
7	+ 9.2%	€8,829
8	+ 6.6%	€7,243
9	+ 8.6%	€6,038
10	+ 6.8%	€5,194
11	+ 6.1%	€5,558
12	+ 6.6%	€5,656
13	+ 5.2%	€5,605
14	+ 8.5%	€6,227
15	+ 7.7%	€6,309
16	+ 10.4%	€6,962
17	+ 6.8%	€5,710
18	+ 9.6%	€5,247
19	+ 9.2%	€4,705
20	+ 6.8%	€4,990

Price Range (€)	Properties
€50,000–75,000	2-bed cottage to renovate in hamlet in Haute-Vienne, Limousin; small house to renovate on 1.1ha in Poitou-Charentes; barn for conversion in Dordogne, Aquitaine; barn for conversion in Vendée, Pays-de-la-Loire; *longère* to renovate on 2ha in Côtes d'Armor, Brittany; restored 3-bed village house in Deux-Sèvres, Poitou-Charentes; 2-bed house + 4 outbuildings to renovate on 1ha in Orne, Lower Normandy; renovated studio flat in Royan, Charente-Maritime; stone farmhouse in need of interior renovation in Mayenne, Pays-de-la-Loire.
€75,000–100,000	2-bed cottage + outbuildings in Somme, Picardy; 2-bed farmhouse + barn & stable to renovate in Loire, Rhône-Alpes; 3-bed house to renovate on 0.3ha in Côtes d'Armor, Brittany; 2-bed farmhouse + barn to renovate in small village in Allier, Auvergne; 1-bed village house in Sarthe, Pays-de-la-Loire; stone village house for renovation in Lot, Midi-Pyrénées; 4-bed farmhouse for renovation in Vienne, Poitou-Charentes; 2-bed village house in Lot-et-Garonne, Aquitaine; 3-bed village house in Aude, Languedoc-Roussillon; 2-bed ski apartment in Hautes-Alpes, PACA; 4-bed village house + outbuildings in Vienne, Poitou-Charentes; 3-bed terraced house in Haute-Vienne, Limousin; 2-bed house in hamlet in Nièvre, Burgundy; 3-bed semi-detached house in Pas-de-Calais.
€100,000–125,000	New studio apartment near Lille in Nord; renovated village house in Midi-Pyrénées; 4-bed house in Corrèze, Limousin; house + 6 outbuildings on 0.4ha in Loire, Rhône-Alpes; new 1-bed apartment in Ille-et-Vilaine, Brittany; 4-bed village house in Brittany; 2-bed semi in village in Nièvre, Burgundy; 1-bed village house + barn for renovation in Burgundy; 1-bed apartment + communal pool near sea in Pyrénées-Orientales, Languedoc-Roussillon; 2-bed cottage on small plot in Sarthe, Pays-de-la-Loire; new 1-bed apartment in Oise, Picardy.
€125,000–150,000	2-bed village house in Hérault, Languedoc-Roussillon; 2-bed semi-detached cottage in Morbihan, Brittany; 3-bed house with outbuildings and large plot in Haute-Vienne, Limousin; 2-bed townhouse in Côte d'Or, Burgundy; 1-bed apartment in Nice, Alpes-Maritimes, PACA; 7-bed partially renovated house in Puy-de-Dôme, Auvergne; 3-bed village semi in Vendée, Pays-de-la-Loire; barn for renovation in Pyrénées-Atlantiques, Aquitaine; 2-bed house with large garden in hamlet in Dordogne, Aquitaine; new studio apartment in village in Haute-Savoie, Rhône-Alpes; 4 adjoining houses for renovation in Aude, Languedoc-Roussillon;

renovated 3-bed townhouse in Pas-de-Calais; 3-bed stone semi on small plot in Manche, Lower Normandy; 2-bed character house in Sarthe, Pays-de-la-Loire; 2-bed cottage in Tarn-et-Garonne, Midi-Pyrénées; 2-bed stone house + two barns in village in Morbihan, Brittany; 3-bed townhouse in Hautes-Alpes, PACA.

€150,000–175,000   1-bed apartment in Courchevel, Savoie, Rhône-Alpes; new 1-bed apartment in Juan-les-Pins, Var, PACA; renovated 3-bed *longère* in Finistère, Brittany; restored 3-bed village house in Tarn-et-Garonne, Midi-Pyrénées; new 1-bed apartment + communal pool in Hérault, Languedoc-Roussillon; restored farmhouse in hamlet in Allier, Auvergne; 2-bed thatched cottage with outbuildings in Manche, Lower Normandy; 3-bed stone house on 0.3ha in Limousin; 2-bed house + barn & outbuildings to renovate on 1.5ha in Haute-Vienne, Limousin.

€175,000–200,000   New 1-bed apartment in village in Savoie, Rhône-Alpes; 2-bed stone house on small plot in Côtes d'Armor, Brittany; restored farmhouse + barn to renovate in Saône-et-Loire, Burgundy; new 2-bed house in Hérault, Languedoc-Roussillon; renovated 3-bed farmhouse in Burgundy; restored 3-bed cottage + pool & outbuilding in Charente; 3-bed townhouse with outbuildings in Burgundy; 3-bed farmhouse in hamlet in Lozère, Languedoc-Roussillon; modern 2-bed house in Auvergne; 3-bed *longère* on 0.6ha in Mayenne, Pays-de-la-Loire; 3-bed village house in Manche, Lower Normandy.

€200,000–225,000   3-bed house + outbuildings on 0.4ha in Morbihan, Brittany; 3-bed half-timbered house with pool on 0.5ha in Calvados, Lower Normandy; 4-bed house on 0.3ha in Poitou-Charentes; renovated 4-bed village house in Aude, Languedoc-Roussillon; renovated 3-bed stone house on 0.8ha in Aveyron, Midi-Pyrénées; 3-bed stone house + outbuildings in Tarn-et-Garonne, Midi-Pyrénées; modern 3-bed house + barn & stables on 1.5ha in Pas-de-Calais; restored 3-bed stone cottage + furniture in Dordogne, Aquitaine; part-renovated 2-bed village house with outbuildings in Indre-et-Loire, Centre; 4-bed house on large plot in Somme, Picardy.

€225,000–250,000   Modern 2-bed house on 2ha including 1.5ha lake in Dordogne, Aquitaine; farmhouse + outbuildings in Gers, Midi-Pyrénées; 2-bed 19th-century house + three *gîtes* on 0.3ha in Loire-Atlantique, Pays-de-la-Loire; renovated 3-bed farmhouse + barn on 1ha in Loire, Rhône-Alpes; renovated large farmhouse + 2 *gîtes* & pool in Puy-de-Dôme, Auvergne; 25ha farm with 3-bed farmhouse and outbuildings to renovate in Haute-Vienne, Limousin; 3-bed house + barn to renovate in Cantal, Auvergne; 3-bed rural house + pool on small plot in Charente-Maritime; 3-bed villa in Hérault, Languedoc-Roussillon; 2-bed cottage for renovation in Pyrénées-Atlantiques, Aquitaine; 4-bed house with small house to renovate in Saône-et-Loire, Burgundy.

€250,000–300,000   2-bed bungalow + pool in Tarn-et-Garonne, Midi-Pyrénées (€245,000); renovated 4-bed farmhouse + *gîte* & outbuildings in Pas-de-Calais; 5-bed manor house on small plot in Calvados, Lower Normandy; 5-bed stone house in Morbihan, Brittany; restored 4-bed *longère* on 2ha in Mayenne, Pays-de-la-Loire; 3-bed farmhouse + pool & outbuildings in Vienne, Poitou-Charentes; 4-bed village house on small plot near Carcassonne in Aude, Languedoc-Roussillon; 4-bed house + barn to renovate on 0.25ha in Dordogne, Aquitaine; restored village farmhouse + outbuildings & two 3-bed *gîtes* in Pas-de-Calais; 3-bed house + *gîte* & outbuildings on 1ha in Côtes d'Armor, Brittany; 3-bed cottage + outbuildings on 0.8ha in Mayenne, Pays-de-la-Loire (€285,000).

€300,000–350,000   Refurbished 4-bed villa + small pool near Carcassonne in Aude, Languedoc-Roussillon; 3-bed house on small plot in Saône-et-Loire, Burgundy; 3-bed 19th-century farmhouse on 0.3ha in Brittany; modern 4-bed house in Charente-Maritime; 3-bed house for renovation in St Céré, Lot, Midi-Pyrénées; new 2-bed house on marina + mooring in Gard, Languedoc-Roussillon; new 2-bed apartments in Juan-les-Pins, Var, PACA; new 3-bed apartment in village in Haute-Savoie, Rhône-Alpes; old 3-bed stone house on small plot in Seine-et-Marne, Ile-de-France; 3-bed house in village centre in Sarthe, Pays-de-la-Loire; renovated 2-bed railway station with outbuildings on 1ha in Burgundy; 4-bed house on 1ha in Manche, Lower Normandy; restored *longère* converted into three *gîtes* on 1 ha in Finistère, Brittany; 6-bed house + barn to renovate on 3.5ha in Creuse, Limousin; renovated 4-bed house + pool & outbuilding in Charente; new 1-bed apartments in Cannes, Var, PACA; 3-bed traditional house + guest suite near coast in Charente-Maritime.

€350,000–400,000   Modern 3-bed village house + mooring on coast in Côtes d'Armor, Brittany; 4-bed *longère* + pool on 0.3ha in Brittany; new 3-bed apartment + communal pool in Hérault, Languedoc-Roussillon; 3-bed 18th-century farmhouse on 1ha in Orne, Lower Normandy; 2-bed apartment on 7th floor in Hauts-de-Seine, Ile-de-France; 1-bed chalet in 10ha including 5ha lake in Burgundy; 3-bed house in Alpes-Maritimes; 3-bed barn conversion on 0.3ha near

Cahors in Lot, Midi-Pyrénées; 3-bed farmhouse + outbuildings for conversion on 6.4ha in Deux-Sèvres, Poitou-Charentes; 5-bed house + pool on 0.65ha in Languedoc-Roussillon.

€400,000–500,000 4-bed house with pool in Gironde, Aquitaine; renovated 4-bed farmhouse + outbuildings & stables on 2ha in Auvergne; two restored houses in village in Aveyron, Midi-Pyrénées; 6-bed 18th-century presbytery on 0.8ha in Manche, Lower Normandy; 3-bed 17th-century stone farmhouse + 3-bed *gîte* + pool & outbuildings in Poitou-Charentes; 4-bed villa + pool on 0.15ha in Languedoc-Roussillon; 4-bed apartment + garage in Montpellier in Hérault, Languedoc-Roussillon; restored 17th-century house on 4ha in Calvados, Lower Normandy; 4-bed farmhouse + outbuildings in Vaucluse, PACA.

€500,000–750,000 Off-plan 2-bed villa in Var, PACA; 4-bed *longère* in Sarthe, Pays-de-la-Loire; 5-bed *maison de maître* with outbuildings in Centre; 3-bed apartment near beach and Biarritz; 5-bed 19th-century house + outbuildings on 0.6ha in Vienne, Poitou-Charentes; 3-bed 19th-century stone farmhouse + 3-bed *gîte* on 2.5ha in Lot-et-Garonne, Aquitaine; modern 5-bed house + pool in Sarthe, Pays-de-la-Loire; 5-bed modern house + pool in Haute-Savoie, Rhône-Alpes; large house + *gîte* & stables on 13.4ha in Midi-Pyrénées; 4-bed house in Paris; 6-bed farmhouse + 3-bed cottage on 4ha in Dordogne, Aquitaine; 2-bed manor house + 2-bed house on 1ha in Pyrénées-Atlantiques, Aquitaine; 3-bed 18th-century half-timbered manor house on 5ha in Seine-Maritime, Upper Normandy.

€750,000–1 million 4-bed ski chalet in Rhône-Alpes; 7-bed *maison de maître* + pool & outbuildings on 0.4ha in Gers, Midi-Pyrénées; chateau in town in Sarthe, Pays-de-la-Loire; 4-bed villa + pool in Hérault, Languedoc-Roussillon; part-renovated apartment/chalet complex on 0.9ha in Languedoc-Roussillon; 4-bed *maison de maître* + two *gîtes*, pool & furniture in Tarn, Midi-Pyrénées; penthouse flat on the Côte d'Azur.

€1 million plus Restored 19th-century convent on 1.1ha in Aisne, Picardy (€1.5m); restored 10-bed 19th-century chateau on 4.5ha including vineyard in Tarn, Midi-Pyrénées (€1.8m); 13th-century 7-bed mill + house on 4ha in Var, PACA (€5.5m); 5-bed villa with 'infinity' pool & sea view near Nice (€7m); 7-bed *maison de maître* with 'infinity' pool & sea view near St Tropez (€15m).

Finally, note that it isn't unusual for French vendors to strip a house bare and take everything, including light fittings, internal doors and the kitchen sink, so when comparing prices make sure you know and allow for what's included (and what isn't) – see **Contracts** on page 123.

Fees

A variety of fees (also called closing or completion costs) are payable when you buy a property in France, which vary considerably according to the purchase price, the age of the property, whether you're buying via an agent (as opposed to buying direct from the vendor), whether you've employed a lawyer and surveyor, and whether you have a French or foreign mortgage. They can amount to almost 40 per cent of the purchase price of a new property and almost 25 per cent for an property over five years old, although they're normally around 15 per cent. Most property fees are based on the 'declared' value of a property.

The fees associated with buying a property in France are listed below, although not all apply to all sales. Fees are payable on the completion of a sale if not before. Before signing a preliminary contract, check exactly what fees are payable and how much they are, and have them confirmed in writing. You should never be tempted to under-declare the purchase price in order to pay lower fees,

as it can have serious consequences if it's discovered.

Notaire's Fees

The *notaire* handling the sale collects all the fees associated with a purchase (except a selling agent's commission and sundry fees – see **Other Fees** below). These are confusingly referred to as the *frais de notaire*, although only around 10 per cent of them are made by the *notaire* himself for his services; these are known as *émoluments et honoraires*. Notaires' fees are calculated as a percentage of the purchase price on the sliding scale shown below, which is fixed by the government. Note, however, that these are the maximum fees they can charge; they can be (and usually are!) considerably more than the actual amount due (allegedly in case of unforeseen expenses) and you can wait up to six months to receive a reimbursement of the amount overpaid.

Portion of Purchase Price	Rate Fee	Cumulative
Up to €45,734.71	5%	€2,286.74
Over €45,734.71	2.5%	

This means that the *notaire*'s fees for a property costing €100,000, for example, would be €3,643.37, to which VAT must be added (see below). In addition, a *notaire* normally charges around €250 for preparing a preliminary contract. Note that British solicitors have challenged the *notaires*' monopoly on conveyancing in France and, should government regulation be abolished, fees will inevitably come down significantly.

Registration Taxes

Registration taxes (*taxes de publicité foncière/TPF*) vary according to whether

you're buying a new or an 'old' (i.e. over five years old) property. On an old property registration taxes (known in this case as *droits de mutation*) total 4.89 per cent, which comprises 3.6 per cent departmental tax (*taxe départmentale*), which is itself subject to 2.5 per cent *frais de recouvrement* making an effective tax of 3.69 per cent, and 1.2 per cent communal tax (*taxe communale* or *taxe additionnelle*). The same rates apply to building plots and commercial property. On a property less than five years old that's being sold for the first time, *TPF* is at just 0.6 per cent of the price excluding VAT, which must also be paid (see below).

Land Registry Fees

Expenses associated with land registration (*droits d'enregistrement*) depend on the size of the mortgage and the number of searches made by the notary in order to draft the deed of sale but usually total around 0.6 per cent of the property's value.

Mortgage Fees

Mortgage arrangement fees may amount to around 1 per cent of the purchase price (see **Fees** on page 120). There's also a fee payable to the *notaire* for registration of the mortgage at the *bureau des hypothèques*, which has recently been reduced by around 15 per cent but is still between around 1 and 1.8 per cent of the mortgage amount depending on the type of mortgage.

Value Added Tax

Value added tax (VAT) at 19.6 per cent must be paid on properties less than five years old when they're sold for the first time. If you sell a new property within five years, you must pay VAT on any profit (plus capital gains tax – see page 198). Since 1998, there has been no VAT on building plots purchased by individuals. Note also that most of the other fees associated with buying property, including *notaires*' fees, are subject to VAT at 19.6 per cent.

Selling Agent's Fee

Where the selling agent is an estate agent (*agent immobilier*), his fee is normally calculated as a commission on the selling price, which can be as high as 10 per cent but is more usually between 3 and 8 per cent, the higher rates normally applying to luxury properties. Advertised selling prices usually include the agent's fee; this is indicated by the terms *commission compris* or *frais d'agence inclus*. The words *net vendeur* indicate that the agent's fee isn't included.

> ☑ SURVIVAL TIP
>
> Before signing a contract, check who must pay the estate agent's fee and what it will be.

When the selling 'agent' is a *notaire*, his fee is generally lower than that of an estate agent and it's **always** paid by the buyer. Where no agent is used, i.e. in a direct sale, no fee is payable, which **should** mean that the purchase price is the relevant percentage lower than those of comparable properties being offered by estate agents and *notaires*.

Other Fees

Other fees may include the following:

● lawyer's fees;

● surveyor's or architect's fees;

● utility connection and registration fees.

Running Costs

In addition to the fees associated with buying a property you must take into account running costs. These include local property taxes, building and contents insurance, standing charges for utilities, community fees for a community property, maintenance (e.g. garden and pool), plus a caretaker's or management fees if you leave a home empty or let it. Annual running costs usually average around 2 to 3 per cent of the cost of a property.

LETTING YOUR PROPERTY

If you buy a property in France but decide not to retire there permanently, you may w ish to consider letting your property while you're abroad to offset maintenance and running costs. Or you may choose to buy property to let in order to increase your monthly pension income. There are essentially three types of letting: letting as holiday accommodation, either as bed and breakfast or as *gîtes*; letting furnished accommodation long term; letting unfurnished accommodation long term. Different criteria and regulations apply to each of these types of letting; all are explained in detail in *Earning Money From Your French Home* by Jo Taylor (Survival Books) and only a brief overview is given here. Information (in French) on letting can be found on the website of the Union des Chambres Syndicales de Proprétaires et Copropriétaires (UNPI, 💻 www.unpi.org – click on '*Questions/Réponses*' for a list of topics).

Rules & Regulations

Income tax is payable in France on rental income (*revenu foncier*) from a French property, even if you live abroad and the money is paid there. All rental income must be declared to the French tax authorities, whether you let a property for a few weeks to friends or 52 weeks a year on a commercial basis. For most letting income, you must complete Form 2044. Furnished property lettings are exempt from VAT, although you may need to charge clients VAT if you offer services such as bed and breakfast, a daily maid, linen or a reception service. The amount of tax you pay and the allowances you're eligible for depend on the type of letting you do, as well as on your residence status.

You must notify your insurance company if a property is to be let. When letting an apartment, you may be required to notify the community's manager; check before buying an apartment that letting is permitted. Property to be let must be registered with the local town hall and (if you're offering B&B accommodation or a hotel with more than five or six rooms) the local *préfecture*, and it must meet appropriate standards and comply with local regulations.

In general, short-term rentals are exempt from the *Loi Mermaz* (1989), which is designed to protect long-term tenants, but the law is complicated and you should check with a lawyer. Information about rules and regulations can be obtained from tourist offices, offices of the Fédération Nationale de l'Immobilier (FNAIM, 💻 www.fnaim.fr) and from the Union Nationale de la Propriété Immobilière (UNPI, 💻 www.

unpi.org – in French only), which publishes a number of *Guides pratiques*.

Contracts

It's a legal requirement to have a contract for all rentals and, although it doesn't have to be in writing, a written contract is obviously desirable. Most people who let a property for holiday accommodation draw up a simple agreement form that includes a property description, the names of the clients, and the dates of arrival and departure. However, if you do regular letting, you may wish to check with a lawyer that your agreement is legal and contains all the necessary safeguards. For example, it should specify the kinds of damage for which the lessor is responsible. Strictly, all descriptions, contracts and payment terms must comply with French laws.

If you're letting through an agent (who must be licensed in France), he will provide a standard contract. Note, however, that if you plan to let to non-English speaking clients you must have a letting agreement in French or other foreign languages.

Rents

Rents vary hugely depending on the season, the region, and the size and quality of a property. A house sleeping six in an average area can be let for around €1,000 to €1,500 per week in high season. A luxury property in a popular area with a pool and accommodation for 8 to 12 can be let for between €4,000 and €6,000 per week in high season (Americans and Britons tend to pay the highest rents). High season generally includes the months of July and August and possibly the first two weeks of September. The mid-season usually comprises June, September and October (and possibly Easter), when rents are usually around 25 per cent lower than in high season; the rest of the year is low season (except in skiing areas, when Christmas, the New Year and Easter are also high season). For long lets in low season, a house sleeping six usually rents for around €500 per week or €2,000 per month in most regions. The tenant usually pays for running costs, including utilities. Note that central heating is essential if you want to let in the winter.

Costs & Expenses

When letting a property, make sure you allow for the numerous costs and expenses that will inevitably reduce the profit you can expect to make. These may include: cleaning between and during lets; laundry of household linen; garden and pool maintenance; maintenance of appliances; replacement of damaged or soiled items; insurance; and utility bills (electricity bills can be high if your property has air-conditioning or electric heating). Some property owners find that costs and expenses account for as much as half the rental income.

Using an Agent

If you're letting a second home, the most important decision is whether to let it yourself or use a letting agent (or agents). If you don't have much spare time, you're better off using an agent, who will take care of everything and save you the time and expense of advertising and finding clients. Agents usually charge commission of between 20 and 40 per cent of the gross rental income, although some of this can be recouped through higher rents. If you want your property to appear in an agent's catalogue, you must usually contact him the summer before you wish to let it (the deadline for catalogues is usually September). Note that although self-catering holiday companies may fall over themselves to take on a luxury property on the Côte d'Azur, the best letting agents turn

down many properties. Take care when selecting an agent, as it isn't uncommon for them to go bust or simply disappear, owing their clients thousands of euro's.

If possible, make sure that your income is kept in an escrow account and paid regularly, or even better choose an agent with a bonding scheme who pays you the rent **before** the arrival of guests (some do). It's absolutely essential to engage a reliable and honest (preferably long-established) company. Anyone can set up a holiday letting agency and there are many 'cowboy' operators. Always ask a management company to substantiate rental income claims and occupancy rates by showing you examples of actual income received from other properties. Ask for the names of satisfied customers and contact them.

Questions to ask a letting agent include:

- When is the letting income paid?

- What additional charges are made?

- Are detailed accounts of income and expenses provided (ask to see a sample)? If not, don't look elsewhere.

- Who does he let to (e.g. which nationalities and whether they include families with young children and singles)?

- How are properties marketed?

- Are you expected to contribute to marketing costs?

- Are you free to let the property yourself and use it when you wish? (Many agents don't permit owners to use a property during the months of July and August.)

Agents may also provide someone to meet and greet guests, hand over the keys and check that everything is in order. The actual services provided usually depend on whether a property is a budget apartment or a luxury villa. A letting agent's representative should also make periodic checks when a property is empty to ensure that it's secure and everything is in order. You may wish to check whether a property is actually empty when the agent tells you it is, as it isn't unknown for some agents to let a property and pocket the rent (you can get a local friend or neighbour to check).

DOING YOUR OWN LETTING

Some owners prefer to let a property to family, friends, colleagues and acquaintances, which allows them more control – and **hopefully** the property will also be better looked after. In fact, the best way to get a high volume of lets is usually to do it yourself, although many owners use a letting agency in addition to doing their own marketing. You must decide whether you want to let to smokers or accept pets and young children – some owners don't let to families with children under five (due to the risk of bed-wetting) or to young, single groups. Note, however, that this will reduce your letting prospects.

Detailed information about letting a property yourself can be found in *Running Gîtes and B&Bs in France* (Survival Books).

HOME SECURITY

Security is obviously an important consideration for anyone buying a home in France (or anywhere else), particularly if it's a seasonal retirement home that will be unoccupied for long periods.

☑ SURVIVAL TIP

While it's important not to underestimate security risks, even in rural areas of France where crime rates are generally low (see Crime on page 251), you should avoid turning your home into a fortress, which will deter visitors as well as would-be thieves!

Bear in mind that your home is generally more at risk from fire and storm damage than from burglary.

Generally, the minimum level of security required by French insurance companies is fairly basic, e.g. security locks on external doors and shutters on windows (small windows generally have bars rather than shutters). If the contents of your home are worth less than around €60,000, this will normally be all that's required unless the property is in Alpes-Maritimes or the Paris area, where burglary rates are the highest in France and many insurers insist on extra security measures, such as two locks on external doors, internal locking shutters, and security bars or metal grilles on windows and patio doors.

In remote areas owners may fit two or three locks on external doors, alarm systems (see below), grilles on doors and windows, window locks, security shutters and a safe for valuables, although such systems are rarely required by insurance companies. The advantage of grilles is that they allow you to leave windows open without inviting criminals in (unless they're **very** slim). You can fit UPVC (toughened clear plastic) security windows and doors, which can survive an attack with a sledge-hammer without damage, and external steel security blinds (that can be electrically operated), although these are expensive.

An insurance policy may specify that all forms of protection on doors must be employed when a property is unoccupied, and that all other protection (e.g. shutters) must also be used after 22.00 and when a property is left empty for two or more days.

When moving into a new home, it's often wise to replace the locks (or lock barrels) as soon as possible, as you have no idea how many keys are in circulation for the existing locks. This is true even for new homes, as builders often give keys to sub-contractors. In any case, it's

wise to change the external locks or lock barrels periodically if you let a home. If they aren't already fitted, it's best to fit high security (double cylinder or dead bolt) locks. Modern properties may be fitted with high-security locks that are individually numbered. Extra keys for these locks cannot be cut at a local hardware store and you need to obtain details from the previous owner or your landlord. Some modern developments and communities have security gates and caretakers.

You may wish to have a security alarm fitted, which is usually the best way to deter thieves and may also reduce your household insurance (see page 214). It should be linked to external doors and windows and infra-red security beams, and it may also include an entry keypad (whose code can be frequently changed and is useful for clients if you let) and 24-hour monitoring. With a monitored system, when a sensor (e.g. smoke or forced entry) is activated or a panic button is pushed, a signal is sent automatically to a 24-hour monitoring station. The duty monitor will telephone to check whether it's a genuine alarm (a code must be given); if he cannot contact you, someone will be sent to investigate. Note, however, that an insurer may require you to have a particular alarm fitted; check before buying one that may not be acceptable. More sophisticated security systems using internet technology are now available, including cameras and sound recorders linked to your computer or mobile phone, e.g. those marketed by Visonic (💻 www.visonic.com).

You can deter thieves by ensuring that your house is well lit at night and not conspicuously unoccupied. External security 'passive infra-red' (PIR) lights (that switch on automatically when a sensor detects movement), random timed switches for internal lights, radios and televisions, dummy security cameras, and tapes that play barking dogs (etc.) triggered by a light or heat detector may all help deter burglars. A real dog can be useful to deter intruders, although it should be kept inside where it cannot be given poisoned food. Irrespective of whether you actually have a dog, a warning sign with a picture of a fierce dog may act as a deterrent. There are systems that control and manage everything from the heating and lighting to the TV and hi-fi, although these can be **very** expensive.

Another alternative is to use a 'home-sitting' service, where someone lives in your home while you're away, either on a fee basis or (preferably) for a free holiday in France.

If not already installed, you should have the front door of an apartment fitted with a spy-hole and chain so that you can check the identity of a visitor before opening the door.

> ☑ SURVIVAL TIP
>
> Remember, prevention is better than cure, as stolen property is rarely recovered.

Holiday homes are particularly vulnerable to thieves and in some areas they're regularly ransacked. No matter how secure your door and window locks, a thief can usually gain entry if he's determined, often by simply smashing a window or even by breaking in through the roof or by knocking a hole in a wall! In isolated areas thieves can strip a house bare at their leisure and an un-monitored alarm won't be a deterrent if there's no-one around to hear it. If you have a holiday home in France, it isn't wise to leave anything of great value (monetary or sentimental) there. If you vacate your home for an extended period, it may be obligatory to notify a caretaker, landlord or insurance company, and to leave a key with someone in case of emergencies. If you have a robbery, you should report it immediately to your local *gendarmerie*,

where you must make a statement (*porter plainte*). You'll receive a copy, which is required by your insurance company if you make a claim.

Another important aspect of home security is ensuring that you have early warning of a fire, which is easily accomplished by installing smoke detectors, although these aren't as widely available in France as, for example, in the UK. Those that are available tend to be of the optical variety or part of a smoke detection 'system' (where detectors are linked so that, if one is triggered, they all sound the alarm) and therefore more expensive than the ionisation detectors available in other countries for around €10, which are nevertheless adequate. In France, Castorama and Leroy-Merlin are two major retailers offering basic smoke detectors. Detectors should be tested regularly to ensure that the batteries aren't exhausted – unless you fit long-life batteries, which can last up to ten years. You should clean (e.g. vacuum) smoke detectors periodically to remove dust. You can also fit an electric-powered gas detector that activates an alarm when a gas leak is detected.

When closing a property for an extended period, e.g. over the winter, you should ensure that everything is switched off and that it's secure.

UTILITIES

As well as electricity and gas, French homes use oil (*fioul* or *fuel*) and wood (*bois*) for heating and hot water, and the government offers tax credits for the installation of energy systems running on renewable fuel (e.g. wood and solar energy). According to the Ministry for Industry, 100KWh of heating costs around €12 using electricity, €5 using natural gas, €9 with bottled gas and €10 with oil. Electricity and gas are supplied by the state-owned Electricité de France/Gaz de France (EDF/GDF, 🖳 www.edf.fr and 🖳 www.gdf.fr), although there are local electricity companies in some areas, and commercial users now have a choice of private suppliers (domestic users, as usual, must wait longer).

For information about making the most efficient use of electricity and gas, contact the Agence de l'Environnement et de la Maîtrise de l'Energie (ADEME, ☎ 08 00 31 03 11, 🖳 www.ademe.fr), which will advise you where to find your nearest *Point Info Energie* (*PIE*).

Electricity

Unlike other developed countries, France generates some 75 per cent of its electricity from nuclear power, the balance coming mostly from hydro-electric power stations. This means that France's electricity is among the cheapest in Europe (it supplies electricity to its neighbours for less than they can produce it themselves and owns nine other European electricity companies, including Seeboard in the UK). Due to the moderate cost of electricity and the high degree of insulation in new homes, electric heating is more common in France than in other European countries.

Connection & Registration

You must usually apply to your local EDF office to have your electricity connected and to sign a contract specifying the power supply installed and the tariff required. To have your electricity connected, you must prove that you're the owner by producing an attestation or a lease if you're renting. You must also show your passport or residence permit (*carte de séjour*). If you wish to pay your bill by direct debit from a bank or post office account, don't forget to take along your account details (*relevé d'identité bancaire*).

To ensure that your electricity supply is connected and that you don't pay for

someone else's electricity, you should contact your local EDF office and ask them to read the meter (*relevé spécial*) before taking over a property. If the property has an existing supply, you must pay an 'access' fee (*frais d'accès*) of around €15. Residents don't usually pay a deposit, although non-residents may be required to pay one. When payable, the deposit is refundable against future bills.

Tariffs

Your standing charge (*abonnement*) depends on the rating of your supply and the tariff you choose, which also affects the amount you pay for electricity consumed (calculated in kilowatt-hours or KWh). EDF offers three domestic tariff options: basic (suitable only for those who use little electricity), off-peak (with different rates for day and night-time use), and *Tempo* (most suitable for those with second homes that are unoccupied for long periods). Details of tariffs are given in *Living and Working in*

France (Survival Books – see page 325). A tax called the *contribution au service public* is applied to all electricity bills at the rate of €0.33 per KWh.

Bills

You're normally billed for your electricity every three months but may receive bi-monthly or monthly bills if your consumption is above a certain level. A number of bills (*facture*) received throughout the year, e.g. alternate bills, are estimated. Bills include the standing charge, VAT and local taxes (*taxes locales*). VAT is levied at 5.5 per cent on the standing charge and 19.6 per cent on the total power consumption.

> Local taxes (*taxe communale/départementale*) are around 12 per cent and where applicable are levied on around 80 per cent of the consumption and standing charge total before VAT is added. VAT at 19.6 per cent is also levied on the local taxes.

Gas

Mains Gas

Mains gas (*gaz de ville*) is available only in around 80 towns and cities and is supplied by the state-owned Gaz de France (GDF), part of the same company as Electricité de France (EDF), and, since July 2007, other companies. If you buy a property without a mains gas supply, you can obtain a new connection (*raccordement*), provided of course mains gas is available in the area. If the property is within 35m (115ft) of a supply, connection costs are around €840 if you're on *base* or *B0* tariff, or around €420 if you're on the *B1* tariff (see below). Contact GDF for an accurate estimate.

When moving into a property already connected to mains gas, you must contact GDF to have the gas switched on and/or have the meter read and to have the account switched to your name. This can usually be done at the same time as you arrange for your electricity supply (see above). There's a connection charge (*mise en service*) of around €15 (or €30 if you have gas and electricity connected at the same time).

You must decide on the type of supply you require, e.g. *base* for cooking only, *B0* for cooking and hot water, *B1* for heating (in a small house) and *B2I* for heating (in a larger house). The annual service charge (*abonnement*) is lower for a limited supply, e.g. around €25 for *base* compared with around €185 for *B2I*, but you're charged more per kWH (e.g. €0.06 for *base* and around €0.03 for *B2I* depending on the town you live in). Details of charges in each town where mains gas is available can be found on the GDF website (💻 www.monagence.gazdefrance.fr). Further information about gas supplies is provided in *Living and Working in France* (Survival Books – see page 325).

Bottled Gas

Most rural homes have cookers and some also have water heaters that use bottled gas. Cookers often have a combination of electric and (bottled) gas rings (you can choose the mix). Check when moving into a property that the gas bottle isn't empty. Keep a spare bottle or two handy and make sure that you ask how to change bottles, as this can be quite a complicated procedure involving safety switches, etc. Bottled gas is more expensive than mains gas. Bottles come in 35kg, 13kg and 5/6kg sizes – a small one used just for cooking will last an average family around six weeks.

The 13kg bottles can be bought and exchanged at most petrol stations and super/hypermarkets. An exchange bottle costs around €25; if you need to buy a new bottle, you'll be asked to register and pay a deposit, e.g. €40 per bottle. Some village shops also sell bottled gas. Note, however, that there are several different types of bottle (e.g. Antargaz, Butagaz, Primagaz and Totalgaz, each a different colour) and the supplier of one type won't accept an empty bottle of another type. (Check **before** you unload your 35kg bottles!) Note also that the connectors usually turn in the opposite direction to most threaded devices.

Some houses keep their gas bottles outside, often under a lean-to. If you do this you must buy propane gas rather than butane, as it can withstand a greater range of temperatures than butane, which is for internal use only (in fact, propane gas bottles **must** be kept outside a house). Note also that butane requires a different demand valve (*détendeur*) from propane, i.e. 28M/bar 1300g/h instead of 37M/bar 1500g/h. If you're planning to buy or rent an apartment, check whether gas bottles are permitted, as they're prohibited in many new apartments.

Gas Tanks

Gas central heating is common in France, although in rural areas the gas supply comes from a gas tank (*citerne*) installed on the property, rather than a mains supply or bottles. Tanks can be hired, from suppliers such as Total and Antargaz, for around €300 per year, or you can pay a deposit of around €1,500, which is refunded if you take out a contract for the supply of gas for a fixed period.

The cost of filling a 1,100kg tank is around €1,000; some suppliers offer monthly payment plans. A family of four in an average house with gas central heating, hot water and cooking uses around 1,150kg per year (around 800kg for heating, 300kg for hot water and 50kg for cooking). **Having a gas tank on your property will increase your insurance premiums**.

⚠ **Caution**

If you take over a property with a gas tank, you must not only pay the deposit but also have it filled and pay for a full tank of gas, irrespective of how much was left in it!

Water

Mains water in France is supplied by a number of private companies, the largest of which are the Saur group (part of Bouygues, which also supplies mobile phone services, 🖳 www.saur.com), Lyonnaise des Eaux (🖳 www.lyonnaise-des-eaux.fr) and Veolia Environment (part of Vivendi, 🖳 www.generale-des-eaux.fr), who between them supply some three-quarters of the water in France. The water supply infrastructure, however, is owned and managed by local communes, so rates vary across the country. Most properties in France are metered, so that you pay only for the water you use. If you need to have a water meter installed, there's a small non-refundable charge. When moving into a new house, ask the local water company to read your meter – and check that it works properly and that there's no leak (turn everything off and see whether the meter moves!). Note that owners of a *copropriété* can have individual meters installed.

Supply & Connection

If you own a property in or near a village, you can usually be connected to a mains water system. Note, however, that connection can be expensive, as you must pay for digging the channels required for pipes. Obtain a quotation (*devis*) from the local water company for the connection of the supply and the installation of a water meter. Expect the connection to cost at least €800, depending on the type of terrain and soil (or rock!) which must be dug to lay pipes. If you're thinking of buying a property and installing a mains water supply, obtain an estimate **before** signing the purchase contract.

Water shortages are rare in towns (although they do occur occasionally) but are fairly common in some rural areas during hot summers, when the water may periodically be switched off. It's possible to have a storage tank installed for emergencies and you should also keep a supply of rainwater or recycled waste water for watering the garden, etc..

If you rely on a well (*puits*) or spring (*source*) for your water, bear in mind that these can dry up, particularly in parts of central and southern France, which continue to experience droughts.

If the source is on a neighbour's land, make sure that there's no dispute over the ownership of the water and your right to use it, e.g. that it cannot be stopped or drained away by your neighbours. You don't pay water charges for well water or water from a stream or river running through your property. If a supply is marked *eau non potable*, the water should

not be drunk, and in any case you should have it tested for safety.

> ☑ SURVIVAL TIP
>
> **Always confirm that a rural property has a reliable water source and check it or have it checked by an expert.**

Cost

It's usual to have a contract for a certain amount of water; if you exceed this amount, you incur a higher charge. There's no flat fee (*forfait*), which has been abolished, although 'special charges' may be levied. French water varies by up to 100 per cent in price from region to region, depending on its availability or scarcity, and is among the most expensive in the world, although rates include sewerage charges. If your property is on mains drainage (*tout à l'égout*), your water can cost as much as €3.60 per cubic metre or as little as €1.75; the national average is around €2.75. If it has a septic tank (*fosse septique*), on the other hand, your water bill will be much lower, e.g. €0.75 per cubic metre, as water rates include charges for sewerage.

Bills

You're billed by your local water company annually or every six months and can pay by direct debit. If an apartment block is owned *en copropriété*, the water bill for the whole block is usually divided among the apartments according to their size. Hot water may be charged by adding an amount per cubic metre consumed by each apartment, to cover the cost of heating the water, or may be shared among apartments in proportion to their size.

Sewerage

Properties in urban areas are normally connected to mains drainage (*tout à l'égout*), whereas those in rural parts usually have individual sewage systems: either cesspits (*puisard*, also known as a *puits perdu* – a 'lost well'!) or septic tanks (*fosse septique*). Note, however, that according to a law passed in January 1992, which came into force in December 2005 (although it won't come into force countrywide until the end of the decade), mains drainage must be installed wherever it's considered cost-effective, which generally means in the centre of all French villages. Where mains drainage is installed, there will be a one-time charge for connection made to all properties within the area of the system, which must be connected within two years of the installation, plus an annual service charge. Charges for mains drainage are normally included in property taxes (see page 195).

☑ SURVIVAL TIP

Before buying a property with its own sewage system, you should have it checked by an expert. If you're planning to buy a property or plot without a sewerage system, you should obtain expert advice as to whether such a system can be installed and at what cost.

If you have a septic tank, you should use enzyme bio-digesters and employ bleach and drain unblockers sparingly, as they kill the friendly bacteria that prevent nasty smells. You mustn't use certain cleaning agents, such as ammonia, in a septic tank, as they will destroy it, and you may need to put specially formulated products into the tank to keep it working properly. A *fosse toutes eaux* must be emptied at least once a year, depending on whether a property is permanently inhabited or not, a *fosse septique* every three to five years; the cost of emptying is around €200.

HEATING & AIR-CONDITIONING

Even in the south of France, there can be extremes of weather and winters can be cold. Unless you plan to visit a property only in the summer, you need to consider central heating, although air-conditioning is a luxury.

Heating

Central heating systems in France may be powered by electricity, gas, oil, solid fuel (usually wood) or even solar power (see below). According to the Ministry for Industry, 100KWh of heating costs around €5 using natural gas, €9 with bottled gas and €12 using electricity or oil. Whatever form of heating you use, it's essential to have good insulation, without which up to 60 per cent of heat is lost through the walls and roof. Insulation is given a high priority in France, particularly in new homes. Some 65 per cent of French homes have central heating, which is essential if you wish to let your home during winter. Many people keep their central heating on a low setting (which can be controlled via a master thermostat) during short absences in winter to prevent pipes from freezing.

If you need to install a hot water boiler and immersion heater, ensure it's large enough for the size of the property, e.g. one room studio (100 litres), two rooms (150 litres), three to four rooms (200 litres) and five to seven rooms (300 litres).

Electric

Electric central heating is the most common form in France, particularly in modern homes with good insulation and a permanent system of ventilation, and is inexpensive to run using off-peak storage heaters. However, electric central heating isn't recommended for old properties with poor insulation. If you install an electric central heating system, you must usually uprate your electricity supply (see **Power**

Supply) to cope with the extra demand.
Note that some stand-alone electric heaters
are expensive to run and are best suited
to holiday homes. See also **Electricity** on
page 128.

Gas

Gas central heating is popular in towns with
mains gas and is the cheapest to run.
Gas is clean, economical and efficient,
and the boiler is usually fairly small and
can be wall-mounted. In rural areas
where there's no mains gas, you can
have a gas tank (*citerne*) installed on your
property. You'll need space for the tank,
which must be installed at least 3m (10ft)
from the house. Tanks can be hired, from
suppliers such as Total and Antargaz,
for around €300 per year, or you can
pay a deposit of around €1,500, which is
refunded if you take out a contract for the
supply of gas for a fixed period. Note that
piping adds to the already considerable
cost of a gas tank, the system needs
regular maintenance, and having a gas
tank on your property will increase your

household insurance. See also **Gas** on
page 129.

Oil

Around 27 per cent of French homes use
an oil-fired heating system (*chauffage au
fioul/fuel*). As with gas, you need space
to install the storage tank. A tank with
a capacity of up to 2,000 litres can be
located in the basement; a larger tank must
be buried in your garden or stored in a
separate location sheltered from frost and
away from the house. Oil costs have risen
dramatically in recent years and are now
over €0.60 per litre. There are two grades of
oil: *ordinaire* and *premier*; note that the only
difference between them is that *ordinaire*
freezes at around -15C and *premier* at
around -25C, so you need to pay extra for
premier only if you have an outdoor tank
and live in an area that experiences severe
winters.

You should expect to use around 2,000
to 3,000 litres per year to heat a three-
bedroom house (including hot water). As
oil causes a rapid build-up of deposits, it's

essential to have your system cleaned and checked annually (costing around €120) and to replace the jet regularly.

☑ SURVIVAL TIP

You should wait at least two hours after an oil delivery before restarting your boiler, in order to allow any foreign bodies in the tank to settle to the bottom.

For information about the use of fuel for heating, contact Chaleur Fioul, an association of petroleum manufacturers, distributors and retailers (☎ 08 10 34 34 34, 💻 www.chaleurfioul.com).

Solar Power

A solar power system can be used to supply all your energy needs, although in France it's usually combined with an electric or gas heating system, as solar power cannot usually be relied upon year-round for heating and hot water. The main drawback is the high cost of installation, which varies considerably with the region and how much energy you require. The cost is between €2,000 and €5,000 for an installation sufficient to operate around eight lights and a small refrigerator (a solar power system must be installed by an expert), although a government grant is available under the *Plan Soleil* scheme; for details contact ADEME (☎ 08 10 06 00 50, 💻 www2.ademe.fr – available in English, although regional office contact details are given only in the French version).

Wood

Almost a quarter of France is covered by forest and some 7m homes rely solely on wood-burning stoves (*chauffage au bois*) for their heating and hot water, particularly in rural areas (and millions more have wood fires simply for effect). Stoves come in a huge variety of sizes and styles and can be purchased second-hand from *brocantes*. Wood for fuel (which should have been seasoned for at least two years) is measured in *stères*; one *stère* is 1m3 of stacked wood, including the spaces between the logs, and roughly equivalent to 150 litres of oil. Check whether your commune supplies wood from local forests (*affouage*); otherwise you'll need to find a commercial supplier (often a local farmer), who will charge around €35 per *stère*.

Air-conditioning

In some regions of France, summer temperatures are often above 30C (86F) and, although properties are usually built to withstand the heat, you may wish to install air-conditioning (*climatisation*). Note, however, that there can be negative effects if you suffer from asthma or respiratory problems. You can choose between a huge variety of air-conditioners, fixed or moveable, indoor or outdoor installation, and high or low power. An air-conditioning system with a heat pump provides cooling in summer and economical heating in winter. Some air-conditioners are noisy, so check the noise level before buying one. Many people fit inexpensive ceiling fans for extra cooling in summer.

Humidifiers & De-humidifiers

Note that central heating dries the air and may cause your family to develop coughs. Those who find the dry air unpleasant can purchase a humidifier to add moisture to the air. Humidifiers that don't generate steam should be disinfected occasionally to prevent nasty diseases. The French commonly use humidifiers, ranging from simple water containers hanging from radiators to expensive electric or battery-operated devices.

On the other hand, if you're going to be using a home only occasionally, it's worthwhile installing de-humidifiers, especially in the bedrooms, to prevent clothes and linen going mouldy.

6.
MAKING THE MOVE

Moving into your new French home is the culmination of your dreams; it can also be a highly stressful experience. However, it's possible to limit the strain on your mental and physical health by careful planning and preparation. This chapter contains checklists that will help to ensure that you don't forget anything important.

SHIPPING YOUR BELONGINGS

It usually takes just a few days to have your belongings shipped from other parts of continental Europe or the UK. From anywhere else the time varies considerably, e.g. around four weeks from the east coast of America, six weeks from the US west coast or the Far East, and around eight weeks from Australasia. Customs clearance is no longer necessary when shipping your household effects from one European Union (EU) country to another. However, when shipping your effects from a non-EU country to France, you should enquire about customs formalities in advance.

⚠ **Caution**

If you fail to follow the correct procedure, you can encounter numerous problems and delays, and can even be charged duty or fined.

The relevant forms to be completed by non-EU citizens depend on whether your French home will be your main residence or a second home. Removal companies usually take care of the paperwork and ensure that the correct documents are provided and properly completed. Major international moving companies usually also provide a wealth of information and can advise on a wide range of matters concerning an international relocation. Check (with a local embassy or consulate) the current procedure for shipping your belongings to France.

It's wise to use a major shipping company with a good reputation. For international moves it's best to use a company that's a member of the International Federation of Furniture Removers (FIDI, Belgium ☎ 02-426 5160, http://fidi.com) or the Overseas Moving Network International (OMNI, UK ☎ 01306-889218, 🖳 www.omnimoving.com), with experience in France. Members of FIDI and OMNI usually subscribe to an advance payment scheme providing a guarantee: if a member company fails to fulfil its commitments to a client, the removal is completed at the agreed cost by another company or your money is refunded. Some removal companies have subsidiaries or affiliates in France, which may be more convenient if

Port de la Ciotat, Provence

you encounter problems or need to make an insurance claim.

You should obtain at least three written quotations before choosing a company, as costs vary considerably. Moving companies should send a representative to provide a detailed quotation. Most companies will pack your belongings and provide packing cases and special containers, although this is naturally more expensive than packing them yourself. Ask a company how fragile and valuable items are packed and whether the cost of packing cases, materials and insurance (see below) is included in a quotation. If you're doing your own packing, most shipping companies will provide packing crates and boxes. Shipments are charged by volume, e.g. the square metre in Europe and the square foot in the US. You should expect to pay from €4,000 to €7,000 to move the contents of a three to four-bedroom house within western Europe, e.g. from London to southern France.

If you're flexible about the delivery date, shipping companies will quote a lower fee based on a 'part load', where the cost is shared with other deliveries. This can result in savings of 50 per cent or more compared with an individual delivery. Whether you have an individual or shared delivery, obtain the maximum transit period in writing, otherwise you may need to wait months for delivery! Note also that lorries are banned from most French towns on Sundays and bank holidays.

Be sure to fully insure your belongings during removal with a well established insurance company. Don't insure with a shipping company that carries its own insurance, as its rates are usually high and it may fight every *centime* of a claim. Insurance premiums are usually 1 to 2 per cent of the declared value of your belongings or a percentage (e.g. 15) of the removal cost, depending on the type of cover chosen. It's prudent to make a photographic or video record of valuables for insurance purposes.

Most insurance policies provide cover for 'all risks' on a replacement value basis. Note that china, glass and other breakables can usually be included in an all-risks policy only when they're packed by the removal company. Insurance usually covers total loss or loss of a particular crate only, rather than individual items (unless they were packed by the shipping company). If there are any breakages or damaged items, they must be noted and listed before you sign the delivery bill (although it's obviously impractical to check everything on delivery).

If you need to make a claim, be sure to read the small print, as some companies require clients to make a claim within a few days, although seven is usual. Send a claim by registered post. Some insurance companies apply an 'excess' of around 1 per cent of the total shipment value when assessing claims. This means that if your shipment is valued at €30,000 and you make a claim for less than €300, you won't receive anything.

If you're unable to ship your belongings direct to France, most shipping companies will put them into storage and some allow a limited free storage period prior to shipment, e.g. 14 days, after which you may be charged between €40 and €80 per month for an average container (measuring 2.25m/8ft x 1.5m/5ft x 2m/6ft), although prices (and the quality of storage facilities) vary greatly. You should ask whether a warehouse is insulated against damp and extremes of temperature, whether there are fire detectors and alarms, and whether insurance is included in the price.

☑ SURVIVAL TIP

If you need to put your household effects into storage, it's imperative to have them fully insured, as warehouses have been known to burn down!

Make a complete list of everything to be moved and give a copy to the removal company. Don't include anything illegal (e.g. guns, bombs or drugs) with your belongings, as customs checks can be rigorous and penalties severe.

Provide the shipping company with **detailed** instructions of how to find your French address from the nearest main road and a telephone number where you can be contacted. If your French home has poor or impossible access for a large truck you must inform the shipping company (the ground must also be firm enough to support a heavy vehicle). Note also that, if furniture needs to be taken in through an upstairs window, you may need to pay extra. You should also make a simple floor plan of your new home with rooms numbered and mark corresponding numbers on furniture and boxes as they're packed, so that the removal company will know where everything is to go and you can leave them to it.

After considering the shipping costs, you may decide to ship only selected items of furniture and personal effects and buy new furniture in France. If you're importing household goods from another European country, you can rent a self-drive van or truck (but bear in mind that you'll probably need to return the van to where you hired it from).

If you plan to transport your belongings to France personally, check the customs requirements in the countries you must pass through. Generally, it isn't wise to do your own move unless it's a simple job, e.g. a few items of furniture and personal effects only. It's no fun heaving beds and wardrobes up stairs and squeezing them into impossible spaces. If you're taking pets with you, you may need to ask your vet to tranquillise them, as many pets are frightened (even more than people) by the chaos and stress of moving house.

If you're moving permanently to France, take the opportunity to sell, give away or throw out at least half of your possessions. It will cut down your removal bill, clear your mind, and make life simpler, plus you'll have the fun of buying new furniture that really suits your new house.

Bear in mind when moving home that everything that can go wrong often does, so allow plenty of time and try not to arrange your move from your old home on the same day as the new owner is moving in; that's just asking for fate to intervene!

PRE-DEPARTURE HEALTH CHECK

If you're planning to retire to France, even for part of the year only, it's wise to have a health check (including general health, eyes, teeth, etc.) before your arrival, particularly if you have a record of poor health or are elderly. If you're already taking medicine regularly, you should note that the brand names of drugs and medicines vary from country to country, and should ask your doctor for the generic name.

IMMIGRATION

France is a signatory to the Schengen agreement, which means that if you arrive in France from another Schengen country (currently Austria, Belgium, France, Germany, Greece, Iceland, Italy, Luxembourg, the Netherlands, Portugal, Spain and Sweden), there are usually no immigration checks or passport controls (although France invoked a 'safeguard' clause in the Schengen agreement to preserve frontier controls because of fears over illegal immigration and cross-border drug trafficking).

If you arrive from a non-Schengen country, you must go through immigration (*police des frontières*) for non-EU citizens. **If you require a visa to enter France and attempt to enter without one, you'll be refused entry**. If you have a single-entry visa, it will be cancelled by the immigration official. If you think you'll need to prove your date of entry, e.g. if your visa is valid

for a limited period, you should obtain a declaration of entry (*déclaration d'entrée sur le territoire*).

Immigration officials may ask non-EU visitors to produce a return ticket, proof of accommodation, health insurance and financial resources (e.g. cash, travellers' cheques and credit cards). If you're a non-EU national coming to France to work, study or live, you may be asked to show documentary evidence that you have a job or home or are enrolled on a course in France. The onus is on visitors to show that they won't violate French law. Immigration officials aren't required to prove that you'll breach the law and can refuse you entry on the grounds of suspicion only.

All foreigners planning to remain in France for longer than 90 days must register with the local authorities within a week of arrival and obtain a residence permit. EU nationals who visit France with the intention of finding employment or starting a business have 90 days in

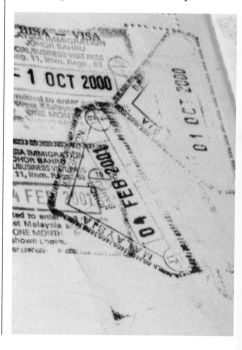

which to find a job. Once employment has been found, an application must be made for a residence permit. If you don't have a regular income or adequate financial resources, your application will be refused. Failure to apply for a residence permit within 90 days is a serious offence and may result in a fine. For further information see **Residence Permits** on page 27.

CUSTOMS

Those arriving from outside the EU (including EU citizens) are subject to customs checks and limitations on what may be imported duty-free. The shipment of personal (household) effects to France from another EU country isn't subject to customs formalities, although an inventory must be provided. There are no restrictions on the import or export of French or foreign banknotes or securities, although if you enter or leave France with €10,000 or more in cash or negotiable instruments, you must make a declaration to French customs.

If you require general information about customs regulations or have specific questions, contact the Centre de Renseignements des Douanes, 84, rue d'Hauteville, 75498 Paris Cedex 10 (☎ 08 25 30 82 63 – on this number you can ask for the telephone number of your nearest centre) or your nearest customs office. The Customs website (🖳 www.douane. gouv.fr) lists local and regional customs office addresses but whereas there used to be a map on which you could simply click, you must now follow a tortuous trail of links, available only on the French version of the website: '*Les coordonnées des services douaniers*' (under '*Connaître la douane*') > '*Les adresses des services douaniers déconcentrés (directions et services)*' > '*Les services douaniers en France métropolitaine*', where you choose your region or department and, under

'*Une direction*' choose '*Douanes et droits indirects*'. (The French love to complicate things.) The same page may be brought up by entering 🖳 www.douane.gouv.fr/ page.asp?id=140#0 (the map referred to shows the areas covered by each regional office but it cannot be clicked on).

Visitors

If you're visiting France (i.e. for less than 90 days), your belongings aren't subject to duty or VAT and may be imported without formality, provided their nature and quantity doesn't imply any commercial aim. This applies to the import of private cars, camping vehicles (including trailers and caravans), motorcycles, aircraft, boats and personal effects. All means of transport and personal effects imported duty-free mustn't be sold, loaned or given away in France and must be re-exported before the end of the 90-day period.

If you enter France from another Schengen country, you may drive (at a walking pace) through the border without stopping. However, any goods and pets that you're carrying mustn't be the subject of any prohibition or restriction (see below). Customs officials may stop anyone for a spot check, e.g. for drugs or illegal immigrants. If you enter France from Spain – particularly if you're a single male in an old car – your vehicle is likely to be searched and 'inspected' by a sniffer dog.

Occasionally you will come across an obstructive customs officer who will insist on inspecting everything in your car, and unfortunately there's nothing you can do to prevent him.

If you arrive at a seaport by private boat, there are no particular customs formalities, although you must show the boat's registration papers if asked. If you arrive at a river port or land border with a boat, you may be asked to produce registration papers for the boat and its outboard motor(s). A foreign-registered boat may remain in France for a maximum of six months in a calendar year, after which it must be re-exported or permanently imported (and duty and tax paid).

Non-EU Nationals

If you're a non-EU national planning to take up permanent or temporary residence, you're permitted to import your furniture and personal effects free of duty. These include vehicles, mobile homes, pleasure boats and aircraft. However, to qualify for duty-free importation, articles must have been owned and used for at least six months. Value added tax must be paid on items owned for less than six months that weren't purchased within the EU. If goods were purchased within the EU, a VAT receipt must be produced.

To import personal effects, an application must be made to the Direction Régionale des Douanes in the area where you will be resident. Customs clearance can be carried out by a customs office in an internal town in France, rather than at the border, in which case you should obtain a certificate (*carte de libre circulation*) proving that you've declared your belongings on entry into France and are entitled to travel with them.

All items should be imported within a year of the date of your change of residence – in one or a number of consignments, although it's best to have one consignment only. After a year's residence in France, you must pay French VAT (*TVA*) on further imports from outside the EU, except in certain circumstances, such as property resulting from an inheritance. A complete inventory of items to be imported (even if they're imported in a number of consignments) must be provided for customs officials, together with proof of residence in your former country and proof of settlement in France. If there's more than one consignment, subsequent consignments should be cleared through the same customs office.

If you use a removal company to transport your belongings, it will usually provide the necessary forms and take care of the paperwork. Many of the forms are now available online, either through the Customs website (🖥 www.douane.gouv.fr – available in 'English') or by following the links on the Service Public site (🖥 www.service-public.fr – in French only: click on '*Impôt, taxe et douane*', then on '*Douane*' and then '*Installation et transfert de biens en France*'). If the removal company packs your belongings, ask for the containers to be marked 'Mover Packed'; this will speed the customs clearance process.

Always keep a copy of forms and communications with customs officials – both in France and in your previous or permanent country of residence. An official record of the export of valuables from any country will allow you to re-import them later.

Prohibited & Restricted Goods

Certain goods are subject to special regulations, and in some cases their import (and export) is prohibited or restricted. This applies in particular to animal products, plants (see below), wild fauna and flora and products derived from them, live animals, medicines and medical products (except for prescribed medicines), guns and ammunition, certain goods and technologies with a dual civil/military purpose, and works of art and collectors' items. If you're unsure whether any goods you're importing fall into the above categories, you should check with French customs.

To import certain types of plant, you must obtain a phytosanitary health certificate (*certificat sanitaire*). Details of the types of plant for which a certificate is required and how to obtain one can be obtained from a regional Service de la Protection des Végétaux or your country's customs department.

If you make it through customs unscathed with your car loaded to the gunwales with illicit goods, don't be too quick to break out the champagne in celebration: France has 'flying' customs officials (*douane volante*) with the power to stop and search vehicles at random anywhere within its borders (they often stop vehicles at motorway toll stations and roundabouts on trunk roads).

REGISTRATION

All foreigners intending to remain in France for longer than 90 days must register with the local authorities within a week of arrival and obtain a residence permit, although this may not be necessary for EU nationals.

> **Caution**
>
> Failure to apply for a residence permit, if required, within 90 days is a serious offence and may result in a fine.

For further information see **Residence Permits** on page 27.

Nationals of some countries must register with their local embassy or consulate after taking up residence. Even if registration isn't mandatory, most embassies like to keep a record of their country's citizens resident in France (it helps them to justify their existence) and it can be to your benefit (e.g. in a national or international crisis).

FINDING HELP

One of the biggest difficulties facing new arrivals in France is how and where to find help with day-to-day problems, particularly as many administrative matters are handled at a regional, departmental or even local level rather than nationally. The availability of local information varies according to your employer, the town or area where you live (e.g. residents of Paris are better served than those living in rural areas), your nationality, your French proficiency (there's an abundance of information available in French, but little in English and other foreign languages) and to some extent your sex (women are better served than men through numerous women's clubs). You should exploit the following sources of local information as well as local clubs and societies.

Friends & Acquaintances

In France it isn't what you know, but who you know that can make all the difference between success and failure. String-pulling (i.e. the use of contacts) is widespread, and when it comes to breaking through the numerous layers of bureaucracy, a telephone call on your behalf from a French neighbour or friend can save you endless frustration. Any contact can be of help, even professionals such as a bank manager or insurance agent (in many cases, such people will become friends). **But take care!** Although friends and acquaintances can often offer advice and invariably mean well, you're likely to receive much irrelevant and even inaccurate information, and you should check everything you're told for yourself.

Local Community

Your local community is usually an excellent source of reliable information, but you usually need to speak French to benefit from it. Your town hall (*mairie*), which is often the local registry of births, deaths and marriages, passport office, land registry, council office, citizens' advice bureau and tourist office, should be your first port of call for most kinds of local information, although even there you may not be given accurate or relevant information.

Ask at your town hall (or look in your local yellow pages) where to find your nearest Centre Local d'Information et de Coordination Gérontologique (CLIC), of which there are over 500 throughout the country. CLICs were established in 2001 as a result of a government initiative to provide help for older people, and they can supply information and advice on rights and entitlements, and healthcare and other services as well as arranging home help where required.

Embassy or Consulate

Most embassies and consulates provide their nationals with local information including details of lawyers, interpreters, doctors, dentists, schools, and social and expatriate organisations, although some are more helpful than others (the British Embassy in Paris is particularly

unapproachable). The American Embassy has a particularly good website (🖳 www.amb-usa.fr), which includes a good deal of information (in English) about living and working in France, including lists of English-speaking professionals, from doctors to private investigators. Much of the information comes from their popular *Blue Book: Guide for U.S. Citizens Residing in France*, which can be downloaded from the site (click on 'U.S. Citizen Services', then 'Living in France' and click in the box top right) or obtained from the US Embassy, 2, avenue Gabriel, 75382 Paris Cedex 08 (☎ 01 43 12 22 22).

Hand-holding Services

A number of English-speaking expatriates offer 'hand-holding' services to new arrivals. As with any service provider, some are worth their weight in gold while others are a complete waste of time and money, so it's essential to ask for and follow up references before paying a joining or annual membership fee (typically around ☐100 each). Services may range from help with house hunting and buying to finding tradesmen and completing tax returns.

> An extensive and well established network of hand-holding services is the Granny Network (☎ 02 51 98 23 96, 🖥 www.grannynetwork. com), which, however, doesn't operate in all areas of France.

Expatriate Organisations

There's usually at least one English-language expatriate organisation in major French cities; in Paris foreigners are well served by English-speaking clubs and organisations (see below) and there are several Anglophone organisations in the Bordeaux area. Contacts can be found through many expatriate magazines and newspapers (see **Appendix B**). An English-speaking counsellor in certain parts of France can be found via 🖥 www. counsellinginfrance.com.

For some, the Anglican church can be a source of help, advice and friendship. To fin an Anglican church in your area, go to 🖥 www.eruope.anglican.org and click on 'CHAPLAINCIES/LOCATIONS', then 'France'.

In Paris, the American Church (☎ 01 40 62 05 00, 🖥 www.acparis.org), runs an annual newcomer's orientation series in October called 'Bloom Where You Are Planted'. The programme is designed to help foreigners adjust to life in France and consists of seminars on topics such as overcoming culture shock, survival skills, personal and professional opportunities, networking, enjoying France and its food, fashion, travel and wine. The capital also houses The Association of American Wives of Europeans (☎ 01 40 70 11 80, 🖥 www. aaweparis.org), which is a member of the Federation of American Women's Clubs Overseas (FAWCO) and publishes the snappily titled *Vital Issues: How to Survive*

Officialdom while Living in France; the Association France Grande-Bretagne (☎ 01 55 78 71 71, 🖥 www.afgb.free.fr), whose aim is to foster links between the two nations; The British & Commonwealth Women's Association (☎ 01 47 20 50 91, 🖥 www.bcwa.org); and WICE (☎ 01 45 66 75 50, 🖥 www.wice-paris.org), an Anglophone expatriate organisation which operates a 'Living in France' programme for newcomers.

Associations outside the capital include Anglophones Pau-Pyrénées (🖥 http://pau. anglophones.com, ✉ pau@anglophones. com), the Association France Grande-Bretagne Cannes (☎ 04 93 99 04 28) and the Mulhouse English Speaking Society (☎ 03 89 66 56 80). There are French 'versions' of the Round Table and 41 Club associations – La Table Ronde Française (🖥 www.trf.asso.fr) and Le Club 41 Français (🖥 www.club41francais.asso. fr) – which may have English-speaking members.

The British Community Committee publishes a free *Digest of British and Franco-British Clubs, Societies and Institutions*, available from British consulates in France (see **Appendix A**). Other local and regional organisations are listed in *The Best Places to Buy a Home in France* (Survival Books – see page 323).

SEL

A *système d'échange local* (*SEL*), like a local exchange trading system (LETS) in the UK, is a system whereby people exchange services and, in some cases, goods rather than buying and selling them. For example, you may be able to have your plumbing or electrical system fixed in exchange for English lessons. The first *SEL* was set up in France in 1994 and there are now almost 400 of them, nationwide, involving some 200,000 people. A *SEL* can be a source not only of 'free' help but of friends. To find a *SEL* near you, ask locally or search the web for 'systeme echange local'. (For example, the Paris *SEL* has its own website at 💻 www. seldeparis.org.)

AVF

An organisation of particular interest to foreigners moving to France is the Union Nationale des Accueils des Villes Françaises (AVF). The AVF is a national organisation comprising over 600 local volunteer associations, which provide a welcome for individuals and families and help them to settle into their new environment. Each association operates a centre where information and advice is available free of charge. The address of local associations can be found on the AVF website (💻 www.avf-accueil.com), where some information is available in English and there's a list of groups in each department as well as details such as whether information and services are available in English. Groups often contain at least one fluent English-speaker. Foreigners planning to move to France can obtain information about particular areas from the Union Nationale des AVF, Relations Internationales (☎ 01 47 70 45 85, 💻 www.avf.asso.fr).

CIRA

If you don't know which administrative department to contact for particular information (which is often the case in France), you can ask your local Centre Interministériel de Renseignements Administratifs (CIRA). As its name suggests, CIRA is a 'pan-governmental' organisation, which can answer questions on a range of subjects, including employment, finance, accommodation, health, consumer affairs, the environment and education. There are nine information centres (in Bordeaux, Lille, Limoges, Lyon, Marseille, Metz, Paris, Rennes and Toulouse) but one central telephone number (☎ 3939).

The Disabled

Disabled people can obtain advice and help from the Association des Paralysés de France (💻 www.apf.asso.fr), which isn't only for those who are paralysed, the Fédération des Associations pour Adultes et Jeunes Handicapés (APAJH, 💻 www.apajh.org) and the Fédération Nationale des Accidentés de Travail et des Handicappés (💻 www.fnath. org).

Disabled people looking for work or employment-related information should contact the Association Gestion du Fonds d'Insertion Personnes Handicappées (AGEFIPH, 💻 www.agefiph.asso.fr, which provides contact details for the 18 regional associations).

> ☑ **SURVIVAL TIP**
>
> If you're seriously and permanently disabled, you should apply to the Commission Technique d'Orientation et de Reclassement Professionel (COTOREP) for an invalidity card (*carte d'invalidité civile*), which entitles you to a number of benefits.

MOVING IN

One of the most important tasks to perform after moving into a new home is to make an inventory of the fixtures and fittings and, if applicable, the furniture and furnishings. When you've purchased a property, you should check that the previous owner hasn't absconded with any fixtures and fittings which were included in the price or anything that you specifically paid for, e.g. carpets, light fittings, curtains, furniture, kitchen appliances, garden ornaments, plants or doors. It's common to do a final check or inventory when buying a new property, which is usually done a few weeks or days before completion.

When moving into a long-term rental property it's necessary to complete an inventory (*inventaire détaillé/état des lieux*) of its contents and a report on its condition. This includes the condition of fixtures and fittings, the state of furniture and furnishings, the cleanliness and state of the decoration, and anything that's damaged, missing or in need of repair. An inventory should be provided by your landlord or agent and may include every single item in a furnished property (even the number of teaspoons).

The inventory check should be carried out in your presence, both when taking over and when terminating a rental agreement. If an inventory isn't provided, you should insist on one being prepared and annexed to the lease. If you find a serious fault after signing the inventory, send a registered letter to your landlord and ask for it to be attached to the inventory.

The inventory can be drawn up (for around €150) by a *huissier*, an official (similar to a bailiff) authorised to prepare factual legal documents. If the inventory is prepared by a *huissier*, you have a good chance of resolving any disputes, as his evidence is indisputable in a court of law. An inventory should be drawn up both when moving into (*état des lieux d'entrée*) and when vacating (*état des lieux de sortie*) a rented property. If the two inventories don't correspond, you must make good any damages or deficiencies or the landlord can do so and deduct the cost from your deposit. Although French landlords are generally no worse than those in most other countries, some will do almost anything to avoid repaying a deposit. Note the reading on your utility meters (e.g. electricity, gas, water) and check that you aren't overcharged on your first bill. The meters should be read by utility companies before you move in, although you may need to organise it yourself.

It's wise to obtain written instructions from the previous owner concerning the operation of appliances, heating and air-conditioning systems, maintenance of grounds, gardens, lawns and swimming pool, care of surfaces such as wooden or marble floors, and the names of reliable local maintenance men who know the property and are familiar with its quirks. Check with your local town hall regarding local regulations concerning such things as rubbish collection, recycling and on-road parking.

Finally, don't expect your new neighbours to come round with a casserole! Remember that it takes time to get to know the French. Nevertheless, you should introduce yourselves to your neighbours at the earliest opportunity – even if your French is basic.

CHECKLISTS

When retiring permanently to France, there are many things to be considered and a 'million' people to be informed. Even if you plan to spend just a few months a year in France, it may be necessary to inform a number of people and companies in your home country. The checklists below are designed to make the task easier and help prevent an ulcer or a nervous breakdown (provided, of course, you don't leave everything to the last minute). Note that not all points are applicable to non-residents or those who spend only a few months a year in France.

Before Arrival

The following are tasks that should be completed (if possible) before your arrival in France:

- Check that your and your family's passports are valid.

- Obtain a visa, if necessary, for you and your family members (see page 26). Obviously this must be done before arrival in France.

- Arrange inoculations and shipment for any pets that you're taking with you.

- If you live in rented accommodation, give your landlord adequate notice (check your contract).

- Arrange to sell or dispose of anything you aren't taking with you, e.g. house, car and furniture. If you're selling a home or business, you should obtain expert legal advice, as you may be able to save tax by establishing a trust or other legal vehicle.

Note that if you own more than one property, you may have to pay capital gains tax on any profits from the sale of second and subsequent homes.

- Arrange shipment of your furniture and belongings by booking a shipping company well in advance).

- Arrange health insurance for yourself and your family. This is essential if you aren't covered by a private insurance policy and won't be covered by French social security.

- Check whether you need an international driving licence or a translation of your national driving licence(s). Note that some foreigners are required to take a driving test before they can buy and register a car in France.

- Open a bank account in France and transfer funds. Give the details to any companies that you plan to pay by standing order (e.g. utility companies).

- If you're exporting a car, you'll need to complete the relevant paperwork in your home country and re-register it locally after your arrival. Contact your local French embassy or consulate for information.

- Check whether you're entitled to a rebate on your road tax, car and other insurance. Obtain a letter from your motor insurance company stating your no-claims discount.

- You may qualify for a rebate on your tax and social security contributions. If you're leaving a country permanently and have been a member of a company or state pension scheme, you may be entitled to a refund or be able to

continue payments to qualify for a full (or larger) pension when you retire. Contact your company personnel office, local tax office or pension company for information.

● It's wise to arrange health, dental and optical check-ups for your family before leaving your home country. Also, obtain a copy of any health records and a statement from your private health insurance company stating your present level of cover.

● Terminate outstanding loan, lease or hire purchase contracts and pay all bills (allow plenty of time, as some companies are slow to respond).

● Return any library books and anything borrowed.

● If you don't already have one, it's wise to obtain an international credit or charge card, which may be useful during your first few months in France, particularly until you've opened a bank account.

Note, however, that credit cards aren't universally accepted in France.

● Don't forget to bring all your family's official documents, including birth certificates, driving licences, marriage certificate, divorce papers or death certificate (if a widow or widower), educational diplomas, professional certificates and job references, school records and student ID cards, employment references, copies of medical and dental records, bank account and credit card details, insurance policies and receipts for any valuables. You'll also need the documents necessary to obtain a residence permit (see page 27) plus certified copies, official translations and some passport-size photographs.

● Inform the following people:

– your town hall or municipality (you may be entitled to a refund of your local property or income taxes).

– the police, if it was necessary to register with them in your home country (or present country of residence).

– your electricity, gas, water and telephone companies (contact companies well in advance, particularly if you need to have a deposit refunded).

– your insurance companies (e.g. health, car, home contents and private pension), banks, post office (if you have a post office account), stockbroker and other financial institutions, credit card, charge card and hire purchase companies, lawyer and accountant, and local businesses where you have accounts.

– your family doctor, dentist and other health practitioners (health records should be transferred to your new doctor and dentist in France, if applicable).

- all regular correspondents, social and sports clubs, professional and trade journals, friends and relatives (give them your new address and telephone number and arrange to have your post redirected by the post office or a friend).

- your local or national vehicle registration office if you have a driving licence or car (return your registration plates if applicable).

● If you're planning to spend only part of the year in France, you may wish to give someone 'power of attorney' over your financial affairs in your home country so that he can act for you in your absence. This can be for a fixed or unlimited period and can be for a specific purpose only.

⚠ Caution

Note that you should take expert legal advice before giving anyone power of attorney over any of your financial affairs!

● Obtain some euros before arriving in France, as this will save you time on arrival and you may obtain a better exchange rate.

● Finally, allow plenty of time to get to the airport or ferry, register your luggage, and clear security and immigration.

After Arrival

The following tasks should be completed after arrival in France (if not done before):

● On arrival at a French airport or port, have your visa cancelled and your passport stamped, as applicable.

● If you've exported a vehicle, re-register it in France.

● If you aren't taking a car with you, you may wish to rent one for a week or two until buying one locally. Note that it's practically impossible to get around in rural areas without a car. If you purchase a car in France, register it and arrange insurance.

● Apply for a residence permit at your local town hall or *préfecture* within a week of your arrival (see page 27).

● Register with your local embassy or consulate.

● Find a local doctor and dentist.

● Arrange whatever insurance is necessary, including health (see page 219) car, household (see page 214) and third party liability (see page 217).

● Make courtesy calls on your neighbours and the local mayor within a few weeks of your arrival. This is particularly important in villages and rural areas if you want to be accepted and become part of the community.

village, Languedoc

7.
HEALTHY LIVING

O ne of the most important aspects of retiring in France is your health – both maintaining good health and obtaining effective treatment when required. The quality of French healthcare and healthcare facilities is among the best in the world (some say the best, including the World Health Organization in a recent survey). The standard of hospital treatment is second to none, and there are virtually no waiting lists for operations or hospital beds. (Many British people obtain treatment in France at the expense of the British National Health Service to avoid long waiting lists in the UK!) One of the few things that usually involves a long wait (four to six months) is an eye test.

Public and private medicine operate alongside one another and there's no difference in the quality of treatment provided by public hospitals and private establishments, although the former may be better equipped. However, local hospital services, particularly hospitals with casualty departments, are limited in rural areas. Nevertheless, private treatment costs around half or even a third as much as similar treatment in the UK (e.g. around GB£900 for a cataract operation, compared with GB£3,000 in the UK).

> France devotes a greater proportion of its GDP to healthcare than to defence or education, around half of it being spent on hospitals, a quarter on doctors' salaries and a fifth on medicines. Yet the system is in dire financial straits.

As a result of the cost of the public health service spiralling out of control (the annual overspend has reached several billion euros!), doctors are now subject to periodic checks on the necessity of their prescriptions and the list of 4,500 treatments reimbursed by the state is gradually being whittled away (almost 1,000 treatments were 'struck off' between 2003 and 20066). A wide-ranging reform of the health service, supposedly aimed at 'treating you better while spending less' but in fact designed to save the government money, was approved by parliament in July 2004 and has already seen the introduction (in January 2005) of the 'regular doctor' (*médecin traitant*) system and of a compulsory €1 levy on all consultations. However, while most French people recognise the need for reform, they're reluctant to lose hospitals (especially those that are half empty) and the right to unlimited second opinions and an endless supply of free pills ...

In general, French healthcare places the emphasis on preventive medicine rather than treating sickness. Alternative medicine (*médecine douce*) is popular, particularly

acupuncture and homeopathy. These treatments are recognised by France's medical council (Ordre des Médecins) and reimbursed by the national health service when prescribed by a doctor. France is the world leader in homeopathy, and some 15 per cent of the population regularly consults homeopathic doctors; many chemists provide free leaflets explaining homeopathic treatments. Other types of treatment (e.g. osteopathy and chiropractic) are available but may not be reimbursed. There are over 3,000 health associations in France – one for every conceivable ailment. A complete list, *L'Annuaire des Associations de Santé*, can be found on 💻 www.annuaire-aas.com.

HEALTH RISKS

France has long been a nation of hypochondriacs (famously satirised by Molière in *Le Malade Imaginaire*) and the French visit their doctors more often than most other Europeans and buy large quantities of medicines, health foods and vitamin pills. Despite the common stereotype of the French as wine-swilling gourmets stuffing themselves with rich foods, many have become health freaks in recent years. Fitness and health centres flourish in most towns, and jogging (*footing*) has become fashionable. Smoking has declined considerably and is now a minority habit, although it's still more prevalent than in many other European countries and is estimated to kill 30,000 people a year. The incidence of heart disease is among the lowest in the world, a fact that has recently been officially contributed in part to the largely Mediterranean diet.

On the other hand, the French have a high incidence of cirrhosis of the liver and other problems associated with excessive alcohol consumption, and there has recently been an increase in the number of sufferers from Alzheimer's disease to over half a million (it affects around 10 per cent of those over 65 and 50 per cent of those over 85). And air pollution (caused by vehicles, not smokers!) is an increasing problem in Paris and other French cities (particularly Grenoble, Lyon and Strasbourg), where it's blamed for a sharp rise in asthma cases. It's estimated that around 16,000 people die prematurely each year as a result of air pollution. There's also a high and increasing rate of stress in cities.

Among expatriates, sunstroke, change of diet, too much rich food and (surprise, surprise) too much alcohol (see below) are the most common causes of health problems. Nevertheless, when you've had too much of *la bonne vie*, you can take yourself off to a spa for a few weeks to rejuvenate your system (in preparation for another bout of over-indulgence). Among the most popular treatments offered is thalassotherapy (*thalassothérapie*), a sea water 'cure' recommended for arthritis, circulation problems, depression and fatigue; it's even available on the national health service!

The claim that drinking red wine helps to reduce heart and other diseases – e.g. in *Your Good Health: The Medicinal Benefits of Wine Drinking* by Dr E. Maury (Souvenir Press) – has recently been challenged by other medical experts. However, it's generally agreed that drinking excessive amounts of red wine (or any alcohol) can destroy your brain and cause liver failure! As French producers sometimes warn buyers: *l'abus d'alcool est dangereux pour la santé, consommez avec modération* (alcohol abuse is dangerous for your health, consume in moderation).

Essential vaccinations, renewable every ten years, are polio and tetanus, which are 65 per cent reimbursed or 100 per cent if given as part of a free health check-up (*bilan de santé*), available to those on *Couverture Maladie Universelle* (*CMU*). Free flu jabs are available in October for over 65s and those with certain complaints.

You can safely drink mains water unless it's labelled as non-drinking (*eau non-potable*), although the wine (especially a Château Mouton Rothschild) is more enjoyable. Those who enjoy swimming in lakes and rivers should be aware of the potentially fatal Weil's disease (leptospirose), transmitted through the urine of rats and other rodents, which is on the increase, particularly in Aquitaine.

Alcoholism

One of France's major health problems is alcoholism, which is directly responsible for the loss of 17,000 lives a year, mostly in poor urban and rural areas (usually as a result of drinking cheap red wine rather than spirits). The legal age for drinking alcohol is 16, although there's virtually no enforcement and children are readily served and sold alcohol everywhere.

Alcoholism can be a problem for expatriates and retirees in France, who often have a lot of time of their hands and

may be encouraged to drink more by the unaccustomed low cost of alcohol and the wealth of social activities which always seem to involve drinking! There are a number of English-speaking Alcoholics Anonymous (*Alcooliques Anonymes*) groups in Paris (☎ 01 48 06 43 68 for information) and other areas, and French-speaking groups throughout France.

BEFORE YOU GO

Pre-departure Health Check

Before leaving for France it's wise to have a health check, particularly if you have a record of poor health or are elderly.

> ☑ SURVIVAL TIP
>
> If you suffer from an existing medical condition ask your doctor to prepare a written report for you to take to France and, if possible, have it translated into French.

As soon as you've registered with a doctor in France, you should give him a copy of the report for your new medical records. If you have an unusual blood group or suffer from allergies to medicine, prepare a list and have it translated into French.

Medicines

If you're already taking regular medication, bear in mind that the brand names of medicines (drugs) vary from country to country, and you should ask your doctor for the generic name. If you wish to match medication prescribed abroad, you need a current prescription with the medication's trade name, the manufacturer's name, the chemical name and the dosage. Most medicines have an equivalent in other countries, although particular brands may be difficult or impossible to obtain.

French chemists provide a wide range of medicines, but you might prefer to bring favourite over-the-counter remedies for flu, headaches, diarrhoea, etc. with you.

Health Insurance

Before you leave for France, one of the most important things you must do is ensure that you have adequate health insurance. You may be covered for emergency treatment for a limited period by a reciprocal health agreement between France and your present country of residence; otherwise, you'll need private health insurance – at least a holiday or travel policy (see page 217) and preferably an international health policy (see page 221). If you're planning to settle in France, you may be eligible for treatment under the national health system (see page 159) or may need private insurance (see page 221).

Reciprocal Health Agreements

If you're entitled to social security health benefits in another EU country or in a country with a reciprocal health agreement with France, you'll receive free or subsidised medical treatment in France. The US doesn't have a reciprocal health agreement with France, so Americans who aren't covered by French social security must have private health insurance or a holiday/travel policy that covers them in France.

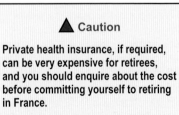

> ⚠ Caution
>
> Private health insurance, if required, can be very expensive for retirees, and you should enquire about the cost before committing yourself to retiring in France.

EU citizens should apply for a certificate of entitlement to treatment at their local social security office (or a post office in the UK) at least three weeks before they plan to travel to France. The paper form called an E111 has now been superseded by a plastic card called a European Health Insurance Card (EHIC), and there have been a number of changes to procedures and conditions of use. First, an EHIC must be applied for (by post, phone or internet) at least a month before travel and cannot simply be obtained the same day from a post office. An EHIC covers only one person and not a family, as did the E111, but is valid for three to five years (an E111 had to be renewed annually). However, you must continue to make social security contributions in the country where it was issued and, if you become a resident in another country (e.g. in France), it becomes invalid in that country.

Although an EHIC entitles you to much better cover than an E111 (which covered only emergency hospital treatment, whereas the EHIC covers 'any necessary medical treatment arising during a temporary stay in another EU

member state'), it still doesn't entitle you to 100 per cent reimbursement of all medical expenses in France. Rather, it gives you entitlement to the same cover as a French resident, i.e. normally around 70 per cent of routine healthcare and treatment costs (some treatments and medicines are fully reimbursed; others aren't covered at all). You're therefore recommended to enquire about the availability of 'top-up' insurance plans, covering the balance of costs.

If you do incur medical costs in France, you must obtain a treatment confirmation (*fueille de soins*) and go to the local Caisse Primaire d'Assurance Maladie/CPAM, the authority which deals with health insurance, to apply for reimbursement, which will be sent to you or credited to your UK bank account. Details of the procedure are included in the booklet that comes with the EHIC form. **Note that it can take months for medical expenses to be reimbursed.**

As soon as you have a permanent address in France, even if this is within the six month period the EHIC covers you for, you must obtain a form E121 (for retirees – you must complete an E121 for **each** member of your household) or a form E106 (for those below retirement age who have been paying contributions for at least three years), which are available in the UK from the Inland Revenue's International Pension Service (☎ 0191-218 7777). These forms entitle you to cover in France: the E121 indefinitely, the E106 for two years, while you transfer out of your home country's system (you must inform the relevant authority, e.g. the Department of Work and Pensions in the UK) and into the French system.

If you're entitled to neither an E121 nor an E106, legislation (apparently deriving from an EU directive) passed in January 2008 no longer allows you to 30 months' cover, as was previously the case; nor does it allow you to pay voluntary contributions to the French social security system in order

to benefit from state health insurance – to qualify for which you must wait 30 months. If this is your case, you must obtain private medical insurance, which starts at around £1,200 per year for a healthy 60-year-old requiring only 'emergency' cover. This restriction shouldn't affect Britons registered as French residents before 23rd November 2007, and the French government has stated that Britons with a chronic illness may be entitled to *CMU* in the interim, but the situation is far from clear.

⚠ Caution

Britons wishing to retire to France before the official retirement age must check their entitlement (or lack of it) to French state healthcare before committing themselves to a move.

British visitors or Britons planning to live in France can obtain further information about reciprocal health treatment in France from the Department of Work & Pensions' Medical Benefits department (☎ 0191-218 7747) or, if you're of pensionable age, the Pension Service (☎ 0191-218 7777) and about the new EHIC from the post office (☎ 0845-606 2030) and via the internet (e.g. 🖥 www.dh.gov.uk/en/Policyandguidance/ Healthadvicefortravellers/index.htm). English-language assistance is available in France on ☎ 08 20 90 42 12 and ☎ 01 45 26 33 41.

EMERGENCIES

France's emergency medical services are among the best in the world but may operate in a slightly different way from those you're used to. The action to take in a medical emergency depends on the degree of urgency. In a life-threatening emergency such as a heart attack, poisoning or serious accident, dial 15 for your nearest *Service d'Aide Médicale d'Urgence* (*SAMU*) unit. *SAMU* is an emergency service that works closely with local public hospital emergency and intensive care units. Its ambulances are manned by medical personnel and equipped with resuscitation equipment. *SAMU* has a central telephone number for each region and the duty doctor decides whether to send a *SAMU* unit, refer the call to another ambulance service, or call a doctor for a home visit. In the most critical situations, *SAMU* can arrange transport to hospital by aeroplane, helicopter or, if appropriate, boat. If you call the fire brigade or police services, they will request a *SAMU* unit if they consider it necessary.

You can also call the local fire brigade (*sapeurs-pompiers* or *pompiers*) in an emergency by dialling 18. The fire brigade and public ambulance services are combined, and the fire brigade is equipped to deal with accidents and emergency medical cases. It operates its own ambulances, which are equipped with resuscitation equipment, and they will arrive with a doctor.

If you need an ambulance but the emergency isn't life-threatening, call the local public assistance (*assistance publique*) or municipal ambulance (*ambulance municipale*) service. There are also private ambulances in most towns providing a 24-hour service, listed by town under *Ambulances* in yellow pages. Ambulance staff are trained to provide first-aid and oxygen. In an emergency an ambulance will take a patient to the nearest hospital equipped to deal with the emergency. In small towns the local taxi service also provides an 'ambulance' service.

You'll be billed for the services of *SAMU*, the fire service or the public ambulance service, although the cost will be reimbursed by social security and your complementary insurance policy, if you have one, in the same way as other medical costs (see **National Health System** on page 159). In an emergency any hospital must treat you, irrespective of your ability to pay.

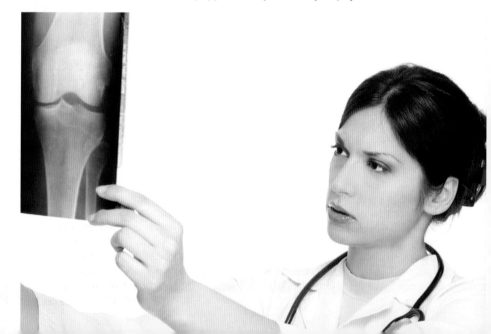

There are 24-hour medical and dental services in major cities and large towns (numbers are listed in telephone directories). For example, in Paris you can call *SOS Médecins* (☎ 01 47 07 77 77) for medical emergencies and *SOS Dentaire* (☎ 01 43 37 51 00) for dental emergencies. Contact numbers for *SOS Médecins* in other parts of France can be found on 🖳 www.sosmedecins-france.fr. *SOS* doctors and dentists are equipped with radio cars and respond quickly to calls. A home visit in Paris costs from around €32 before 19.00 and €48 after 19.00, plus the cost of any treatment. In Paris and other main cities, there are emergency medical telephone boxes at major junctions marked '*Services Médicaux*', with direct lines to emergency services.

If someone has swallowed poison, the number of your local poison control centre (*centre anti-poison*) is listed at the front of telephone directories. The 'morning-after pill' (*contraception d'urgence*) can be purchased without a prescription from chemists'.

If you're unsure who to call, telephone your local police, who will tell you who to contact or call the appropriate service for you. Whoever you call, give the age of the patient and if possible, specify the type of emergency. **Keep a record of the telephone numbers of your doctor, local hospitals and clinics, ambulance service, poison control, dentist and other emergency services (e.g. fire, police) next to your telephone**.

If you're able, you can go to a hospital emergency or casualty department (*urgences*). Check in advance which local hospitals are equipped to deal with emergencies and the quickest route from your home. **This information could be of vital importance in the event of an emergency, when a delay could mean the difference between life and death**.

Emergency Numbers	
Number	**Service**
☎ 15	Ambulance (*Service d'Aide Médicale d'Urgence/SAMU*) or to contact a duty doctor out of hours
☎ 17	Police (*police-secours*)
☎ 18	Fire (*sapeurs-pompiers/feu centrale d'alarme*)

NATIONAL HEALTH SYSTEM

France has an excellent, although expensive, national health system. If you qualify for healthcare under the national health system (see **Entitlement** below), you and your family are entitled to subsidised or (in certain cases) free medical and dental treatment. Benefits include general and specialist care, hospitalisation, laboratory services, medicines, dental care, maternity care, appliances and transportation. Those who don't automatically qualify can contribute voluntarily or take out private health insurance (see page 219).

Entitlement

Your entitlement to French state healthcare depends on whether a reciprocal social security agreement exists between your 'home' country and France (see page 63).

EU Citizens

Retirees receiving a state pension from another EU country are entitled to the same health benefits as French retirees. EU retirees over 60 going to live permanently in France aren't required to contribute to French social security, but must register with their local CPAM (and present forms E106 and E121). You're now required to have a form E121 for **each** member of your household. If you're receiving a state pension in another EU country, you may be subject to an annual check that you're still receiving it.

EU citizens who retire before qualifying for a state pension can receive French social security health cover for up to 30 months by obtaining a form E106 from their country's social security department; you must have made full contributions in your home country during the last two years. You need to register at your local CPAM, where you must present a copy of your *carte de séjour/résident* or your temporary authorisation of residence (*récépissé de demande de carte de séjour*), proof of your relationship with any dependants who don't qualify in their own right (e.g. a marriage certificate), and your bank account details (*relevé d'identité bancaire*). If the temporary cover expires before you reach retirement age, you must take out private health insurance (see page 219) or make voluntary social security contributions in order to qualify for benefits, with contributions based on your income (which must be confirmed by your tax return).

If you're of retirement age but are still working, you may qualify for an E106 and obtain health benefits for up to 30 months.

Non-EU Citizens

Certain non-EU citizens are covered for some or all French state healthcare benefits, depending on the existence and extent of reciprocal social security agreements (see page 63). You should check with your 'home' country's social security organisation what, if any, entitlements you'll have as a retiree in France.

Registration

You must register for national healthcare at your local CPAM), of which there are around 130 throughout the country (at least one in each department) and which deal with everyday matters and reimbursements. Your town hall will give you the address or you can find it under *Sécurité Sociale* in your local yellow pages. In certain cases, you must visit the Relations Internationales department of social security, e.g. if you're retired with a pension in another EU country.

You must provide your personal details, including your full name, address, country of origin, and date and place of birth. You will also need to produce passports, *cartes de séjour* and certified birth certificates for your dependants, plus a marriage certificate (as applicable). You may need to provide copies with official translations, but check first, as translations may be unnecessary. You will also need proof of residence such as a rental contract or an electricity bill.

When you've registered, you'll receive a registration card (*Carte Vitale*), which looks like a credit card and contains an electronic ('smart') chip (*puce*). The card has your name and your social security number (*No. d'Immatriculation de l'Assuré*) printed on the front. (Social security numbers are issued by l'Institut National de la Statistique et des Études Economiques/INSEE.) Additional information is coded into the chip, which is needed to process any claim for reimbursement or services. Contrary to some fears, there's no detailed information regarding your health or medical condition on the chip. However, at the beginning of 2007, the *Carte Vitale* began to be superseded by the *Carte Vitale 2*, which carries a photograph of

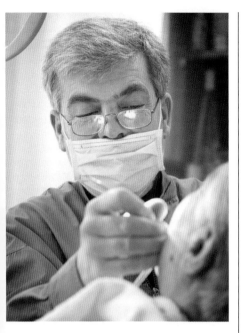

the holder and the following additional information:

- the name of your regular doctor (*médecin traitant*) ;
- details of your complementary insurance, if any;
- details of a person to contact in an emergency;
- your permission to donate organs if applicable.

The *Carte Vitale 2* is linked to a computerised system known as a *dossier médical personnel* (*DMP*), containing all your medical records and vital information such as your blood group and allergies. The cards are being issued initially to those making their first social security registration, and it will take up to seven years for all existing cards to be updated. The idea behind the new system (like most health service innovations) is to save the government money by reducing

a phenomenon known as *nomadisme*, whereby patients seek opinions on the same ailment from several doctors, which is estimated to cost €3bn per year. Nevertheless, the new card costs only €2.70, compared with the €3.66 charged for the original *Carte Vitale* when it was introduced in 1998.

Along with a *Carte Vitale*, you'll receive a certificate (*attestation*) containing a list of those entitled to benefits on your behalf (*bénéficiaires*), i.e. your dependants, and the address of the office where you must apply for reimbursement of your medical expenses. (This address is normally indicated in small type just above your name and address and is easy to miss.) Dependants include your spouse (if they aren't personally insured), dependent children under the age of 16 (or under the age of 20 if they're students or unable to work through illness or invalidity), and ascendants, descendants and relatives by marriage supported by you and living in the same household.

If you move home, acquire or need to change or transfer beneficiaries or find any errors in the information on your attestation, you must inform your CPAM. If a social security official makes a regular visit to your town hall, you may be able make changes to your records and ask questions during a scheduled visit.

The date when your entitlement to social security benefits expires is shown on the certificate (*droits jusqu'au…*). If no date is shown, your entitlement is indefinite. Just before the end of the year when your benefits expire (if applicable), you should receive a new certificate, along with instructions as to how and where to update your card; this is normally every three years. There are machines in most public hospitals and in some town halls in which you can simply insert your *Carte Vitale* and update the chip. Alternatively, you can post the card to the office that sent it to you and ask for it to be updated.

☑ SURVIVAL TIP

Make sure you keep your certificate in a safe place, as you may be required to show it if you require services from a medical practitioner chemist who isn't linked to the card system or whose computer is out of order.

Benefits & Reimbursement

Under the national health system, health treatment is assigned a basic monetary value (*tarif de convention*), which is often lower than what you actually pay, and social security pays or reimburses a proportion of this basic value, as follows:

The figures below are intended only as a guide and should be confirmed with social security and practitioners, as they can vary with your circumstances and social security 'status'. For example, certain patients classified as needing serious long-term treatment, e.g. diabetic, cancer and cardiac patients, receive 100 per cent reimbursement for all treatment. The cost of buying or hiring medical instruments such as walking sticks, wheelchairs and special pillows and mattresses is reimbursed up to specified limits. The reimbursement you receive from social security applies to the *tarif de convention*, which is not necessarily the same as the amount you pay.

For example, if a blood test costs €75 and the *tarif de convention* is €60, you'd be reimbursed 70 per cent of €60 (€42) leaving you with a bill of €33. The balance of medical bills, called the *ticket modérateur*, can be paid by a complementary health insurance scheme, to which many people subscribe (see page 219).

When you visit a medical practitioner whose fees are wholly or partly refundable by social security, simply present your *Carte Vitale* and reimbursement will be automatically 'triggered', although you must still pay the doctor and wait for your bank account to be reimbursed (which should take place within five days).

If a medical practitioner isn't linked to the *Carte Vitale* system or isn't able to access a computer, he will complete a paper form

---

National Health System - Reimbursements

Practitioner/Treatment	Reimbursement
Maternity-related care	100 per cent
Hospitalisation	80 per cent
Doctor, dentist and midwife services; consultations as an out-patient; basic dental care; miscellaneous items, e.g. laboratory work, apparatus, ambulance services	70 per cent
Spectacles	65 per cent
Services of medical auxiliaries, e.g. nurses and therapists	60 per cent
Medicines	0 to 100 per cent

called a 'treatment sheet' (*feuille de soins*). The treatment provided and the cost of the consultation are listed on the form, which must be sent to your local CPAM for reimbursement. **Don't forget to put your social security number (*numéro d'immatriculation*) and date of birth on the form (if not already printed), and also to sign it before sending it.** If forms aren't correctly completed, they will be returned and this will delay your reimbursement (which may take up to 13 days in any case).

If your doctor prescribes medicines, he will give you a prescription (*ordonnance*) to take to a chemist (pharmacists). Many chemists have systems enabling them to deduct the appropriate percentage of the bill reimbursed by social security, leaving you to pay only the unreimbursed portion. Some are also 'linked' to certain complementary insurance schemes, so that once you've registered with the chemist, you won't have to pay anything. Simply present your *ordonnance* to the chemist. If your chemist isn't computerised or doesn't recognise your complementary insurer (see page 219), you must pay 100 per cent for your medicines and make a claim for reimbursement later. In this case, the chemist will give you a copy of the *feuille de soins*, with confirmation that the medicines have been issued, for you to send to your CPAM or insurer.

If you're requesting a reimbursement for auxiliary services prescribed by a doctor, you must accompany the *feuille de soins* with a copy of the doctor's original prescription. You can save a number of *feuilles de soins* and send them together.

The refund will be paid directly into the bank or post office account that was designated when you registered with social security and you'll receive a statement from the office, confirming the amount refunded. Normally, you'll also automatically receive reimbursement of the 'complementary' sum (*ticket modérateur*) from your complementary insurance policy (sometimes before the social security refund). If you don't, you must send the social security statement to your complementary insurer. Always keep a copy of your *feuilles de soins* and check that reimbursements are received and correct, especially for large sums.

To be reimbursed by social security for certain medical treatment, you must obtain prior approval from your CPAM. This may include physical examinations, non-routine dental care, contact lenses and non-standard lenses for glasses, certain laboratory and radiology tests, physiotherapy and speech therapy, and thermal and therapeutic treatments. Your medical practitioner will give you a proposal form (*demande d'entente préalable*) and, unless treatment is urgently required, you should apply at least 21 days before the proposed treatment and obtain a receipt for your application (if made in person) or send it by registered post. If you don't receive a reply from your CPAM within ten working

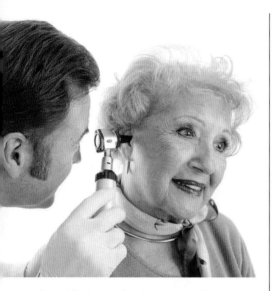

practitioners who perform specialist treatment (*dépassement exceptionnel*) and those with a particular qualification or expertise (*dépassement permanent*). If you're in any doubt, you should ask what the fee is for a consultation or treatment and what percentage will be reimbursed by social security.

If you're a non-resident you may be asked to pay in cash, although cheques drawn on a French bank are acceptable. If you're unable to pay your portion of the bill, you can apply to your social security payment centre (Caisse Primaire d'Assurance Maladie/CPAM) for a waiver (*prise en charge*). In the case of urgent or necessary treatment, approval is a formality.

days, it's deemed to have agreed to the request.

> Since 1st January 2005, €1 has been deducted from all reimbursements except those relating to treatment for those on *CMU*, in order to reduce the social security debt.

When choosing a medical practitioner, e.g. a doctor or dentist, it's important to verify whether he has an agreement (*convention*) with social security. If he has an agreement, he's known as *conventionné* and will charge a fixed amount for treatment as specified under the *tarif de convention*. If he has no agreement, he's termed *non-conventionné* and the bill may be two to five times the *tarif de convention*; some *non-conventionné* practitioners are approved (*agréé*) by social security, but only a small proportion of their fees are reimbursed. A few medical professionals are classified as *conventionné honoraires libres*; although they're *conventionné*, they're permitted to charge higher fees than the standard rates. These include

HOSPITALS

France boasts a higher number of hospital beds in proportion to its population than most other European countries (8.7 per 1,000 compared with 7.6 in Spain and Italy and 6.9 in the UK), although the introduction of the 35-hour week and a recent shortage of doctors and nurses, particularly in the provinces, have led to the closure of many wards, and in the summer months, when staff are on holiday, some hospitals are forced virtually to close. There's also a shortage of certain specialists, e.g. anaesthetists, gynaecologists and ophthalmologists, partly due to a recent increase in malpractice lawsuits.

All cities and large towns have at least one hospital (*hôpital*) or clinic (*clinique*), indicated by the international hospital sign of a red 'H' on a white background. Hospitals are listed in the yellow pages under *Hôpitaux et Hospices*. There are many types of hospital, both public and private (see below). Like doctors and other medical practitioners, hospitals are either *conventionné* or *non-conventionné*

Every large town has at least one *hôpital conventionné*, which may be public or private, usually with a direct payment agreement with social security. Private hospitals and clinics that are *non-conventionné* may also have an agreement (*agréé*) with social security, whereby around 30 per cent of the fees are usually paid by social security.

For non-urgent hospital treatment, check in advance the reimbursement made by social security and, if applicable, the amount your complementary insurance policy or other private health insurance will pay. If you're admitted to a hospital or other medical institution, you should be given a document outlining your rights (*charte des droits et libertés*).

Public Hospitals

There are generally three categories of public hospital: hospital centres or short-stay hospitals (*hôpital de court séjour*), medium-stay centres (*centre de moyen séjour*) and long-term treatment centres (*centre et unité de long séjour*). Hospital centres include general hospitals, *assistance publique* (*AP*) hospitals in Paris, specialist hospitals and regional centres (*centre hospitalier régional/ CHR* or *centre hospitalier universitaire/ CHU* when associated with a university). Public hospitals must accept all patients in an emergency irrespective of their ability to pay.

Medium-stay hospitals are usually for patients who have previously been treated in a short-stay hospital centre. They contain facilities for convalescence, occupational and physical therapy, and recuperative treatment for drug and alcohol abuse and mental illness. Long-term treatment centres are for those who are unable to care for themselves without assistance and include psychiatric hospitals and nursing homes for the aged (*maisons de retraite*).

There are over 35 *CHU*s in France (12 in Paris), where medical students do their training. *CHU*s are among the best hospitals in France (indeed in the world), and professors and senior staff must undergo intensive training to secure appointments. Rural community hospitals are also classified as hospital centres, although they're usually less well equipped than other short-stay hospitals and you should go to a large hospital if possible.

☑ **SURVIVAL TIP**

Not all hospitals have accident and emergency (*urgences*) departments, and you should check where your nearest A&E centre is to be found.

Private Hospitals & Clinics

Most private hospitals (*hôpital privé*) and clinics (*clinique*) specialise in inpatient care in particular fields of medicine, such as obstetrics and surgery, rather than being full-service hospitals (the American Hospital in Paris is a rare exception). You should check in advance. The cost of treatment in a private hospital or clinic is generally much higher than in a public hospital, where a large proportion of costs is reimbursed by social security. However, some private hospitals participate in the French social security system and operate in the same way as public hospitals. These include the Hertford British and International hospitals in Paris (see below).

If your French is poor, you may prefer to be treated at a private hospital or clinic with English-speaking staff, as most public hospitals make little or no allowance for foreigners who don't speak French. There are a number of expatriate hospitals in the Paris area, including the American Hospital in Paris (☎ 01 46 41 25 25, 🖳 www. american-hospital.org) and the Hertford

British Hospital, also known as the Hôpital Franco-Britannique (☎ 01 46 39 22 22, 🖳 www.british-hospital.org), which specialises in maternity care. Most staff at all levels in these hospitals speak English. Fees at the American hospital are much higher than at French hospitals, although they can usually be reclaimed through the French social security system and most *mutuelles* (see page 220) and are accepted by most American medical insurance companies.

Accommodation

The basic hospital accommodation that is reimbursed at 80 per cent by social security is a two- or three-bed room (*régime commun*). A supplement must be paid for a private room (if available), although it may be paid in part or in full by your complementary or other private health insurance. You can usually rent a radio, TV or telephone for a small daily fee if they aren't included in the room fee. A bed is also usually provided for relatives

if required. You must normally provide your own pyjamas, robes, towels and toiletries. The best hospital accommodation is similar to five-star hotels with food and wine (and prices!) to match. Catering in basic accommodation varies from good to adequate.

Procedure

Except in an emergency, you're admitted or referred to a hospital or clinic for treatment only after a recommendation (*attestation*) from a doctor or a specialist. Normally you're admitted to a hospital in your own *département*, unless specialist surgery or treatment is necessary which is unavailable there. If you wish to be treated in hospital by your own doctor, you must check that he's able to do so. Except in the case of emergencies, you must provide the following documents on admission to a public hospital in order to receive reimbursement from social security:

- your social security registration card (*carte d'immatriculation*) or *Carte Vitale* – see **Registration** on page 143;

- a doctor's certificate (*attestation*) stating the reason for hospitalisation;

- documents provided by your social security office (*caisse*) stating the conditions under which you're insured, e.g. if you're unemployed you need a document stating that you're entitled to unemployment benefits.

If you aren't covered by social security, you must provide evidence of your health insurance (e.g. a European Health Insurance Card) – or your ability to pay! If you have no insurance and are unable to pay, you may be refused treatment at a private hospital or clinic, except in an emergency.

Upon admission to a hospital you should receive an information booklet (*livret d'accueil*) containing meal schedules, visiting hours, floor plan, doctors' names, hospital rules, and a description of the uniforms and name tags worn by hospital staff. (If you don't, ask for one.) Visiting hours are usually from 13.30 or 14.00 to 20.30 or 21.00 daily but tend to be flexible for immediate family members; visits can be made outside these hours in exceptional circumstances. In a private clinic there may be no restrictions on visiting hours.

Hospital stays are kept to a minimum, and much treatment is performed on an outpatient basis (*hôpital de jour*); your convalescence takes place at home (*hospitalisation à domicile/HAD*), supervised by visiting doctors and nurses. You can usually leave hospital at any time without a doctor's consent by signing a release form (*décharge de responsabilité*).

Costs

Hospital bills can be **very** high, e.g. €150 to €250 per day for medicine, accommodation and meals plus €250 to €300 for surgery, or much more for a major operation.

☑ **SURVIVAL TIP**

If you're paying a bill yourself for elective surgery, you should shop around, not just in France but in other countries, as the cost can vary considerably.

Note, however, that some operations are performed in France for half or a third of the price in some other European countries. If you're covered by French social security, 80 per cent of your hospital bill will normally be paid by the state. (Some types of plastic surgery are also paid for, e.g. breast reduction in certain circumstances and some ear and nose operations.)

Patients covered by social security are charged a fixed daily fee (*forfait journalier/ indemnité journalière*) for meals of around

€16, unless hospitalisation was due to an accident at work or you're exempt on the grounds of low income, although some hospitals waive the charge on the day of admission. This fee is usually reimbursed by complementary health insurance.

If a medical bill is expected to be above a certain amount (which is increased annually in line with inflation), you can apply to social security for a *prise en charge*, which means that the full bill will be sent directly to social security. Otherwise, you must pay the bill when you leave hospital, unless you've made prior arrangements for it to be paid by your insurance company. You must pay for hospital outpatient treatment in the same way as a visit to a doctor or specialist.

Certain patients, classified as needing serious long-term treatment, receive 100 per cent reimbursement, e.g. cardiac, diabetes and cancer patients. Pensioners receive free hospital treatment under social security, although up to 90 per cent of their pension may be deducted to compensate for the cost of treatment (while in hospital). A stay at a spa is usually reimbursed at 70 per cent or higher when recommended by a doctor and approved by social security. Convalescence after a serious illness is often paid 100 per cent by social security.

Long-term Care

The elderly are better catered for in France than in many other countries, although the great majority of old people are looked after at home by relatives (adult children are obliged by law to support ageing parents according to their means) and the cost of retirement homes and other accommodation can be prohibitive. Nevertheless, there are some 5,000 retirement homes in France, including public and private establishments (see **Retirement Homes** on page 112).

A new social security allowance, *allocation personnalisée à l'autonomie*

(*APA*), was introduced in 2001 to help those over 60 requiring long-term care. The maximum allowance (in the case of severe 'loss of autonomy') is around €1,200 per month. Application should be made to the Conseil Général of the *département* in which you're living. Details (in French) can be found on ⌨ http://vosdroits.service-public.fr/particuliers/F2112.xhtml.

It's also possible to insure against becoming a burden on your children (see page 219).

DOCTORS

There are around 3.4 doctors (*médecins*) per 1,000 population in France (compared with 1.7 in the UK, 4.4 in Spain and 5.9 in Italy), around 45 per cent women, and there are excellent doctors throughout the country, most of whom speak some English and many of whom are fluent. Many embassies and consulates maintain a list of doctors and specialists in their area who speak English (and other foreign languages), and your employer, colleagues or neighbours may be able to recommend someone. Town halls and chemists keep a list of local practitioners. You can obtain a list of doctors registered with social security from your local social security office. General practitioners or family doctors (*médecin généraliste*) are listed in the yellow pages under *Médecins Généralistes* and specialists under *Médecins Qualifiés* followed by their speciality, e.g. *Gynécologie Médicale*. (There are as many specialists as general practitioners.) All French doctors and specialists are registered with the Ordre des Médecins.

Until recently, you could choose to see any doctor or specialist at any time and weren't required to register with a particular doctor, which made it easy to obtain a second opinion, should you wish to do so. You're now required to appoint an 'regular doctor' (*médecin traitant*) and to obtain a

referral from him before seeing another doctor or specialist, including a medical auxiliary such as a nurse, physiotherapist or chiropodist, or a gynaecologist, ophthalmologist or paediatrician. In some cases, you can go directly to a specialist but you may have to pay more than on referral.

Most doctors have two or three 'open surgery' hours each day, when no appointment is necessary. At all other times you must have an appointment.

Many French doctors are specialists in acupuncture and homeopathy, both of which are reimbursed by social security when performed or prescribed by a doctor or practitioner who is *conventionné*. It's normal practice to pay a doctor or other medical practitioner after each visit, whether you're a private or social security patient, and then seek reimbursement. A routine visit to the doctor costs €22 and home visits around €40, although these are seldom available.

The standard fee for a consultation with a specialist is €27, but a visit to a psychiatrist, neuro-psychiatrist or neurologist will cost you €37, and specialists who are *non-conventionné* can charge €45 or more.

Many doctors are in single practices but an increasing number work in group practices, and there are also healthcare centres (*centre médical et social*), which may offer services that are usually unavailable at doctors' surgeries, e.g. health screening, vaccinations, dental care (*soins dentaires*) and nursing care (*soins infirmiers*). Some centres specialise in a particular field of medicine, such as cancer or heart treatment. For example, as part of a Health Department initiative to fight breast cancer, women aged between 50 and 74 can obtain free screening (*dépistage*) at centres listed on www.rendezvoussanteplus.net. As when visiting a doctor, check whether the centre is *conventionné*. In some areas, there are outpatient services (*centre de soins*) run by private organisations such as the Red Cross. You can obtain a list of local healthcare centres from your town hall.

MEDICINES & CHEMISTS'

The French take a lot of medicines (*médicaments – drogues* are narcotics!). Those prescribed by doctors represent over 80 per cent of sales, and doctors habitually prescribe three or four different remedies for each ailment. The French have traditionally been prescribed more antibiotics than any other Europeans, a third of which are reckoned to be unnecessary or ineffective, and have the highest incidence of anti-biotic-resistant bacteria in Europe, with the result that the government is now campaigning (among both doctors and patients) for a reduction in antibiotics prescription. The cost of prescription medicines is controlled by the government (prices are reviewed twice a year), although there are no price controls on non-prescription medicines.

Social security pays the whole cost of essential medication for certain illnesses or conditions, e.g. insulin and heart pills (labelled '100 per cent'), 65 per cent of medicines designated as important (with white labels), and 35 per cent for *médicaments de confort* (with blue labels)

A few medicines aren't reimbursed at all, including those deemed to be 'ineffective' (of the 100 most-prescribed medicines in France, 23 are reckoned to fall into this category!) and those that can be bought over the counter, although in some cases over-the-counter medicines can be obtained free or at reduced cost on prescription (check with your doctor or a chemist). Information (in French only) about medicines commonly prescribed in France can be found on the website of the Association Française de Sécurité Sanitaire des Produits de Santé (AFSSAPS, 💻 http://agmed.sante.gouv.fr).

> ⚠️ **Caution**
>
> **If you must pay for your own medicines, it can be expensive, e.g. €100 or more for a course of antibiotics.**

The brand names for medicines often vary from country to country, so if you regularly take a particular medicine you should ask your doctor for the generic name. If you wish to match a medicine prescribed abroad, you need a current prescription with the medicine's trade name, the manufacturer's name, the chemical composition and the dosage. Although you aren't obliged to accept it, a chemist may propose a generic product which is cheaper than the brand on your prescription (as part of the government's scheme to reduce health spending).

Despite an almost 100 per cent increase in the use of generic medicines between 2002 and 2005, the French are second only to the Spanish in the European league of preferring branded products, only 6.4 per cent of them accepting generic alternatives compared with 20.6 per cent of Britons and 22.7 per cent of Germans. **Note, however, that under legislation which became effective in July 2003 social security reimbursement (see page 293) is based on the generic equivalent of branded medicines (if one exists).** Generic products, which are up to a third cheaper than branded products, are usually identified by the prefix '*Gé*'. Most foreign medicines have an equivalent in France, although particular brands may be difficult or impossible to obtain. It's possible to have medicines sent from abroad and no import duty or value added tax (*TVA*) is payable. If you're visiting France for a short period, you should take sufficient medicines to cover the length of your stay. In an emergency, a local doctor will write a prescription (*ordonnance*) that can be filled

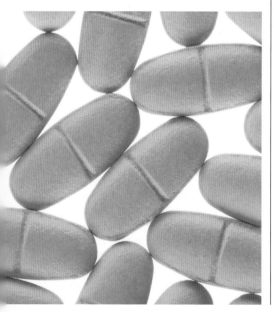

by a local chemist, or a hospital may refill a prescription from its own pharmacy.

A triangular 'traffic' sign with a red border and a black car symbol on a medicine packet indicates that it can cause drowsiness and that you shouldn't drive or operate machinery when taking it, but colour-coded packaging is being introduced to indicate the level of drowsiness caused by each medicine: yellow means 'drive with care', orange 'drive only with your doctor's permission' and red 'don't drive'.

Prescription and non-prescription medicines are obtained from chemists' (*pharmacie*), denoted by a sign consisting of a green cross on a white background (which is usually illuminated and flashing when the shop is open). A chemist must own and run his own shop (chain chemists are illegal) and their numbers are strictly controlled, although there's at least one chemist in every town and many villages. Most chemists' are open from 09.00 to 19.00 or 19.30 from Mondays to Saturdays, although many close for lunch from 12.00 or 12.30 to 14.00. Some are closed on Mondays and others may be closed on Saturday afternoons since the introduction of the 35-hour week. Outside normal opening hours, a notice giving the address of the nearest duty chemist (*pharmacie de garde*) is displayed in the windows of chemists' (the telephone numbers of local doctors on call may also be shown). This information is also published in local newspapers and listed in monthly bulletins issued by town halls. In most cities, several chemists' are open until late evening or early morning and in Paris a 24-hour service is provided by the Pharmacie Les Champs, 84 avenue des Champs-Elysées, 75008 Paris (☎ 01 45 62 02 41). There are also American and British chemists in the capital, stocking familiar American and British medicines.

Chemists are trained and obliged to give first aid and they can also perform tests such as blood pressure. They can supply a wider range of medicines over the counter without a prescription than is available in Britain and the US, although some medicines sold freely in other countries require a doctor's prescription in France. A chemist will recommend non-prescription medicines for minor ailments and may also recommend a local doctor, specialist, nurse or dentist. (Some chemists regard this type of recommendation as unethical and will prefer to give you a list of practitioners). Chemists are trained to distinguish between around 50 species of edible and poisonous fungi (*champignon*) and will tell you whether those you've picked are delicious or deadly. They're also trained to identify local snakes to enable them to prescribe the correct antidote for bites. Crutches (*béquilles*) can be hired from chemists for around €3 per week, plus a deposit of around €15.

French chemists' aren't cluttered with the non-medical wares found in American and British chemists, although many sell cosmetics and toiletries and most stock animal medicines and baby products (e.g. feeding bottles). A few chemists' are called *parapharmacies*; these don't stock some common medicines, such as painkillers. Chemists' are cheaper than a *parfumerie* for cosmetics but more expensive than a supermarket or hypermarket. Only a limited range of non-prescription medicines can be purchased in supermarkets and hypermarkets.

> A *droguerie*, which is a sort of hardware store selling toiletries, cleaning supplies, a wide range of general household goods, paint, garden supplies, tools and DIY supplies, shouldn't be confused with an American drug store.

Prescriptions may be printed or handwritten; in the latter case, as in most countries, they're invariably illegible but a chemist will (usually!) be able to decipher them and will explain to you (and write on the medicine boxes) what you need to take when. Whereas you must pay the full cost of non-prescription medicines, prescription medicines may be partly or wholly reimbursed by social security and/or your complementary insurance policy. You don't have to wait for a prescription to be 'made up' (as, for example, in the UK); medicines are pre-packaged and all a chemist has to do is find them, although some may be out of stock and need ordering. Many French doctors prescribe homeopathic medicines, stocked by all chemists, many of which specialise in homeopathy.

DENTISTS

There are excellent dentists (*dentiste*) throughout France, where there are around 330 dentists per 100,000 inhabitants – similar to Germany, Switzerland and the US, but fewer than Italy (550 per 100,000) and more than the UK (around 300). Few French dentists speak fluent English – 'Aaargh!' is the same in any language! Many embassies keep a list of dentists speaking their national language, and your employer, colleagues or neighbours may be able to recommend someone. Town halls maintain lists of local dentists, and local chemists may recommend someone or narrow the choice for you. You can obtain a list of dentists registered with social security from your local social security office.

Dentists are listed in the yellow pages under *Dentistes*. Usually only names, addresses and telephone numbers are listed, and information such as specialities, surgery hours and whether they treat children (some don't) isn't provided. Many 'family' dentists are qualified to perform non-routine treatment, e.g. endodontics (*endodontie*) or periodontics (*paradontie*), carried out by specialists in many other countries, but some treatment is available only from a 'surgeon dentist' (*chirurgien dentiste*).

Dentists also usually carry out routine teeth cleaning themselves, and hygienists are rare.

Dental treatment can be expensive, e.g. €1,500 for a crown fitted by a 'specialist', although the normal charge is between €300 and €600. A standard check-up costs €20, fillings (*reconstitution coronaire*) between around €15 and €35, and plaque removal (*détartrage*) around €30. There's no additional €1 charge as for doctor's consultations. As with doctors, however, you should check whether a dentist is *conventionné* if you want costs to be reimbursed (see **National Health System** on page 159). Social security pays 70 per cent of the cost of dental care and prosthetic treatment, e.g. crowns and bridges. For orthodontic work, which is generally restricted to children under 12, you must obtain a written description of the treatment required and an estimate of the cost for social security in advance and should be reimbursed 100 per cent of the cost.

These percentages apply to the theoretical cost of treatment as established by social security, which is often far lower than the actual cost. For example, the official cost of a crown is €107.50, so that the state will reimburse you only €75.25, whereas the cheapest crown usually costs around €350, and a ceramic crown can set you back up to €1,000 (dentists can charge what they like). You must pay the full cost of false teeth. Sometimes it pays to have private treatment, as social security pays dentists only a small amount for some jobs (such as cleaning teeth) and they're therefore less likely to do a thorough job.

Always obtain a written estimate before committing yourself to a large bill. If you or your family require expensive cosmetic dental treatment, e.g. crowns, bridges, braces or false teeth, it may be cheaper to have treatment abroad (e.g. in the UK). Alternatively, ask your dentist if he can reduce the cost by reducing the work involved.

Like doctors, dentists may give you a treatment form (*feuille de soins*), on which is listed the treatment provided and the cost. It's normal practice to pay a dentist after a course of treatment is completed, although if you're having expensive treatment such as a crown or bridge, you may be asked for a deposit.

OPTICIANS

There are no free eye tests for elderly people in France, where to obtain reimbursement (at 70 per cent) from social security it's necessary to have your eyes examined by an ophthalmologist (*ophtalmologue*), although you may have to wait weeks or even months for an appointment (the number of registered ophthalmologists is dwindling). An ophthalmologist is a specialist medical doctor trained in diagnosing and treating disorders of the eye, performing sight tests, and prescribing spectacles and contact lenses. As with doctors, some ophthalmologists are *conventionné*, meaning that they charge the basic rate of €27 for a consultation, whereas others (roughly half) aren't, which means that they charge more but you'll be reimbursed only at the basic rate. Treatment, including surgery, is reimbursed at just 65 per cent.

If spectacles are necessary, an ophthalmologist will write a prescription which you take to an optician (*opticien*). You must have your eyes tested by an ophthalmologist every three years but, since April 2007, opticians are allowed to test your eyes in the interim and adjust your prescription accordingly.

To be reimbursed, you must choose an optician who's approved (*agréé*) by social security. Social security pays for 65 per cent of the cost of lenses and a 'basic' frame, provided your vision has changed or your spectacles are broken beyond repair. Note, however, that the approved cost of a basic frame is a mere €2.84 and of standard lenses €7.32, so your social security refund may be as little as €6.60 (hardly worth the paperwork!). The balance may be picked up by a *mutuelle* if you have one. Larger refunds are available for contact lenses, bifocals or tinted lenses, but you may need prior approval from your *caisse*; if applicable, your optician will complete the necessary documents for social security.

Laser treatment for short-sightedness isn't reimbursed and costs between €250 and €400 per eye for the latest treatment.

Some opticians test eyes as well as supplying glasses but these aren't reimbursed by social security, although some *mutuelles* cover the cost of optician-prescribed glasses. In Paris and other cities, there are large optical chains where spectacles can be made within an hour. Prices for spectacles and contact lenses aren't controlled and are generally higher than in some other European countries (for example, soft contact lenses are cheaper in the UK and Germany), so it's wise to shop around and compare costs. The French generally prefer spectacles to contact lenses, as the former are often a fashion accessory (or even a fashion 'statement'), but both are widely available. Always obtain an estimate for lenses and ask about charges for eye tests, fittings, adjustments, lens-care kits and follow-up visits. Non-standard lenses can increase the cost of spectacles considerably. Ask the cost of replacement lenses; if they're expensive, it may be worthwhile taking out insurance. Many opticians and retailers provide insurance against accidental damage for a nominal fee.

It isn't necessary to register with an ophthalmologist or optician. You simply make an appointment with the optician of your choice. Ask your colleagues, friends or neighbours if they can recommend someone. Opticians are listed in the yellow pages under *Opticiens* and ophthalmologists under *Ophtalmologues*.

☑ **SURVIVAL TIP**

It's wise to have your eyes tested before you arrive in France and to bring a spare pair of spectacles and/or contact lenses with you. You should also bring a copy of your prescription in case you need to obtain replacement spectacles or contact lenses urgently.

MEDICAL TREATMENT ABROAD

If you're entitled to social security health benefits in France, you can take advantage of reciprocal healthcare agreements in other EU countries (as well as certain other countries, e.g. Algeria and Morocco). In some cases you must obtain a form (e.g. E101 and E106 for temporary workers) or a European Health Insurance Card (EHIC) from your CPAM before leaving France. Within the EU, the cost of treatment will normally be covered by the national health service of the country you're in. Outside the EU, full payment (possibly in cash) must usually be made in advance, although you may be reimbursed on your return to France (you must obtain detailed receipts).

Note that reimbursement is based on the cost of comparable treatment in France, which may be far below what you're charged abroad. In certain countries, e.g. Canada, Japan, Switzerland and the US, medical treatment is **very** expensive and you're advised to take out travel or holiday insurance (see page 217) when visiting these countries. In fact insurance is wise wherever you're travelling, as it provides considerably better medical cover than reciprocal healthcare agreements and includes many additional benefits such as repatriation. If you travel abroad frequently, it's worthwhile having an international health insurance policy (see page 221). Check also what cover is provided by your French bank's international credit card and your car insurance policy.

DYING IN FRANCE

When someone dies in France, the attending doctor completes a death certificate (*constatation de décès*), but the medical cause of death is treated as confidential and doesn't appear on death certificates. This can lead to problems if the body is to be sent abroad for burial, when a foreign coroner may require a post mortem examination. If a death takes place at home in Paris, a coroner (*médecin de l'état civil/médecin légiste*) must be called, although in the provinces a family doctor can complete the death certificate. An inquest (*enquête judiciaire*) must be held when a death occurs in a public place or when it could have been caused by a criminal act. In the case

of the death of a French resident, you should make several copies of a death certificate.

Anyone can register a death, but you must present your own identification and that of the deceased. If the deceased was a foreigner, the town hall will require his passport or *carte de séjour*. The family record book (*livret de famille*) is required for a French citizen. Deaths of foreign nationals in France should also be registered at your local consulate or embassy.

> A death must be registered within 24 hours at the town hall in the district where it took place.

Within a week of a death, you should inform banks, employer, retirement fund, insurers and *notaire*, as appropriate, as well as next of kin; within a month, a surviving spouse should apply for any pension refund (*réversion*); and within six months you should provide a *déclaration des revenus* (on form 2042N) to the tax office showing all the income of the deceased's household between 1st January last and the date of death. See also **Wills** on page 394.

Euthanasia is illegal in France, although the current Health Minister has vowed to press for its legalisation.

Burial & Cremation

Cemeteries (*cimetière*) are secular and are usually owned by local authorities, who license a local undertaker (*pompes funèbres*) to perform burials. Before a burial can take place, the town hall must issue an 'act of death' (*acte de décès*) and a burial or cremation permit (*permis d'inhumer/de crémation*), as well as a permit to transport the body if it's to be buried outside the commune. You also need the mayor's permission to be buried in the commune where you have a second home. You should obtain at least six copies of the *acte de décès*. Bodies are normally buried or cremated within six days of death.

It's possible to reserve a burial plot (*concession*) for 15, 30 or 50 years or indefinitely. (You can even dig your own grave if you wish!) If a plot hasn't been reserved, the body will be buried in communal ground (*terrain communal*), where graves are maintained free of charge by the local authority for five years. After this period, the remains are disinterred and buried in a common grave. You're allowed to erect any monument but are responsible for the upkeep of a grave. There may be a diagram at the entrance to a cemetery indicating which plots are reserved and for how long.

It's common for a coffin to be left uncovered while friends and relatives pay their last respects, and you should inform the undertakers if you want the coffin closed.

Until recently there weren't many crematoria (*crématoire*), although they can now be found in most large cities. You're entitled to scatter ashes anywhere except on a public right of way. Further information about funerals can be obtained from the Association Française d'Information Funéraire (www.afif.asso. fr).

Costs

Dying in France is expensive and is best avoided if at all possible. However, the cost has recently been reduced, at least in the Paris area, with the opening of 'supermarkets for the dead' by the Roc-Eclerc chain (www.roceclerc.com) – not without considerable opposition from undertakers. Always obtain a quotation (*devis*) for a funeral in advance and make sure you aren't paying for anything you

don't want. The cost of a basic funeral
is set by the commune and is usually
around €400 to €600, although the
average funeral costs around €1,000
and top-of-the-range funerals €3,000
(undertakers can bury you only once and
have to make the most of it!). Many people
take out an insurance policy to pay for
their funerals. Although banks will block
the deceased's accounts (unless joint
accounts), the next of kin may withdraw up
to €5,300 to pay for a funeral, on production
of the *acte de décès* and an undertaker's
bill. The spouse or partner of a person
who dies before retirement is also entitled
to a death benefit (*capital décès*) to offset
funeral costs, etc..

A 30-year burial plot can cost between
€150 and €500 depending on the area,
and a perpetual plot between €1,500 and
€4,000. The cost of cremation is around
half that of a burial, unless you want the
ashes scattered from a helicopter on top of
Mont Blanc!

8.
MONEY MATTERS

Moving to another country inevitably complicates the management of
your finances, although it can have advantages, such as paying less tax.
This chapter deals with transferring and changing money, banking and
obtaining a mortgage, French taxes and making a will for your French assets.

If you're planning to invest in property
in France that's financed with funds in a
non-euro currency (e.g. GB£ or US$), it's
important to consider both the present and
possible future exchange rates. If you need
to borrow money to buy property in France,
you should carefully consider where and in
what currency to raise finance.

 Caution

Bear in mind that if your pension or other
income is paid in a currency other than
euros it can be exposed to risks beyond
your control when you live in France,
particularly regarding inflation and
exchange rate fluctuations.

If you own a home in France, you can
employ a French accountant or tax adviser
to look after your financial affairs there and
declare and pay your local taxes. You can
also have your financial representative
receive your bank statements, ensure that
your bank is paying your standing orders
(e.g. for utilities and property taxes) and
that you have sufficient funds to pay them.
If you let a home in France through a
French company, it may perform the above
tasks as part of its services.

Foreigners, particularly retirees, often
under-estimate the cost of living and
some are forced to return to their home
countries after a year or two. You should
ensure that your income is (and will
remain) sufficient to live on, bearing in
mind devaluations (if your income isn't
paid in euros), rises in the cost of living
(see page 53), unforeseen expenses
such as medical bills and anything else
that may reduce your income (such as
stock market crashes and recessions!).

Although the French prefer to pay in
cash or by cheque or debit card rather
than use credit or charge cards, it's
wise to have at least one credit card
when visiting or living in France (Visa
and MasterCard are the most widely
accepted), although you should ensure
that you have a card with a microchip,
as 'swipe' cards are regarded with deep
suspicion by the French. Even if you
don't like credit cards and shun any
form of credit, they do have their uses,
for example no-deposit car rentals, no
pre-paying hotel bills (plus guaranteed
bookings), obtaining cash 24 hours a
day, simple telephone and mail-order
payments, greater security than cash and,
above all, convenience. Note, however,

that not all French businesses accept credit cards, even with a microchip.

FRENCH CURRENCY

The euro replaced the franc as France's official currency (*monnaie*) on 1st January 2002, though the franc, which is worth €0.15, continues to be the official currency of Monaco, French overseas territories, such as Guadeloupe and Martinique, and many former French colonies. Nevertheless, many people (even bank managers!) still automatically think and talk in francs, which they often call *balles*. In fact, some French people, and not just the elderly, sometimes talk in old francs (a hundred times smaller than a 'new' franc), which were abolished in 1958, particularly when discussing large numbers such as house prices. When house-buying in France, it pays to have an interpreter and a calculator handy!

The euro (€) is divided into 100 cents (nostalgically called *centimes* by the French) and coins are minted in values of 1, 2, 5, 10, 20, 50 *centimes*, €1 and €2. The 1, 2 and 5 *centimes* coins are brass-coloured, the 10, 20 and 50 *centimes* copper-coloured. The €1 coin is silver-coloured in the centre with a brass-coloured rim, and the €2 coin has a brass-coloured centre and silver-coloured rim. The reverse ('tail' showing the value) of euro coins is the same in all euro-zone countries, but the obverse ('head') is different in each country; French coins show Marianne, symbol of the Revolution, liberty, equality and fraternity, etc..

Euro banknotes (*billets*) are identical throughout the euro-zone and depict a map of Europe and stylised designs of buildings (because the original 12 countries couldn't agree which actual buildings should be shown!). Notes are printed in denominations of €10, €20, €50, €100, €200 and €500 (worth over £300 or $500!). The size of notes increases with their value (who said size doesn't matter?) and they've been produced using all the latest anti-counterfeiting devices. Nevertheless, euro notes are said to be the most counterfeited notes in the world and you should be particularly wary of €200 and €500 notes – if only because of the risk of losing them! Note that money is *argent* in French and *monnaie* means currency or change (*change* means exchange, as in *bureau de change*). To pay 'in cash' is *en espèces*, *en liquide* or *cash*.

The euro symbol may appear before the amount (as in this book), after it (commonly used by the French, who have been used to putting F after the amount) or even between the euros and centimes, e.g. 16€50. Values below one euro are invariably written using the euro symbol, e.g. €0,75 (the French put a comma and not a point before decimals), rather than with an American-style cent symbol.

It's wise to obtain some euro coins and banknotes before arriving in France and to familiarise yourself with them. You should have some euros in cash, e.g. €75 to €150 in small notes, when you arrive. This will save you having to change money on arrival at a French port or airport, although you shouldn't carry a lot of cash and should avoid high value notes, which sometimes aren't accepted, particularly for small purchases or on public transport.

IMPORTING & EXPORTING MONEY

Shop around for the best exchange rate and the lowest costs when transferring money to France. Banks are often willing to negotiate on fees and exchange rates when you're transferring a large amount of cash.

☑ SURVIVAL TIP

Don't be too optimistic about the exchange rate, which can change at short notice and can cost you tens of thousands of euros (or pounds or dollars) more than you planned.

It's possible to 'fix' the exchange rate to guard against unexpected devaluations by buying a 'forward time option' from your bank or through a specialised currency exchange firm such as those that advertise in the expatriate press (see **Appendix B**); the further in advance you buy, the more you pay. By fixing the exchange rate, you know exactly how much you'll have to pay, even over a long period (e.g. if you're having a house built), and won't have to worry about losing thousands of euros owing to a sudden change in the exchange rate. The downside (apart from the cost) is that you may regret doing so if there's a big swing in your favour!

If the exchange rate is poor and you're hoping it will improve before you need to pay for your home, you can buy a 'limit order'. You set a target exchange rate and a time limit. If that rate is achieved within the time limit, your money is exchanged at that rate; if it isn't, you must accept the current rate at the time of exchange, although you can pay for a 'stop loss order', which fixes the lowest rate you'll accept (the higher the minimum, the more the order costs).

Declaration

There are no limits on the import or export of funds to/from France, but sums in excess of €7,500 deposited abroad, other than by regular bank transfers, must be reported to the Banque de France. Similarly if you enter or leave France with €7,500 or more in French or foreign banknotes or securities (e.g. travellers' cheques, letters of credit, bills of exchange, bearer bonds, giro cheques, stock and share certificates, bullion, and gold or silver coins quoted on the official exchange), you must declare it to French customs. **If you exceed the €7,500 limit, you can be fined over €1,500**. If you send or receive any amount above €1,500 by post, it must be declared to customs. If you're a French resident, you may open a bank account in any country and export an unlimited amount of money from France; however, you must inform the French tax authorities of any new foreign account in your annual tax return.

Transfers

When transferring or sending money to (or from) France you should be aware of the alternatives available:

● **Bank draft (*chèque de banque*)** – A bank draft should be sent by registered post but, if it's lost or stolen, it's impossible to stop payment and you

must wait six months before a new draft can be issued. In France, bank drafts must be cleared, like personal cheques.

- **Bank transfer (*virement*)** – A 'normal' transfer should take three to seven days, but usually takes much longer, and an international bank transfer between non-affiliated banks can take weeks! (It's usually quicker and cheaper to transfer funds between branches of the same bank than between non-affiliated banks.) In fact, the larger the amount the longer it often takes, which can be particularly awkward when you're transferring money to buy a property.

- **SWIFT transfer** – One of the safest and fastest methods of transferring money is via the Society of Worldwide Interbank Financial Telecommunications (SWIFT) system. A SWIFT transfer should be completed in a few hours, funds being available within 24 hours, although even SWIFT transfers can take five working days, especially from small branches

that are not used to dealing with foreign transfers. Australian and British members of the SWIFT system are listed on the Society's website (www. swift.com). The cost of transfers varies considerably – not only commission and exchange rates, but also transfer charges – but is usually between around €30 and €50.

- **Currency dealer** – It may be quicker to use a specialist currency dealer to carry out the transfer for you, and you may obtain a better exchange rate than from a bank.

⚠ Caution

You should verify claims by companies that offer 'better exchange rates than banks', as these aren't always justified, and there may be hidden charges.

When you have money transferred to a bank in France, ensure that you give the name, account number, branch number (*code agence*) and the bank code (*clé*) – known as a bank's IBAN. Otherwise, your money can be 'lost' while being transferred to or from a French bank account and it can take weeks to locate it.

☑ **SURVIVAL TIP**

If you plan to send a large amount of money to France or abroad for a business transaction such as buying property, you should ensure you receive the commercial rate of exchange rather than the tourist rate.

Always check bank charges and exchange rates in advance and agree them with your bank (you may be able to negotiate a lower charge or a better exchange rate).

Note that it isn't wise to close your bank accounts abroad, unless you're certain that you won't need them in the future. Even if you're resident in France, it's cheaper to keep money in local currency in an account in a country that you visit regularly than to pay commission to convert euros. Many foreigners living in France maintain at least two accounts: a foreign bank account for international transactions and a local account with a French bank for day-to-day business.

BANKS

There are two main types of bank in France: commercial and co-operative. The largest commercial banks have branches in most large towns and cities and include the Banque Nationale de Paris (BNP Paribas), Crédit Lyonnais (now part of Crédit Agricole – see below) and Société Générale. All three have now been privatised and, in order to compete with other larger European banks, are intent on merging, the latest proposal being a union between BNP and Société Générale. Village banks are rare, although in many villages there are bank offices (*permanence*), which usually open only one morning a week.

The largest co-operative banks are Crédit Agricole, Crédit Mutuel and BRED Banque Populaire. They began life as regional, community-based institutions working for the mutual benefit of their clients, although most are now represented nationally and offer a full range of banking services. Unlike commercial banks, each branch office of a co-operative bank is independent and issues its own shares. Anyone can become a member and invest in their shares, which is usually mandatory if you wish to take out a mortgage or loan but isn't necessary to open a current account.

Crédit Agricole is the largest co-operative bank (and the biggest landholder) in France. It's the largest retail bank in Europe with around 10,000 branches and some 17m customers and has an English-language service (see **Foreign Banks** below). The top four French banks (Crédit Agricole, Crédit Lyonnais, Société Générale and BNP Paribas) are among the world's top ten banks. (In 2003, Crédit Agricole bought Crédit Lyonnais, which has, however, continued to trade as Crédit Lyonnais, albeit with fewer branches, many of which closed as a result of the take-over.)

The Banque de France is the authority which sets interest rates and regulates other banks; you cannot open an account with the Banque de France.

All banks, including foreign banks, are listed in the yellow pages under *Banques*. For further information about French banks, refer to *Living and Working in France* (Survival Books – see page 325).

Post Office Banking

As in many other countries, the most popular banking facility in France is operated by the post office (*La Poste*), which also offers some of the 'cheapest' banking. In terms of the amount of money handled, *La Poste* is the country's third-largest bank (after Crédit Agricole and Caisse d'Epargne – see below). In rural areas, where the nearest bank is often many kilometres away, many people use the post office as their local 'bank'. Another advantage of the post office is that many branches are open for longer hours than banks, although many aren't. Post office accounts provide the same services as bank accounts, including international money transfers (by post and telegraph to many countries) and payment of bills. Post office account holders are issued with a (free) cash card for withdrawals from cash machines (ATMs) located outside main post offices. Every transaction is confirmed with a receipt by post.

Savings Banks

There are also savings banks in France, the major bank being Caisse d'Epargne

with a network of over 400 regional institutions. Savings banks are similar to British building societies and American savings and loan organisations and offer savings schemes and loans for property and other purchases, although general banking services are limited compared with commercial and co-operative banks.

Foreign Banks

Foreign-owned banks in France number some 175 – more than in any other European country except the UK – although they have a small market share. However, competition from foreign banks is set to increase, as EU regulations allow any bank trading legitimately in one EU country to trade in another. Among foreigners in France, the British are best served by their national banks, both in Paris and in the provinces, particularly on the Côte d'Azur. The most prominent British bank is Barclays with around 100 branches, including at least one in all major cities. National Westminster has branches in most major cities, the Abbey National has around 12 branches, and Lloyds and HSBC one each (in Paris).

If you do a lot of travelling abroad or carry out international business transactions, you may find that the services provided by a foreign bank are more suited to your needs. They're also more likely to have staff who speak English and other foreign languages. Note, however, that many foreign banks (and some French banks) handle mainly corporate clients and don't provide banking services for individuals. And whereas most major foreign banks are present in Paris, branches are rare in the provinces.

The UK bank HSBC (formerly Midland) owns a French bank, CSF, and can therefore make life easy for Britons wishing to open an account in France without leaving home, as well as simplifying transfers between the UK and French accounts.

The Crédit Agricole has an English-language service, called 'Britline', based at its Caen branch (Lower Normandy), 15 esplanade Brillaud de Laujardière, 14050 Caen Cedex (☎ 02 31 55 67 89, 🖥 www. britline.com). Only some of its forms are printed in English, but an English-speaker always answers the telephone. Note, however, that branches of Crédit Agricole in other parts of France aren't familiar with dealing with Britline and, if you have an account in Caen, you cannot pay cheques into any branch outside Calvados.

Similarly, Barclays Bank has a branch offering an English-language service, at 15 rue Jeanne d'Arc, 76000 Rouen (☎ 02 35 71 70 63) and via its website (🖥 www. barclays.fr – in English; go to 'Destination France'). Some other French banks have English-language helplines, including the Charente-Périgord branch of Crédit Agricole (☎ 05 45 20 49 60).

Opening an Account

You can open a bank account in France whether you're a resident or a non-resident (see below). It's better to open a French bank account in person than by correspondence from abroad. Ask friends, neighbours or colleagues for their recommendations and just go to the bank of your choice and introduce yourself. You must be aged at least 18 and provide proof of identity, e.g. a passport (be prepared to produce other forms of identification), and of your address in France if applicable (an electricity bill usually suffices).

If you wish to open an account with a French bank while you're abroad, you must first obtain an application form, which is usually downloadable from the bank's website. You need to select a branch, which should be close to where you'll be living in France. If you open an account by correspondence, you must provide a reference from your current bank, including a certificate of signature or a signature witnessed by a solicitor. You also need a photocopy of the relevant pages of your passport and a euro draft to open the account.

Any account holder can create a joint account by giving his spouse (or anyone else) signatory authority. A joint account can be for two or more people. If applicable, you must state that cheques or withdrawal slips can be signed by any partner and don't require all signatures.

Non-residents

If you're a non-resident (i.e. spend at least six months per year outside France), you're only entitled to open a non-resident account (*compte non-résident*). There's little difference between non-resident and resident accounts and you can deposit and withdraw funds in any currency without limit, although there may be limits on the amount you can transfer between accounts (an anti-money-laundering measure). Non-resident accounts have a ban on ordinary overdrafts (*découverts*), although loans for a car or house purchase are often possible. Note, however, that banks are increasingly imposing minimum deposit levels on non-resident accounts and you may need €3,000 or more to open one, although it's unlikely that a bank will close an account if your balance subsequently falls below the opening level.

⚠ Caution

Note that in the event of the death of a partner, a joint account will be blocked until the will has been proven.

If you're a non-resident with a second home in France, it's possible to survive without a French account by using travellers' cheques and credit cards, although this isn't wise and is an expensive option. If you're a non-resident, you can have documentation (cheque books, statements, etc.) sent to an address abroad.

Residents

You're considered to be a resident of France if you have your main centre of interest there, i.e. you live or work there more or less permanently. To open a resident account you must usually have a residence permit (*carte de séjour*) or evidence that you have a job in France.

MORTGAGES

Mortgages or home loans (*hypothèque*) are available from all major French banks (for both residents and non-residents) and many foreign banks. The French post office also offers mortgages, but you must have been contributing to a *plan* or *compte d'épargne logement* (*PEL/CEL*) for at least 18 months to qualify. It's possible to obtain a foreign currency mortgage, other than in euros, e.g. GB£, Swiss francs or US$.

If you need to obtain a mortgage to buy a home in France, you should shop around and compare interest rates, terms and fees (which can be very high) from a number of banks and financial institutions – not just in France but also in your home country.

⚠ Caution

Bear in mind that mortgages in France are generally for a shorter period than in the UK and US, and therefore your repayments may be much higher.

It's generally recognised that you should take out a loan in the currency in which you're paid or in the currency of the country where a property is situated. In this case, if the foreign currency is devalued you'll have the consolation of knowing that the value of your French property will have increased by the same percentage when converted back into the foreign currency. When choosing between a euro loan and a foreign currency loan, be sure to take into account all costs, fees, interest rates and possible currency fluctuations. You should be extremely wary before taking out a foreign currency mortgage, as interest rate gains can be wiped out overnight by currency swings and devaluations.

However you finance the purchase of a second home in France, you should obtain professional advice from your bank manager and accountant. Most French banks offer euro mortgages on French property through foreign branches in EU and other countries. Most financial advisers recommend borrowing from a large reputable bank rather than a small one. Crédit Agricole is the largest French lender, with a 25 per cent share of the French mortgage market. UCB is part of the French BNP Paribas group and specialises in arranging mortgages for foreign buyers (in conjunction with the Abbey building society).

Both French and foreign lenders have tightened their lending criteria in the last few years as a result of the repayment problems experienced by many recession-hit borrowers in the early '90s. Some foreign lenders apply stricter rules than French lenders regarding income, employment and the type of property on which they will lend, although some are willing to lend more than a French lender. It can take some foreigners a long time to obtain a mortgage in France, particularly if they have neither a regular income nor assets there. Note also that it can be difficult for a single woman to obtain a mortgage in France.

It's possible to remortgage or take out a second mortgage on an existing property, either abroad or in France.

Types of Mortgage

Most French mortgages are repaid using the capital and interest (repayment) method (known as a *prêt amortissable*); endowment and pension-linked mortgages aren't normally offered, although it's possible to take out a *prêt in fine*, which is similar to an endowment mortgage in including a compulsory investment that 'matures' at the end of the mortgage term. Lenders are now also beginning to offer full-term interest-only mortgages. (Interest-only repayments were previously available for only the first ten years of a mortgage, followed by 5 to 15 years of capital repayment.) However, certain conditions apply – the loan must be for at least €100,000 and you must have assets worth at least one-and-a-half times the loan amount – and interest rates tend to be higher than with capital repayment mortgages.

Interest rates can be fixed or variable, the fixed rate being higher than the variable rate to reflect the increased risk to the lender. The advantage of a fixed rate is that you know exactly how much you must pay over the whole term. Variable rate loans may be fixed for the first two or more years, after which they're adjusted up or down on an annual basis in line with prevailing interest rates, but usually within preset limits, e.g. within 3 per cent of the original rate.

You can usually convert a variable rate mortgage to a fixed rate mortgage at any time. There's normally a redemption penalty, e.g. 3 per cent of the outstanding capital, for early repayment of a fixed rate mortgage, although that isn't usual for variable rate mortgages. If you think you may want to repay early, you should try to have the redemption penalty waived or reduced before signing the agreement.

An alternative to a *hypothèque* is a *privilège de prêteur de deniers* (*PDD*), which is marginally cheaper but has certain restrictions (e.g. you can only take out a *PDD* at the time of purchase and may not take out a *PDD* for more than the purchase price of a property).

Terms & Conditions

It's customary in France for a property to be held as security for a loan taken out on it; in other words, the property is 'owned' by the lender until the loan is repaid in full. However, some foreign banks won't lend on the security of a French property.

French law doesn't permit French banks to offer mortgages or other loans where repayments are more than 30 per cent of your net income. Joint incomes and liabilities are included when assessing a couple's borrowing limit (usually a French bank will lend to up to three joint borrowers). Note that the 30 per cent limit includes existing mortgage or rental payments, both in France and abroad. Earned income isn't included if you're aged over 65.

French mortgages are usually limited to 70 or 80 per cent of a property's value (although some lenders limit loans to just 50 per cent). A mortgage can include renovation work, when written quotations must be provided with a mortgage application. Note that you must add expenses and fees, totalling around 10 to 15 per cent of the purchase price on an 'old' property, i.e. one over five years old. For example, if you're buying a property for €75,000 and obtain an 80 per cent mortgage, you must pay a 20 per cent deposit (€15,000) plus 10 to 15 per cent fees (€7,500 to €11,250), making a total of €22,500 to €26,250.

Mortgages can be obtained for any period from 2 to 20 years, although the usual term is 15 years (some banks won't lend for longer than this). In certain cases mortgages can be arranged over terms of up to 25 years, although interest rates are higher and a mortgage must usually be paid off before you reach the age of 70 (in some cases 65). Generally the shorter the period of a loan, the lower the interest rate.

All lenders set minimum loans, e.g. €15,000 to €30,000, and some set minimum purchase prices. Usually there's no maximum loan amount, which is subject to status. As a condition of a French mortgage, you must take out a life (usually plus health and disability) insurance policy equal to 120 per cent of the amount borrowed. The premiums are included in mortgage payments. An existing insurance policy may be accepted, although it must be assigned to the lender. A medical examination may be required, although this isn't usual if you're under 50 years of age and borrowing less than €150,000. A borrower is responsible for obtaining building insurance (see page 215) on a property and must provide the lender with a certificate of insurance.

Fees

There are various fees associated with mortgages. All lenders charge an administration fee (*frais de dossier*) for setting up a loan, usually 1 per cent of the loan amount. There's usually a minimum fee, e.g. €350 plus VAT (*TVA*), and there may also be a maximum.

Although it's unusual for buyers to have a survey in France, foreign lenders usually insist on a 'valuation survey' (costing around €250) for French properties before they will grant a loan.

If a loan is obtained using a French property as security, additional fees and registration costs are payable to the notary (*notaire*) for registering the charge against the property at the *bureau des hypothèques*, which amounts to around 2.5 per cent of the amount borrowed.

If you borrow from a co-operative bank (see **Banks** on page 183), you're obliged to subscribe to the capital of the local bank. The amount (number of shares) is decided by the board of directors and you'll be sent share certificates (*certificat nominatif de parts sociales*) for that value. The payment (e.g. €75) is usually deducted from your account at the same time as the first mortgage repayment. When the loan has been repaid, the shares are reimbursed (if required).

Note that if you're resident in France and take out a foreign currency mortgage or are a non-resident with a euro mortgage, you must usually pay commission charges each time you make a mortgage payment or remit money to France.

However, some lenders will transfer mortgage payments to France each month free of charge or for a nominal amount.

If you're buying a new property off plan, when payments are made in stages, a bank will provide a 'staggered' loan, where the loan amount is advanced in instalments as required by the *contrat de réservation*. During the period before completion (*période d'anticipation*), interest is payable on a monthly basis on the amount advanced by the bank (plus insurance). When the final payment has been made and the loan is fully drawn, the mortgage enters its amortisation period (*période d'amortissement*), when payments are made as for a 'normal' mortgage.

TAXATION

An important consideration when you're planning to retire in France, even if you don't plan to live there permanently, is taxation, which includes property tax, wealth tax, capital gains tax (CGT) and inheritance tax. You'll also have to pay income tax if you live permanently in France or earn an income from a property there, even if you don't have a salaried job.

France is one of the highest taxed countries in the European Union (EU) when income tax, social security contributions, VAT (*TVA*) at 19.6 per cent and other indirect taxes are taken into consideration. If you aren't employed, however, you won't have to make social security contributions. Before deciding to retire in France permanently, you should obtain expert advice regarding French taxes. This will (hopefully) ensure that you take maximum advantage of your current tax status and that you don't make any mistakes that you'll regret later.

As you'd expect in a country with millions of bureaucrats, the French tax system is inordinately complicated and most French people don't understand it. It's difficult to obtain accurate information from the tax authorities and, just when you think you have it cracked, (ho! ho!) the authorities change the rules or hit you with a new tax. Taxes are levied at both national and local levels, although even 'national' taxes such as income tax are usually calculated and paid locally. (It's even possible to meet your tax man – or woman – if you should

so wish!) There's a five-year statute of limitations on the collection of taxes in France: i.e. if no action has been taken during this period to collect unpaid tax, it cannot be collected. On the other hand, late payment of any tax bill usually incurs a surcharge of 10 per cent.

INCOME TAX

Personal income tax (*impôt sur le revenu des personnes physiques/IRPP*) in France is below average for EU countries, particularly for large families, and accounts for only some 20 per cent of government revenue. The government has been reducing income tax levels for the past decade; on the other hand, social security contributions are constantly increasing, which means that average net income is a mere 50 per cent of gross salary.

Employees' income tax **isn't** deducted at source by employers in France (although the government is considering introducing such a system, in line with those of other EU countries), and individuals are responsible for declaring and paying their own income tax. Most taxpayers pay their tax a year in arrears in three instalments, although it can be paid in ten monthly instalments.

Tax is withheld at flat rates and at source only for non-residents who receive income from employment and professional activities in France, who must file a statement with the Centre des Impôts des Non-Résidents (9 rue d'Uzès, 75094 Paris Cedex 02, ☎ 01 44 76 18 00) each year.

Families are taxed as a single entity, although you can elect for a dependent child's income to be taxed separately if this is advantageous (a dependant's income up to a certain amount is exempt from income tax). The French income tax system favours the family, as the amount of income tax paid is directly related to the number of dependent children. Tax rates are based on a system of coefficients or 'parts' (*parts*), reflecting the family status of the taxpayer and the number of dependent children. The number of parts is known as the *quotient familial* (*QF*).

French law distinguishes between living with someone on an 'unofficial' basis (*en union libre*) and cohabiting with a spouse or 'official' partner (*en concubinage*). A partner can be made 'official' by entering into an agreement called a *pacte civil de solidarité* (*PACS*). If you live *en union libre*, you're treated for tax purposes as two single people, whereas if you live *en concubinage*, you're treated as a couple and are entitled to a number of tax advantages.

It's difficult to obtain accurate information from the tax authorities, and errors in tax assessments are commonplace.

The information below applies only to personal income tax (*Impôt sur le Revenu des Personnes physiques/ IRPP*) and not to company tax. A list of registered tax consultants is available from the Conseil Supérieur de l'Ordre des Experts-Comptables (🖥 www. experts-comptables.fr). Details of Franco-British tax consultants are available from the French Chamber of Commerce in London (UK ☎ 020-7304 4040). Unless your tax affairs are simple, it's prudent to employ an accountant (***expert comptable***) to complete your tax return and ensure that you're correctly assessed. In fact, a good accountant will help you (legally) to save more in taxes than you'll pay him in fees.

Many books are available to help you understand and save taxes, and income tax guides are published each January, including the *Guide Pratique du Contribuable*. The Service Public website (🖥 www.service-public.fr) also has extensive tax information under '*Impôt,* axe et douane'. If your French isn't up to deciphering tax terminology, refer to *Taxation in France* by Charles Parkinson (PKF Publications).

Liability

Your liability for French taxes depends on where you're domiciled. Your domicile is normally the country you regard as your permanent home and where you live most of the year. A person can be resident in more than one country at any given time, but can be domiciled only in one country. The domicile of a married person isn't necessarily the same as his spouse's but is determined using the same criteria as for anyone capable of having an independent domicile. Your country of domicile is particularly important regarding inheritance tax (see page 199).

Under the French tax code, domicile is decided under the 'tax home test' (foyer fiscal) or the 183-day rule. You're considered to be a French resident and liable to French tax if any of the following applies:

- Your permanent home, i.e. family or principal residence, is in France.

- You spend over 183 days in France during any calendar year.

- You carry out paid professional activities or employment in France, except when secondary to business activities conducted in another country.

- Your centre of economic interest, e.g. investments or business, is in France.

If you intend to live permanently in France, you should notify the tax authorities in your present country (you'll be asked to complete a form, e.g. a form P85 in the UK). You may be entitled to a tax refund if you depart during the tax year. The tax authorities may require evidence that you're leaving the country, e.g. evidence of having bought or rented a property in France. If you'll be undertaking paid work in France, you must register with the local tax authorities (Centre des Impôts) soon after your arrival.

Taxable Income & Exemptions

Income tax is calculated upon both earned income (*impôt sur le revenu*) and unearned income (*impôt des revenus de capitaux*). Pension income is taxable, but if you have an average or low income (e.g. a pension) and receive interest on bank deposits only, tax on unearned income won't apply, as it's deducted from bank interest before you receive it.

In general, single people earning less than €11,264 and couples earning less than €16,982 (2007) pay no income tax.

Taxation of Property Income

French income tax is payable on rental income (*revenu foncier*) from a French property, even if you live abroad and the money is paid there. All rental income must be declared to the French tax authorities, whether you let a property for a few weeks to a friend or 52 weeks a year on a commercial basis. For most letting income, you must complete Form 2044. Furnished property lettings are exempt from VAT, although you may need to charge clients VAT if you offer services such as bed and breakfast, a daily maid, linen or a reception service.

> The amount of tax you pay and the allowances you're eligible for depend on the type of letting you do as well as on your residence status, as detailed below.

Residents

Resident property owners are eligible for deductions such as repairs, maintenance, security and cleaning costs, mortgage interest (French loans only), management and letting expenses (e.g. advertising), local taxes, and an allowance to cover depreciation and insurance, unless they're claiming a fixed tax deduction (which should cover all the above). You should seek professional advice to ensure that you're claiming everything to which you're entitled. An additional tax called the *contribution additionelle à la contribution représentative du droit de bail* (*CACRDB*) is charged at 2.5 per cent. You should contact your local tax office to clarify your position (don't rely on your accountant).

If your net letting income is over €23,000 or comprises more than half the income of your household, you're considered to be a landlord and must make a business registration. This will also mean that you'll pay higher social security contributions.

If you run a *gîte* or B&B, you'll also normally be liable for *taxe professionelle*, although you may be granted exemption if you let for less than half the year and/or the property is also your principal residence.

Finally, if your property is over 15 years old, you may be liable for a letting tax called *contribution sur les revenus locatifs* (*CRL*).

Non-residents

Non-resident property owners who receive an income from a French source must file a tax return, *Déclaration des Revenus* (Cerfa 2042/2042C), available from local tax offices in France or French consulates abroad. Completed forms must be sent to the Centre des Impôts de Non-Résidents (9 rue d'Uzès, 75094 Paris Cedex 02, ☎ 01 44 76 18 00) before 30th April each year. It's wise to keep a copy of your return and send it by registered post (*lettre recommandée*) so that there's no dispute over whether it was received. Like residents, you can take advantage of various tax allowances, depending on the tax regime you choose or qualify for.

Some months after filing you'll receive a tax assessment detailing the tax due.

There are penalties for late filing and non-declaration, which can result in fines, high interest charges and even imprisonment. The tax authorities have many ways of detecting people who are letting homes and not paying tax and have been clamping down on tax evaders in recent years.

Non-residents must also declare any income received in France on their tax return in their country of residence, although tax on French letting income is normally paid only in France. However, if you pay less tax in France than you'd have paid in your home country, you must usually pay the difference. On the other hand, if you pay more tax in France than you'd have paid on the income in your home country, you aren't entitled to a refund!

Note that if you're a non-resident of France for tax purposes and own residential property there that's available for your use, you may be liable for French income tax on the basis of a deemed rental income equal to three times the real rental value of the property (usually calculated to be 5 per cent of its capital value). There are, however, exceptions, e.g. if you have French source income that exceeds this level or when you're protected by a double-taxation treaty. Consult a tax accountant to clarify your position.

⚠ Caution

There are severe penalties for failing to declare property income to the French tax authorities, who can impose tax on 52 weeks' letting income and cancel your entitlement to tax deductions in future.

Allowances

Your taxable income can be considerably reduced by allowances (*abattement*). These include social security payments, which aren't taxable, although the 'general

deduction' (*abattement général*) of 20 per cent on certain categories of income, including pensions and life annuities, applicable until 2007, has now been 'incorporated' in the tax rates (see below).

Those over 65 (in the relevant tax year) are entitled to a reduction of €2,202 if their taxable income is below €13,550 and of €1,101 if it's between €13,550 and €21,860; all these amounts are doubled for a couple if both are over 65. The figure you arrive at after deducting all allowances is your net taxable income (*revenu net imposable*) or 'tax base'.

Tax Rates

The income tax rates for a single person for 2007 income (2008 tax return) are shown in the table below. To calculate the taxable income for a couple without children, double the figures in the left column.

Reductions & Credits

Once you've calculated your tax due, you should deduct any reductions (*réductions*) or credits (*crédits*) to which you're eligible. For example, tax credits may apply to major expenditure on home improvements and VAT on major items of domestic equipment purchased from and installed by a VAT-registered company.

The self-employed should join their regional Association Agréé des Professions Libérales (commonly known as a *centre de gestion*), a government-sponsored body that regulates the income tax declarations of self-employed people, in order to benefit from tax reductions.

Income Tax Rates		
Taxable Income	**Tax Rate**	**Cumulative** Tax
Up to €5,614	0%	€0
€5,614 to €11,198	5.5%	€307.12
€11,198 to €24,872	14%	€2,221.48
€24,872 to €66,679	30%	€14,763.58
Over €66,679	40%	

Tax Return

You should be sent an annual tax return (*déclaration des revenus*) by the tax authorities in late February or early March of each year. If you aren't sent a form, you can obtain one from your local town hall or tax office (look in the telephone book under '*Impôts, Trésor Public*').

French tax returns are complicated, despite attempts to simplify them in recent years. The language used is particularly difficult to understand for foreigners (and many French people). You can make an appointment for a free consultation with your local tax inspector at your town hall. However, unless your French is excellent you'll need to take someone with you who's fluent. Local tax offices (Centre des Impôts) are usually helpful and will help you complete your tax return. The Centre des Impôts also offers assistance via telephone (☎ 08 20 32 42 52 – between 08.00 and 22.00 Mondays to Fridays and from 09.00 to 19.00 on Saturdays) and the internet (💻 www.impots.gouv.fr). Alternatively, you can employ a tax accountant (*expert comptable/ conseiller fiscal*).

Note that tax declarations can be made online, but not the first time you make a declaration in France; once you've been issued with a taxpayer number, you can use the online facility, which is free and allows you an extension of one to three weeks on the filing deadline.

If you pay income tax abroad, you must return the form uncompleted with evidence that you're domiciled abroad. Around a month later you should receive a statement from the French tax authorities stating that you have no tax to pay (*vous n'avez pas d'impôt à payer*). The French tax authorities may request copies of foreign tax returns. Americans who are going to be abroad on 15th April should ask for an Extension Form. Note that US income tax returns cannot be filed with the Internal Revenue Service (IRS) in Paris but must be sent to the IRS in the US. The information contained in IRS Publication 54, *Tax Guide for US Citizens and Resident Aliens Abroad*, is displayed on the IRS website (💻 www.irs.gov/publications/p54/ar01.html).

Tax returns must usually be filed by late April, though the exact date varies from year to year. **Late filing, even by one day, attracts a penalty of 10 per cent of the amount due.**

Payment

Some time between August and December, you'll receive a tax bill (*avis d'imposition*). There are two methods of paying your tax bill in France: in three instalments (*tiers provisionnels*) or in ten equal monthly instalments (*mensualisation*).

Note that you become liable for French tax as soon as you establish your principal residence in France (see **Liability** on page 191), which normally means the day you move into your French home. Therefore, if you arrive in France in September 2008, you won't make your first tax payment until September 2009, and then only for the last three or four months of the year 2008, so you won't need to pay any significant income tax until two years after your arrival, i.e. September 2010, although you may of course also be liable for tax in your previous country of residence for the first part of the year of your move.

WEALTH TAX

France imposes a wealth tax (*impôt sur la fortune/ISF*), which is payable by each 'fiscal unit' (*foyer fiscal*), e.g. couple or family, when its annual income exceeds €750,000. Wealth tax is assessed on the net value of your assets on 1st January each year and is payable by the following 15th June by French residents (15th July for other European residents and 15th August for all others). The rates shown below apply to 2007 assets.

Certain exemptions apply, e.g. PERP and PERCO savings plans, antiques and fine art, business assets (strictly defined) and income from long-term letting of rural property. If you're domiciled in France, the value of your estate is based on your worldwide assets. If you're resident in France but not domiciled there, the value of your estate is based on your assets in France only.

☑ **SURVIVAL TIP**

If you think you'll be liable for wealth tax, you should consult a tax expert, as there may be ways you can legally avoid it.

PROPERTY TAXES

There are four types of local property tax (*impôt local*) in France: *taxe d'habitation* (referred to here as 'residential tax'), *taxe foncière* (referred to as 'property tax'), *taxe assimilée* ('sundry tax') and *taxe professionelle* ('professional tax'). Taxes pay for local services, including rubbish collection, street lighting and cleaning, local schools and other community services, and include a contribution to departmental and regional expenses. You may be billed separately for rubbish collection. As professional tax applies only to those who use their homes as business premises, it isn't considered here.

Both residential and property taxes are payable whether a property is a main or a second home and whether the owner is a French or a foreign resident. Both taxes are

Wealth Tax		
Assets	**Rate**	**Cumulative Liability**
Up to €760,000	0%	€0
€760,000 to €1.22m	0.55%	€2,530
€1.22m to €2.42m	0.75%	€11,530
€2.42m to €3.80m	1.00%	€25,330
€3.80m to €7.27m	1.30%	€70,440
€7.27m to €15.81m	1.65%	€211,350
Over €15.81m	1.80%	

calculated according to a property's notional 'cadastral' rental value (*valeur locative cadastrale*), which is reviewed every six years. If you think a valuation is too high, you can contest it.

Property and residential taxes vary from area to area and are generally higher in cities and towns than in rural areas and small villages, where few community services are provided. They also vary with the type and size of property and will be significantly higher for a luxury villa than for a small apartment. If you're renting a property, check whether you're required to pay part of the **taxe foncière** as well as the **taxe d'habitation**.

Note that there's no reduction in either residential or property tax on a second home (*résidence secondaire*); in fact, your *taxe d'habitation* is likely to be higher, as there's a reduction for principal residences (*maison principale*).

Forms for the assessment of both residential and property tax are sent out by local councils and must be completed and returned to the regional tax office (Centre des Impôts) by a specified date, e.g. 15th November or 15th December for residential tax. They will calculate the tax due and send you a bill. You may be given up to two months to pay and a 10 per cent penalty is levied for late payment. It's possible to pay residential tax monthly (in ten equal instalments from January to October) by direct debit from a French bank account, which helps soften the blow.

Property Tax

Property tax (*taxe foncière*) is paid by owners of property in France and is similar to the property tax (or rates) levied in most countries. It's payable even if a property isn't inhabited, provided it's furnished and habitable. Property tax is levied on land, whether or not it's built on, and all 'shelters' for people or goods, including warehouses and houseboats (fixed mooring). The tax is

split into two amounts: one for the building (*taxe foncière bâtie*) and a smaller one for the land (*taxe foncière non bâtie*). Buildings and land used exclusively for agricultural or religious purposes, government and public buildings are exempt, and certain other exemptions apply (see below).

The amount of property tax payable varies by up to 500 per cent with the region, and even between towns or villages within the same region, and may be as little as €300 or as much as €1,500 per year for the same kind of property, although there are plans to make the application of the tax 'fairer'. Strangely, the Paris area has some of the country's lowest rates.

Note that many village properties are to be connected to mains drainage in the near future and owners will be charged a connection fee, which will be added to the *taxe foncière*; you should therefore check whether this will affect the property you plan to buy and, if so, what will be the cost.

Note also that, if you move permanently to France, you should notify the local Service du Cadastre (part of the Tax Office) **and** the local Trésorerie; otherwise, you may find that your first property tax bill is sent to your previous address (even if this is abroad) and, when you fail to pay (because you haven't received it), you're charged for late payment!

Exemptions

New and restored buildings used as main or second homes are exempt from property tax for two years from 1st January following the completion date (new houses and apartments financed by certain types of government loan or purchased by an association for letting to people on low incomes may be exempt for 10 or 15 years). An application for a temporary exemption from property tax must be made to your local property tax office (Centre des Impôts Fonciers) or Bureau du Cadastre before 31st December for exemption the following year. Applications must be made within 90 days of the completion of building work.

Certain people (e.g. those aged over 75 and those receiving a disability pension below a certain level) are exempt from property tax, and others (e.g. those over 65 on low incomes) may qualify for a discount (*allègement*) of around €100. If you sell a property part of the way through the year, the purchaser isn't legally required to reimburse you for a proportion of the property tax due (or paid) for that year. However, it's customary for property tax to be apportioned, by the notary handling the sale, between the seller and buyer from the date of the sale (a clause to that

effect should be included in the *promesse de vente*). Therefore, if you purchase a property in July, you'll normally be asked to 'reimburse' the vendor for half the annual property tax. Because you aren't obliged to do so, you can negotiate the amount (or the purchase price of the property), although you may not make yourself popular with the vendor!

Residential Tax

Residential tax (*taxe d'habitation*) is payable by the owner or (if different) occupier on 1st January of any habitable (i.e. furnished) property; this includes tenants and those staying in a property rent-free, although they may have an agreement with the owner whereby he pays the tax on their behalf.

 Caution

Note that, even if you vacate or sell a property on 2nd January, you must pay residential tax for the whole year and have no right to reclaim part of it from a new owner.

Residential tax is payable on residential properties (used as main or second homes), outbuildings (e.g. accommodation for servants, garages) located less than a kilometre from a residential property, and on business premises that are an indistinguishable part of a residential property. It's calculated on the living area of a property, including outbuildings, garages and amenities, and takes into account factors such as the quality of construction, location, renovations, services (e.g. mains water, electricity and gas) and amenities such as central heating, swimming pool, covered terrace and garage. Properties are ranked in eight categories ranging from 'very poor' to

However, residential tax isn't paid by residents whose income is below a certain level (e.g. €16,290 for a single person), nor by those over 60 whose income in the preceding year was below €10,993 (plus around €2,000 for each dependant).

Regional or Sundry Tax

In some areas – especially popular tourist resorts, where the local authorities must spend more than usual on amenities and the upkeep of towns – a regional or sundry tax (*taxe assimilée*) is levied.

CAPITAL GAINS TAX

Capital gains tax (*impôt sur les plus-values*) is payable on the profit from the sale of certain assets in France, including antiques, art and jewellery, securities and property. Gains net of capital gains tax (CGT) are added to other income and are liable to income tax (see page 189). Capital gains are also subject to social security contributions at 8 per cent. Changes to the capital gains regulations were made in the Finance Act, 2004, which also requires a *notaire* handling a property sale to calculate and pay CGT on behalf of the vendor.

Principal Residence

CGT isn't payable on a profit made on the sale of your principal residence in France, provided that you've occupied it since its purchase (or for at least five years if you didn't occupy it immediately after purchase). You're also exempt from CGT if you're forced to sell for family or professional reasons, e.g. you're transferred abroad by your employer. Income tax treaties usually provide that capital gains on property are taxable in the country where the property is located.

'luxurious'. Changes made to a building, such as improvements or enlargements, must be notified to the land registry within 90 days, as these can alter your tax category.

Residential tax is levied by the town where the property is located and varies by as much as 400 per cent from town to town. As with property tax (see above), the Paris area has some of the country's lowest rates. Generally, you should expect to pay around half the amount paid in *taxe foncière*. Residential tax is usually payable in autumn of the year to which it applies.

Exemptions

Only premises used exclusively for business, farming and student lodging are exempt from residential tax.

If you move to France permanently and retain a home in another country, this may affect your position regarding capital gains. If you sell your foreign home before moving to France, you'll be exempt from CGT, as it's your principal residence. However, if you establish your principal residence in France, the foreign property becomes a second home and is thus liable to CGT when it's sold. **Note that EU tax authorities may co-operate in tracking down CGT dodgers.**

Second Homes

Capital gains tax is payable, by both residents and non-residents, on profits of more than €20,000 per owner from the sale of a second home in France up to 15 years after purchase (until 2004, the period was 22 years). The basic rates of CGT are 26 per cent for residents, 16 per cent for non-resident citizens of EU countries, Norway or Iceland, and 33.3 per cent for non-resident citizens of other countries. Any inheritance or gift tax paid at the time of purchase is taken into account when determining the purchase price, and there are certain exemptions to the above tax rates, as follows:

● If you've owned a property for more than five years but less than 15, you're entitled to a 10 per cent reduction in CGT for every year of ownership over five (i.e. 10 per cent for six years' ownership, 20 per cent for seven years', etc.).

● If you've owned a property for at least five years and can produce proof of substantial expenditure on improving it (e.g. receipts for work done by professionals), you can claim a further deduction of 15 per cent of the property's purchase price against CGT (irrespective of the actual cost of the work), but you're no longer entitled to claim for work you've done yourself,

nor any materials purchased for DIY improvements.

⚠ Caution

The purchase price of a property is no longer 'indexed' to increases in the cost of living and, if you make a loss on the sale of a second home, you cannot claim this against other CGT payments, nor against income tax!

Before a sale, the *notaire* prepares a form calculating the tax due and appoints an agent (*agent fiscal accrédité*) or guarantor to act on your behalf concerning tax. If the transaction is straightforward, the local tax office may grant a dispensation (*dispense*) of the need to appoint a guarantor, provided you apply **before** completion of the sale. If you obtain a dispensation, the proceeds of the sale can be released to you in full after CGT has been paid. The *notaire* handling the sale must apply for the dispensation and must declare and pay CGT on your behalf; you're no longer required to make a CGT declaration.

INHERITANCE & GIFT TAX

As in most other developed countries, giving away your assets, either while you're living or when you die, doesn't free you (or your inheritors) from the clutches of French tax inspectors. France imposes both gift and inheritance taxes on its inhabitants, as detailed below.

Inheritance Tax

Inheritance tax (*droits de succession*), called estate tax or death duty in some countries, is levied on the estate of a deceased person. Both residents and non-residents are subject to inheritance tax if they own property in France. The country where you pay inheritance tax is decided by your domicile (see **Liability** on page

191). If you're living permanently in France at the time of your death, you'll be deemed to be domiciled there by the French tax authorities. If you're domiciled in France, inheritance tax applies to your world-wide estate (excluding property); otherwise it applies only to assets located in France. It's important to make your domicile clear, so that there's no misunderstanding on your death.

When a person dies in France, an estate tax return (*déclaration de succession*) must be filed within six months of the date of death (within 12 months if the death occurred outside France). The return is generally prepared in France by a notary. Any tax due may be paid in instalments over five or, in certain cases, ten years.

The rate of tax and allowances varies according to the relationship between the beneficiary and the deceased. French succession laws have traditionally been restrictive compared with those in many other countries, but they're gradually being relaxed. If a married couple have shared ownership of a property (see **Avoiding Inheritance Tax** below), no inheritance tax is payable on the death of the first spouse. If they don't, inheritance tax is payable on the 'inheritance' of the deceased spouse's share of the property to the surviving spouse and children. However, the surviving spouse has an allowance (*abattement*) of €76,000 and the children each have an allowance of €50,000 – in addition to which there's a 'global' allowance of €50,000 to be shared between the surviving spouse and children. After the relevant allowance has been deducted, inheritance tax is payable at the rates shown in the table below.

Note that it's the individual beneficiaries who are taxed on their share of the inheritance and not the estate which is taxed (as in the UK, for example). Note also that since January 2007 a child has been able to renounce his share in favour of a sibling or his own children, who will thus inherit tax-free from their grandparents. Childless couples may nominate brothers, sisters, nephews or nieces as heirs and any person may now make a tax-free legacy of up to €5,000 to brothers and sisters.

Unmarried couples with a French *PACS* agreement qualify for an allowance of €57,000 (the limitation that the agreement had to be in place for at least two years no longer applies). Inheritances from a deceased *PACS* partner above that amount are taxed at 40 per cent up to

Inheritance Tax Allowances		
Spouse	**Children**	**Tax Rate**
Up to €7,600	Up to €7,600	5%
€7,600 to €15,000	€7,600 to €11,400	10%
€15,000 to €30,000	€11,400 to €15,000	15%
€30,000 to €520,000	€15,000 to €520,000	20%
€520,000 to €850,000	€520,000 to €850,000	30%
€850,000 to €1.7m	€850,000 to €1.7m	35%
Above €1.7m	Above €1.7m	40%

€15,000 and at 50 per cent above €15,000. It's expected that these allowances will be extended to cover those who enter into a similar relationship outside France.

If you've been resident in France for more than six years and receive an inheritance from abroad, you're subject to French inheritance tax.

You may make tax-free gifts every ten years to a spouse (up to €76,000), child (up to €46,000) or grandchild (up to €30,000). Each of these figures is increased by €46,000 if the recipient is handicapped. To brothers, sisters, nephews, nieces and grandchildren you may make a single tax-free gift of up to €5,000. Gift tax is payable on gifts made between spouses in France, so assets should be equally shared before you're domiciled there.

Gift tax (*droits de donation*) is calculated in the same way as inheritance tax (see above), according to the relationship between the donor and the recipient and the size of the gift, although there's a reduction of 50 per cent if the donor is aged over 70 and 35 per cent if over 80. Any gifts made within six years of the death of the donor (*en avancement d'horie*) must be included in the inheritance tax return and are valued at the time of death rather than at the time of donation.

Payment of gift tax can be spread over a number of years, except in the case of the donation of a business.

Avoiding Inheritance Tax

It's important to understand French inheritance laws, which apply to both residents and non-residents with property in France.

First, property is divided into 'movable' and 'immovable' property: *meubles*, including not only furniture but all belongings except land and buildings,

and *immeubles*, including land and buildings. Immovable property must be handed down to your heirs (disposed of) in accordance with French law, irrespective of whether you're resident or non-resident in France, whereas movable property is subject to French law only if you're resident (or spend the majority of your time) in France.

Second, all property subject to French law is divided into a 'disposable part' (*quotité disponible*) and a 'heritary part' (*réserve héréditaire*). Irrespective of your will(s), the hereditary part **must** be disposed of according to French law. The size of the hereditary part depends on how many children you have. If you have one child, half of your affected property must be left to the child; if you have two children, they must inherit two-thirds; three or more children three-quarters. If you have no children, surviving parents or grandparents no longer (from January

2007) automatically inherit, although they can be made beneficiaries in a will.

A couple's marital status is also of relevance to inheritance. French couples normally enter into a marriage contract, whereby their assets are either shared (*communauté universelle*) or owned separately (*séparation de biens*). Foreign couples who don't have a marriage contract will normally be regarded as having separate ownership unless they state otherwise in the property purchase contract. It's important to do so because otherwise, if one spouse dies, the other retains ownership only of his half of the property and the deceased's part is disposed of as explained above, the beneficiaries being subject to inheritance tax (see page 199). If, on the other hand, you've specified that your marital 'arrangement' is similar to the French *communauté universelle*, ownership of all property will pass to the surviving spouse on the death of the other and the surviving spouse will be exempt from inheritance tax, although there may be a small fee (e.g. 1 or 2 per cent of the property's value) for the re-registration of the property in the surviving spouse's name. Note that since January 2007 married couples with stepchildren or 'illegitimate' children can adopt shared ownership, which wasn't previously possible.

If you don't have shared ownership, you can limit or delay the impact of French inheritance by inserting a *clause tontine* into the purchase contract. The *clause tontine* (or *pacte tontinier*) – an obscure law relating to an archaic finding system set up by an Italian banker in the 17th century and hardly used by French people – allows a property to be left entirely to a surviving spouse and not shared among the children. Because it places the entire inheritance tax burden on the surviving spouse, rather than sharing it among the spouse and children, it's particularly advantageous for inexpensive properties; with more expensive property, it may be advantageous only for married couples, who are entitled to higher inheritance tax allowances (see above). In any case, a *clause tontine* is likely to be valid only if both spouses have a similar life expectancy (otherwise, it could be argued that it was used expressly as a way of disinheriting children). Another consideration to be made before using a *clause tontine* is that, if you want to sell the property but your spouse objects, there's nothing you can do to force a sale; for this reason French *notaires* generally dislike the *clause tontine*.

A surviving spouse can also be given a life interest (*usufruit*) in an estate in priority to children or parents through a gift between spouses (*donation entre époux*). This is also known as a 'cross-purchase' (*achat croisé*). This means that the spouse may occupy the property for life and take any income generated by it but may not sell or otherwise dispose of it; on the other hand, the property cannot be sold or otherwise disposed of without the spouse's consent. A gift between spouses therefore delays the inheritance of an estate by any surviving children, who will have a 'reversionary interest' (*nue-propriété*) in it, i.e. ownership reverts to them on the death of the spouse. A *donation* must be prepared by a *notaire* and signed in the presence of the donor

Château de Chenonceau, Loire Valley

and the beneficiary. You must take along your passports, marriage certificate, birth certificates, *titres de séjour* (if applicable) and evidence of your address and occupations; a *donation entre époux* costs around e160. **It may not apply to non-residents, who are normally governed by the law of their home country.**

Note that French law doesn't recognise the rights to inheritance of an unmarried partner, unless a *PACS* agreement has been signed, although there are a number of solutions to this problem, e.g. a life insurance policy.

Another way to reduce your inheritance liability is to make a *donation partage* to your children or (from January 2007) stepchildren or grandchildren or (if you have none of these) to brothers, sisters, nephews or nieces, although gift tax will be payable (see above). It's even possible to make a gift or legacy to a child with the instruction that the asset concerned be passed to his child or children on his death – an arrangement similar to a British trust. You can also register your home in your child(ren)'s name(s).

In the latter case, however, if a child dies before you or divorces, part of your home will count among the child's assets, which could make matters **very** complicated. **Seek expert advice before registering a property in children's names.**

Finally, you might consider buying property through a company (see **Buying Through a Company** on page 245).

Whatever your marital situation, it's important to make a French will (even if you already have a foreign will that's valid in France), which can help to reduce your French inheritance tax liability or delay its payment.

 Caution

French inheritance law is an extremely complicated subject, and professional advice should be sought from an experienced lawyer who understands both French law and that of any other country involved.

WILLS

It's an unfortunate fact of life that you're unable to take your hard-earned assets with you when you take your final bow. All adults should make a will (*testament*), irrespective of how large or small their assets. The disposal of your estate depends on your country of domicile (see **Inheritance & Gift Tax** above). As a general rule, French law permits a foreigner who **isn't** domiciled in France to make a will in any language and under the law of any country, provided it's valid under the law of that country.

Note, however, that 'immovable' property (*immeubles*) in France, i.e. land and buildings, must be handed down (on death) in accordance with French law. All other property in France or elsewhere (defined as 'movables' – *meubles*) may be disposed of in accordance with the law of your

country of domicile. Therefore, it's extremely important to establish where you're domiciled under French law. A possibility for a non-resident who wishes to avoid French inheritance laws regarding immovable property located in France is to buy it through a French holding company, in which case the shares of the company are 'movable' assets and are therefore governed by the succession laws of the owner's country of domicile.

The part of a property that must be inherited by certain heirs (*héritiers réservataires*) is called the legal reserve (*réserve legale*). Once the reserved portion of your estate has been determined, the remaining portion is freely disposable (*quotité disponible*). French law is restrictive regarding *héritiers réservataires* and gives priority to children, including illegitimate and adopted children, although changes to inheritance law which came into force in January 2007 removed the entitlement of the living parent(s) of a deceased person to inherit in preference to a spouse.

Under French law (*code Napoléon*) you cannot disinherit your children, who have first claim on your estate, even before a surviving spouse. However, a surviving spouse has the right to at least a quarter of an inheritance: if you die leaving one child, he must inherit half of your French estate, and two children must inherit at least two-thirds; if you have three or more children, they must inherit three-quarters of your estate. There are, however, many legal ways to safeguard the rights of a surviving spouse, some of which are mentioned above under **Avoiding Inheritance Tax**. If a couple has no surviving children, the deceased's spouse inherits the whole estate apart from family possessions, half of which must go to any surviving brothers or sisters of the deceased. Only when there are no descendants or ascendants is the whole estate freely disposable – or in the unlikely event that an heir signs a *pacte successorale* renouncing his entitlement in favour of someone else (e.g. a child or grandchild).

Note the following information regarding wills in France:

● In France, marriage doesn't automatically revoke a will, as in some other countries, e.g. the UK.

● Wills aren't made public in France and aren't available for inspection.

● **Where applicable, the rules relating to witnesses are strict; if they aren't followed precisely, a will may be rendered null and void.**

● Under French law, the role of the executor is different from that in many other countries; his duties are supervisory only and last for a year and a day. He's responsible for paying your debts and distributing the balance of the inheritance in accordance with your will. The executor who's dealing with your affairs in France must file a *déclaration de succession* within a year of your death. At your death your property passes directly to your heirs and it's their responsibility to pay inheritance tax and any debts relating to that property. Winding up an estate takes much longer than in many other countries and usually isn't given priority by *notaires*.

● You should keep a copy of your will(s) in a safe place and another copy with your solicitor or the executor of your estate. Don't leave them in a bank safe deposit box, which in the event of your death is sealed for a period under French law. Keep information regarding bank accounts, pensions and benefits, investments and insurance policies with your will(s), but don't forget to tell someone where they are! You should also make a separate note of your last wishes (e.g. regarding funeral arrangements) where your next-of-kin can find it immediately after your death, along with your social security number, birth, marriage, divorce and spouse's death certificates (as applicable) and the names and whereabouts of any children.

> ☑ SURVIVAL TIP
>
> French inheritance law is a complicated subject and it's important to obtain professional legal advice when writing or altering a will.

It's possible to make two wills, one relating to French property and the other to foreign property. Opinion differs on whether you should have separate wills for French and foreign property, or a foreign will with a codicil (appendix) dealing with your French property (or vice versa). However, most experts believe it's better to have a French will from the point of view of winding up your French estate (and a will for any country where you own immovable property). **If you have French and foreign wills, make sure that they don't contradict one another (or, worse, cancel each other out, e.g. when a will contains a clause revoking all other wills).**

Types of Will

There are three kinds of will in France: holographic (*olographe*), authentic (*authentique*) and secret (*mystique*), described below.

Holographic Will

The most common form of will used in France. It must be written by hand by the person making the will and be signed and dated by him. No witnesses or other formalities are required. In fact it shouldn't be witnessed at all, as this may complicate matters. It can be written in English or another language, although it's preferable if it's written in French (you can ask a *notaire* to prepare a draft and write a copy). A holographic will must be handed to a *notaire* for filing. He sends a copy to the local district court, where the estate is administered. A holographic will can be registered in the central wills registry (*fichier de dernières volontés*). For anyone with a modest French estate, e.g. a small second home in France, a holographic will is sufficient.

Authentic or Notarial Will

This is used by some 5 per cent of French people. It must be drawn up by a *notaire* in the form of a notarial document and can be handwritten or typed. It's dictated by the person making the will and must be witnessed by two *notaires* or a *notaire* and two other witnesses. Unlike a holographic will, an authentic will is automatically registered in the central wills registry. An authentic will costs around e80.

Secret Will

A secret will is rarely used and is a will written by or for the person making it and signed by him. It's sealed in an envelope in the presence of two witnesses. It's then given to a *notaire*, who records on the envelope that it has been handed to him and that the testator has affirmed that the envelope contains his will. The *notaire* then files the will and sends a copy to the local district court where the estate is administered.

Villefrance-sur-mer, Alpes-Maritimes

9.
PEACE OF MIND: INSURANCE

An important consideration when planning to retire to France is insurance (*assurance*), not only for your home and its contents, but also for you and your family when you're spending time there. It's unnecessary to spend half your income insuring yourself against every eventuality from the common cold to being sued for your last *centime*, but it's important to insure against any event that could precipitate a major financial disaster, such as a serious illness or accident or your house falling down.

When buying insurance, shop till you drop! Obtain recommendations from friends and neighbours, and compare the costs, terms and benefits provided by a number of companies before making a decision.

> ☑ SURVIVAL TIP
>
> Simply collecting a few brochures from insurance agents or making a few telephone calls could save you a lot of money.

Further information about insurance can be found on the Service Public website (🖥 www.service-public.fr) and from the Fédération Française des Sociétés d'Assurances (🖥 www.ffsa.fr).

CAR INSURANCE

As in most other countries, car insurance is essential in France and driving without it is a serious offence, for which you can be fined up to €7,500 and imprisoned for up to six months. All imported motor vehicles plus trailers and semi-trailers must also be insured. If you arrive in France with a vehicle without valid insurance, you can buy a temporary policy valid for 8, 15 or 30 days from the vehicle insurance department of the French customs office at your point of entry. However, motorists insured in an EU country or Liechtenstein, Norway or Switzerland are automatically covered for third-party liability in France (see **Green Card** below). The following categories of car insurance are available in France:

● **Third-party** – Third-party insurance (known variously as *assurance responsabilité civile/minimale/tiers illimitée/au tiers*) is the minimum required by law in France and includes unlimited medical costs and damage to third-party property.

- **Third-party, Fire & Theft** – Third-party, fire and theft (TPF&T; *assurance tiers personnes/restreinte/intermédiaire/vol et incendie*) insurance, which is known in some countries as part comprehensive, includes cover against fire, natural hazards (e.g. rocks falling on your car), theft and legal expenses (*défense-recours*). TPF&T includes damage to (or theft of) contents and radio.

- **Multi-risk Collision** – Multi-risk collision (*multirisque collision*) covers all risks listed under TPF&T (see above) plus damage caused to your own vehicle in the event of a collision with a person, vehicle, or animal belonging to an 'identifiable person'.

- **Comprehensive** – Comprehensive insurance (*multirisque tous accidents/tous risques*) covers all the risks listed under TPF&T and multi-risk collision (see above) and includes damage to your vehicle however caused and whether a third party can be identified or not. Note, however, that illegally parked cars automatically lose their comprehensive cover. Comprehensive insurance is usually compulsory for lease and credit-purchase contracts.

Glass breakage (*bris de glace*) is often included in TPF&T comprehensive insurance, but you should check, as there may be an additional premium. Driver protection (*protection du conducteur/assurance conducteur*) is usually optional. It enables the driver of a vehicle involved in an accident to claim for bodily injury to himself, including compensation for his incapacity to work or for his beneficiaries should he be killed. However, if you have an accident while breaking the law, e.g. drunken driving or illegal parking, your comprehensive insurance may be automatically downgraded to third party only – or nullified altogether. This means that you must pay for your own repairs and medical expenses, which can be **very** expensive.

You should also check whether your insurance policy covers items stolen from your car.

 Caution

When motoring in France (or anywhere else), don't assume that your valuables are safe in the boot of your car, particularly if the boot can be opened from the inside.

Green Card

Although all motorists insured in an EU country or Liechtenstein, Norway or Switzerland are automatically covered for third-party liability in France, British motorists should note that British insurance companies usually insist on your applying for a certificate of motor insurance (commonly known as a 'green card') if you're driving in France (or any other European country). Note also that most companies will issue a green card for a maximum of 90 days per year. (This is because British insurers know that you're far more likely to have an accident when driving on the right!) Nevertheless, you should shop around, as some companies allow drivers a green card for up to six months a year. Another way round the restriction is to return to the UK for at least 24 hours after 90 days and obtain another green card!

If you're British and have comprehensive insurance, a green card is essential, as it extends your comprehensive insurance abroad; otherwise you may be insured only for third-party liability. There's usually no charge for a green card for a short period abroad (e.g. up to five days) but thereafter there may be a small charge (e.g. around £1 per day).

and receive a definitive contract (*police définitive*) a few weeks later. With the contract is a green tear-off tab (*vignette*), which you must display in the windscreen of your vehicle as confirmation of insurance (*attestation d'assurance*). A *vignette* holder is usually provided. Each tab is valid for a limited period (e.g. six months) and you're sent a replacement automatically (provided you've paid your premiums!). Non-display of the tab, even if it has fallen off the windscreen and is in the car, can result in a fine of around €150. You must also sign the updated insurance document (to which the *vignette* is attached) on the back and carry it when driving. It isn't necessary to sign the *vignette*, although some French policemen claim that this is a requirement and attempt to fine drivers who fail to do so!

If you drive a British-registered car and spend over three (or six) months a year on the continent, you may need to take out a special (i.e. expensive) European insurance policy or obtain insurance with a European company. If you wish to import a foreign-registered car into France permanently, you may find that your (foreign) insurance company will refuse to insure it, although since 1st January 1993, EU residents can theoretically insure their cars in any EU country. A French insurance company may insure it, but usually for a limited period only, so you may have no option but to buy a new car in France.

All French insurance companies provide an automatic green card (*carte internationale d'assurance automobile/carte verte* – even though it's yellow in France!), extending your normal insurance cover to most other European countries.

Contracts

You'll initially be given a provisional insurance contract (*police d'assurance provisoire*) by a French insurer or broker

Premiums

Insurance premiums are high in France – a reflection of the high accident rate, the large number of stolen and vandalised cars, and the high taxes (around 35 per cent) levied on car insurance. Premiums vary considerably according to numerous factors, including the type of insurance and car, your age and accident record, and where you live. For example, premiums are highest in Paris and other cities and lowest in rural areas; they're lower for cars over three years old, while drivers with less than three years' experience usually pay a 'penalty' and drivers under 25 pay higher premiums. However, the maximum penalty for young drivers is 100 per cent or double the normal premium. A surcharge is usually made when a car isn't garaged overnight. Some premiums are based on the number of kilometres (*kilométrage*) driven each year. Value added tax (*TVA*) at 19.6 per cent is payable on insurance premiums.

Always shop around and obtain a number of quotations. You can reduce your premium by choosing to pay a higher excess (*franchise*), e.g. the first €300 to

€750 of a claim instead of the usual €125 to €250. It's possible to insure a vehicle for less than a year (e.g. three months) and you can also insure a vehicle for a single journey over 1,000km (620mi).

If you're convicted of drunken or dangerous driving, your premium will be increased considerably, e.g. by up to 150 per cent. Separate insurance can be purchased for contents and accessories such as an expensive car stereo system.

A car with a value of over €15,250 must have an approved alarm installed and the registration number must be engraved on all windows.

No-claims Bonus

A foreign no-claims bonus is usually valid in France, but you must provide written evidence from your present or previous insurance company, not just an insurance renewal notice. You may also need an official translation. Always insist on having your no-claims bonus recognised, even if you don't receive the same reduction as you received abroad (shop around!). If you haven't held car insurance for two years, you're usually no longer entitled to a no-claims bonus in France.

A French no-claims bonus isn't as generous as those in some other countries and is usually 5 per cent for each year's accident-free driving up to a maximum of 50 per cent after ten years. If you have an accident for which you're responsible, you're usually required to pay a penalty (*malus*) or your bonus (*bonus*) is reduced. Your premium will be increased by 25 per cent each time you're responsible for an accident or 12.5 per cent if you're partly to blame, up to a maximum premium three-and-a-half times the standard premium. If you're judged to be less than 30 per cent responsible, you won't usually lose your no-claims bonus.

However, if you've had the maximum bonus for three years, one accident won't reduce it even if you were at fault. All penalties are cancelled if you have no accidents for two years. There's no premium increase if your car is damaged while legally parked (although you must be able to prove it and identify the party responsible) or as a result of fire or theft, and you should still receive your bonus for the current year. The same normally applies to glass breakage.

Claims

In the event of an accident, claims are decided on the information provided in accident report forms (*constat amiable d'accident de voiture/constat européen d'accident*) completed by drivers, as well as in reports by insurance company experts and police reports. You must notify your insurance company of a claim resulting from an accident within a limited period, e.g. two to five days. In the case of a stolen car report, 30 days must elapse before an insurance company will consider a claim. **It often takes a long time – even years! – for claims to be resolved in France**.

If your car is damaged in an accident, you may take it to any reputable repairer (*carrosserie*), where the damage must usually be inspected and the repair sanctioned by your insurance company's assessor (*expert*), although sometimes an independent assessment may be permitted. Assessors normally visit different repairers on different days of the week, so you should arrange to take your car on the relevant day. (Some assessors have a weekly 'clinic' at their office where you can have damage inspected.) You should tell your insurer at least a day in advance so that he can advise the assessor. You may then be able to leave the car with the repairer or you may have to return it another day

for the repair to be carried out. For minor repairs, an inspection may be unnecessary.

Cancellation

French insurance companies are forbidden by law to cancel third-party cover after a claim, except in the case of drunken driving or when a driver is subsequently disqualified from driving for longer than a month. A company can, however, refuse to renew your policy at the end of the current contract period, although it must give you two months' notice. If you find it difficult to obtain cover, the Bureau Central de Tarification can demand that the company of your choice provide you with cover, the premium being fixed by the Bureau.

Like other French insurance policies, a car insurance policy is automatically renewed annually unless you cancel it (*résilier*) in writing, and you must do so at least two months before the end of your annual insurance period, although the notice period is sometimes a month and in a few cases three months, so you must check. You may cancel your insurance without notice if the premium is increased by more than the official index (*indice*), based on the Index of Construction Costs published by INSEE, the terms are altered, or your car has been declared a write-off or stolen. Policies can also be cancelled without notice for certain personal reasons, such as moving house, a change of job, divorce and retirement. Standard cancellation letters (*lettre type de résiliation*) are usually provided by insurance companies and brokers.

Breakdown Insurance

Breakdown insurance (*assurance dépannage*) is provided by car insurance companies and motoring organisations. If you're motoring abroad or you live abroad and are motoring in France, it's important to have breakdown insurance (which may include limited holiday and travel insurance – see page 217), including repatriation for your family and your car in the event of an accident or breakdown. Most foreign breakdown companies provide multi-lingual, 24-hour centres where assistance is available for motoring, medical, legal and travel problems. Some organisations also provide economical annual motoring policies for those who frequently travel abroad, e.g. owners of holiday homes in France.

⚠ Caution

If your car is registered outside France, you may be unable to obtain breakdown insurance from a French insurance company.

French insurance companies provide an optional accident and breakdown service (*contrat d'assistance*) for policyholders for around €30 per year, which is adopted by some 90 per cent of French motorists. The breakdown service usually covers the policyholder, his spouse, single dependent children, and parents and grandparents living under the same roof. The 24-hour telephone number of the breakdown

service's head office is shown on the insurance tab affixed to your windscreen. If you break down anywhere in France, you simply call the emergency number and give your location, and a recovery vehicle is sent to your aid.

Although accidents are covered anywhere in France, in the event of a breakdown you need to be at least a certain distance from your home, e.g. 25 or 50km (15 to 30mi). The service provides for towing your vehicle to the nearest garage and contributes towards the expenses incurred as a result of a breakdown or an accident, e.g. alternative transport and hotel bills. If your car is unusable for more than 48 hours in France or more than five days abroad, your insurance company will usually pay for alternative transport home, e.g. first-class rail travel or car hire in France or tourist-class air travel abroad. The retrieval of your vehicle is also guaranteed from within France or abroad. Such policies may include cover for personal accident, injury and illness even when you aren't using your car, although they aren't adequate as holiday and travel insurance (see page 217).

HOUSEHOLD INSURANCE

Household insurance in France generally includes third-party liability (*responsabilité civile*), building and contents insurance, all of which are usually contained in a multi-risk policy (*assurance multirisques habitation*). Nine out of ten French homeowners have a multi-risk policy, but not all policies cover the same risks: for example, while over 90 per cent of policies cover water damage, fewer than 90 per cent include third-party liability, only around 75 per cent include theft, and barely more than half cover you for glass breakage.

All buildings under construction or undergoing major renovation or repair work must be covered by insurance for damages (*assurance dommages*) that guarantees the work for ten years after completion. It's the builder who is responsible for taking out this cover and during the first ten years of the building's life it passes automatically to a new owner, covering him for damage caused by faults in the original construction.

Building

Although it isn't compulsory for owners, it's wise to take out building (*bâtiment*) insurance covering damage due to fire, water, explosion, storm, freezing, snow, theft, malicious damage, acts of terrorism and natural catastrophes, which are usually covered by a multi-risk policy (see above). However, in some cases, claims for certain kinds of property damage aren't considered unless the government declares the situation a natural catastrophe or 'act of God'. This has happened with floods in southern France in recent years, where many people found that their household insurance didn't cover them for water coming in from ground level, only for water seeping in through the roof. Read the small print and, if floods are one of your concerns, ensure that you're covered. It's particularly important to have insurance for storm damage in France, which can be severe in some areas. Note, however, that if you live in an area that's hit by a succession of natural disasters (such as floods), your household insurance may be cancelled. You may need to take out additional cover for *catastrophes naturelles*, which should cost only a small amount (e.g. €10 per year).

Note also that theft is covered only under certain conditions (e.g. that doors and windows were locked and that a thief had to break in). Property insurance is based on the cost of rebuilding your home and is increased each year in line with an industry-agreed inflation figure.

> ☑ **SURVIVAL TIP**
>
> Make sure that you insure your property for the current cost of rebuilding.

Apartments

If you're a *copropriétaire*, building insurance is included in your service charges, although you should check exactly what's covered. You must, however, still be insured against third-party liability in the event that you cause damage to neighbouring apartments, e.g. through flooding or fire.

Rented Accommodation

If your accommodation is rented, your landlord will usually insist that you have third-party liability insurance. A lease requires you to insure against 'tenants' risks' (*risques locatifs*), including damage you may make to a rental property and to other properties if you live in an apartment, e.g. due to floods, fire or explosion. You can choose your own insurance company and aren't required to use one recommended by your landlord, but your landlord is entitled to void your lease if you don't provide him with proof of adequate cover within a specified time (usually a month or two after moving in).

Contents

Contents (*contenu*) are usually insured for the same risks as a building (see above) and are insured for their replacement value. Items of high value must usually be itemised and photographs and documentation (e.g. a valuation) provided. When claiming for contents, you should produce the original bills if possible (always keep receipts for expensive items) and bear in mind that replacing imported items in France may be much more expensive than buying them abroad. Note that contents policies usually contain security clauses and if you don't adhere to them a claim won't be considered.

Premiums

Premiums are usually based on the size of a property – either the habitable area in square metres or the number of rooms – rather than its value. Usually the sum insured (house and contents) is unlimited, provided the property doesn't exceed a certain size, e.g. 1,200m^2 (12,900ft^2) or seven rooms (excluding kitchen, bathrooms and toilets), and is under a certain age, e.g. 200 years. However, some companies restrict home insurance to a maximum value of contents, e.g. €50,000. The cost of multi-risk property insurance in a low risk area is around €120 to €150 per year for a property with one or two bedrooms, €180 to €240 for three or four bedrooms and around €240 to €275 for five or six bedrooms. Premiums are much higher in high-risk areas (especially Paris and the Côte d'Azur) and increase annually. If you have an index-linked policy, your cover is automatically increased each year in line with inflation.

French and foreign insurers may not charge an excess (deductible) unless a property is left unoccupied for long periods (e.g. more than a month), in which case you may have to pay the first €200 or more of a claim. Note also that French insurance premiums include relevant taxes.

Claims

If you wish to make a claim, you must usually inform your insurance company in writing (by registered letter) within two to five days of the incident or 24 hours in the case of theft. Thefts should also be reported to the local police within 24 hours, as the police statement (*déclaration de vol/plainte*), of which you receive a copy for your insurance company, is required when submitting a claim. Check whether you're covered for damage or thefts that occur while you're away from a property and are therefore unable to inform the insurance company immediately.

Cancellation

Like other French insurance policies, a household policy is automatically renewed annually unless you cancel (*résilier*) in writing, in which case you must usually give at least two months' notice (i.e. cancel at least two months before the end of your annual insurance period), although the notice period is sometimes only a month and in a few cases three months, so you should check.

There are certain circumstances in which you're entitled to a refund for the unexpired period of the insurance contract, including the following:

- moving home;

- selling the property;

- changing your marital status (e.g. becoming divorced);

● changing your profession (if the change is relevant to your home ownership) or retiring;

● if the insurance company increases your premiums by more than the official index, based on the Dwelling Rents Reference Index (*indice de référence des loyers*) published by INSEE (🖳 www.insee.fr – click on 'dwelling rents reference index' on the English version of the site).

If you cancel a policy for any other reason, you won't receive a refund. Standard cancellation letters (*lettre type de résiliation*) are usually provided by insurance companies and brokers.

THIRD-PARTY LIABILITY INSURANCE

It's customary in France to have third-party liability insurance (*assurance responsabilité civile*, sometimes called *responsabilité civile vie privée*) for all members of a family. This covers you for damage done or caused by you, your children and even your pets, e.g. if your dog bites someone, although where damage is due to negligence benefits may be reduced.

> ☑ **SURVIVAL TIP**
>
> Check whether insurance covers you against accidental damage to your home's fixtures and fittings.

Third-party liability insurance is usually combined with household insurance (see above). The cost of third-party liability insurance when not included in household insurance is around €160 per year and you may need to pay an excess, e.g. the first €75 to €150 of a claim.

If you're self-employed or run a business, you must also have third-party liability insurance for 'managers' (*assurance responsabilité civile chef d'entreprise*), the cost of which depends on your line of work.

If you're letting a property, ensure that you're covered for third-party liability in respect of your tenants, as most home insurance policies exclude such 'commercial' liability.

HOLIDAY & TRAVEL INSURANCE

Holiday and travel insurance (*assurance voyage*) is recommended for those whose health and possessions aren't covered by an existing policy while travelling. As you're no doubt already aware, innumerable things can (and often do) go wrong with a holiday, sometimes before you even reach the airport or port, particularly when you **don't** have insurance.

Travel insurance is available from many sources, including travel agents, insurance agents, motoring organisations, transport companies and direct from insurance companies. Package holiday companies also offer insurance policies, most of which don't provide adequate cover. It isn't wise to depend on travel insurance provided by charge and credit card companies, household or car insurance policies or private medical insurance, none of which usually provide adequate cover (although you should take advantage of what they offer). For example, car insurance may include personal accident and health insurance (e.g. through Mondial Assistance) even if you don't take your car but won't cover you for belongings or cancellation of flights.

Before taking out travel insurance, carefully consider the level of cover you require and compare policies. Most policies include cover for loss of deposit or holiday cancellation, missed flights, departure delay at both the start and the end of a holiday (a common occurrence), delayed baggage, lost or stolen money, luggage and other belongings, medical expenses and accidents (including repatriation if necessary), personal liability, legal expenses and a tour operator or airline going bankrupt.

Medical expenses are an important aspect of travel insurance and you shouldn't rely on reciprocal health arrangements. The minimum medical insurance recommended by experts is €500,000 in France and the rest of Europe and €1-2m in North America and some other destinations, e.g. Japan. If applicable, check whether pregnancy-related claims are covered and whether there are restrictions for those aged over 65 or 70. Third-party liability cover should be around €1.5m in Europe and €3m in North America. **Always check any exclusion clauses in contracts by obtaining a copy of the full policy document** (all relevant information isn't included in the insurance leaflet).

The cost of travel insurance varies considerably according to your destination and the duration of your trip. Usually the longer the period, the lower the daily or weekly cost. You should expect to pay around €40 for a week's insurance for one person in Europe, €60 for two weeks and €80 for a month and around twice as much for a family. Premiums are around double for travel to North America, where medical treatment costs an arm and a leg (although they also accept dollars!). Premiums may be higher for those aged over 65 or 70. Some insurance companies offer annual travel policies from around €200 that are good value for frequent travellers, although you should check exactly what's covered (or omitted), as these policies may not provide adequate cover. Note, however, that many French insurance companies don't offer annual policies. Note also, that many UK insurers won't offer foreign residents travel insurance; exceptions in the UK include Expat Health Direct (🖥 http://www.expathealthdirect.co.uk) and Travel Protection Group (☎ 028-9032 0797).

Although travel insurance companies gladly take your money, they aren't usually so keen to honour claims and you may have to persevere before they pay up.

Always be persistent and make a claim **irrespective** of any small print, as this may be unreasonable and therefore invalid in law. Insurance companies usually require you to report a loss (or any incident for which you intend to make a claim) to the local police (or carriers) within 24 hours and obtain a written report. Failure to do this usually means that a claim won't be considered.

PRIVATE HEALTH INSURANCE

If you aren't eligible for healthcare under the French national health system (see page 159), it's essential that you have private health insurance to cover any necessary treatment while in France. If you're planning on being resident in France, this will be in the form of a 'voluntary insurance' (*assurance volontaire*) policy; if you only visit France (and other countries) from time to time, you may require an international health policy. Even if you are covered by the French healthcare system, you may wish to take out a complementary policy, which covers some or all of the costs not reimbursed by the state. These options are discussed below.

It's also possible to insure against becoming a burden on your children in old age or following an illness or accident (*assurance dépendance*). This can cost €500 or more per month, however. Policies can normally be taken out between the ages of 45 and 75, and premiums are tax free.

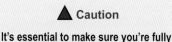

⚠ Caution

It's essential to make sure you're fully covered in France before you receive a large bill. If you or your family aren't adequately insured, you could be faced with some very high medical bills.

Private Insurance in France

If you aren't covered by French social security, it's essential that you have private health insurance. Even if you are covered, you may wish to take out a complementary or 'top-up' insurance (see below).

Complementary Insurance

If you're eligible for French social security, which will cover you for most of your medical expenses, you may wish to take out a complementary health insurance (or 'top-up') policy (*assurance complémentaire maladie*, commonly called a *mutuelle*, although strictly a *mutuelle* is a particular kind of benefit organisation – see below), which pays the portion of medical bills that isn't paid by social security. As complementary insurance contributions are high for retirees and the national health service provides 100 per cent cover for treatment for life-threatening illnesses and accidents, it may not be worth your while to take out such insurance. Carefully consider the costs and benefits before committing yourself to a policy.

Top-up insurance is provided by three types of organisation. *Mutuelles* (see below), which represent roughly 60 per cent of the market, non-profit provident institutions and private insurance companies (including both for-profit and non-profit carriers).

A mutual benefit organisation (*mutuelle*) is an association made up of individuals who are grouped together, e.g. by profession or area, in order to insure themselves for a favourable premium. There are two kinds of *mutuelle*: one is a sort of provident society or sick fund, which is a non-profit organisation that ploughs its profits back into the fund, and the other an insurance company operating at a profit (or not). A provident *mutuelle* provides fixed tariffs irrespective of the number of claims

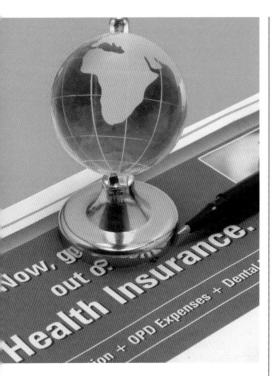

Mutualité Française (💻 www.mutualite. com – in French only; click on 'Trouver une mutuelle' at the top of the home page) and under *Mutuelles d'Assurances* in the yellow pages.

> The *Loi Madelin* allows you to deduct your contributions from taxable income provided you join a *mutuelle*, which costs around €15.

Many *mutuelles* base their reimbursements on those of social security (see page 64) and reimburse a patient only after social security has paid a proportion of the fee. Therefore, in a case where social security doesn't contribute, e.g. when a medical practitioner isn't part of the national health system (*non-conventionné, non-agréé*), a complentary fund may also pay nothing. However, some *mutuelles* pay the whole cost or part of the cost of treatment or items that aren't covered or are barely covered by social security, such as false teeth and spectacles. Note that not all *mutuelles* reimburse the statutory €1 charge on all consultations introduced in October 2004.

Reimbursement applies only to the standard medical charges (*tarif de convention*). For example, if a blood test costs €50 and the *tarif de convention* is €40, your complentary fund will normally pay only the 30 per cent of the €40 that isn't refunded by social security. You must pay the €10 charged in excess of the *tarif de convention* yourself. However, for a higher premium you can insure yourself for the actual charge (*frais réels*). Most policies offer different levels of cover. It's sometimes necessary to have been a member of a complentary fund for a certain period before you're eligible to make a claim, e.g. three months for medical claims and six months for dental claims.

and is **greatly preferable** to an insurance company.

There are around 400 *mutuelles*, and if you aren't in a particular trade or profession you're free to choose one. Different health practitioners 'recognise' different *mutuelles*, i.e. reimbursement is triggered automatically in the case of those that are recognised, but must be applied for in the case of those that aren't, which will involve you not only in a certain amount of paperwork but also in delays before receiving reimbursement. Unfortunately, it's almost impossible to find out which *mutuelles* are most widely recognised. However, if you're likely to be using a particular practitioner (e.g. acupuncturist or physiotherapist) regularly, you should ask which *mutuelles* he recognises and consider joining one of those. Details of *mutuelles* in your area can be found on the site of the Fédération Nationale de la

> ⚠ **Caution**
>
> Premiums are normally quoted as a flat rate per person covered, so unlike social security health cover, insuring a large family will cost considerably more than insurance for just a single person.

There are few foreign insurance companies which offer top-up policies for expatriates living in France. For UK nationals, they include Amariz (☎ 0117-974 5770, 🖳 www.amariz.co.uk) and Goodhealth Worldwide (☎ 0870-442 7376, 🖳 www.goodhealthworldwide.com). Bilingual insurers based in France include Agence Eaton (☎ 02 97 40 80 20, 🖳 www.french-insurance.com).

When choosing a complementary fund, compare the costs, terms and benefits provided by a number of funds before making a decision. It's wise to choose an insurer that is regulated by the *Loi Evan*, which means that after a certain period (e.g. two years) he isn't permitted to alter your terms and conditions, increase the premiums if your health deteriorates with advancing years or refuse to continue your insurance after an accident or illness.

Comprehensive Insurance

French private health insurance providers (rightly) assume that almost everyone is covered for the majority of your healthcare needs by the social security system and therefore provide mainly complementary or top-up policies; few offer comprehensive health insurance for those who aren't covered by social security, which is known as *assurance volontaire*, although it isn't difficult to find companies that do. Not surprisingly, however, it's expensive, and there's usually an upper age limit by which you must take out a policy, e.g. 65. Monthly premiums for a 55-year-old in good health (most insurers require you to complete a health questionnaire) start at start at around €150; if you're older and/or have health problems, you'll pay more – possibly much more.

Note that the 'voluntary old-age insurance' (*assurance volontaire vieillesse*) offered by the French social security system is only for those who have been in receipt of income support (*RMI*), which wouldn't apply to most foreign retirees.

International Health Insurance

Non-residents who spend time in different countries should take out an international health policy (sometimes referred to as private medical insurance or PMI), which should provide the following:

● immediate emergency healthcare;

● immediate access to a doctor;

● referral to a specialist if required;

● routine treatment, including dental treatment – if necessary in a hospital.

Cover for treatment of chronic conditions is rarely included in individual policies – Allianz Worldwide Care (see below) is one of the few major insurers to offer it, although several insurers include it in group policies. Most private health insurance policies don't pay standard doctors' consultation fees or pay for medicine that isn't provided in a hospital (or they charge a high 'excess', e.g. €100, which often exceeds the cost of treatment). Most will, however, pay for 100 per cent of specialist fees and hospital treatment in the best French hospitals. If pregnancy is a possibility, you should carefully check what's included and what isn't (e.g. regarding complications), as there may be a fixed monetary limit on claims; you may also have to wait ten months before becoming eligible for pregnancy benefits.

Before choosing a policy, compare not only costs but also benefits and conditions, or use an independent broker to do so for you, which shouldn't cost you any more. A broker can also help with claims or any difficulties you might encounter in dealing with an insurer. You should check, however, that a broker is reputable, e.g. by contacting the relevant regulatory body (the Financial Services Authority in the UK, ☎ 020-7066 1000, 🖥 www.fsa.gov.uk) or a recognised brokers' association, e.g. in the UK the Association of Medical Insurance Intermediaries (🖥 www.amii.org.uk) or the British Insurance Brokers' Association (☎ 0901-814 0015, 🖥 www.biba.org.uk). A policy should have a 'cooling-off' period of 14 to 30 days.

It's an advantage to be insured with a company that will pay large medical bills directly, because if you're required to pay bills and claim reimbursement from the insurance company, it can take you several months to receive your money. All French health insurance companies pay hospital bills directly, unlike some foreign companies. Some foreign companies limit your choice of hospitals to those with which they have a specific contract for rates and services. If you're planning to use the American Hospital of Paris, for example, make sure that your private insurer will cover the costs (and ideally, will make payment directly to the hospital), as treatment there isn't covered under all private insurance plans.

Most international insurance companies offer health policies for different areas, e.g. Europe, worldwide excluding North America, and worldwide including North America. Most companies offer different levels of cover, e.g. basic, standard, comprehensive and prestige. There's always an annual limit on medical costs, which should be at least €500,000 (although many provide cover of up to €1.5m), and some companies also limit the charges for specific treatment or care such as specialists' fees, operations and hospital accommodation.

> Most private health insurance policies don't pay family doctors' fees or pay for medicines other than those provided in a hospital or they charge a high excess (deductible), e.g. you must pay the first €75 of a claim, which often exceeds the cost of treatment. Most will, however, pay 100 per cent of specialists' fees and hospital treatment.

A medical examination isn't usually required for international health policies, although 'pre-existing' health problems are excluded for a period, e.g. one or two years. Most international health policies include repatriation or evacuation, which may also cover shipment (by air) of the body of a person who dies abroad to his home country for burial. An international policy also allows you to have non-urgent medical treatment in the country of your choice.

Claims are usually settled in most major currencies, and large claims are usually settled directly by insurance companies (although your choice of hospitals may be limited). Check whether an insurance company will settle large medical bills directly; if you're required to pay bills and claim reimbursement from an insurance company, it can take several months before you receive your money (some companies are slow to pay). It isn't usually necessary to have bills translated into English or another language, although you should check a company's policy. Most international health insurance companies provide emergency telephone assistance.

When choosing an insurer, ask the following questions:

● Who owns the company?

● Who underwrites its insurance?

- What is its financial standing? (Ask for a copy of its annual report and accounts.)

- How long has it been operating? (If it's a new company, ask whether the directors or managers have experience of international health insurance provision.)

- Is it a member of the relevant governing body (e.g. the Financial Services Authority/FSA or the General Insurance Standards Council/GISC in the UK)?

- Who administers claims? (Small companies may use a third-party administrator/TPA.)

- Which international emergency assistance company does it use? (The most widely used is International SOS.)

- Is cover available only up to a certain age?

- Is critical illness cover and/or income protection provided and, if so, at what cost?

- Is hospital treatment available only in certain hospitals?

- Is cover still valid if you return to your home country?

You should also consider whether the insurer has a French office or offices, which at least demonstrates that it's committed to providing a high-quality service in France.

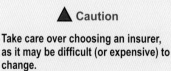

⚠ **Caution**

Take care over choosing an insurer, as it may be difficult (or expensive) to change.

If you already have private health insurance in another country, it may be possible to extend it to cover you in France. You should bear in mind, however, that in some countries, e.g. the UK, if you inform your insurance companies that

you're moving abroad permanently they may automatically cancel your insurance policies without even notifying you!

When changing health insurance companies, it's also wise to inform your old company if you have any outstanding bills for which they're liable.If you're planning to change your health insurance company, you should ensure that no important benefits are lost, e.g. existing medical conditions won't usually be covered by a new insurer.

The cost of international health insurance varies considerably according to your age and the extent of cover. Note that with most international insurance policies, you must enrol before you reach a certain age, usually between 60 and 75, to be guaranteed continuous cover in your old age. Premiums can sometimes be paid monthly, quarterly or annually, although some companies insist on payment annually in advance. When comparing policies, carefully check the extent of cover and exactly what's included and excluded from a policy (often indicated only in the

very small print), in addition to premiums and excess charges. In some countries, premium increases are limited by law, although this may apply only to residents in the country where a company is registered and not to overseas policyholders.

Although there may be significant differences in premiums, generally you get what you pay for and can tailor premiums to your requirements. The most important questions to ask yourself are: does the policy provide the cover required and is it good value? If you're in good health and are able to pay for your own out-patient treatment, such as visits to your family doctor and prescriptions, the best value is usually a policy covering specialist and hospital treatment only.

When deciding on the type and extent of private health insurance, make sure that it covers **all** your present and future health requirements in France **before** you receive a large bill. A health insurance policy should cover you for **all** essential health care whatever the reason, including accidents (e.g. sports accidents) and injuries, whether they occur in your home or while travelling. Don't take anything for granted, but check in advance.

 Caution

Some foreign insurance companies don't provide sufficient cover to satisfy French regulations, and you should check the minimum cover necessary with a French consulate in your country of residence.

Sauzon, Belle-Ile, Morbihan

10.
KEEPING OCCUPIED

Retirement makes possible – even necessary – a plethora of leisure pursuits, the chance to engage in activities and pastimes you previously didn't have time for. However, some retirees find it difficult to know what to do with their increased free time and end up doing little or nothing, becoming lonely and bored: they no longer have daily contact with colleagues in a workplace and suddenly find themselves (initially at least) with a much smaller circle of friends – especially if they retire to France! Your leisure time therefore needs careful planning if you're to keep healthy and active, stimulate your mind and, most importantly, enjoy yourself. Don't forget, however, that you don't have to give up work entirely; you might find a part-time job (even a voluntary one) provides you with a suitable challenge and an opportunity to meet and socialise with people – although the French are generally disinclined to socialise with work colleagues.

France offers a wealth of leisure possibilities for retirees, outdoor activities, sports, entertainment, social clubs (including arts and crafts societies), and church groups, and travel, most of which aren't expensive. This chapter contains a summary of the opportunities available in each of these areas, including information about holidays and travel reductions for seniors. A useful website for news of offers, products and services relevant to retirees is 🖳 www.senioractu.com – in French only.

☑ SURVIVAL TIP

While there are few English-language activities outside Paris and a few other popular expatriate areas, joining in French-speaking activities will do wonders for your command of the language.

EMPLOYMENT OPPORTUNITIES

For some retirees, the whole point of retiring in France is to forget all about their previous working life and start a new life of leisure; others, on the other hand, miss challenge, discipline and routine of employment (a common experience) as well as daily contact with colleagues, customers and suppliers. If you fall into the latter category, a part-time job could be the solution; it's also a good way to meet people, improve your French and supplement your pension.

Regulations

In most countries, including France and the UK, remuneration received for part-time employment has no effect on state-pension payments, but it's worth checking your tax liabilities. Additional income from part-time work may, however, increase your tax

liability (see **Income Tax** on page 189). Once you start work, your employer should register you with the social security system and monthly contributions may also be deducted from your pay.

Some pensioners in France take part-time jobs that are paid in cash by their employer, whereby both parties save on tax payments and possibly social security contributions. Be aware, however, that this is illegal and penalties are severe if you're caught.

Which Job?

Your employment opportunities depend on where you live and your skills, not least your French language proficiency. Some popular part-time jobs include shop assistant, gardener, odd-job man and baby minder. There are also opportunities for seasonal work, e.g. in bars and cafés in tourist areas during the summer.

It's also worth considering turning a hobby into a business – for example, if you're interested in furniture restoration, computing (English-speaking 'PC doctors' are in demand in some areas) or car maintenance – and you may wish to consider consultancy work in your area of expertise, which can often be done via the internet. Buying and selling (e.g. antiques) on the internet (e.g. via eBay) or at a local market can be lucrative as well as a way of making use of your free time. Writing is another possibility, and there are opportunities with the various magazines and newspapers that cover France (see **Appendix B**). Note, however, that it's no longer possible to act as a 'property finder' for an estate agency without the appropriate qualifications. Job sharing is another possibility, although this is much less common in France than in the UK, for example.

Voluntary Work

An excellent way to fill your day while helping others – provided you don't need to earn any money! – is to become a volunteer. Wherever you live in France, there are organisations which would be more than grateful for a few hours of your time: charities, self-help organisations and support groups are constantly seeking helpers. Volunteer work consists of a variety of jobs such as helping out at a charity shop; driving sick, disabled or non-car owners to hospital or medical appointments; listening and offering advice to those in need; providing company to the lonely; and helping to run charity events. For information about local charities and organisations, check your local newspapers or enquire at your town hall. If your French is up to it, you can even put yourself forward for election to your local municipal council – you'll probably be welcomed with open arms – although you must be a French citizen before you can run for *maire*!

The websites 🖳 www.benevolat.com and 🖳 www.espacebenevolat.org (in French only) will help you to find voluntary work (*bénévolat*).

Starting a Business

Setting up a business in France isn't for the faint-hearted, although thousands of foreigners have successfully launched businesses, and the paperwork and red tape alone will take up hours of your time even if you hire the services of an accountant or lawyer to help.

 **⚠ Caution**

Once you've completed the paperwork, long working hours are required in order to establish a business and get it firmly off the ground. In short, this is probably not the ideal activity for retirement!

However, if you're intent on starting your own business in France, our sister publication *Making a Living in France* (see page 321) provides comprehensive information and advice, as well as many business ideas.

If you think that offering bed and breakfast accommodation (*chambres d'hôte*) or converting part of your home or an outbuilding into a *gîte* might usefully supplement your income as well as provide you with valuable 'human contact', refer to *Running Gîtes and B&Bs in France* (Survival Books) – which may make you think twice!

OUTDOOR ACTIVITIES

Most of France has a pleasant climate for much of the year and this lends itself to an outdoor life.

Camping & Caravanning

Camping and caravanning are extremely popular, with both the French and the many thousands of tourists who flock to France each year to spend their holidays in the open air (*en plein air*). The French are the keenest campers in Europe and have elevated *le camping* to a high level of sophistication and chic. There are over 11,500 campsites in France, including over 2,000 rural and farm sites (*camping à la ferme*), although these may have few or no facilities. France is also Europe's largest camper van (*camping-car*) market with around 18,000 vehicles sold annually.

Note that permission is required to park or camp on private property or anywhere outside official campsites (including beaches); farmers may shoot first and ask questions afterwards! Off-site camping (*camping sauvage*) is restricted in many areas, particularly in the south of France, due to the danger of fires. For example, you need permission from the local Office des Eaux et Forêts to camp in state forests (*forêts domaniales*). Many campsites are open from June to September only and most have fewer than 150 pitches.

Information

The Fédération Française de Camping et de Caravanning (FFCC) publishes a *Guide Officiel* describing in detail the facilities at around 11,500 sites, including naturist and farm sites. It's available direct from La Fédération Française de Camping et de Caravanning (FFCC), 78 rue de Rivoli, 75004 Paris (☎ 01 42 72 84 08, 🖳 www. ffcc.fr) and from bookshops and camping, caravanning and motoring organisations.

Camping and caravanning guides are published for all areas and are available from local regional tourist offices. There are also many national camping guides, including *Camping à la Ferme* published by Gîtes de France, Alan Rogers' *Good Camps Guide*, *France* (Deneway Guides), the *Michelin Green Guide – Camping and Caravanning* and *Caravan and Camping in France* by Frederick Tingey (Mirador). The

French Government Tourist Office (FGTO) publishes an excellent free booklet, *The Camping Traveller in France*. If you wish to rent a mobile home, caravan or tent on site, Alan Rogers' *Rented Accommodation on Quality Sites in France* (Deneway Guides) provides a comprehensive list.

Fishing

Although not particularly well known internationally, France is a paradise for fishermen (and women) with over 4,800km (3,000mi) of coastline, 240,000km (150,000mi) of rivers and streams, and 120,000ha (300,000 acres) of lakes and ponds. There's excellent fishing in rivers, lakes and ponds throughout France, many of which are stocked annually with trout, grayling and pike. Fishing (*pêche*) is enjoyed regularly by around 4m French people and irregularly by some 20 per cent of the population, and is claimed by many to be France's national sport (football fans would disagree).

Fishing is permitted on beaches and other public areas of seafront (though not in ports) but there are restrictions on the type of equipment you may use and the kind of fish you may catch (e.g. you aren't allowed to catch young fish); the amount of shellfish (especially sea urchins and oysters) you may gather is strictly limited.

Rivers are divided into two categories. The first category (*première catégorie* or *salmonidés dominants*) covers headwaters and rivers suitable for salmon, trout and grayling, where maggots are banned as bait. The second category (*deuxième catégorie* or *salmonidés non dominants*) usually includes the lower stretches of rivers populated mainly by coarse fish, where bait can include practically anything except fish-eggs.

Almost all inland waters, from the tiniest stream to the largest rivers and lakes, are protected fishing areas. Fishing rights may be owned by a private landowner, a fishing club or the state, as described below. Wherever you fish, however, you must pay a fishing tax (*taxe piscicole*) by means of a *timbre fiscal* (obtainable from tobacconists'), which varies between around €10 and €40 depending on the type of water and the kind of fishing (e.g. you pay more to fish salmon, which are now rare in French rivers). You can pay a supplement of €15 to use your permit in another area (a scheme known as *réciprocité*). A permit known as a *vignette UPIF* is available for all fishing in the Ile-de-France region, costing €25. Permits are sold by fishing tackle shops, who can also advise you of the best local fishing spots, and in some cases by local cafés. Always carry your fishing permit with you, as wardens (who patrol most waters) may ask to see it.

For a list of associations, ask at a tackle shop or contact the Fédération Nationale de la Pêche en France, 17 rue Bergère, 75009 Paris (☎ 01 48 24 96 00, 💻 www.unpf.fr), whose website contains a useful list of related contacts (click on '*Adresses utiles*').

> To obtain a permit to fish state-controlled waters, you must in effect join a recognised fishing association, which will issue your *carte de pêche* (there are various types) as part of the annual membership.

Stretches of a river are often divided between local clubs, and anglers must join a local fishing club to fish there. In addition to club fees, you may have to pay an annual fee (e.g. €15 to €30) to the local federation of clubs. You need a passport-size photograph for your membership card.

Signs such as *pêche réservée/gardée* are common and denote private fishing. Many of the best fishing waters are in private hands, although it may be possible to obtain permission to fish from the owners.

The fishing season varies with the area and type of fish but is typically from around 1st March to 15th September for category 1 waters and from 15th January to 15th April for category 2. Fishing regulations vary from department to department, but you're generally permitted to fish from half an hour before sunrise until half an hour after sunset; night fishing is forbidden on all rivers (although permitted in certain lakes and ponds). There are limits on catches in most areas. Boats can be hired on inland waters and from sea ports, where deep-sea fishing expeditions are organised. Sea fishing is better in the Atlantic than the Mediterranean.

Information

Further information can be obtained from the Union Nationale pour la Pêche en France (see above). Various websites offer information about fishing in France, including 💻 www.peche-direct.com (available in English) and (for trout fishers) 💻 www.pechetruite.com (available in 'English'). A brochure, *Angling in France*, is available from the FGTO. There are a number of books on fishing in France, including *Fly Fishing in France* and *Pêche Française* by Phil Pembroke.

Hiking

France has some of the finest hiking (*tourisme pédestre*) areas in western Europe. Almost nowhere else offers the same combination of good weather, variety of terrain and outstanding natural beauty. Spring and autumn are the best seasons for hiking, when the weather is cooler and the routes less crowded, although the best time for mountain flowers is between May and August. There are pleasant walks in all regions but most serious walkers head for the Alps, Pyrenees, Vosges, Auvergne and Jura mountains. France has six national parks, all with an inner zone where building, camping and hunting are prohibited, and

85 state-run natural reserves, created to preserve the most-threatened areas of national heritage, which are ideal for hikers.

France has the finest network of walking trails in Europe, including some 30,000km (18,600mi) of footpaths known as *Grande Randonnée* (*GR*). The *GR* network was started in 1947 and has since been expanded into every corner of France under the guidance of the Fédération Française de la Randonnée Pédestre (FFRP), 64 rue du Dessous des Berges, 75013 Paris (☎ 01 44 89 93 93, 🖥 www. ffrandonnee.fr – in French only). The FFRP issues permits and provides insurance, although these aren't compulsory. A *GR de pays* is a country walk and a *Promenade Randonnée* (*PR*) a one-day or weekend excursion from a *GR*.

There are hiking clubs in most areas, all of which organise local walks, usually on Sundays. Local footpaths include forest paths (*routes forestières*) and 'little walks' (*petites randonnées*), usually between 2km and 11km.

Hunting

Hunting (*la chasse*) is viewed as a privilege hard won (during the Revolution) from the aristocracy and is indulged in by a large proportion of the rural population. France has 1.6m registered hunters (*chasseurs*) – more than all other European countries combined. Hunting is a key part of the masculine culture (fewer than 2 per cent of hunters are women). It's even a way of doing business (*chasses d'affaires*) and companies often invite their most important clients to shoots. Hunting rights are jealously guarded and hunters pay €1,500 per year or more for rights in some areas.

If you're thinking of joining a hunt, you should take precautions. French hunters are notoriously bad marksmen and around 50 people (often other hunters) are killed each year. Many hunters are inexperienced and some are downright dangerous, especially if they've been at the bottle before taking to the land. Although they won't deliberately shoot you (unless you're a conservationist or *garde-chasses*), it's advisable to steer clear of the countryside during the hunting season. The tendency in recent years has been towards stricter regulation of hunting, largely to prevent human accident and the following regulations must be observed:

● Hunters must have comprehensive accident insurance (costing from around €20).

● Hunting within 150m (500ft) of a dwelling is forbidden.

● All hunters must be clearly visible against foliage, usually by wearing fluorescent bibs and caps. The rule extends to dogs, which are collared in similar fashion.

- Roaming is no longer permitted and stalking of prey discouraged. Muster points are easily recognisable by the roadside, usually signposted 'point de chasse'.

- Guns must be carried in the 'broken' position to prevent accidental discharge.

A licence isn't required for a shotgun, which can be bought by mail-order or in a shop, but a permit (permis de chasser) is necessary. Hunters must pass a practical as well as a theoretical exam set by the Fédération Départementale des Chasseurs/ FDC (see below). An application form can be obtained from your local mairie and the exams cost €15 (which is effectively a membership fee for the FDC). When you pass the exams, you receive a permit, which costs around €30 (plus a supplement for certain types of hunting) and is renewable annually.

Non-residents can obtain temporary permits (licence de chasse) from local préfectures, for which they require two passport-size photographs, a passport and a shotgun licence (with a French translation). Permits are valid for nine consecutive days and you may obtain up to three per year. However, non-resident permits are severely restricted and are expensive (e.g. around €150) owing to the scarcity of game and the already fierce competition among local hunters. For further information about permits, contact the FDC or the ONCFS (see below).

Popular prey includes wild boar, deer, partridge, pheasant, duck, snipe, pigeon, rabbit, hare and (for timid hunters) snails. Hunting is legal from September to February, although the exact dates vary according to the department and the prey, e.g. the close season for snails is 1st April to 30th June. No hunting is permitted during the breeding and suckling periods, and the species and numbers of game that can be shot is (at least in theory)

carefully controlled. The wildfowl hunting season was recently shortened to the end of January to protect migrating birds during their return to breeding grounds (despite angry objections by hunters, who are notorious for their often violent attacks on anyone who threatens to restrict their 'right' to hunt).

▲ Caution

Before buying a rural property or erecting any fencing or walling, you should check the hunting rights on or adjacent to the land. Although hunters don't have the right to hunt on private land (propriété privée) without permission, when land has traditionally been used by hunters they won't bother to ask.

Where hunting is forbidden it's usually shown by a sign ('chasse interdite/gardée'). Certain areas are denoted as réservé pour repeuplement, which means that hunting access is prohibited in order to allow wildlife to reproduce; red public notices are attached to the perimeter.

For further general information contact the Office National de la Chasse et de la Faune Sauvage (ONCFS, 🖳 www. oncfs.gouv.fr). Local information, including the dates of the hunting season, can be obtained from your Direction Départementale de l'Agriculture et de la Forêt or Fédération Départementale des Chasseurs (obtain contact details from your mairie or town hall). There are many magazines devoted to hunting in France.

Music

Choral singing is a popular activity among both French and foreigners and there are numerous amateur choirs (chorale) throughout the country. A Coeur Joie (🖳 http://acj.musicanet.org – in French) is a grouping of some 500 choirs, many for

seniors only, which organise courses, festivals and other activities; click on 'Contacts?' on the website for a list of contacts. A list of regional contacts for what used to be called *centres d'art polyphonique* but now come under the obscure title *missions voix* can be found on 🖳 http://missionvoixalsace.org – in French only: click on 'Mission Voix' and then on 'Le réseau des Missions Voix'. There's no shortage of instrumental teachers (including typically French instruments such as the accordion); the website of the Fédération des Centres Musicaux Ruraux (🖳 www. cmr-musicites.org – in French only) is a good source of information on classes and 'musical holidays'; click on 'Le résau' and then 'Contact'.

On the other hand, there are fewer amateur orchestras, bands and other instrumental groups than in the UK, for example. However, the national Association des Musiciens Amateurs (🖳

http://membres.lycos.fr/ffama – in French only) may lead you to a local group: click on 'REGIONS' on the above web page for a list of regional contacts (there isn't one in every region).

Naturism

France is the naturist capital of Europe (having supplanted the former Yugoslavia), with numerous naturist beaches, villages and over 60 holiday centres, including a huge number of superbly equipped naturist camping centres (for those who don't want to bother with laundry while on holiday). Topless bathing is accepted almost everywhere, even in Paris along the banks of the Seine, but nude bathing should be confined to naturist beaches. The main naturist areas include Aquitaine, Brittany, Corsica, Languedoc, Provence and the Midi-Pyrénées. Cape d'Agde on the Languedoc coast is the largest naturist resort in the world, with a population of 40,000 from Easter to September. Naked day trippers are allowed in most resorts, although single male visitors aren't usually admitted.

Information about naturist holidays can be obtained from the FGTO, which publishes *France, a Land for all Naturisms*. If you aren't a member of a naturist association in another country, you must join the Fédération Française de Naturisme, 5 rue Regnault, 93500 Pantin (☎ 08 92 69 32 82, 🖳 www. ffn-naturisme.com), or pay a fee for the duration of your stay.

SPORTS

Almost any sport you care to name can be enjoyed somewhere in France, including cricket. The following is a selection of sports that are widely practised and may be suitable for retirees. For further information about sport in France, refer to *Living and Working in France* (Survival Books – see page 325).

The Fédération Française de la Retraite Sportive (FFRS, 12, rue des Pies, BP 20, 38360 Sassenage, ☎ 04 76 53 09 80, ✉ ffrs38@free.fr, 💻 www.ffrs-retraite-sportive. org – in French only) is an association of sport and activity clubs for older people. Click on 'Implantation' on the website home page to find a list of clubs in your region (or a contact telephone number if there aren't any).

Boules

Boules has been unkindly referred to as a 'glorified game of marbles', probably by some poor foreign loser. There are in fact three principal games of *boules* (which is also the word used for the balls themselves): *boules lyonnaise*, *pétanque* and *le jeu provençal* (or *La Longue*), from which *pétanque* derived. In *le jeu provençal*, which is still played in Provence, players take three running steps before 'shooting' and the game is played on a pitch (*piste* or *terrain*) measuring 21m by 15m (68ft by 49ft). *Boules lyonnaise* is also played on a large pitch and with larger *boules* than the more popular *pétanque*, which uses a pitch measuring 10m by 6m (33ft by 20ft) and requires the player to keep his feet together when throwing. (The word *pétanque* derives from *pieds tanqués*, southern dialect for 'feet together', and the game supposedly originated when one Jules Le Noir, a champion *jeu provençal* player from La Ciotat, a little port between Marseille and Toulon, was confined to a wheelchair as a result of an accident and was therefore unable to take a run-up.) It's generally recognised that *pétanque* is easier to play, as no special playing area is required and the rules are simpler.

There are also a number of regional variations of *boules* – there's even a game played in central France using square *boules* (*boules de fort*)!

> The British claim that *boules* derives from a game invented in the UK and played with cannon balls and that it was a game of *boules* and not bowls that Sir Francis Drake famously refused to interrupt when informed of the impending arrival of the Spanish Armada.

For most people, *pétanque* is a pastime or social game rather than a serious sport. However, it managed to earn recognition as an Olympic demonstration 'sport' in the Barcelona Olympics in 1992 and even has World Championships, which are held in Marseille. It's played throughout France, but particularly in the south, where most village squares have a pitch (*piste*) and many towns have an arena called a *boulodrome*. It isn't unusual, however, to find people playing on almost any patch of ground – even in the middle of the road! The more uneven the surface the better (grass is totally unsuitable). The other essential requirement is an unlimited supply of *pastis*.

In the last decade, the number of registered *boules* players has doubled and the Fédération Française de Pétanque et Jeu Provençal, 13 rue Trigance, 13002 Marseille (☎ 04 91 14 05 80, 💻 www. petanque.fr) now has over 500,000 members. Although traditionally a male dominated game, many young players now are female. Beware of hustlers and **never** play locals for money!

Cycling

France is one of Europe's foremost cycling countries, and cycling is both a serious sport and a relaxing pastime, though not without its dangers. French motorists usually give cyclists a wide berth when overtaking (apart from Parisians, who respect nobody else's right to use the road), although tourists aren't always so generous, particularly those towing caravans. Bicycles aren't expensive in France, where you can buy an 18-gear racing bike for around €250 and a 'shopping' bike for around €150. Mountain bikes (*vélo tout terrain/VTT*) with 21 or more gears cost as little as €100 (children's mountain bikes cost from around €80) and can be bought in supermarkets and hypermarkets. An 'all-purpose' bicycle, called a *vélo tout chemin/VTC*, can be bought for around €200. At the other extreme, you can pay up to €4,000 for a *VTT* fit to conquer Mont Blanc and €6,000 or more for a road racing machine – not to mention the Tour-de-France-style gear that's *de rigueur* for all serious cyclists. There are *VTT* bike trails in many areas, although bikes aren't permitted on hiking tracks.

Associations & Clubs

Keen cyclists may wish to join the Fédération Française de CycloTourisme (FFCT), 12 rue Louis Bertrand, 94207 Ivry-sur-Seine Cedex (🖳 www.ffct.org) or the Fédération Française de Cyclisme (FFC), 5 rue de Rome, 93561 cedex, Rosny-sous-Bois (☎ 01 49 35 69 00, 🖳 www.ffc.fr).

Golf

Golf is one of the fastest growing sports in France, where there are over 200,000 registered players and the second-highest number of golf courses (over 500) in any European country after the UK, the majority of which were built in the last decade. The largest number of clubs is found in Normandy (especially the department of Calvados), Brittany (especially Ille-et-Vilaine), the south-west (especially Gironde), the Côte d'Azur (especially Alpes-Maritimes and Var) and the Paris region, where there are no fewer than 24 courses in the department of Yvelines. Many courses have magnificent settings (seaside, mountain and forest) and they're often linked with property developments. Properties on or near golf clubs, which may include life membership, are becoming increasingly popular with foreigners seeking a permanent or second home.

> Due to the relatively small number of players, golf is a more relaxed game in France than in many other countries and queues are virtually unknown. Many players treat the game as a leisurely stroll after lunch. Dress regulations are almost non-existent.

A few golf courses offer reduced green fees for seniors; these can be found on 🖳 www.golfmoinscher.com (in French only; look for 'Green fee senior' – yes, that's French!).

Information

For more information about golf contact the Féderation Française de Golf (🖳 www.ffgolf.org). A free magazine, Golf in France, is published by Regional Golf (☎ 01761-472468, 🖳 www.regionalgolf.net). A useful website for French golfers is 🖳 www.golf.com.fr. The Institut Géographique National (IGN) publishes a general golf map of France (ref. 910).

Racket Sports

Tennis is by far the most popular racket sport in France; squash and badminton are also played, but facilities can be poor. There are two main kinds of racket club: sports centres open to all, and private clubs. Sports centres require no membership or membership fees and anyone can book a court. Clubs tend to have little or no social aspect, as for example in the UK, but are principally facilities for playing a sport; there may not even be club nights or tournaments. Costs are around €8 per hour for a squash or indoor tennis court at a centre, €4 per hour for an outdoor court or €6 if it's floodlit.

Club membership can cost as little as €50 per year. Most towns and villages have municipal courts that can be rented for €3 to €5 per hour. Some hotels have their own tennis and squash courts, and organise coaching holidays throughout the year.

Tennis

The French invented tennis – or so they would have you believe – and the country has over 2.5m players and some 10,000 clubs. Tennis's popularity has grown tremendously in the last few decades and there are courts in most towns and villages, although in small villages there may be one court only and it may be in poor repair. Courts are usually hard (*court en dur*), although clay courts (*court en terre battue*) are also popular; many courts are floodlit. One of the reasons for the popularity and high standard of tennis in France is that there are hundreds of covered and indoor courts, allowing tennis to be played year round.

Tennis was long regarded as an elite sport in France and remains that way in

many private clubs, which are usually expensive and exclusive and rarely accept unaccompanied visitors. Membership runs to several hundred euros per year and most clubs have long waiting lists. At an elite private club you can pay €30 per hour for a court. France has many tennis schools and resorts, and in Paris and other cities there are huge tennis complexes with as many as 24 courts, open from 07.00 to 22.00 daily. Many tennis clubs provide saunas, whirlpools, solariums and swimming pools, and most have a restaurant.

Squash & Badminton

There are squash clubs in most large towns, although many have only one or two courts. There are also many combined tennis and squash clubs. The general standard of squash is low due to the lack of experienced coaches and top competition, although it's continually improving. Rackets and balls for squash and racketball (a 'simplified' version of squash played with a larger, bouncier ball and shorter rackets) can be hired from most squash clubs.

Some tennis centres also provide badminton courts and there are around 600 badminton clubs, although facilities tend to be poor.

Information

Further information about racket sports can be obtained from the Fédération Française de Tennis (🖥 www.fft.fr), the Fédération Française de Squash (🖥 www.ffsquash.com) and the Fédération Française de Badminton (🖥 www.ffba. org). Local information is available from racket clubs, travel agents and tourist offices.

Skiing

Both downhill skiing (*ski alpin*) and cross-country skiing (*ski de fond/ski nordique*) are popular, although downhill skiing is greatly preferred. France is Europe's number one destination for serious downhill skiers and some 15 per cent of the French population ski regularly. The French mountain ranges have the largest number of resorts and the most extensive network of ski lifts in the world (over 4,000). France boasts over 3,000km^2 (over 1,150mi^2) of skiing areas spread over five mountain ranges.

> The ski season runs from December to April (or May in the higher resorts, which are the best choice for early or late season skiing).

The major skiing area is, of course, the French Alps, but there's cheaper skiing in some 35 resorts in the French Pyrenees, e.g. Barèges and Cauterets, (plus those of neighbouring Andorra and Spain), nine resorts in the Massif Central (Auvergne) and a number of resorts in the Vosges and Jura mountain ranges along the German border, although these resorts cater mostly for beginners and intermediates rather than experts.

Alpine skiing areas include a number of vast, inter-linked regions with over 300km (186 miles) of runs (*piste*) and some with over 600km (372mi), e.g. the Portes du Soleil, the Trois Vallées and the recently formed 'Paradiski' area (combining Les Arcs and La Plagne), providing the largest skiing area in the world. There are many long runs, including the *Vallée Blanche* at Chamonix (24km/15mi), the *Aiguille Rouge* at Les Arcs and the *Sarenne* at Alpe d'Huez (both 16km/10mi). A number of French resorts are linked with Italian and Swiss resorts (don't forget your passport!).

The French invented the purpose-built ski resort, where you jump out of bed in the morning directly onto the slopes (but put your salopettes and skis on first!). Purpose-built resorts are mostly lacking in character and charm (some are downright ugly), although France also has many traditional village resorts rivalling the best in Austria and Switzerland. The main advantages of purpose-built resorts are that they're situated at high altitude where there's reliable snow and are designed so you can ski from door-to-door (in some resorts almost all runs start and finish in the village), and the trend nowadays is away from monolithic concrete blocks and back to traditional wooden chalets.

The largest and most famous French ski resorts include Alpe d'Huez, Les Arcs, Argentières, Avoriaz, Chamonix, Courchevel, Les Deux Alpes, Flaine, Les Menuires, Megève, Méribel, Morzine, La Plagne, Tignes, Val d'Isère, Valmorel and Val Thorens (the highest resort in Europe). Chamonix, Courchevel and Megève are France's most fashionable (i.e. expensive) ski resorts. Many French resorts are situated at high altitude and have excellent snow records, even when most of the rest of the Alps is without snow. Many resorts also boast snow cannons, enabling them to guarantee skiing for most of the season.

Information

For further information about skiing and other winter sports contact the Club Alpin Français (🖳 www.ffcam.fr), the Fédération Française de Ski (🖳 www.ffs.fr) or the Association des Maires des Stations Française de Sports d'Hiver (also known simply as SkiFrance, 🖳 www.skifrance.fr – available in 'English'). The latest weather and snow conditions are available via telephone (☎ 08 92 68 08 08), internet (e.g. the France Météo website, 🖳 www.meteofrance.com), teletext, daily newspapers and direct from resorts. The FGTO (see page 402) publishes a *Winter Holiday Guide*. General information on health and safety for skiing can be obtained from the

flag' (*pavillon bleu*) categories (A and B) for the quality of their water, although many that fail the tests are dangerously polluted. The dirtiest beaches are on the northern coast between Calais and Cherbourg, the cleanest around Nice (although not all). The pollution count must be displayed at the local town hall: blue = good quality water, green = average, yellow = likely to be temporarily polluted, and red = badly polluted. A list of blue flag beaches can be found on the Blue Flag website (🖥 www.blueflag.org – in English) and a list of 'black flag' beaches on that of the Surfrider Foundation Europe (🖥 www. surfrider-europe.org – the 'English' version of the site is 99 per cent in French!), which draws attention to what it considers to be unacceptably high levels of pollution.

Swimming can be dangerous at times, particularly on the Atlantic coast, where some beaches have very strong currents. Most beaches are supervised by lifeguards who operate a flag system to indicate when swimming is safe. When a beach is closed or swimming is prohibited, it's shown by a sign ('*baignade interdite*'). You should always observe flags and other beach warning signs. There are stinging jellyfish in parts of the Mediterranean and along the Atlantic coast but no (dangerous) sharks.

Médecins de Montagne website (🖥 www. mdem.org).

Swimming

Not surprisingly, given France's generally hot summer weather and miles of beautiful beaches (*plage*) as well as numerous public swimming pools (*piscine*), swimming (*natation*) is one of the country's favourite sports and pastimes. Beaches vary considerably in size, surface (sand, pebbles, etc.) and amenities, and most are notable for their cleanliness. Most resorts provide beach clubs for the young (*club des jeunes*) and all but the smallest beaches have supervised play areas where you can leave young children for a fee. Deckchairs and umbrellas can be hired on most beaches, which are usually free, although there are private beaches in some areas (notably along the Mediterranean coast).

In a few areas, public beaches are dirty and overcrowded, although this is very much the exception. The vast majority of French beaches are in the top two EU 'blue

Watersports

France is a paradise for watersports enthusiasts, which is hardly surprising considering its immense coastline, numerous lakes, and thousands of kilometres of rivers and canals. Popular watersports include sailing, windsurfing, waterskiing, jet-skiing, rowing, canoeing, kayaking, surfing, barging, rafting and subaquatic sports. Wetsuits are recommended for windsurfing, waterskiing and subaquatic sports, even in summer. Rowing and canoeing are possible on most lakes and rivers, where canoes and kayaks can usually be hired (rented). France has

Europe's best surfing beaches, on the extreme south-west Atlantic coast, including Biarritz (the capital of European surfing), Capbreton, Hossegor and Lacanau. Scuba diving and snorkelling are especially popular off the coasts of Brittany, the French Riviera and Corsica. There are clubs for most watersports in all major resorts and towns throughout France, where instruction is usually available.

Offshore windsurfers, jet-bikers and motorboaters must use marked channels, on beaches as well as in the sea, and give priority to swimmers, even in channels. There's a speed limit of 10kph (6mph) within 300m of a coast and a distance limit of 1.8km (3mi). If you need rescuing, you must pay between around €90 and €125 per hour (swimmers are rescued free – if they're lucky!).

France has 8,500km (5,300mi) of inland waterways, controlled by Voies Navigables de France (VNF, 🖥 www.vnf. fr), and it's possible to navigate from the north coast to the Mediterranean along rivers and canals. These aren't just for pleasure craft, and millions of tonnes of freight are transported on them annually. Life on France's waterways continues at a leisurely pace, not least due to maximum speed limits of as little as 5kph (3mph). The principal inland boating regions are Alsace, Brittany, Burgundy, Champagne-Ardenne and Picardy. The most popular waterway is the Canal du Midi in the south of France. Except for parts of the Moselle river, all French waterways provide free access, although you must have a licence to drive a boat with a motor larger than 9hp (see below).

Some rivers have strong currents and require considerable skill and experience to navigate. It's sensible to wear a life-jacket, whether you're a strong swimmer or a non-swimmer. On some rivers there are quicksand-like banks of mud, silt or shingle where people have been sucked under.

> ⚠ **Caution**
>
> **Be sure to observe all warning signs on lakes and rivers. Take particular care when canoeing, as even the most benign of rivers have 'white water' patches that can be dangerous for the inexperienced.**

Boating holidays are popular in France, where boats vary from motorboats for two to four people to barges or houseboats (*pénichette*) with accommodation for 10 to 12 people. A boat with four to seven berths costs from around €850 per week in low season and from around €1,500 per week in high season depending on the specification. If you prefer to let someone else do the work, there are hotel barges, some with heated swimming pools, air-conditioning, and suites with four-poster beds!

France has hundreds of harbours, and sailing has always been a popular sport – there are some 750,000 yacht owners in France. Boats of all shapes and sizes can be hired in most resorts and ports, where there are also sailing clubs and schools. If you have a few (thousand) euros to spare and wish to impress your friends, you can even rent a luxury yacht with crew for a modest €100,000 to €200,000 per week (plus tips!). The French have a long tradition of seafaring and are prominent in international yachting, particularly long-distance races, which are avidly followed by the general public.

French residents must obtain a certificate of competence to pilot motorboats of 9 to 50hp; separate certificates are required for inland waters (*permis fluvial*) and coastal waters, including rivers within 5 nautical miles of a harbour (*permis mer*). If you're inexperienced, you should steer well clear of jet-skis, which can be deadly in the wrong hands.

Information

Further information about inland waterways can be obtained from Voies Navigables de France (VNF, 💻 www.vnf. fr). The FGTO publishes a free booklet, *Boating on the Waterways*. A book which may be of interest to boat owners is *The French Alternative: The Pleasure and Cost-Effect of Keeping your Boat in France* by David Jefferson (Waterline).

ENTERTAINMENT

France offers numerous possibilities for live entertainment, ranging from amateur productions to world-class acts, and even the smallest towns usually have a programme of cultural events. Amateur theatre and dance groups are, however, few and far between.

Finding Out What's On

Events generally aren't well advertised (or advertised at all), so it pays to ask neighbours and friends as well as 'official' sources what's going on locally and to keep an eye out for posters in shop windows and on information boards. Officially, information about local events and entertainment is available from tourist offices and is published in local newspapers and magazines, as well as in many foreign publications (see **Appendix B**). In most cities there are magazines and newspapers devoted to entertainment, and free weekly or monthly programmes are published by tourist organisations in major cities and tourist centres. Many city newspapers publish weekly magazines or supplements containing a detailed programme of local events and entertainment.

Tourist Offices

Most towns have a tourist office – usually called an *office de tourisme*, although the quaintly old-fashioned term *syndicat d'initiative* is still in use in some areas. Each department and region of France (see **Appendix E**) has a tourist authority, and many of the regions have tourist offices in Paris. The main tourist office in Paris is the Office de Tourisme de Paris, 127 avenue des Champs Elysées, 75008 Paris (☎ 08 92 68 30 00, 💻 http://en.parisinfo. com – both in English). There are also tourist offices at the Gare de Lyon and the Eiffel Tower, which can be contacted via the above telephone number. There are tourist offices at international airports in Paris and other cities, where you can make hotel bookings. The Maison de la France (💻 www.franceguide.com) provides tourist information about most regions and will send information. (Its office in avenue Opéra isn't open to the public.) Information in English can also be found on 💻 www.v1.paris.fr/ en. A recent development is a computerised tourist information service available in motorway rest areas (*aires d'autoroute*).

Cinema

French cinema (known as the 'seventh art') has resisted the threat of television (which is generally poor in France) far better than the cinema in most other developed countries – and France has resisted the invasion of US-made films better than most other countries. (Some 200 French films are made each year; only India and South Korea have a better record.) The French are huge film fans: some 200m tickets are sold annually, which means that on average every inhabitant goes to the cinema more than three times a year.

Paris is the cinema capital of the world, with some 350 cinemas, most of which are packed every day (Parisians buy some 80 per cent of all cinema tickets sold in France). You can literally see a different film (in a different cinema) every day of the year, and every film you ever wanted to see (and lots more that you wouldn't watch if you were paid to) is usually showing somewhere. Many cinemas in Paris show old films or reruns (*reprises*) of classics and many hold seasons and festivals featuring a particular actor, director or theme.

> Film lovers shouldn't miss the 'cinema days' (*journées du cinéma*) in summer, when films are shown non-stop for 24 hours at low prices.

As in other developed countries, most old cinemas have been replaced by modern multiplexes, with ten or more screens and state-of-the-art technology. Cinemas listed as *grande salle* or *salle prestige* have a large screen (*grand écran*), comfortable seats and high projection and sound standards. Smoking isn't permitted in cinemas, some of which are air-conditioned (a relief in summer). There are also private *ciné-clubs* in most cities.

In Paris and other major cities, foreign films are shown in their original version (*version originale/VO*) with French subtitles (*sous-titres français*); elsewhere, however, it can be difficult to find *VO* screenings and most foreign films are dubbed (labelled *VF* for *version française*). You may also come across *VA* (*version anglaise*), denoting an English-language film made by a French-speaking director (beware!). Note that French translations of English film titles often bear little relationship to the original, although an increasing number of titles aren't translated.

Museums & Galleries

France has around 7,000 museums and many important historical collections. There are over 100 museums and some 500 historic monuments in and around Paris alone, ranging from one of the largest museums and galleries in the world, the Musée National du Louvre, to some of the smallest and most specialised. The Louvre, which is over 200 years old, is the most

important museum in France and houses, among many famous exhibits, the Mona Lisa and the Venus de Milo. It takes around a week to see everything in the Louvre (if you really want to), which is also the world's largest (ex-)royal palace and a national treasure in itself (💻 www.louvre.fr).

One of Paris's most popular art venues is the Centre National d'Art et de Culture Georges Pompidou (known as the Centre Pompidou), housing the Musée National d'Art Moderne, the Public Reference Library, with over a million French and foreign books, the Institute of Sound and Music and the Industrial Design Centre. Other important Paris museums and galleries include the Musée Rodin, Musée Picasso, Musée d'Orsay and the Cité des Sciences et de l'Industrie. In addition to its national galleries, Paris boasts around 300 commercial galleries displaying the most innovative contemporary art (admission is free but the prices can be astronomical!).

France also has a wealth of provincial museums devoted to such varied subjects as farming, local history, industry, crafts, cultural heritage, transport, archaeology, art, textiles, folklore, war, technology, pottery and nature. You can also visit numerous manor houses (*manoir*) and *châteaux*.

An experiment started in January 2008 meant that entry to some museums and 'monuments' is free, although this applied to only 14 places in Paris, only on one night of the week and only to 18- to 25-year-olds!

Information

Useful websites for museum information include 💻 www.museums-of-paris.com and 💻 www.rmn.fr (site of the Réunion des Museés Nationaux, which operates 32 museums across France).

Music

Although the French don't have a reputation as music lovers, France boasts some 5m amateur musicians and stages over 300 music festivals a year.

Classical Music

France has no world-renowned orchestra and few internationally famous performers, yet there's no shortage of classical music concerts, especially in Paris, which boasts several major classical music concert halls, including the recently refurbished Salle Pleyel, the Théâtre des Champs-Elysées, the Théâtre du Châtelet (see above), the Salle Gaveau and the Maison de Radio France. These feature leading foreign orchestras and soloists as well as performances by the Orchestre de Paris, the Orchestre Philharmonique de Radio France and various other national and provincial orchestras (among the best are those of Bordeaux, Lille, Lyon and Toulouse).

The Parisian concert season runs from October to June. Students at the Conservatoire National perform regularly in the Paris *métro* and on the city's streets as well as at the Cité de la Musique in north-east Paris, where there's a fascinating museum of musical instruments. Recitals of organ and sacred music are often held in churches and cathedrals, including Notre Dame de Paris, and many churches sponsor concerts with good soloists and excellent choirs. Paris also has a number of music halls where top international artists regularly perform. There's plenty of classical music outside the capital, although much of it is poorly advertised.

> There are discounts at classical music concerts for senior citizens on production of identification or a *Carte Senior*.

The main agency for tickets to almost any concert or cultural event in Paris is FNAC at 136 rue de Rennes, 6ᵉ (☎ 08

92 68 36 22, 🖳 www.fnac.com) and in the Forum des Halles Level 3, 1-5 rue Pierre-Lescot, 1er (☎ 08 92 68 36 22). You can also buy tickets from the Virgin Megastore, 52 avenue des Champs Elysées, 8e (☎ 01 49 53 50 00).

Popular Music

French popular music is something of an acquired taste, being based on the traditional *chanson*, in which the words are far more important than the music. Even French rock music is rooted in this style and therefore, to American and British ears, a generation 'out of date'. This is reflected in the fact that the 1960s rock star Johnny Hallyday, who is now over 60, and octogenarian crooner Charles Aznavour remain France's biggest box office draws. Foreign bands are much better known to French fans than any French group.

Most pop venues can be divided into those where you sit and listen and dance clubs. The former (in Paris) include Bataclon, Bercy, Bobigno, Olympia, the Palais des Congrès and Zénith, although none of these is an 'automatic' stop on the world tour. Tickets for club performances cost around €15 and concerts €25 or more. Drinks are expensive in music clubs and may run to €15 for a beer.

Jazz

Paris is possibly Europe's leading jazz venue and attracts the world's best musicians, while France as a whole hosts many excellent jazz festivals, including the Festival de Jazz in Paris in autumn, the Antibes-Juan-les-Pins Festival and the Nice Jazz Festival in July, one of the most prestigious jazz and blues festivals in Europe. France even has a nationally-funded National Jazz Orchestra.

Most jazz is performed in cellar clubs, where there's usually a cover charge and expensive drinks. Music starts at around 22.00 and lasts until around 04.00 at weekends and includes everything from trad to be-bop, free jazz to experimental.

Music Festivals

Open-air music festivals are common and popular in summer throughout the country, many of them staged in spectacular venues such as cathedrals and *châteaux*. Music festivals embrace all types of music, including classical, opera, chamber music, organ, early music, piano, popular, jazz and folk, many of which are listed in a booklet, *Festive France*, available from French Tourist Offices (see page 241).

Every year in around 40 towns, over a weekend in May, the bandstand (*kiosque à musique*) is given over to the performance of music of the Belle Epoque and 21st June is a national Fête de la Musique, when every French town becomes an open-air concert venue.

Information

French music magazines include the *Guide des Concerts* and *Les Activités Musicales*. Two publications provide a guide to what's on in Paris: *L'Officiel des Spectacles* and *Pariscope*, the latter having an English supplement.

Theatre, Ballet & Opera

High quality theatre, opera and ballet performances are staged in all major cities, many by resident companies.

Theatre

Parisian theatres include the famous Comédie Française (classics), founded by Louis XIV, and the Théâtre National Populaire (contemporary). Other than the classics (Molière, Racine, Corneille, Feydeau, etc.), most French-language shows are translated hits from London and New York. There are also many café-theatres, where performances may not always be memorable but are usually enjoyable. Children's theatres in Paris and other cities perform straight plays, pageants and magic shows. There are also a number of English-language theatre venues in Paris, including the Théâtre Marie Stuart, ACT, Theatre Essaion, Voices and the Sweeney Irish Pub.

In the provinces, performances are often held in theatres that are part of a cultural centre (*maison de la culture or centre d'animation culturelle*), and the only national theatre outside the capital is the Théâtre National de Strasbourg. In total over 400 theatre companies receive state subsidies, including 150 in Paris.

In addition to the large and luxurious state-funded theatres, there are many good medium and small theatres where performance quality varies from excellent to poor, although there's plenty of variety. Performances usually start at 20.30 or 21.00 and theatres close one day a week. As in cinemas, smoking isn't permitted.

> Tickets usually cost between €5 and €45 for national theatres (although you can obtain half-price tickets if you subscribe to ⬚ www.theatreonline.com – in French only) and between €8 and €20 for private theatres.

Midweek matinee subscriptions are available at reduced rates. The Kiosque Théâtre (place de la Madeleine, 75008 Paris) in Paris sells half-price tickets on Tuesdays to Saturdays from 12.30 to 20.00 for shows on performance days, and many theatres provide student discounts. Just before a show starts, seats are often available at huge discounts. Students can also obtain reduced price tickets from the Centre Régional des Oeuvres Universitaires et Scolaires/CROUS. Ushers expect a small tip (and will usually remind you if you overlook the fact!).

Obtaining theatre tickets in advance is difficult in Paris, where many theatres accept bookings only one or two weeks in advance. Many theatres don't accept credit card bookings and don't use ticket agencies, although bookings can be made up to three weeks in advance via the website 🖳 www.theatreonline.com.

Drama festivals are also popular and include the world-renowned Festival d'Avignon in July/August, encompassing drama, dance, film, concerts, exhibitions and many other events.

Ballet & Modern Dance

The Paris Opéra Ballet has a history going back three centuries and is one of the world's foremost ballet companies (it no longer stages opera). Although tickets are cheaper than their equivalents in London and New York, they're hard to obtain, as most seats are sold by subscription months in advance. For information and booking details, see **Opera** below. Paris also

boasts the Théâtre du Châtelet in the 1st *arrondissement*, where a variety of shows are staged, including ballet productions and classical music concerts (🖥 www.chatelet-theatre.com – in French only). Modern and contemporary dance thrives and the Centre Pompidou stages some 'interesting' avant-garde programmes by French and international dance companies. Many small dance companies perform in small theatres and dance studios.

Opera

The new Opéra de la Bastille, 2 bis place de la Bastille, 75012 Paris is France's major opera venue, although it has been plagued by problems (e.g. lack of funding, sackings and strikes) since its opening. Paris also boasts the celebrated Opéra Garnier in the 9th *arrondissement*. For details of performances and bookings for both Paris operas call ☎ 08 92 89 90 90 or visit 🖥 www.opera-de-paris.fr (in French only). The Théâtre du Châtelet in the 1st

arrondissement stages a variety of shows, including opera productions (🖥 www.chatelet-theatre.com). France also has 12 regional opera companies, most notably in Bordeaux, Lille, Lyon and Toulouse.

SOCIAL CLUBS & ORGANISATIONS

There are many social clubs and organisations catering for both foreigners and the French. These include Ambassador Clubs, American Women's and Men's Clubs, Anglo-French Clubs, Kiwani Clubs, Lion and Lioness Clubs and Rotary Clubs, along with clubs for business people and others. Paris is home to a plethora of clubs and societies founded and run by expatriates. During October, many organisations hold 'open houses' or other events to induct new members.

In the Paris region, there are several arts groups, including The English Cathedral Choir of Paris, The International Players (an amateur drama group), the Paris Decorative and Fine Arts Society and The Royal Scottish Country Dance Society. There's also an English Language Library for the blind in the 17th *arrondissement*.

Outside the capital, there are Anglophone clubs and societies in certain areas only, such as Dordogne, Bordeaux and the Côte d'Azur, although most are in the Ile-de-France. The British Consulate publishes a free *Digest of British and Franco-British Clubs, Societies and Institutions* (published by the British Community Committee and available free from the British Embassy in Paris – see **Appendix A**). Details of English-language clubs are also included in *The Best Places to Live in France* (Survival Books). Other sources of information about English-speaking clubs are *The Connexion* and *The News* (see **Appendix B**) and English-speaking churches, a directory of which is published by the Intercontinental Church Society (ICS, 1 Athena Drive, Tachbrook Park, Warwick CV34 6NL, UK, ☎ 01926-430347, 💻 www.ics-uk.org).

For French speakers (although many groups have at least one English-speaker), the Accueil des Villes Françaises (AVF), a French organisation designed to welcome newcomers to an area, is an option (see page 146). Many local clubs organise activities and pastimes such as chess, bridge, art, music, sports activities and sports outings, theatre, cinema and local history. Joining a local club is one of the easiest ways to meet people and make friends. If you want to integrate into your local community or French society in general, one of the best ways is to join a local French club. Ask at your local town hall (*mairie*) for information.

HOLIDAYS

A number of organisations offer holidays tailored to the requirements of seniors, including Club Monde Attitude (💻 http://club-monde-attitude.typepad.fr – in French only), the Union Nationale des Associations de Tourisme (UNAT, 💻 www.unat.asso.fr – in French only; click on '*Vacances seniors*' for details) and Vacances Bleues (💻 www.vacancesbleues.fr – available in English), while others offer holiday and travel reductions to those over 60 or 65, including the following:

● Air France (💻 www.airfrance.fr – in French only) – up to 75 per cent off standard fares for the over 60s under its *Evasion Jeune/Etudiants/Senior* scheme: details may be found on 💻 www.airfrance.fr/FR/fr/local/resainfovol/achat/gamme_tarifaire_metro.htm;

● Center Parcs (💻 www.centerparcs.fr – available in English; click on '*MODIFIER*' at the top right of the home page, then select '*Grande-Bretagne*' and select your village top right) – offers a 15 per cent reduction for seniors at its three French parks (and parks in other countries);

● Thomas Cook (💻 www.thomascook.fr – in French only) – offers 'long-stay' holidays at reduced rates.Cheap flights and holidays may be found on 💻 www.anyway.fr, 💻 www.directours.com, 💻 www.ebookers.fr, 💻 www.fr.lastminute.com, 💻 www.look-voyages.fr and 💻 www.nouvelles-frontieres.fr (all in French only).

DAY & EVENING CLASSES

Adult day and evening classes – formal and informal – are run by various organisations in all cities and large towns and even in many small towns and villages. The range and variety of subjects offered is endless and includes French and foreign languages, handicrafts, hobbies and sports, and business-related courses.

Many expatriate clubs and organisations organise day and evening classes in a variety of subjects. These include WICE (☎ 01 45 66 75 50, 💻 www.wice-paris.org), an Anglophone expatriate organisation.

Some expatriate organisations provide classes for children (e.g. English), particularly during school holidays. French universities run non-residential language and other courses during the summer holiday period.

For those whose French is up to it, there are dozens of institutions offering home study and other courses for adults. The Centre d'Enseignement à Distance (💻 www.cned.fr) is equivalent to the British Open University and offers a plethora of correspondence courses. There are also some 18 'Third Age Universities' in France, whose contact details can be found on the website of the Association Internationale des Universités du Troisième Age (💻 http://aiuta.org – available in English; click on 'Universities', then on 'Europe' and 'France et Dom-Tom').

Among the most popular classes with foreigners are those concerned with cooking (and eating). A full list of companies offering cookery courses and gastronomic breaks is included in the *Reference Guide to Travellers in France* available from the French Tourist Office. The most famous French cookery school is the École Cordon Bleu (💻 www.cordonbleu.edu – in English). Many famous French chefs have founded cookery schools, including Auguste Escoffier, Michel Guérard, Roger Vergé and Paul Bocuse, the 'English' version of whose website (💻 www.bocuse.fr) includes the following description of the renowned Restaurant Bocuse: 'Located at 4 km in the north of Lyon on the edges of Saone not far from the bridge of Collonges, this house of family became the road of all the greedy ones.'

Montmartre grape harvest festival, Paris

11.
ODDS & ENDS

This chapter contains (in alphabetical order) miscellaneous information relevant to retirees in France, including crime and security, culture shock, legal and general advice, religion, the French police, social customs and voting rights – as well as a few key facts about France. For comprehensive information about just about all aspects of living in France, see our sister publication *Living and Working in France* by David Hampshire (Survival Books).

CRIME

France has a similar crime rate to most other European countries and in common with them crime has increased considerably in recent years; the number of reported crimes has almost doubled in a decade: an estimated 18m offences are reported to the police each year (over half of which are related to noise!), 5m resulting in an official crime report (*procès verbal/PV*) and 1.3m in legal proceedings, 650,000 in court, although more than half of these cases are dropped. Such figures have been compiled only since 2003, when the government set up the Observatoire National de la Délinquance, and available to the public only since February 2006 (go to 🖳 www.inhes.interieur.gouv.fr and click on '*OND*' and then '*Bulletins mensuels*').

Stiffer sentences have failed to stem the spiralling crime rate, and prisons are bursting at the seams with almost 60,000 inmates (around 95 per cent of them men) – nearly 12,000 more than their official capacity, some housing almost twice as many prisoners as they were designed for, although new prisons are under construction and the 'occupancy rate' is much lower than the UK's: 88 prisoners per 10,000 population compared with 143 (and 724 in the US!). More than 35 per cent of those sentenced to prison terms manage to avoid them, and over 1,000 convicted offenders are on parole, wearing an electronic bracelet. There's no death penalty in France, where the maximum prison sentence is 30 years.

Although most crimes are against property, violent crime is increasing, particularly in the Ile-de-France. Mugging is on the increase throughout France, although it's still rare in most cities. In some towns in southern France pensioners have been the target of muggers and even truffle hunters have been robbed of their harvest at gunpoint.

⚠ **Caution**

Sexual harassment (or worse) is common in France, where women should take particular care late at night and never hitchhike alone.

The worst area for crime is the Mediterranean coast (one of the most corrupt and crime-ridden regions in Europe), particularly around Marseille and Nice, where most crime is attributable to a vicious underworld of racketeers and drug dealers. Marseille is notorious as the centre of organised crime such as drug-trafficking, money-laundering, robbery and prostitution. There's a growing use of guns in urban crime, and gang killings are fairly frequent in Marseille and Corsica, where separatist groups such as the *Front Libéral National Corse* (*FLNC*), *Cuncolta Naziunalist* and the *Mouvement pour l'Autodétermination* (*MPA*) have become increasingly violent in recent years.

Thefts are soaring (around half of crimes involve theft) and burglary has reached epidemic proportions in some areas (holiday or second homes are a popular target). Many people keep dogs as a protection or deterrent against burglars and fit triple-locked and steel-reinforced doors. However, crime in rural areas remains low and it's still common for people in villages and small towns not to lock their homes or cars.

Car theft and theft from cars is rife in Paris and other cities. Foreign-registered cars are a popular target, particularly expensive models, which are often stolen to order and spirited abroad.

Car burning has become a popular 'sport' among urban youth gangs. An average of 200 cars are set alight in various cities (especially Mulhouse and Strasbourg) every weekend. Other 'games' include driving without lights at night and shooting at the first car to flash its headlights!

Pickpockets and bag-snatchers have long been a plague in Paris, where the 'charming' street urchins (often gypsies) are highly organised and trained. They surround and distract you, and when your attention is diverted pick you clean without your noticing. Keep them at arm's length, if necessary by force, and keep a firm grip on your valuables. Always remain vigilant in tourist haunts, queues and on the *métro*. **Never** tempt fate with an exposed wallet or purse or by flashing your money around and hang on tight to your bags. One of the most effective methods of protecting your passport, money, travellers' cheques and credit cards, is with a money belt. Tourists and travellers are the targets of some of France's most enterprising criminals, including highwaymen (see page 220) and train robbers.

You can usually safely walk almost anywhere at any time of day or night and there's no need for anxiety or paranoia about crime. However, you should be 'street-wise' and take certain elementary precautions. These include avoiding high-risk areas at night, such as tower block suburbs, which are inhabited or frequented by the unemployed, drug addicts, prostitutes and pickpockets.

Street people (*clochards*) in Paris and other cities may occasionally harass you, but they're generally harmless. You can safely travel on the Paris *métro* (and other *métros* in France) at any time, although some stations are best avoided late at night and you should **always** beware of pickpockets, who tend to snatch bags and jump off trains just as the doors are closing.

When you're in an unfamiliar city, ask a policeman, taxi driver or other local person whether there are any unsafe neighbourhoods – and avoid them!

Note that it's a criminal offence not to attempt to help someone who has been a victim of crime, at least by summoning assistance.

CULTURE SHOCK

The story is all too familiar among retirees abroad and France is no exception: During the initial 'honeymoon' period life is new and exciting; the sun is shining and you've got a tan to prove it; dining out is cheap; and your fellow retirees at home are green with envy. However, after those initial blissful few weeks the novelty starts to wear off and you become frustrated: the plumber who promised he would fix the bathroom tap last week still hasn't appeared, the red tape seems interminable, you're finding

it difficult to make new friends, you can never find what you want in the shops, nobody seems to understand your rusty school French and you cannot understand half of what is said to you. You even find yourself missing the drizzle back home and wondering why you ever retired to France.

The above pattern of emotions form part of a well documented condition known as 'culture shock' – you may find it reassuring to know that most expatriates go through the same feelings when they move abroad. Some retirees (the minority) give in to the negative feelings and return to their home country, but the majority persevere with their new life abroad and go on to enjoy a fulfilling and happy retirement in France. There's much you can do to help settle in and ensure that you're among the retirees whose retirement in France is a triumph rather than a failure. Below are some tips to smooth your move to France and help make settling in easier.

Before You Go

● Do as much research as possible about France and the area you're moving to before leaving home. Visit some of the many websites (see **Appendix C**) about France which have expatriate forums. Forewarned is forearmed and settling into a new place is much easier if you have a good idea of what to expect.

● Take a course in French; English isn't widely spoken in France and even those who do speak it are often reluctant to do so (other than a few basic words and phrases). If you speak French, you'll feel less helpless and local people will warm to you more. See **Learning the Language** on page 47 for further information.

● Keep your expectations realistic: for example, not all of France has a

marvellous climate; the Mediterranean coast and Corsica may be pleasant for much of the year, but it can (and frequently does) pour with rain for days on end in winter and many properties don't have central heating and are cold and damp. In complete contrast, the summer months can be swelteringly hot.

Accommodation

- When you first move to France, it's better initially to rent a property (rather than buy), which allows you time to get a feel for an area without the commitment and expense of buying a property – then, if you don't like the location, you can move somewhere else relatively easily.

- Don't burn your bridges and, if you can afford it, maintain your home abroad until you're sure you want to spend your retirement in France. Even if you're sure you don't want to return to your home country, it's comforting to know that you have an escape route if you need it. Retirees who sell up and cut all ties with

their home country can feel trapped in France, particularly if things go wrong.

- Move to somewhere with good ferry and/ or flight connections with your home town so that you can pop back easily and cheaply if you wish to. See **Getting There** on page 28 for more information.

Arrival

- Make an effort to get out and meet people, as the French generally won't come to you. Join a local club or society, even if there isn't an activity you're particularly interested in – at least you'll have the opportunity to meet other people and talk to them.

- Be as flexible as possible and try to accept unusual and frustrating aspects of French life: make allowances for the slower, more formal approach (see **Social Customs** on page 257) and remember that French paperwork is relentless and the red tape frustrating for everyone, including the French – you can save yourself time and stress by paying a professional to sort it out.

- **Finally, allow yourself time to adapt – expect it to take at least six months – but most of all, enjoy it!**

See also **Finding Help** on page 143 for further advice and tips on settling in.

FACTS ABOUT FRANCE

Capital: Paris.
Population: around 62m.
Largest cities: Paris (pop. 2.6m), Lyon (1.6m), Marseille (1.4m) and Lille (1.1m).
Geography: France is the largest country in western Europe and covers an area of 550,000km² (212,300mi²), stretching 1,050km (650mi) from north to south and almost the same distance from west to east. Its land and sea border extends for

,800km (around 3,000mi) and includes some 3,200km (2,000mi) of coast.
Government: Republican and traditionally highly centralised, although more responsibilities have recently been delegated to regional and departmental administrations.
Health: Number of doctors per thousand population 3.37; dentists 0.67; nurses 7.24; midwives 0.26; chemists 1.06 (source: World Health Organization).
Time: GMT plus one hour in winter; GMT plus two hours in summer (i.e. always one hour ahead of the UK). Times in France are usually written using the 24-hour clock, e.g. 3pm is 15h.

POLICE

There are three main police forces in France: the *police nationale*, the *gendarmerie nationale* and the *Compagnie Républicaine de la Sécurité* (*CRS*).

French policemen are addressed formally as *monsieur/madame l'agent* and colloquially called *flics* (cops), although there are many less polite names.

The *police nationale* are under the control of the Interior Ministry and are called *agents de police*. They deal with all crime within the jurisdiction of their police station (*commissariat de police*) and are most commonly seen in towns, distinguished by the silver buttons on their uniforms. At night and in rain and fog, they often wear white caps and capes.

The *gendarmerie nationale/gardes-mobiles* is part of the army and under the control of the Ministry of Defence, although it's at the service of the Interior Ministry. *Gendarmes* wear blue uniforms and traditional *képis*, and are distinguished by the gold buttons on their uniforms. They deal with serious crime on a national scale and general law and order in rural areas and are responsible for motorway patrols, air safety, mountain rescue, and air and coastal patrols. *Gendarmes* include police motorcyclists (*motards*), who patrol in pairs. The 3,600 brigades of *gendarmes* are to be linked into groups of three or four to improve law enforcement in rural areas.

The *CRS* is often referred to as the riot police, as it's responsible for crowd control and public disturbances, although it also has other duties, including life-saving on beaches in summer. Over the years the *CRS* has acquired a notorious reputation for its violent response to demonstrations (*manifestations*) and public disturbances, although often under extreme provocation. The mere appearance of the *CRS* at a demonstration is enough to raise the temperature (in fact, provoking its appearance is the undeclared aim of many demonstrators!), although it has been trying to improve its public image.

In addition to the three kinds of police mentioned above, most cities and medium-size towns have a municipal police (*police municipale/corps urbain*), who deal mainly with petty crime, traffic offences and road accidents, and there's a general movement in favour of 'neighbourhood policing' (*îlotage*) throughout France. Municipal policemen traditionally wore a *képi* (like *gendarmes*), although this has been replaced by a flat, peaked cap. While officers of the *gendarmerie nationale*, the *police nationale* and the *CRS* are armed, *police municipale* aren't, unless the local *préfet* and *maire* decide that they should be.

In general, French police (of any type) aren't popular with the public and have an unenviable reputation, particularly among ethnic groups. Police 'brutality', usually directed towards racial minorities, has resulted in riots in some areas; in autumn

2005, the worst disturbances in Paris since 1968 were allegedly the outcome of police harassment. On the other hand, an increase in attacks on police in recent years prompted the government in 2001 to pledge over €300m for the recruitment of some 2,700 police to patrol the streets and, following the 2002 election, the new Prime Minister announced measures to recruit an additional 13,500 officers within the police and *gendarmerie* over the following five years. It's also planned to 'encourage' the police and *gendarmes* to work together, which they've traditionally been loath to do.

The police can stop you and demand identification at any time (*contrôle de papiers*), so it's advisable to carry your passport or residence permit (*carte de séjour*) at all times and, if you're driving, your vehicle documents (i.e. *carte grise*, driving licence and insurance certificate). If you don't have any identification, you can be arrested. If your identification documents are stolen or lost, you must report immediately to the nearest police station, where you must make a *déclaration de perte ou de vol*. You'll be given a receipt, which will be accepted by the authorities until new documents are issued. It's wise to keep copies of all important documents (e.g. passport, visa and *carte de séjour*) in a safe place so that replacements are easier to obtain.

If you're arrested, you're required to state your name, age and permanent address only. **Never** make or sign a statement without legal advice and the presence of a lawyer. Unless your French is fluent, you should make it clear that you don't understand French and, in any case, ask permission to call your lawyer or embassy. Someone from your embassy should be able to provide a list of English-speaking lawyers.

The police can hold you in custody for 24 hours, although you're entitled to see a lawyer within three hours of arrest.

After 24 hours they need the authority of a magistrate. If the offence under investigation involves state security, two further 48-hour extensions can be granted, making a total of five days. If you're accused of a serious offence, such as possession of, or trafficking drugs, it may be difficult to obtain bail. A Council of Europe commission recently stated that suspects in France ran a 'not inconsiderable risk' of being mistreated while in police detention.

The police don't prosecute criminal cases in France, which is done by a public prosecutor. Police can fine offenders (and do so, particularly if they're non-residents) on the spot for motoring offences, such as speeding and drunken driving, and fines must be paid in cash. You're entitled to ask the name and particulars of any policeman who stops you, although it may be better to do this **after** you've found out what you've been stopped for!

All French residents have a police record (even if it's blank!) and you may be asked to produce it (e.g. if you need to travel to or work in certain countries). To obtain a copy of your record (*extrait de casier judiciaire*), you should send details of your date and place of birth and a copy of your passport and *carte de séjour* to the Service du Casier Judiciaire, 107 rue du Landreau, 44079 Nantes Cedex.

> If you need to contact the police in an emergency, dialling 17 will put you in touch with your local *gendarmerie* or *commissariat de police*, listed at the front of your local telephone directory.

If you lose anything or are the victim of a theft, you must report it in person at a police station and complete a report (*déclaration de vol/plainte*), of which you'll receive a copy. This must usually be done within 24 hours if you plan to make a claim

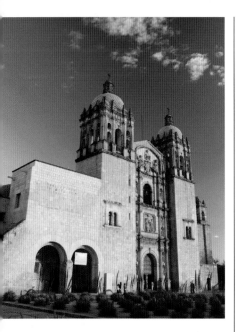

on an insurance policy. Don't, however, expect the police to be the slightest bit interested in your loss.

RELIGION

France has officially been a secular state since the Revolution and therefore has a long tradition of religious tolerance; every resident has total freedom of religion without hindrance from the state or community, and the majority of the world's religious and philosophical movements have centres or meeting places in Paris and other major cities. Few French people are atheists, although many are agnostics. The majority of the population is Christian, by far the largest number belonging to the Catholic faith (around 62 per cent of the population) and a mere 2 per cent Protestants. The second-largest religious group is Muslims (6 per cent), mostly immigrants from North Africa, and France is home to some 700,000 Jews. Details of mosques in France can be found on 🖳 http://mosquee.free.fr and a list of synagogues on 🖳 www.pages jaunes.fr (enter *Synagogues* in the first box and then the name of the town where you're looking for a synagogue).

Religious observance is declining and attendance at Catholic mass has dropped to around 15 per cent (attendance is lowest in Paris and among those aged 18 to 35). Only some 50 per cent of marriages are consecrated in a church and 60 per cent of babies baptised. Parish priests have lost much of their traditional influence and there's a serious shortage of recruits for the priesthood. The most important religious shrine in France is that of Our Lady at Lourdes, which receives hundreds of thousands of visitors every year in search of a miracle cure.

Church and state were officially divorced in 1905 and direct funding of the church by the state is illegal, which means that many churches are in poor repair. The Catholic church is prominent in education, where it maintains many private schools separate from the state education system, although largely funded by the state. An attempt to abolish state funding for religious schools by the Socialists in the '80s generated fierce opposition and was quickly abandoned.

There are over 50 Anglican churches in France, and details of English-language services throughout France (and indeed the world) are contained in the *Directory of English-Speaking Churches Abroad*, published by the Intercontinental Church Society, 1 Athena Drive, Tachbrook Park, Warwick, CV34 6NL, UK (☎ 01926-430347, 🖳 www.ics- uk.org).

SOCIAL CUSTOMS

All countries have particular (and peculiar) social customs and France is no exception. As a foreigner you'll probably be excused if you accidentally insult your hosts, but it's better to be aware of accepted taboos and courtesies, especially as the French are much more formal than most foreigners (especially Americans and Britons) imagine.

Greeting

When you're introduced to a French person, you should say 'good day, Sir/Madam' (*bonjour madame/monsieur*) and shake hands (a single pump is enough – neither limp nor knuckle-crushing). *Salut* (hi or hello) is used only among close friends and young people. When saying goodbye, it's customary to shake hands again. In an office, everyone shakes hands with everyone else on arrival at work **and** when they depart. It's also customary to say good day or good evening (*bonsoir*) on entering a small shop and goodbye (*au revoir madame/monsieur*) on leaving. *Bonjour* becomes *bonsoir* around 18.00 or after dark, although if you choose *bonsoir* (or

bonjour), don't be surprised if the response isn't the same. *Bonne nuit* (good night) is used when going to bed or leaving a house in the evening. On leaving a shop you may be wished *bonne journée* (have a nice day) or variations such as *bon après-midi, bonne fin d'après-midi, bon dimanche* or *bon week-end*, to which you may reply *vous aussi, vous de même* or *et vous*. The standard and automatic reply to *merci* is *je vous en prie* (you're welcome).

Titles should generally be used when addressing or writing to people, particularly when the person is elderly. The president of a company or institution should be addressed as *monsieur* (madame) *le président* (*la présidente*), a courtesy title usually retained in retirement. The mayor must be addressed as *Monsieur/Madame le Maire* (even female mayors are *le Maire*!). Don't

address someone as *cher/chère* (dear) unless you know them very well!

Kissing

To kiss or not to kiss, that is the question. It's best to take it slowly when negotiating this social minefield and to take your cue from the French. You shouldn't kiss (*faire la bise*) when first introduced to an adult, although young children will expect to be kissed. If a woman expects you to kiss her, she will offer her cheek. (Note that men kiss women and women kiss women but men don't kiss men, unless they're relatives or very close friends.) The 'kiss' isn't usually a proper kiss, more a delicate brushing of the cheeks accompanied by kissing noises, although some extroverts will plant a great wet smacker on each side of your face.

The next question is which cheek to kiss first. Again, take your cue from the natives, as the custom varies from region to region (and even the natives aren't always sure where to start).

Finally, you must decide how many kisses to give. Two is the standard number, although many people kiss three or four or even six times. It depends partly on where you are in France. The British travel agent Thomas Cook recently published a *French Kissing Guide*, according to which four kisses are the norm in northern France, three in the mid-west and southern central areas and two in the west, east and extreme south, a single kiss being acceptable only in the department of Charente-Maritime! However, much also depends on how well you know the person concerned: acquaintances might kiss twice, friends four times and old friends six!

Kissing usually takes place when you take your leave as well as when you greet someone. (It's also customary to kiss everyone in sight – including the men if you're a man – at midnight on New Year's Eve!)

Vous & Tu

When talking to a stranger, use the formal form of address (*vous*). Don't use the familiar form (*tu/toi*) or call someone by his first name until you're invited to do so. Generally the older, more important or local person will invite the other to use the familiar *tu* form of address (called *tutoiement*) and first names; in fact, the switch may suddenly happen and you should pick up on it immediately or you'll forever be stuck with the *vous* form. The familiar form is used with children, animals and God, but almost never with your elders or work superiors. However, the French are becoming less formal and the under 50s often use *tu* and first names with work colleagues (unless they're of the opposite sex, when *tu* may imply a special intimacy!), and will quickly switch from *vous* to *tu* with new social acquaintances, although older people may be reluctant to make the change.

> Some people always remain *vous*, such as figures of authority (the local mayor) or those with whom you have a business relationship, e.g. your bank manager, tax officials and policemen.

Gifts

If you're invited to dinner by a French person (which is a sign that you've been accepted into the community), take along a small present of flowers, a plant or chocolates. Gifts of foreign food or drink aren't generally well received unless they're highly prized in France (such as scotch whisky); foreign wine, however good the quality, isn't recommended! Some people say you must never take wine, as this implies that your hosts don't know what wine to buy, although this obviously depends on your hosts and how well you know them. If you do take wine, however, don't be surprised if your hosts put it to one side for a future occasion; they will already have planned the wine for the meal and know that a wine needs to settle before it can be drunk. Flowers can be tricky, as to some people carnations mean bad luck, chrysanthemums are for cemeteries (they're placed on graves on All Saints' Day), red roses signify love and are associated with the Socialists and yellow roses have something to do with adultery, while marigolds (*soucis*) simply aren't *de rigueur*. If in doubt, ask a local florist for advice; as likely as not, he will know your hosts and their taste in flowers!

Eating & Drinking

French meals can go on for a **very** long time; four or five hours isn't unusual. You

shouldn't serve any drinks (or expect to be served one) before all guests have arrived – even if some are an hour or more late! If you're offered a drink, wait until your host has toasted everyone's health (*santé*) before taking a drink. **Never** pour your own drinks (except water) when invited to dinner. If you aren't offered a(nother) drink, it's time to go home. Always go easy on the wine and other alcohol; if you drink to excess you're unlikely to be invited back! The French say *bon appétit* before starting a meal and you shouldn't start eating until your hosts do. It's polite to eat everything that's put on your plate. Cheese is served before dessert.

Conversation

The French love detailed and often heated discussions, but there are certain topics of conversation that need handling with care. These include money, which is generally avoided by the French; it's a major *faux pas* to ask a new acquaintance what he does for a living, as his job title will often give an indication of his salary. Far safer to stick to discussions of food and drink. When conversing, even in the midst of a heated debate, avoid raising your voice, which is considered vulgar. Note also that the French often stand close when engaging in conversation, which you may find uncomfortable or even threatening at first.

Gesticulating

Like the Italians, the French talk with their hands – often more than with their tongues – but the art of gesticulation can be as difficult to master (and as full of pitfalls for the unwary) as the spoken language. Here are a few tips that could help you avoid a *faux pas*: never point with your index finger, which is considered rude, but use an open hand (which should also be used when 'thumbing' a lift); similarly, beckon with your four fingers, palm down; the thumb is used to mean 'one' when counting, not

he index finger; to indicate boredom, rub
your knuckles against your cheek, to show
surprise, shake your hand up and down,
and to convey disbelief pull down your lower
eyelid; tapping your fingers on the opposite
forearm while raising the forearm slightly
indicates an impending or actual departure
- usually as a result of boredom! The classic
French shrug is perhaps best left to the
natives!

Cards

The sending of cards, other than birthday
cards, isn't as common in France as in
some other countries. It isn't, for example,
usual to send someone a card following a
bereavement or after passing a driving test.
Instead of Christmas cards, the French send
New Year cards, but only to people they
don't normally see during the year.

Dress

Although the French are often formal in their
relationships, their dress habits, even in the
office and at occasions such as weddings
and funerals, are often extremely casual.
Note, however, that the French tend to judge
people by their dress, the style and quality
being as important as the correctness for the
occasion (people often wear 'designer' jeans
to dinner). You aren't usually expected to
dress for dinner, depending of course on the
sort of circles you move in. On invitations,
formal dress (black tie) is *smoking exigé/
tenue de soirée* and informal dress is *tenue
de ville*.

Phone Calls

Always introduce yourself before asking to
speak to someone on the telephone.

Surprisingly it's common to telephone at meal
times, e.g. 12.00 to 14.00 and around 20.00,
when you can usually be assured of finding
someone at home.

If you call at these times, you should
apologise for disturbing the household. It
isn't always advisable to make calls after
14.00 in the provinces, when many people
have a siesta.

Noise

It's common for there to be noise restrictions
in French towns and villages, particularly
with regard to the use of lawnmowers and
other mechanical tools. Restrictions are
imposed locally and therefore vary, but in
general, noisy activities are prohibited before
around 08.00 or 09.00 every day, after 19.00
on weekdays and Saturdays and after 12.00
on Sundays, and additionally at lunchtime
(e.g. 12.00 to 15.00) on Saturdays.

VOTING

As a resident of France, you're entitled to
vote in municipal or communal elections
(e.g. for a new *maire*) and European
elections but not French national elections
(e.g. for the president), unless you become
a French citizen. To be entitled to vote, you
must register with your *mairie* or town hall
(a simple form must be completed) – voting
rights apply to the year after registration
(from 1st January).

Whether or not (and for how long) you
retain your voting rights in your 'home'
country or previous country of residence
depends on the country. British subjects may
continue to vote in UK elections for 15 years
after leaving the country, provided they
retain a British passport and an electoral
registration. To check whether you're
registered, contact the electoral registration
office for your previous residential address
(this can be found via ☐ www.aboutmyvote.
co.uk or, for former Northern Ireland
residents, ☐ www.eoni.org.uk). If you aren't
registered, you must complete and return
an electoral registration form (downloadable
from the same website).

12.
RETURNING HOME

While many retirees dream of permanent retirement in France, it's a harsh fact of life that many of those who retire there will be forced (or choose) to return permanently to their home country at some time. The reasons are many and varied but are mostly due to personal circumstances, which can change dramatically overnight. Exact statistics are difficult to obtain because many people never register as residents in France or their home country and therefore don't 'exist' on official statistics, but it's estimated that at least one-third of those who retire to France return to their home country after a period.

Financial problems are the most common reason for leaving France. These may include being unable to meet capital gains or inheritance tax bills when your partner dies, struggling to make ends meet on a fixed pension, discovering that your monthly income doesn't cover care during ill health or disability, and investments that perform badly and dramatically reduce your income.

 Caution

The death of a partner is also a widespread cause of retirees leaving France and returning home. The widow or widower not only has to cope with possible financial hardship but also with the paperwork associated with inheritance (for many people, this is the first time they have to deal directly with French bureaucracy) and with loneliness. Many people find the situation impossible to bear and need the support of their family in their home country.

Ill health and disability are another reason retirees are forced to return to their home country. Retirees' home countries may not provide better facilities but, of course, offer treatment in their native language, and for many retirees it's a logical decision to return home.

Other retirees who make the decision to go home cite family ties as their main motive and it's easy to underestimate how much you'll miss your family (particularly grandchildren) and friends when you're in France.

If you do find that your retirement in France hasn't worked out as you'd planned or that there are no longer compelling reasons to stay, don't regard it as a failure on your part but simply as an adventure that turned out to be temporary rather than permanent. Once you've decided to leave France and return to your home country, however, it's important to plan ahead to ensure that you make the right financial and practical decisions.

This chapter is designed to help you plan your return home and includes information about timing, selling your home and settling your affairs in France, and practical tips for your return to a country you left many years ago and which may have changed considerably in the interim.

CAN YOU AFFORD IT?

Many northern European countries have a higher cost of living than France and you may find that your pension income isn't sufficient when you return home. The cost of property in your home country is another major financial concern, although if you sell your home in France for a profit (see **Selling Your Home** below), this may not be a problem.

Before you return, check whether you're entitled to allowances and benefits in your home country. Returning nationals are usually entitled to state benefits, but there may be conditions and requirements, e.g. a certain number of years' social security contributions in your home country. British nationals returning to the UK should contact the International Pension Centre (IPC) of the Department for Work and Pensions, Tyneview Park, Newcastle-upon-Tyne, NE98 1BA, UK (☎ 0191-218 7777, 💻 www.dwp.gov.uk) for information about benefits and allowances. The IPC publish a useful free booklet, *GL28 Coming from abroad and social security benefits*, which can be downloaded from its website.

TIMING

As with any life-changing decision, the timing of your departure from France is the key to success. Start planning your departure as far in advance as you can – at least six months, if possible. **Whatever your reasons for leaving and however distressing you find it to stay, try to avoid leaving in a rush.**

Taxation

If you're a resident in France, obtain expert advice on the timing of your move for tax purposes. In most countries, the annual tax year is the calendar year (i.e. from 1st January to 31st December), but some countries, e.g. the UK, have different tax years. Depending on your tax circumstances, it may be more advantageous to move at a certain time of the year.

Before leaving France, foreigners should pay any tax due for the previous year and the year of departure by applying for tax clearance. A tax return should be filed before departure and include your income and deductions from 1st January of the departure year up to the date of departure. Your local tax office will calculate the tax due and provide a written statement. In most cases, the previous year's taxes will be applied; if this results in overpayment, a claim must be made for a refund. It may pay you to keep your

French home for a while until the market improves and rent a property in your home country.

SELLING YOUR HOME

If you'll need to sell a home before leaving France, it's worth considering the following points.

Price & Property Market

Needless to say, the best way of ensuring a quick sale (or any sale) is to ask a realistic price. What this is will naturally depend on the property market in your area at the time you wish to sell. You must also, of course, take into account the property market in the area you plan to move to in your home country, because the price you obtain for your property in France will determine what sort of property you can buy when you return to your home country.

The national property market in France was generally stable between 2003 and 2006, with steady rises in most regions (generally well above inflation); in the first two years of the 21st century, annual increases of 20 per cent weren't unusual in the most popular areas (e.g. the Côte d'Azur, where available property is now in short supply). If you bought your property before 2002 you're likely to make a substantial profit, even if you sell below the current market value. If, however, you bought after 2002 the chances of making a profit are smaller and in some cases (particularly if you bought in the last few years), negligible, especially when you take the buying and selling costs into account. For further information about the French property market, see page 78.

To find out the market value of your property, you can ask an estate agent – most will provide a free appraisal of a home's value – or you can compare your home with others on the market or that have recently been sold. You should be prepared to drop the price slightly (e.g. 5 to 10 per cent) and should set it accordingly, but don't over-price it as it will deter buyers. You also need to decide how quickly you need to sell your home: if you're in a hurry it might be worth dropping the price for a quick sale. On the other hand, if you can wait six months there may be no need to reduce the price. In today's market, expect to wait at least three months for a definite offer and sale (six months in some areas).

Presentation

As well as accurate pricing, the best way to ensure a quick sale lies in the presentation of the property. First impressions (inside and out) are essential when potential buyers view your property, so it's important to present it in its best light and make it as attractive as possible. It pays to invest in a coat of paint (interior and exterior), a few touches of decoration (e.g. fresh flowers and plants) and a kitchen facelift (e.g. new cupboard doors).

> ☑ SURVIVAL TIP
>
> Be conservative in your decoration, avoid 'loud' colours and make sure that your home isn't cluttered.

It isn't always worth modernising your kitchen and bathroom unless you're sure the cost will be recouped in the sale price; it may be cheaper (and definitely less stressful) to reduce the asking price.

Who Sells Your Home?

Although the majority of properties in France are sold through estate agents (*agent immobilier*), a large number of owners sell their own homes. You must, however, appoint a *notaire* to handle the sale and hold the deposit, and you're strongly advised to obtain legal advice regarding contracts, etc..

The legal procedure is the same as for buying a property, but a few points are worth noting. You may be asked by an agent to sign a conditional clause in the sales contract that the sale is dependent on the buyer selling another property; **you aren't obliged to do so and should be wary of agreeing to such a clause**, particularly if the buyer is selling a property in the UK, where sales can be cancelled at any stage – you won't be able to cancel your agreement even if another would-be buyer offers you cash. Secondly, if a buyer wants to have the property inspected or surveyed, it's wise to have this done before contracts are signed.

Selling a Home Yourself

While certainly not for everyone, selling your own home is a viable option for many people and is particularly recommended when you're selling an attractive home at a realistic price in a favourable market. Saving estate agent's fees (which may be 10 per cent or even more) may allow you to offer the property at a more appealing price, which could be an important factor if you're seeking a quick sale.

How you market your home will depend on the type of home, the price, and the country or area from where you expect your buyer to come. For example, if your property isn't of a type and style and in an area desirable to local inhabitants, it's usually a waste of time advertising it in the local press. In any case, the first step is to get a professional looking 'for sale' sign made (showing your telephone number) and to erect it somewhere visible. Do some research into the best publications for advertising your property (if appropriate), and place an advertisement in those that look the most promising. If you own a property in an area popular with foreign buyers, it may be worthwhile using an overseas agent (see below) or advertising in foreign newspapers and magazines,

such as the English-language publications listed in **Appendix B**.

You could also have a leaflet printed (with pictures) extolling the virtues of your property, which you could drop into local letter boxes or have distributed with a local newspaper (many people buy a new home in the vicinity of their present home). You may also need a 'fact sheet' printed if your home's vital statistics aren't included in the leaflet mentioned above and could offer a finder's fee (e.g. €750) to anyone finding you a buyer. Don't omit to market your home around local companies, schools and organisations, particularly if they have many itinerant employees. Finally, it may help to provide information about local financing sources for potential buyers.

With a bit of effort and practice you may even make a better job of marketing your home than an agent! Unless you're in a hurry to sell, set yourself a realistic time limit for success, after which you can try an agent.

Using an Agent

Most owners prefer to use the services of an agent or notary, either in France or in their home country, particularly when selling a second home. If you purchased the property through an agent, it's often wise to use the same agent when selling, as he will already be familiar with it and may still have the details on file.

> You should take particular care when selecting an agent, as they vary considerably in their professionalism, expertise and experience (the best way to investigate agents is by posing as a buyer).

Note that many agents cover a relatively small area, so you should take care to choose one who regularly sells properties in your area and price range.

Capital Gains Tax

Capital gains tax (*impôt sur les plus-values*) is payable on the profit from sale of certain assets in France, including antiques, art and jewellery, securities and property. Gains net of capital gains tax (CGT) are added to other income and are liable for both income tax (see page 189) and social security contributions. Changes to the capital gains regulations were made in the Finance Act, 2004, which also requires a *notaire* handling a property sale to calculate and pay CGT on behalf of the vendor. For further information, see page 198.

TERMINATING A RENTAL CONTRACT

If you live in rented accommodation in France it's relatively easy to sort out your accommodation affairs. Most rental contracts state that the tenant should give the landlord three months' notice of the termination of the contract by registered letter (*lettre recommandée avec accusé de réception*).

Find out about the conditions for the return of your deposit. Some landlords accept the deposit in lieu of the last month's rental payment, but others require a month's rental payment and only return the deposit (or part of it) once they've checked the accommodation for damage and missing items. Some landlords charge tenants for cleaning at the end of the tenancy, although it's usually cheaper to clean the property yourself or pay a cleaner to do it for you. Be aware, however, that some landlords don't accept this and will present a bill for cleaning irrespective of whether you've cleaned it.

When your tenancy ends, ensure that you pay all outstanding utility bills and cancel any direct debits – it isn't uncommon for old tenants to find themselves paying the new tenants' bills!

SETTLING YOUR AFFAIRS IN FRANCE

When leaving France, there are many things to be considered and sorted out. The following checklist provides a guide to the essential tasks and should help make them easier (provided you don't leave everything to the last minute).

Checklist

● Arrange shipment of your furniture and belongings – book a removal or shipping company well in advance.

● Arrange to sell or dispose of anything you aren't taking with you.

● Check the immigration procedure for non-resident nationals in your home country.

● Cancel your residence permit.

● Inform the tax office that you're no longer resident and pay any outstanding income or capital gains tax or apply for a rebate. It's advisable to obtain expert advice regarding this (see **Timing** on page 264).

- Inform your utility companies (e.g. electricity, gas, water and telephone) in writing of your departure well in advance, particularly if you need to get a deposit refunded.

- Cancel all insurance policies unless they're valid in your home country.

- Close your bank account in France (unless you need to keep it open to pay bills or receive future payments) and cancel your direct debits.

- Check that you've paid all outstanding bills (e.g. utility, community).

- Ensure that you'll have adequate healthcare cover in your home country and while travelling there. You may need to take out a private health insurance policy.

- Return any library books and anything else you've borrowed.

- If you need to leave some loose ends when you depart (e.g. you haven't sold your house), you can give 'power of attorney' to a lawyer or professional you trust in France.

ARRIVAL IN YOUR HOME COUNTRY

Returning to a country you left a number of years ago can be a daunting prospect. Many things will have changed and the return home may not be an easy experience. It will hopefully be a happy one, but at the same time may be fraught with difficulties as you adjust to a new lifestyle that you may have idealised, particularly if you've left France because of problems there. You may also have financial problems, especially if the cost of

living in your home country is higher than in France and you cannot afford to buy a comparable home.

⚠ Caution

Be extremely careful before giving anyone power of attorney over your financial affairs in France (or anywhere else), as it isn't unknown for a lawyer or other professional to sell assets illegally and abscond with the money. If you must do it, it should be for a specific reason only and for a limited period.

You'll probably suffer from reverse culture shock (see **Culture Shock** on page 253) with much the same symptoms as you experienced when you first retired to France, and you may be surprised to find how long it takes for you to re-adapt to life in your home country. Expect to find your family and friends interested in your life in France at first, but bear in mind that most will lose interest after a while.

To make your return home as smooth as possible, you should follow the same advice for retiring abroad. Above all, try not to look on your return as a failure but the end of an adventure or a chapter in your life. Don't dwell on the past (if you must look back, try to remember the good times!) but look forward to getting acquainted with your home country all over again – like meeting an old friend after many years – and facing new and rewarding experiences.

coastline, Brittany

APPENDICES

APPENDIX A: USEFUL ADDRESSES

Embassies & Consulates

F oreign embassies are located in the capital Paris (those for selected English-speaking countries are listed below), and many countries also have consulates in other cities (all British consulates are listed below). Embassies and consulates are listed in the yellow pages under *Ambassades, Consulats et Autres Représentations Diplomatiques*.

Australia: 4 rue Jean Rey, 15e (☎ 01 40 59 33 00).

Ireland: 4 rue Rude, 16e (☎ 01 44 17 67 00).

Jamaica: 60 avenue Foch, 16e (☎ 01 45 00 62 25).

Malta: 92 avenue Champs Elysées, 8e (☎ 01 56 59 75 90).

New Zealand: 7ter rue Léonard de Vinci, 16e (☎ 01 45 01 43 43).

South Africa: 59 quai Orsay, 7e (☎ 01 53 59 23 23).

United Kingdom: 35 rue Faubourg St Honoré, 8e (see below) and 18 bis rue Anjou, 8e (☎ 01 44 51 31 02).

United States of America: 2 rue St Florentin, 1e (☎ 08 10 26 46 26) and 2 avenue Gabriel, 1e (☎ 01 43 12 22 22).

British Consulates-General

Consulates-General are permanently staffed during normal office hours.

Bordeaux: 353 boulevard du Président Wilson, BP 91, 33073 Bordeaux (☎ 05 57 22 21 10). Covers the departments of Ariège, Aveyron, Charente, Charente-Maritime, Corrèze, Creuse, Dordogne, Haute-Garonne, Gers, Gironde, Landes, Lot, Lot-et-Garonne, Pyrénées-Atlantiques, Hautes-Pyrénées, Deux-Sèvres, Tarn, Tarn-et-Garonne, Vienne and Haute-Vienne.

Lille: 11 square Dutilleul, 59800 Lille (☎ 03 20 12 82 72). Covers the departments of Aisne, Ardennes, Nord, Pas-de-Calais and Somme.

Lyon: 24 rue Childebert, 69288 Lyon Cedex 1 (☎ 04 72 77 81 70). Covers the departments of Ain, Allier, Ardèche, Cantal, Côte d'Or, Doubs, Drôme, Isère, Jura, Loire, Haute-Loire, Puy-de-Dôme, Rhône, Haute-Saône, Saône-et-Loire, Savoie, Haute-Savoie and the Territoire de Belfort.

Marseille: 24 avenue du Prado, 13006 Marseille (☎ 04 91 15 72 10). Covers the departments of Alpes-de-Haute-Provence, Hautes-Alpes, Alpes-Maritimes, Aude, Bouches-du-Rhône, Gard, Hérault, Lozère, Pyrénées-Orientales, Var and Vaucluse, as well as Corsica.

Paris: 35 rue du Faubourg Saint Honoré, 75008 Paris (☎ 01 44 51 31 02). Covers the departments of Aube, Calvados, Cher, Côtes d'Armor, Eure, Eure-et-Loir, Finstère, Ille-et-Vilaine, Indre, Indre-et-Loire, Loir-et-Cher, Loire, Loire-Atlantique, Loiret, Maine-et-Loire, Manche, Marne, Haute-Marne, Mayenne, Meurthe-et-Moselle, Meuse, Morbihan, Moselle, Nièvre, Oise, Bas-Rhin, Sarthe and Vosges, as well as the whole of the Ile-de-France and the overseas departments and territories.

British Honorary Consulates

Honorary consulates aren't permanently staffed and should be contacted **in emergencies only** (e.g. for urgent passport renewals or replacements).

Boulogne-sur-Mer: c/o Cabinet Barron et Brun, 28 rue Saint Jean, 62200 Boulogne-sur-Mer (☎ 03 21 87 16 80).

Cherbourg-Octeville: c/o P&O Ferries, Gare Maritime, BP46, 50652 Cherbourg-Octeville (☎ 02 33 88 65 60).

Dunkerque: c/o Lemaire Frères & Fils, 30 rue de l'Hermitte, BP 2/100, 59376 Dunkerque (☎ 03 28 58 77 00).

Le Havre: c/o LD Lines, 124 boulevard de Strasbourg, 76600 Le Havre (☎ 02 35 19 78 88).

Montpellier: 271 Le Capitole, Bâtiment A, 64 rue Alcyone, 34000 Montpellier (☎ 04 67 15 52 07).

Nantes: 16 boulevard Gabriel Giust'hau, BP 22026, 44020 Nantes Cedex 1 (☎ 02 51 72 72 60).

Toulouse: c/o English Enterprises, 8 allée du Commingues, 317700 Colomiers, 31300 Toulouse (☎ 05 61 30 37 91).

Tours: 7, rue des Rosiers, 37510 Savonnières (☎ 02 47 43 57 97).

Miscellaneous

Alliance Française, 101 boulevard Raspail, 75270 Paris Cedex 06 (☎ 01 42 84 90 00, 🖥 www.alliancefr.org). Famous language-teaching school.

Blevins Franks Tax Advisory Service (☎ 020-7015 2126, 🖥 www. blevinsfranks.com). International tax planning experts.

Brit Consulting, 11 rue Félix Faure, 75015 Paris (☎ 06 23 86 30 21, 🖥 www.britconsulting.com). A project management service for people building or renovating property in France.

British Association of Removers (BAR) Overseas, Tangent House, 62 Exchange Road, Watford, WD18 0TG, UK (☎ 01923-699480, 🖥 www. removers.org.uk).

Centre des Impôts de Non-Résidents, 9 rue d'Uzès, 75094 Paris Cedex 02 (☎ 01 44 76 18 00).

Centre Renseignements Douaniers (🖳 www.douane.gouv.fr). Customs information.

Chambre des Notaires, 12 avenue Victoria, 75001 Paris (☎ 01 44 82 24 00, 🖳 www.paris.notaires.fr).

Compagnie Nationale des Experts Immobiliers, 18 rue Volney, 75002 Paris (☎ 01 42 96 18 46, 🖳 www.expert-cnei.com).

Conseil Supérieur du Notariat, 31 rue du Général Foy, 75383 Paris Cedex 08 (☎ 01 44 90 30 00, 🖳 www.notaires.fr).

Department for Environment, Food & Rural Affairs (DEFRA), Nobel House, 17 Smith Square, London SW1P 3JR, UK (☎ 020-7238 6951/0845-933 5577, 🖳 www.defra.gov.uk).

Fédération Nationale de l'Immobilier (FNAIM), 129 rue du Faubourg St Honoré, 75008 Paris (🖳 www.fnaim.fr).

Federation of Overseas Property Developers, Agents and Consultants (FOPDAC), First Floor, 618 Newmarket Road, Cambridge CB5 8LP (☎ 0870-350 1223, 🖳 www.fopdac.com).

Gîtes de France, 59 rue St Lazare, Paris 75439 Cedex 09 (☎ 01 49 70 75 75, 🖳 www.gites-de-france.fr).

Office du Tourisme, 25 rue des Pyramides, 75001 Paris (☎ 08 92 68 30 00, 🖳 www.parisinfo.com).

De Particulier à Particulier, 40 rue du docteur Roux, 75724 Cedex 15 (☎ 01 40 56 33 33, 🖳 www.pap.fr).

Société d'Aménagement Foncier et d'Etablissement Rural (SAFER), 91 rue du Faubourg St Honoré, 75008 Paris (☎ 01 44 69 86 00, 🖳 www.safer.fr).

Union Nationale des AVF (Accueils des Villes Françaises), 3 rue de Paradis, 75010 Paris (☎ 01 47 70 45 85, 🖳 www.avf.asso.fr).

Property Exhibitions

Below is a list of the main exhibition organisers in the UK and Ireland. Note that you may be charged a small admission fee.

Homes Overseas Exhibition (UK ☎ 020-7002 8300, 🖥 www. blendoncommunications.co.uk). The largest organisers of international property exhibitions, who stage over 30 exhibitions each year at a range of venues in the UK and Ireland.

International Property Show (UK ☎ 01252-720652, 🖥 www. internationalpropertyshow.com). Takes place several times a year in London and Manchester.

A Place in the Sun Exhibition (UK ☎ 0870-352 8888, 🖥 www. aplaceinthesunlive.com). A new annual show in London.

World Class Homes (UK ☎ 01582-832001/0800-731 4713, 🖥 www. worldclasshomes.co.uk). Exhibitions are held in small venues around the UK and include mainly British property developers.

World of Property Show (UK ☎ 01323-726040, 🖥 www. outboundpublishing.com). The *World of Property* magazine publishers (see **Appendix B**) organise three large property exhibitions a year, two in the south of England and one in the north.

APPENDIX B – FURTHER READING

This appendix lists the major English-language publications about France and books on France published by Survival Books, which can be ordered at 🖳 www.survivalbooks.net. Other books and magazines are mentioned in the relevant chapters.

English-language Newspapers & Magazines

The Connexion (☎ 04 93 32 16 59, 🖳 www.connexionfrance.com). Monthly newspaper.

Everything France Magazine, Brooklands Magazines (UK ☎ 01342-828700, 🖳 www.everythingfrancemag.co.uk). Bi-monthly lifestyle magazine.

Focus on France, Outbound Publishing (UK ☎ 01323-726040, 🖳 www.outboundpublishing.com). Quarterly property magazine.

France Magazine, Archant Life (UK ☎ 01242-216050, 🖳 www.francemag.co.uk). Monthly lifestyle magazine.

France Review (☎ 05 53 91 65 44, 🖳 www.francereview.com). Bi-monthly magazine in French and English.

France-USA Contacts (☎ 01 56 53 54 54, 🖳 www.fusac.fr). Free bi-weekly magazine.

French News, SARL Brussac (☎ 05 53 06 84 40, 🖳 www.french-news.com). Monthly newspaper.

French Property News, Archant Life (UK ☎ 020-8543 3113, 🖳 www.french-property-news.com). Monthly property magazine.

The Irish Eyes Magazine (☎ 01 41 74 93 03, 🖳 www.irisheyes.fr). Monthly Paris cultural magazine.

Living France, Archant Life (UK ☎ 01858-438832, 🖳 www.livingfrance.com). Monthly lifestyle/property magazine.

Normandie & South of England Magazine (☎ 02 33 77 32 70, 🖳 www. normandie-magazine.fr). News and current affairs about Normandy and parts of southern England, published eight times a year in English and French.

Paris Voice/Paris Free Voice (☎ 01 47 70 45 05, 🖳 www.parisvoice. com). Free weekly newspaper.

The Riviera Reporter (☎ 04 93 45 77 19, 🖳 www.riviera-reporter.com). Bi-monthly free magazine covering the Côte d'Azur.

The Riviera Times (☎ 04 93 27 60 00, 🖳 www.rivieratimes.com). Monthly free newspaper covering the Côte d'Azur and Italian Riviera.

Books

The books listed below are just a selection of the hundreds written about France. The publication title is followed by the author's name and the publisher.

Culture

Culture Wise France, Joe Laredo (Survival Books). The essential guide to French customs and etiquette.

The Essence of Style, Joan Dejean (Free Press).

France, the Land (Lands, Peoples & Cultures), Greg Nickles (Crabtree Publishing).

French Cinema: From its Beginnings to the Present, Henri Fournier Lanzoni (Continuum International Publishing Group).

Paris Jazz: A Guide, Luke Miner (The Little Bookroom).

Savoir Flair, Polly Platt (Distri Books).

The Alps: A Cultural History, Andrew Beattie (Signal Books).

The Complete Merde, Genevieve (Harper Collins).

Food & Drink

Best Street Markets in France, M Anderson & R Fennell (Travellers Temptation Press).

Bistro, Laura Washburn, Ryland (Peters & Small).

The French Kitchen, Joanne Harris & Fran Warde (Doubleday).

The Great Wines of France, Clive Coates (Mitchell Beazley).

Love Food Love Paris, Kate Whiteman (AA Travel Publications).

Out to Lunch in Provence, Mike Aalders (Kenneth Mason).

The Rubbish on our Plates, Fabien Perucca & Gérard Pouradier (Prion).

Truffles and Tarragon, Anne Gregg (Bantam).

Vegetarian France, Alex Bourke & Alan Todd (Vegetarian Guides).

Vintcents French Food Dictionary, Charles Vintcent (Harriman House Publishing).

Why French Women Don't Get Fat, Mireille Guiliano (Chatto & Windus).

History

Agincourt: A New History, Anne Curry (Tempus Publishing).

The French Revolution, Christopher Hibbert (Penguin).

The Measure of All Things: The Seven-year Odyssey that Transformed the World, Ken Alder (Little, Brown).

Napoleon, Vincent Cronin (HarperCollins).

That Sweet Enemy: The British and the French from the Sun King to the Present, Robert & Isabelle Tombs (Pimlico).

The Unfree French: Life under the Occupation, Richard Vinen (Penguin).

La Vie en Bleu: France and the French since 1900, Roderick Kedward (Penguin).

The White Cities, Joseph Roth (Granta Books).

Language

101 French Idioms, Jean-Marie Cassagne (Passport Books).

101 French Proverbs, Jean-Marie Cassagne (Passport Books).

Better French, Monique Jackman (Studymates).

Colloquial French, C. Kirk-Greene (Foulsham).

Conversational French Made Easy, Monique Jackman (Hadley Pager Info.).

French Idioms and Expressions, C. Kirk-Greene (Foulsham).

French Language Survival Guide (Harper Collins).

Insider's French, Eleanor & Michel Levieux (The University of Chicago Press).

Rude French, Georges Pilard (Harrap).

Slang & Colloquialisms, Georgette Marks & Charles Johnson (Harrap).

Living

Buying a Home in France, David Hampshire (Survival Books). All you will ever need to know to successfully buy, rent or sell property in France.

Find Out About France, Duncan Crosbie (Barron's Educational).

Living and Working in France, David Hampshire (Survival Books)

Living in Provence, Dane McDowell & Christian Sarramon (Flammarion).

More More France Please, Helena Frith-Powell (Gibson Square).

Paris Shops & More, Angelika Taschen (Taschen).

Rural Living in France, Jeremy Hobson (Survival Books). Everything you need to know to create your very own French rural idyll.

People

50 Reasons to Hate the French, Jules Eden & Alex Clarke (Quetzal Publishing UK).

French or Foe, Polly Platt (Distri Books).

How to be French, Margaret Ambrose (New Holland Publishers).

Sixty Million Frenchmen Can't Be Wrong, Jean-Benoit Nadeau (Robson Books).

Tourist Guides

AA Explorer France (AA Publishing).

Cruising French Waterways, Hugh McKnight (Adlard Coles Nautical).

The Food Lover's Guide to France, Patricia Wells (Workman Publishing).

France and the Grand Tour, Jeremy Black (Palgrave Macmillan).

France (Eyewitness Travel Guides) (Dorling Kindersley).

France (Lonely Planet Country Guide), Nicola Williams (Lonely Planet).

France (Rough Guide Travel Guides) (Rough Guides).
Provence A-Z, Peter Mayle (Profile Books).

Via Ferrata: A Complete Guide to France, Philippe Poulet (Cordee).

Travel Literature

France in Mind: An Anthology, Powers Leccese (Vintage Books).

Next Stop France, Claire Boast (Heinemann).

Paris: a Literary Companion, Ian Littlewood (Franklin Watts).

Paris & Elsewhere: Selected Writings, Richard Cobb (New York Review of Books).

This is Paris, Miroslav Sasek (Universe Publishing).

Something to Declare: Essays on France, Julian Barnes (Alfred A. Knopf).

Travels with a Donkey in the Cévennes, Robert Louis Stevenson (Oxford).

A Year in Provence, Peter Mayle (Profile Books).

We'll Always Have Paris: American Tourists in France since 1930, H. Levenstein (University of Chicago Press).

APPENDIX C – USEFUL WEBSITES

B elow is a selection of useful websites not otherwise mentioned in the text, which are listed under headings in alphabetical order.

General Information

Adminet (🖥 http://adminet.com). Information about selected towns in France.

AFP (🖥 www.afp.com). World news in French.

All About France (🖥 www.all-about-france.com).

Alliance Française (🖥 www.alliancefr.org). The famous French language school.

Alliance française in Paris (🖥 www.paris.alliancefr.fr).

Anglo Info (🖥 www.angloinfo.com). Information and forums specific to Aquitaine, Brittany, Normandy, Poitou-Charentes and Provence.

Australian Embassy in France (🖥 www.ambafrance-au.org). Plenty of useful information and fact sheets, not only relevant to Australia.

Bonjour (🖥 www.bonjour.com). French tuition.

Box424 (🖥 www.box424.com). Information and entertainment for Expats in France and worldwide.

British Association of Tour Operators to France (🖥 www.holidayfrance.org.uk).

Cityvox (🖥 www.cityvox.com). Information about eating out, accommodation, foreign food shops, etc. in selected towns in France.

EDF (🖥 http://nucleaire.edf.fr). Information about nuclear power stations in France.

Electricité de France (⌨ www.edf.fr).

L'Etudiant (⌨ www.letudiant.fr). Information for students in French.

Europa Pages (⌨ www.europa-pages.com). List of language schools offering French courses.

European Council for International Schools (⌨ www.ecis.org).

France Guide (⌨ www.franceguide.fr). Tourist information in English.

French-at-a-Touch (⌨ http://french-at-a-touch.com). General information on France and links to many other sites.

French Embassy in London (⌨ www.ambafrance-uk.org).

French Entrée (⌨ www.frenchentree.com). Information on every aspect of living in France and a useful forum.

French Tourist Board (⌨ www.franceguide.com).

Gaz de France (⌨ www.gdf.fr).

INSEE (⌨ www.insee.fr). Office of national statistics: population, unemployment, salaries, etc. (in English and French).

Invest in France Agency (⌨ www.invest-in-france.org). Useful information on living and working in France.

Legifrance (⌨ www.legifrance.gouv.fr). Official legal information.

Living France (⌨ www.livingfrance.com). The site of the eponymous magazine, providing useful information about all aspects of living in France and a lively discussion forum with over 6,000 members.

Météo France (⌨ www.meteofrance.com). Weather and climate in France.

Ministry of Culture & Communications (⌨ www.culture.fr).

Moving to France Made Easy (🖥 www.moving-to-france-made-easy. com). Plenty of information about life in France.

Online Newspapers (🖥 www.onlinenewspapers.com/france.htm). Links to dozens of French newspaper publishers' sites.

Pages Jaunes (🖥 www.pagesjaunes.fr). The French yellow pages.

Paris Info (🖥 www.parisinfo.com). The site of the Paris Convention & Visitors' Bureau.

Paris Notes (🖥 www.parisnotes.com). A subscription newsletter about Paris, published ten times a year.

Pavillon Bleu (🖥 www.pavillonbleu.com). A list of 'blue flag' beaches in France (awarded by the Foundation for European Education and Environment).

Le Point (🖥 www.lepoint.fr). Articles and surveys on all aspects of French life from the consumer magazine *Le Point*.

Pratique (🖥 www.pratique.fr). Practical information about life in France (in French).

Le Progrès (🖥 www.leprogres.fr). General information in French.

Que Choisir (🖥 www.quechoisir.org). Reports and articles from the consumer magazine *Que Choisir*.

Radio France (🖥 www.radiofrance.fr).

Senior Planet (🖥 www.seniorplanet.com). Information for older people

Sense Habitat (🖥 www.sernsehabitat.net). Information and courses on ecological methods of property construction, insulation and heating.

Service Public (🖥 www.service-public.fr). Official French government portal, with links to all ministry and other sites.

This French Life (💻 www.thisfrenchlife.com). Articles about setting up a variety of necessary services, from bank accounts to internet connection, as well as some of the more enjoyable things about life.

Union Nationale des Retraitées et des Personnes Agées (💻 www. unrpa.fr). Site of the National Union of Retired and Old People.

US Embassy in Paris (💻 www.amb-usa.fr).

US Embassy in Paris (💻 www.amb-usa.fr/consul/acs/guide/doc.pdf). A list of English-speaking doctors and hospitals.

Webvivant (💻 www.webvivant.com). Online community for English-speakers in France and Francophiles everywhere.

World Health Organization (💻 www.who.int).

Government Ministries

Ministries of the Economy and Finance and of Budgets and Accounting (💻 www.finances.gouv.fr). Economic and tax information.

Ministry of Education (💻 www.education.gouv.fr).

Ministry of Foreign & European Affairs (*sic*) (💻 www.diplomatie.gouv.fr/en). Information (in English) about French foreign policy.

Prime Minister (💻 www.premier-ministre.gouv.fr/en). Information (in English) about the French Prime Minister's role and function.

Property & Accommodation

Sites in English or with an English Version

123 Immo (💻 www.123immo.com). Displays over 4,000 estate agencies' advertisements.

1st for French Property (💻 www.1st-for-french-property.co.uk). Property in most areas.

A Place in France (💻 www.aplaceinfrance.co.uk). New property in all areas.

AB Real Estate (💻 www.ab-real-estate.com). Property in southern France.

Agence L'Union (💻 www.agencelunion.com). Property in Aveyron, Lot, Tarn and Tarn-et-Garonne.

L'Affaire Française (💻 www.french-property-net.com). Property in southwest France.

Association Nationale pour l'Information sur le Logement (💻 www.anil.org). Property information.

Century 21 (💻 www.century21.fr). Estate agent with offices throughout France.

Coast & Country (💻 http://coast-country.com). English-speaking estate agents on the Côte d'Azur.

Cognac Property Services (💻 www.cognacproperty.com). English-speaking estate agent covering the Cognac/Angoulême area.

De Particulier à Particulier (💻 www.pap.fr). Advertisements in the French property magazine *De Particulier à Particulier*.

Dream Properties Dordogne (💻 www.dreampropertiesdordogne.com). Property in Dordogne.

Francophiles (💻 www.francophiles.co.uk). Property in most areas.

Gîtes de France (💻 www.gites-de-france.com). Principal national organisation regulating self-catering accommodation.

Granny Network (💻 www.grannynetwork.com). A relocation, property search and 'hand-holding' service in many parts of France.

Green-Acres Services (💻 www.green-acres.com). Property agents.

Hexagone France (💻 www.hexagonefrance.com). Property 'within an hour of the Channel ports'.

Guy Hoquet (⌨ www.guy-hoquet.com). Property company for buying or renting private or business premises.

ImmoStreet (⌨ www.immostreet.com). Properties for sale and rent; also has automatic calculator showing repayment amounts for mortgage purchases.

Internet French Property Co. (⌨ www.french-property.com). Property in most areas.

JB French Houses (⌨ www.jbfrenchhouses.co.uk). Property in north-west and western France

Latitudes (⌨ www.latitudes.co.uk). Property in most areas.

Leggett Immobilier (⌨ www.frenchestateagents.com). Property in Poitou-Charentes, Dordogne, Gironde, Limousin and Lot-et-Garonne.

Logic-immo (⌨ www.logic-immo.com). Monthly magazine publishing houses for sale and rent.

Notaires de France (⌨ www.notaires.fr). Property listed with *notaires* and information on buying.

Orpi (⌨ www.orpi.com). Displays over 1,000 estate agencies' advertisements.

Propriétés de France (⌨ www.proprietesdefrance.com). Website specialising in advice and estate agents for top of the range property.

Rent a Place in France (⌨ www.rentaplaceinfrance.com). Specialises in rents of over a month.

Salut France (⌨ http://salut-france.com). French property search agents.

Se Loger (⌨ www.seloger.com). Properties for sale and rent plus quotations for insurance, removals and building work.

Southwest France Property Services (⌨ www. southwestfrancepropertyservices.com). Property agents.

Total France (💻 www.totalfrance.com). Properties to buy and rent, plus information, advertisements and a useful forum.

Transaxia France (💻 www.transaxia.fr). Property in most areas.

VEF (💻 www.vefuk.com). Property in most areas.

Vialex International (💻 www.vialex.com). Property in south-west France.

Vivre en France (💻 www.vefuk.com). Property agents.

Waterside Properties International (💻 www.watersideproperties-int. co.uk). Waterside properties in all parts of France.

Websites in French

3d Immo (💻 www.3d-immo.com). Portal displaying advertisements from individuals and estate agents.

Aaterrains (💻 www.aaterrains.com). Information on buying land.

Abimmo (💻 www.abimmo.com). Many properties for sale – new and old, houses and apartments.

Abonim (💻 www.abonim.com). Displays advertisements from individuals and estate agents.

Allobat (💻 www.allobat.fr). Building land for sale.

Appelimmo (💻 www.appelimmo.fr). Properties for sale and rent.

L'Argus du Logement (💻 http://universimmo.servicesalacarte.orange.fr/ argus). Estimates of property values.

A Vendre et à Louer (💻 www.avendrealouer.fr). Properties for sale and rent.

Faire Construire sa Maison (💻 www.construiresamaison.com). Site of the magazine *Faire Construire sa Maison*.

FNAIM (🖳 www.fnaim.fr). French national estate agents' organisation with advice and advertisements on buying property.

Foncia (🖳 www.foncia.fr). Rental accommodation specialists.

Immonot (🖳 www.immonot.com). Property listed with *notaires* and information on buying.

Immoprix (🖳 www.immoprix.com). Average property and building land sale prices by type, size, town, area, department and region.

Journal des Particuliers (🖳 www.journaldesparticuliers.com). Advertisements in the French property magazine *Le Journal des Particuliers*.

Logic-Immo (🖳 www.logic-immo.com). French estate agents' property advertisements.

Panorimmo (🖳 www.panorimmo.com). Links to property websites.

Le Partenaire Européen (🖳 www.partenaire-europeen.fr). Property search agent helping buyers and sellers of property throughout France.

Le Site Immobilier (🖳 www.lesiteimmobilier.com). Website containing many estate agents' advertisements for properties for sale and rent.

Terrains (🖳 www.terrain.fr). Building land for sale and information on buying land.

Le Tuc (🖳 www.letuc.com). Estate agent with offices throughout France.

Communications

Airlines

Aéroports Français (🖳 www.aeroport.fr). Details of and links to all French airports.

Air France (🖳 www.airfrance.com).

Bmi (🖳 www.flybmi.com).

British Airways (⌨ www.britishairways.co.uk).

EasyJet (⌨ www.easyjet.com).

Flybe (⌨ www.flybe.com).

Ryanair (⌨ www.ryanair.com).

Ferry Companies

Brittany Ferries (⌨ www.brittanyferries.com).

Condor Ferries (⌨ www.condorferries.co.uk).

Norfolkline (⌨ www.norfolkline.com).

P&O Ferries (⌨ www.poferries.com).

Sea France (⌨ www.seafrance.com).

Transmanche (⌨ www.transmancheferries.com).

Other Public Transport

Eurolines (⌨ www.eurolines.com). International coach services.

Eurostar (⌨ www.eurostar.com). International rail services.

Eurotunnel (⌨ www.eurotunnel.com). Car transport through the Channel Tunnel.

Motorail (⌨ www.frenchmotorail.com). Travelling by rail with your car in France.

National Express (⌨ www.nationalexpress.com). International coach services.

Rail Europe (⌨ www.raileurope.com). Eurostar/*TGV* link.

RATP (⌨ www.ratp.fr). Parisian regional transport authority.

SNCF (⌨ www.sncf.fr). French national railways.

Trans'bus (⌨ www.transbus.org). Information about urban public transport in France.

Motoring

ASFA (🖥 www.autoroutes.fr). Information about French motorways and tolls.

Automobile Association/AA (🖥 www.theaa.co.uk).

Bison Futé (🖥 www.bison-fute.equipement.gouv.fr). French road traffic reports.

Mappy (🖥 www.iti.fr). Road route planning through France.

Royal Automobile Club/RAC (🖥 www.rac.co.uk).

APPENDIX D - WEIGHTS & MEASURES

F rance uses the metric system of measurement. Those who are more familiar with the imperial system of measurement will find the tables on the following pages useful. Some comparissons shown are only approximate, but are close enough for most everyday uses. In addition to the variety of measurement systems used, clothes sizes often vary considerably with the manufacturer. The website ▣ www.onlineconversions.com allows you to make instant conversions between different measurement systems

Women's Clothes

Continental	34	36	38	40	42	44	46	48	50	52
UK	8	10	12	14	16	18	20	22	24	26
US	6	8	10	12	14	16	18	20	22	24

Pullovers

	Women's						Men's					
Continental	40	42	44	46	48	50	44	46	48	50	52	54
UK	34	36	38	40	42	44	34	36	38	40	42	44
US	34	36	38	40	42	44	sm	med	lar	xl		

Men's Shirts

Continental	36	37	38	39	40	41	42	43	44	46
UK/US	14	14	15	15	16	16	17	17	18	-

Men's Underwear

Continental	5	6	7	8	9	10
UK	34	36	38	40	42	44
US	sm	med		lar	xl	

Note: sm = small, med = medium, lar = large, xl = extra large

Children's Clothes

Continental	92	104	116	128	140	152
UK	16/18	20/22	24/26	28/30	32/34	36/38
US	2	4	6	8	10	12

Children's Shoes

Continental	18	19	20	21	22	23	24	25	26	27	28	29	30	31	32
UK/US	2	3	4	4	5	6	7	7	8	9	10	11	11	12	13

Continental	33	34	35	36	37	38
UK/US	1	2	2	3	4	5

Shoes (Women's and Men's)

Continental	35	36	37	37	38	39	40	41	42	42	43	44
UK	2	3	3	4	4	5	6	7	7	8	9	9
US	4	5	5	6	6	7	8	9	9	10	10	11

Weight

Imperial	Metric	Metric	Imperial
1oz	28.35g	1g	0.035oz
1lb*	454g	100g	3.5oz
1cwt	50.8kg	250g	9oz
1 ton	1,016kg	500g	18oz
2,205lb	1 tonne	1kg	2.2lb

Length

British/US	Metric	Metric	British/US
1in	2.54cm	1cm	0.39in
1ft	30.48cm	1m	3ft 3.25in
1yd	91.44cm	1km	0.62mi
1mi	1.6km	8km	5mi

Capacity

Imperial	Metric	Metric	Imperial
1 UK pint	0.57 litre	1 litre	1.75 UK pints
1 US pint	0.47 litre	1 litre	2.13 US pints
1 UK gallon	4.54 litres	1 litre	0.22 UK gallon
1 US gallon	3.78 litres	1 litre	0.26 US gallon

Note: An American 'cup' = around 250ml or 0.25 litre.

Area

British/US	Metric	Metric	British/US
1 sq. in	0.45 sq. cm	1 sq. cm	0.15 sq. in
1 sq. ft	0.09 sq. m	1 sq. m	10.76 sq. ft
1 sq. yd	0.84 sq. m	1 sq. m	1.2 sq. yds
1 acre	0.4 hectares	1 hectare	2.47 acres
1 sq. mile	2.56 sq. km	1 sq. km	0.39 sq. mile

Temperature

°Celsius	°Fahrenheit	
0	32	(freezing point of water)
5	41	
10	50	
15	59	
20	68	
25	77	
30	86	
35	95	
40	104	
50	122	

Notes: The boiling point of water is 100°C / 212°F.

Normal body temperature (if you're alive and well) is 37°C / 98.6°F.

Temperature Conversion

Celsius to Fahrenheit: multiply by 9, divide by 5 and add 32. (For a quick and approximate conversion, double the Celsius temperature and add 30.)

Fahrenheit to Celsius: subtract 32, multiply by 5 and divide by 9. (For a quick and approximate conversion, subtract 30 from the Fahrenheit temperature and divide by 2.)

Oven Temperatures

Gas	Electric	
	°F	°C
-	225–250	110–120
1	275	140
2	300	150
3	325	160
4	350	180
5	375	190
6	400	200
7	425	220
8	450	230
9	475	240

Air Pressure

PSI	Bar
10	0.5
20	1.4
30	2
40	2.8

Power

Kilowatts	Horsepower	Horsepower	Kilowatts
1	1.34	1	0.75

APPENDIX E: MAPS OF FRANCE

On the following pages are maps of France showing the regions/departments, cities and airports, and TGV rail lines. The map opposite shows the 22 regions and 96 departments of France, which are listed below. The departments are (mostly) numbered alphabetically from 01 to 89. Departments 91 to 95 come under the Ile de France region, which also includes Ville de Paris (75), Seine et Marne (77) and Yvelines (78), shown in detail opposite.

01 Ain	32 Gers	64 Pyrénées Atlantiques
02 Aisne	33 Gironde	65 Hautes Pyrénées
02 A Corse-du-Sud	34 Hérault	66 Pyrénées Orientales
02 B Haute-Corse	35 Ille et Vilaine	67 Bas Rhin
03 Allier	36 Indre	68 Haut Rhin
04 Alpes de Hte Provence	37 Indre et Loire	69 Rhône
05 Hautes Alpes	38 Isère	70 Haute Saôn
06 Alpes Maritimes	39 Jura	71 Saône et Loire
07 Ardèche	40 Landes	72 Sarthe
08 Ardennes	41 Loir et Cher	73 Savoie
09 Ariège	42 Loire	74 Haute Savoie
10 Aube	43 Haute Loire	75 Paris
11 Aude	44 Loire Atlantique	76 Seine Maritime
12 Aveyron	45 Loiret	77 Seine et Marne
13 Bouches du Rhône	46 Lot	78 Yvelines
14 Calvados	47 Lot et Garonne	79 Deux Sèvres
15 Cantal	48 Lozère	80 Somme
16 Charente	49 Maine et Loire	81 Tarn
17 Charente Maritime	50 Manche	82 Tarn et Garonne
18 Cher	51 Marne	83 Var
19 Corrèze	52 Haute-Marne	84 Vaucluse
21 Côte d'Or	53 Mayenne	85 Vendée
22 Côtes d'Armor	54 Meurthe et Moselle	86 Vienne
23 Creuse	55 Meuse	87 Haute Vienne
24 Dordogne	56 Morbihan	88 Vosges
25 Doubs	57 Moselle	89 Yonne
26 Drôme	58 Nièvre	90 Territoire-de-Belfort
27 Eure	59 Nord	91 Essonne
28 Eure et Loir	60 Oise	92 Hauts de Seine
29 Finistère	61 Orne	93 Seine Saint Denis
30 Gard	62 Pas de Calais	94 Val de Marne
31 Haute Garonne	63 Puy de Dôme	95 Val d'Oise

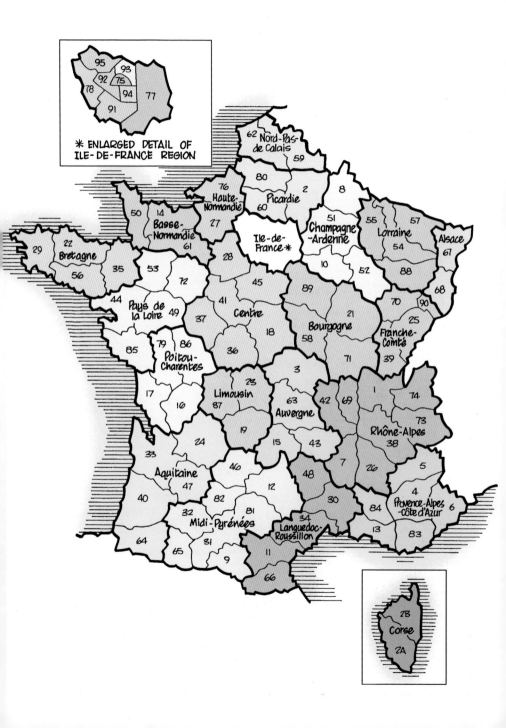

95 93
92 75
78 94 77
91

✳ ENLARGED DETAIL OF
ILE-DE-FRANCE REGION

62 Nord-Pas-
de Calais
59

80   2   8

76
Haute-
Normandie   Picardie
60

50 14
Basse-
Normandie   27   51   55   57
61   Champagne   Lorraine
-Ardenne   54

Ile-de-   Alsace
France✳   67

28   10   52   88

22   Bretagne   35   53   45   89   70   68
29   90
56   72   25

44   41   21   Franche-
Pays de   Centre   Comté
la Loire   49   37   18   Bourgogne   39
58
79 86
85   Poitou-   36   71
Charentes   3

17   23   42 69   1   74
10   Limousin   63
87   Auvergne   73
19   Rhône-Alpes
24   15   43   38

33   46   7   26   5
Aquitaine   48
40   47   12   30   84   4
82   Provence-Alpes   6
32   81   34   13   -côte d'Azur
Midi-Pyrénées   Languedoc-   83
64   Roussillon
65   31   11
9
66

2B
Corse
2A

AIRPORTS & FERRY PORTS

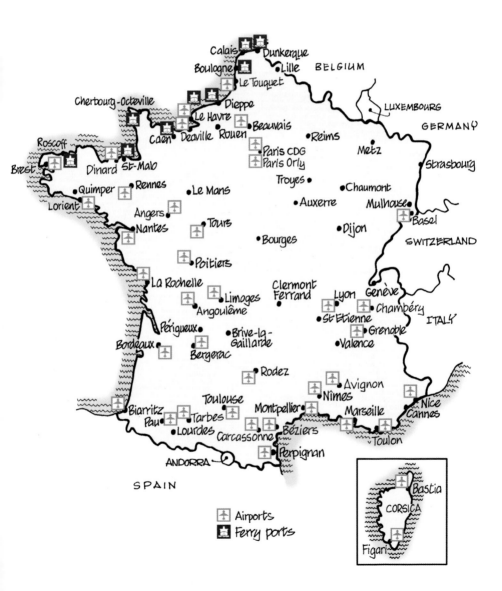

TGV RAIL LINES

APPENDIX F: AIRLINES & AIRPORTS

The information on the following pages indicate where direct scheduled flights operate from UK, Irish and North American airports to France. Airline and airport telephone numbers (where available) and website addresses are also shown below. Details were current in January 2008. As flight schedules change regularly, you're advised to check services before committing yourself to the purchase of a property – or even a long-term rental.

Airline	Telephone/Website
Aer Arann	UK ☎ 0870-876 7676, IRL ☎ 0818-210210, 🖥 www.aerarann.com
Air Canada	CA/US ☎ 888-257 2262, 🖥 www.aircanada.com
Air France	UK ☎ 0870-142 4343, 🖥 www.airfrance.com
Aer Lingus	UK ☎ 0870-876 5000 Ire ☎ 0818-365000 🖥 www.aerlingus.com
Air Transat	Ca/US ☎ 877-872 6728 🖥 www.airtransat.com
American Airlines	US ☎ 800-433 7300 🖥 www.aa.com
British Airways	UK ☎ 0870-850 9850 🖥 www.britishairways.com
BMIbaby	UK ☎ 0871 224 0224 🖥 www.bmibaby.com

Airline	Telephone/Website
BMI	UK ☎ 0870-607 0555 ⌨ www.flybmi.com
Continental Airlines	Ca/US ☎ 800-231 0856 ⌨ www.continental.com
Delta	US ☎ 800-221 1212 ⌨ www.delta.com
EasyJet	UK ☎ 0905-821 0905 ⌨ www.easyjet.com
Flybe	UK ☎ 0871-700 2000 ⌨ www.flybe.com
Flyglobespan	UK ☎ 0871-271 0415 ⌨ www.flyglobespan.com
GB Airways (British Airways)	UK ☎ 0870-850 9850 ⌨ www.ba.com
Jet 2	UK ☎ 0871-226 1737 ⌨ www.jet2.com
Northwest Airlines	US ☎ 800-225 2525 ⌨ www.nwa.com
Ryanair	UK ☎ 0871-246 0000 ⌨ www.ryanair.com
Skysouth	UK ☎ 01273-463673 ⌨ www.skysouth.co.uk
United Airlines	US ☎ 800-538 2929 ⌨ www.united.com
US Airways	US ☎ 800-428 4322 ⌨ www.usairways.com

Airport	Telephone/Website
Aberdeen	UK ☎ 0870-040 0006 💻 www.aberdeenairport.com
Belfast International	UK ☎ 028-9448 4848 💻 www.belfastairport.com
Birmingham	UK ☎ 0870-733 5511 💻 www.bhx.co.uk
Bristol	UK ☎ 0871-334 4444 💻 www.bristolairport.co.uk
Cardiff	UK ☎ 01446-711111 💻 www.cwifly.com
Cork	Ire ☎ 021-431 3131 💻 www.corkairport.com
Dublin	Ire ☎ 01-814 1111 💻 www.dublin-airport.com
Edinburgh	UK ☎ 0870-040 0007 💻 www.edinburghairport.com
Exeter	UK ☎ 01392-367433 💻 www.exeter-airport.co.uk
Glasgow Prestwick	UK ☎ 0871-223 0700 💻 www.gpia.co.uk
Leeds/Bradford	UK ☎ 0113-250 9696 💻 www.lbia.co.uk
Liverpool	UK ☎ 0871-521 8484 💻 www.liverpoolairport.com
London City	UK ☎ 020-7646 0088/00 💻 www.londoncityairport.com

Airport	Telephone/Website
London Gatwick	UK ☎ 0870-000 2468 💻 www.gatwickairport.com
London Heathrow	UK ☎ 0870-000 0123 💻 www.heathrowairport.com
London Luton	UK ☎ 01582-405100 💻 www.london-luton.co.uk
London Stansted	UK ☎ 0870-000 0303 💻 www.stanstedairport.com
Manchester	UK ☎ 0871-271 0711 💻 www.manchesterairport.co.uk
Newcastle	UK ☎ 0871-882 1131 💻 www.newcastleairport.com
Norwich	UK ☎ 01603-411923 💻 www.norwichairport.co.uk
Nottingham/East Midlands	UK ☎ 0871-919 9000 💻 www.eastmidlandsairport.com
Shannon	UK ☎ 061-712000 💻 www.shannonairport.com
Southampton	UK ☎ 0870-040 0009 💻 www.southamptonairport.com

Flights from the UK & Ireland

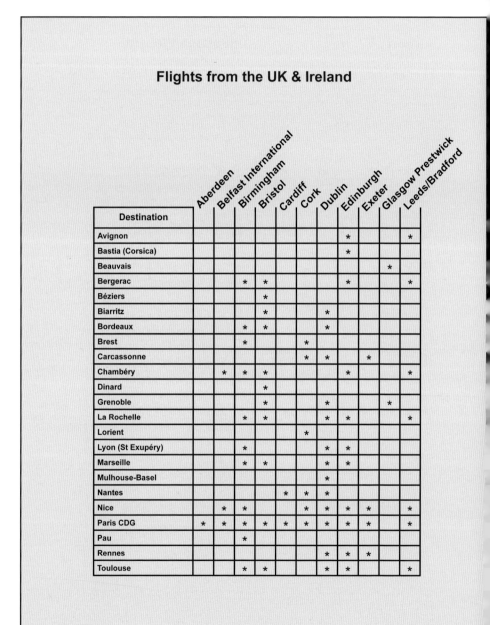

Destination	Aberdeen	Belfast International	Birmingham	Bristol	Cardiff	Cork	Dublin	Edinburgh	Exeter	Glasgow Prestwick	Leeds/Bradford
Avignon								*			*
Bastia (Corsica)								*			
Beauvais										*	
Bergerac		*	*					*			*
Béziers			*								
Biarritz			*				*				
Bordeaux		*	*				*				
Brest			*			*					
Carcassonne						*	*		*		
Chambéry		*	*	*				*			*
Dinard			*								
Grenoble			*				*			*	
La Rochelle		*	*				*	*			*
Lorient						*					
Lyon (St Exupéry)			*				*	*			
Marseille		*	*				*	*			
Mulhouse-Basel							*				
Nantes					*	*	*				
Nice		*	*				*	*	*		*
Paris CDG	*	*	*	*	*	*	*	*	*		*
Pau			*								
Rennes							*	*	*		
Toulouse			*	*			*	*			*

Destination	Liverpool	Lon City	Lon Gatwick	Lon Heathrow	Lon Luton	Lon Stansted	Manchester	Newcastle	Norwich	Nott's/E.Mids	Shannon	Shoreham	Southampton
Angers													*
Angoulême						*							
Avignon													*
Beauvais										*			
Bergerac	*					*	*			*			*
Biarritz						*							
Bordeaux			*	*		*							*
Brest				*		*							*
Caen											*		
Carcassonne	*					*				*			
Chambéry			*			*	*						*
Deauville											*		
Dinard						*				*			
Figari (Corsica)						*							
Grenoble	*				*	*							
La Rochelle													*
Le Havre												*	
Le Touquet												*	
Limoges	*					*				*			*
Lourdes-Tarbes							*						
Lyon (St Exupéry)			*	*		*	*	*					
Marseille			*			*	*						
Montpellier						*							
Mulhouse-Basel						*							
Nantes						*				*			
Nice	*	*	*	*	*	*	*	*		*			*
Nîmes	*				*		*	*	*	*			
Paris CDG	*	*		*	*	*	*	*	*	*			*
Paris Orly		*											
Paris Cergy-Pontoise											*		
Pau						*							
Perpignan						*	*						*
Poitiers						*							
Rennes							*						*
Rodez						*							
Toulon						*							
Toulouse			*				*						
Tours						*							

Flights from North America to France

Airpoorts	Paris CDG	Bordeaux	Nice
Atlanta	*		
Boston	*		
Chicago	*		
Cincinnati	*		
Dallas	*		
Detroit	*		
Houston	*		
Los Angeles	*		
Miami	*		
Montreal		*	
New York JFK	*		*
New Orleans	*		
Newark	*		
Philadelphia	*		
Pittsburgh	*		
San Francisco	*		
Saint Louis	*		
Seattle	*		
Toronto	*		
Washington DC	*		

APPENDIX G - STATISTICS

In December 2007, *L'Express* magazine published the results of a survey into the suitability for retirees of each of France's 96 departments, entitled 'The departments where you can grow old well ... and not so well.' The departments were assessed according to four main criteria, each marked out of 20: the extent and quality of social services for the elderly; the availability of healthcare; the health of the inhabitants; 'quality of life. The results were as follows – the highest scores indicating the best places to retire (shown in blue), the lowest the worst.

Department	Social Services	Healthcare	Health	Quality of Life	Average	Rank
01 Ain	14.5	12.5	12.5	7.5	11	60
02 Aisne	16.5	16.5	6	8.5	11.9	56
2A Corse-du-Sud	11	11	13.5	13.5	12.3	45
2B Haute Corse	9	18	16	14.25	12.3	45
03 Allier	11	11.5	9.5	11	10.8	74
04 Alpes-de-Hte-Provence	13	13.5	12	11.75	12.6	34
05 Hautes-Alpes	**14**	**17.5**	**16.5**	**9.5**	**14.4**	**9**
06 Alpes-Maritimes	7.5	11	14	13	11.4	65
07 Ardèche	**19.5**	**11**	**14**	**12.25**	**14.2**	**10**
08 Ardennes	9.5	14	7	9.5	10.1	88
09 Ariège	14	10.5	17	14	13.9	17
10 Aube	14.5	11.5	9	6.75	10.4	83
11 Aude	8.5	9	16	15.75	12.3	45
12 Aveyron	**15**	**10..5**	**19.5**	**14.5**	**14.9**	**6**
13 Bouches-du-Rhône	11.5	14	11	13.5	12.5	40
14 Calvados	**17.5**	**14**	**13.5**	**11.75**	**14.2**	**10**
15 Cantal	16	14.5	13.5	10.25	13.6	22
16 Charente	17	11	17	11.5	14.1	12
17 Charente-Maritime	11	7.5	17.5	12	12	53
18 Cher	12	9.5	6.5	10	9.5	93
19 Corrèze	12	13	13	11.25	12.3	45
21 Côte-d'Or	16.5	17	13.5	8.5	13.9	17
22 Côte-d'Armor	17.5	12	14	11.5	13.8	19
23 Creuse	12.5	13	12.5	10	12	53
24 Dordogne	15.5	9	14	12.5	12.8	30

Department	Social Services	Healthcare	Health	Quality of Life	Average	Rank
25 Doubs	8	15	11	8.25	10.6	78
26 Drôme	12	12	13	11	12	53
27 Eure	17	6	6.5	7.75	9.3	96
28 Eure-et-Loir	11.5	11.5	11.5	6.75	10.3	85
29 Finistère	16	14.5	10.5	12.75	13.4	25
30 Gard	12	10	12.5	14.25	12.2	49
31 Haute-Garonne	**14**	**15**	**19.5**	**11**	**14.9**	**6**
32 Gers	13	11	18	14.5	14.1	12
33 Gironde	16	15	13	10.25	13.6	22
34 Hérault	13	13.5	15.5	14.5	14.1	12
35 Ille-et-Vilaine	**17.5**	**17**	**14.5**	**12.25**	**15.3**	**2**
36 Indre	10	10	12.5	9.75	10.6	78
37 Indre-et-Loire	14	13.5	16	7	12.6	34
38 Isère	11.5	13.5	12	10	11.8	60
39 Jura	11.5	9.5	12	10	10.8	74
40 Landes	12.5	13	13.5	11.75	12.7	33
41 Loir-et-Cher	11	7	17	8.25	10.8	74
42 Loire	18	12.5	9	10.75	12.6	34
43 Haute-Loire	18	11.5	11	12.25	13.2	28
44 Loire-Atlantique	13.5	14.5	12	10.25	12.6	34
45 Loiret	13.5	8.5	17	6.25	11.3	67
46 Lot	16	9.5	19	10.75	13.8	17
47 Lot-et-Garonne	10	9.5	16.5	10.75	11.7	62
48 Lozère	**19.5**	**15.5**	**13.5**	**14.25**	**15.7**	**1**
49 Maine-et-Loire	**15**	**15**	**18.5**	**12.25**	**15.2**	**3**
50 Manche	14.5	10	12.5	13.25	12.6	34
51 Marne	16	13	8	5.75	10.7	77
52 Haute-Marne	9.5	12	8.5	9.25	9.8	91
53 Mayenne	**18**	**11**	**18.5**	**12.75**	**15.1**	**4**
54 Meurthe-et-Moselle	16	15	6	7.25	11.1	71
55 Meuse	12	13	7	8.75	10.2	87
56 Morbihan	16.5	10	8	12.25	11.7	62
57 Moselle	13	12.5	6.5	7.75	9.9	90
58 Nièvre	11.5	11	5.5	9.75	9.4	95
59 Nord	14	16	7.5	9	11.6	64
60 Oise	13	13.5	7.5	7.25	10.3	85
61 Orne	18	12.5	14.5	11.5	14.1	12

Department	Social Services	Healthcare	Health	Quality of Life	Average	Rank
62 Pas-de-Calais	12	14.5	12	12.75	12.8	30
63 Puy-de-Dôme	13.5	14.5	9.5	12.5	12.5	40
64 Pyrénées-Atlantiques	10	13	12.5	13.25	12.2	49
65 Hautes-Pyrénées	12.5	16	11	13.5	13.3	26
66 Pyrénées-Orientales	7	8.5	13.5	14.75	10.9	72
67 Bas-Rhin	13.5	12.5	7.5	8.25	10.4	83
68 Haut-Rhin	16.5	15.5	7.5	8.75	12.1	51
69 Rhône	14.5	15.5	13.5	7.75	12.8	30
70 Haute-Saône	15	12	10	10.75	11.9	56
71 Saône-et-Loire	15.5	12	11.5	10.75	12.5	42
72 Sarthe	15.5	12.5	16.5	10	13.6	22
73 Savoie	15.5	14	12	9	12.6	34
74 Haute-Savoie	10.5	14	14	6.5	11.3	67
75 Paris	9.5	15.5	12.5	6	10.9	72
76 Seine-Maritime	19.5	11.5	6.5	10	11.9	56
77 Seine-et-Marne	15.5	13	6	4.75	9.8	91
78 Yvelines	14.5	12.5	16	5.25	12.1	51
79 Deux-Sèvres	15.5	8.5	18.5	12.5	13.8	19
80 Somme	13.5	18.5	10	11	13.3	26
81 Tarn	**15.5**	**10.5**	**19**	**15**	**15**	**5**
82 Tarn-et-Garonne	12	8.5	20	9	12.4	42
83 Var	9.5	9.5	11	12.5	10.6	78
84 Vaucluse	14	13.5	11	11.25	12.4	42
85 Vendée	**16.5**	**11.5**	**16**	**15**	**14.8**	**8**
86 Vienne	14	13	19.5	9.75	14.1	12
87 Haute-Vienne	12	16	15	9	13	29
88 Vosges	16.5	13	8	10	11.9	56
89 Yonne	15	12.5	8.5	9.25	11.3	67
90 Territoire de Belfort	13	16	6.5	6.75	10.6	78
91 Essonne	12.5	14	14	5.25	11.4	65
92 Hauts-de-Seine	11.5	12.5	15	5.75	11.2	70
93 Seine-Saint-Denis	11	11.5	9	6.5	9.5	93
94 Val-de-Marne	9.5	12.5	15.5	5	10.6	78
95 Val-d'Oise	13.5	14	8	4.75	10.1	80

Old (Vieux) Port, Cannes, Alpes-Maritimes

INDEX

Survival Books

Survival Books was established in 1987 and by the mid-'90s was the leading publisher of books for people planning to live, work, buy property or retire abroad.

From the outset, our philosophy has been to provide the most comprehensive and up-to-date information available. Our titles routinely contain up to twice as much information as other books and are updated frequently. All our books contain colour photographs and some are printed in two colours or full colour throughout. They also contain original cartoons, illustrations and maps.

Survival Books are written by people with first-hand experience of the countries and the people they describe, and therefore provide invaluable insights that cannot be obtained from official publications or websites, and information that is more reliable and objective than that provided by the majority of unofficial sites.

Survival Books are designed to be easy – and interesting – to read. They contain a comprehensive list of contents and index and extensive appendices, including useful addresses, further reading, useful websites and glossaries to help you obtain additional information as well as metric conversion tables and other useful reference material.

Our primary goal is to provide you with the essential information necessary for a trouble-free life or property purchase and to save you time, trouble and money.

We believe our books are the best – they are certainly the best-selling. But don't take our word for it – read what reviewers and readers have said about Survival Books at the front of this book.

Order your copies today by phone, fax, post or email from:
Survival Books, PO Box 3780, Yeovil, BA21 5WX, United Kingdom.
Tel: +44 (0)1935-700060, email: sales@survivalbooks.net,
Website: www.survivalbooks.net

Buying a Home Series

Buying a home abroad is not only a major financial transaction but also a potentially life-changing experience; it's therefore essential to get it right. Our Buying a Home guides are required reading for anyone planning to purchase property abroad and are packed with vital information to guide you through the property jungle and help you avoid disasters that can turn a dream home into a nightmare.

The purpose of our Buying a Home guides is to enable you to choose the most favourable location and the most appropriate property for your requirements, and to reduce your risk of making an expensive mistake by making informed decisions and calculated judgements rather than uneducated and hopeful guesses. Most importantly, they will help you save money and will repay your investment many times over.

Buying a Home guides are the most comprehensive and up-to-date source of information available about buying property abroad – whether you're seeking a detached house or an apartment, a holiday or a permanent home (or an investment property), these books will prove invaluable.

Living and Working Series

Our Living and Working guides are essential reading for anyone planning to spend a period abroad – whether it's an extended holiday or permanent migration – and are packed with priceless information designed to help you avoid costly mistakes and save both time and money.

Living and Working guides are the most comprehensive and up-to-date source of practical information available about everyday life abroad. They aren't, however, simply a catalogue of dry facts and figures, but are written in a highly readable style – entertaining, practical and occasionally humorous.

Our aim is to provide you with the comprehensive practical information necessary for a trouble-free life. You may have visited a country as a tourist, but living and working there is a different matter altogether; adjusting to a new environment and culture and making a home in any foreign country can be a traumatic and stressful experience. You need to adapt to new customs and traditions, discover the local way of doing things (such as finding a home, paying bills and obtaining insurance) and learn all over again how to overcome the everyday obstacles of life.

All these subjects and many, many more are covered in depth in our Living and Working guides – don't leave home without them.

The Expats' Best Friend!

Culture Wise Series

Our **Culture Wise** series of guides is essential reading for anyone who wants to understand how a country really 'works'. Whether you're planning to stay for a few days or a lifetime, these guides will help you quickly find your feet and settle into your new surroundings.

Culture Wise guides:

- Reduce the anxiety factor in adapting to a foreign culture
- Explain how to behave in everyday situations in order to avoid cultural and social gaffes
- Help you get along with your neighbours
- Make friends and establish lasting business relationships
- Enhance your understanding of a country and its people.

People often underestimate the extent of cultural isolation they can face abroad, particularly in a country with a different language. At first glance, many countries seem an 'easy' option, often with millions of visitors from all corners of the globe and well-established expatriate communities. But, sooner or later, newcomers find that most countries are indeed 'foreign' and many come unstuck as a result.

Culture Wise guides will enable you to quickly adapt to the local way of life and feel at home, and – just as importantly – avoid the worst effects of culture shock.

Culture Wise – The Wise Way to Travel

The essential guides to Culture, Customs & Business Etiquette

Other Survival Books

Investing in Property Abroad: Essential reading for anyone planning to buy property abroad, containing surveys of over 30 countries.

The Best Places to Buy a Home in France/Spain: Unique guides to where to buy property in Spain and France, containing detailed regional profiles and market reports.

Buying, Selling and Letting Property: The best source of information about buying, selling and letting property in the UK.

Earning Money From Your Home: Income from property in France and Spain, including short- and long-term letting.

Foreigners in France/Spain: Triumphs & Disasters: Real-life experiences of people who have emigrated to France and Spain, recounted in their own words.

Making a Living: Comprehensive guides to self-employment and starting a business in France and Spain.

Renovating & Maintaining Your French Home: The ultimate guide to renovating and maintaining your dream home in France.

Retiring in France/Spain: Everything a prospective retiree needs to know about the two most popular international retirement destinations.

Running Gîtes and B&Bs in France: An essential book for anyone planning to invest in a gîte or bed & breakfast business.

Rural Living in France: An invaluable book for anyone seeking the 'good life', containing a wealth of practical information about all aspects of French country life.

Shooting Caterpillars in Spain: The hilarious and compelling story of two innocents abroad in the depths of Andalusia in the late '80s.

Wild Thyme in Ibiza: A fragrant account of how a three-month visit to the enchanted island of Ibiza in the mid-'60s turned into a 20-year sojourn.

For a full list of our current titles, visit our website at www.survivalbooks.net

RURAL LIVING IN FRANCE

Many people dream of moving to rural France – somewhere warm and sunny where days can be spent al fresco basking in the shade of a tree. In their mind's eye they see themselves relaxing over a leisurely lunch of newly-baked baguettes from the village boulangerie, fresh produce from the garden, mouth-watering fromage and charcuterie from the local market, and a few bottles of chilled vin blanc from a local vineyard.

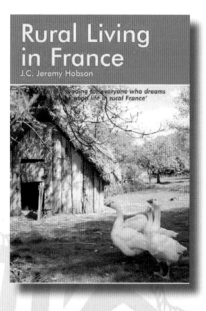

Rural Living in France points out the pitfalls as well as the pleasures of rural life and provides comprehensive practical advice on everything from buying property and land to selling products and produce; from keeping poultry and other livestock to using machinery and hiring plant. Whatever your need or interest, you'll find it in this book.

Rural Living in France is the only book especially written for those who yearn for a slice of the 'good life' in rural France and is essential reading for newcomers – it's guaranteed to help readers overcome or avoid the pitfalls of rural living and smooth their way to a happy and rewarding future in their new home.

Buy your copy today at www.survivalbooks.net

Survival Books - The Expat's Best Friend

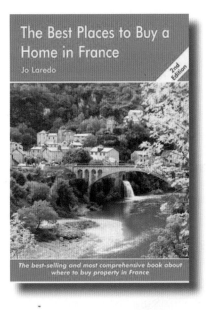

CULTURE WISE
FRANCE

The Essential Guide to Culture, Customs & Business Etiquette

Travellers often underestimate the depth of cultural isolation they can face abroad, particularly in a country with a different language. To many people, France may seem an 'easy' option, with it's millions of visitors from around the globe and hundreds and thousands of foreign residents. However, sooner or later, most newcomers find France a very 'foreign' country indeed. **Culture Wise France** will help you understand France and its people, adapt to the French way of life and quickly feel at home.

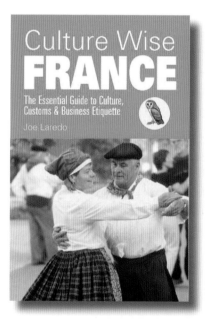

PRINTED IN COLOUR!

Inside you'll discover:

♦ How to overcome culture shock

♦ The historical and political background to modern France

♦ French attitudes and values – at home and at work

♦ Do's, don'ts and taboos

♦ How to enjoy yourself in French style

♦ Business and professional etiquette

♦ France's spoken and body language

♦ Getting around France safely

♦ Shopping the French way

The **Culture Wise** series of guides is essential reading for visitors and residents who want to understand how a country really works. Whether you're planning to stay for a few weeks or a lifetime, they will help you quickly find you feet after arrival, settle in smoothly and integrate into your new surroundings.

Buy your copy today at www.survivalbooks.net

Culture Wise - The Wisest Way to Travel

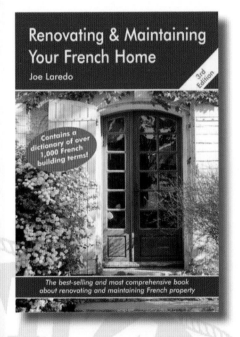

📷 Photo Credits